The Principle of Indemnity in Marine Insurance Contracts

Kyriaki Noussia

The Principle of Indemnity in Marine Insurance Contracts

A Comparative Approach

Springer

Dr. Kyriaki Noussia
University of Birmingham
School of Law
Edgbaston, Birmingham B15 2TT
United Kingdom
k.p.noussia@bham.ac.uk

Library of Congress Control Number: 2006938304

ISBN 978-3-540-49073-9 Springer Berlin Heidelberg New York

Springer is part of Springer Science+Business Media

springer.com

Production: LE-TEX Jelonek, Schmidt & Vöckler GbR, Leipzig
Cover-design: Erich Kirchner, Heidelberg

SPIN 11926276 64/3100YL - 5 4 3 2 1 0 Printed on acid-free paper

For George & Robert

Preface

Marine Insurance is considered one of the oldest of the many forms of commercial protection. It has flourished through the establishment of the institution of the *"coffee-houses"*, wherein *"underwriting"* was being conducted and from where the evolution and dominance of the Lloyd's has stemmed as the world's most famous insurance market. Marine insurance contracts are special in that they have special characteristics and also because they are contracts of indemnity.

This book examines the *principle of indemnity* within marine insurance contracts. The legal problems related to the principle, in theory and in practice, are discussed and evaluated through the citation and critical analysis of the relevant case law in England as well in some of the most representative common law and continental law jurisdictions, together with an analysis comprising thoughts and proposals on possible extensions, further research options, and a possible future law reform.

The book comprises of six (6) chapters: chapter one (1) discusses the history of marine insurance in England and the policy reasoning behind the enactment of the various English statutes as well as the history, legal framework and the way marine insurance is regulated in the other jurisdictions. Chapter two (2) discusses the concept and importance of insurable interest in relation to indemnity marine insurance contracts and the coverage offered under such contracts both in England and in the other legal systems. Chapter three (3) discusses types of losses in England and the rest of the law regimes. Chapter four (4) discusses valuation and the measure of indemnity available according to the type of contract each time as well as in the case of double insurance, both in England and in the rest of the legal systems. Chapter Five (5) examines the legal issues related to the rights of insurer on payment, in all jurisdictions. Chapter six (6) draws some general comparative conclusions and also explores the scope and nature of a reform in the area, in light also of the ongoing attempt for unification, which has been undertaken since 1998 by the *Comité Maritime Internationale* (CMI).

The book is an updated version of the Ph.D. thesis of the author, which was submitted, defended and accepted from the School of Law, University of Southampton, UK in 2004.

I am indebted to the Max Planck Society for the bursary which allowed me to read as a guest scholar at the Max Planck Institute of Comparative and Private International Law in Hamburg (April 2002). I am also indebted to the Research Council of Norway for the research scholarship which enabled me to visit and research at the Scandinavian Institute of Maritime Law, within the Faculty of Law of the University of Oslo in Norway (November 2002). I would also like to thank Prof. Y. Tassel of the University of Nantes, France for providing me with the opportunity to read as a guest scholar at the *Centre de Droit Maritime et Océanique* of the University of Nantes in France (March 2003).

The law is stated as at October 1st, 2006.

Birmingham, October 2006 Kyriaki Noussia

Contents

Abbreviations

AC	Appeal Court
Australian ICA	Australian Insurance Contracts Act
Australian MIA 1909	Australian Marine Insurance Act 1909
AIMU	American Institute of Maritime Underwriters
AK	Αστικός Κώδιξ
All ER	All England Law Reports
ALRC	Australian Law Reform Commission
AMC	American Maritime Cases
ANZ Cases	Australia & New Zealand Cases
App Cas	Appeal Cases
Αρμ	Αρμενόπουλος
B&PNR	Bosanquet & Pullet's New Reports
Bos & Pul (NR)	Bosanquet & Pullet's New Reports
B&C.	Barnwall & Cresswells' King's Bench Reports
B&Ad	Barnwall & Adolphus' King's Bench Reports
Bing NC	Bingham's New Cases
Brod & B	Broderip & Bingham's Common Pleas Reports
Burr	Burrow's King's Bench Reports
CA	Cours d' Appel
Camp	Campbells' Nisi Prius Cases
CB	Common Bench Reports
CCA	Consolidated Case Annotations
C&F	Clark & Fineelly's House of Lords Cases
Ch	Law Reports Chancery Division
c.i.f.	Cost Insurance Freight
CMI	Comité Maritime Internationale
Circ	Circuit
CLC	Common Law Cases
Com Cas	Commercial Cases
CPD	Law Reports Common Pleas Division

CPML	Code of Private Maritime Law
DMF	Droit Maritime Francais
East	East's Term Reports, King's Bench
ΕΕμπΔ	Επιθεώρηση Εμπορικού Δικαίου
ΕλΔ	Ελληνική Δικαιοσύνη
ΕΝαυτΔ	Επιθεώρηση Ναυτικού Δικαίου
Ex	Exchequer Reports
Exch	Exchequer Reports
ExD	Law Reports, Exchequer Division
FCas	Federal Cases
Fed Rep	Federal Reporter
F 2d	Federal Reporter, Second Series
Fed Supp	Federal Supplement
HL	Clark & Finelly's House of Lords Reports
H&C	Hurlstone & Coltman's Exchequer Reports
HL Cas	House of Lords Cases
Holt NP	Holt's Nisi Prius Law Reports
ICA	Insurance Contracts Act
ICC	International Cargo Clauses
IJOSL	International Journal of Shipping Law
IntILR	International Insurance Law Review
IHC	International Hull Clauses
ISC(C)	Institute Strike Clauses (Cargo)
IWC(C)	Institute War Clauses (Cargo)
JBL	Journal of Business Law
JMarLC	Journal of Maritime Law and Commerce
KB	King's Bench
ΚΙΝΔ	Κώδιξ Ιδιωτικού Ναυτικού Δικαίου
ΚΔΝΔ	Κώδιξ Δημοσίου Ναυτικού Δικαίου
LlLRep	Lloyd's Law Reports
LMCLQ	Lloyd's Maritime and Commercial Law Quarterly
LOF	Lloyd's Standard Form of Salvage
LR	Law Reports
LRCP	Law Reports Common Pleas
LRHL	Law Reports House of Lords
LRQB	Law Reports Queen's Bench
Lloyd's Rep.	Lloyd's Reports
LT	Law Times Reports
MIA	Marine Insurance Act
MIA RSBC	Marine Insurance Act Republic

	State of British Columbia
MIA RSM	Marine Insurance Act Republic State of Manitoba
MIA RSNB	Marine Insurance Act Republic State of New Brunswick
MIA RSO	Marine Insurance Act Republic State of Ontario
NMIP	Norwegian Marine Insurance Plan
NoB	Νομικό Βήμα
NSWLR	New South Wales Law Review
P&I	Protection and Indemnity
PIB	Provisional Insurance Bureau
ppi	Policy Proof Interest
QB	Queen's Bench
SCt.	Supreme Court
SCR	New Supreme Court Reports
SDNY	State District of New York
SDNYDC	State District of New York District Court
SG Policy	Ship and Goods Policy
Shaw	Shaw's Session Cases
S&M	Sweet & Maxwell
Sup Ct (NSW)	Supreme Court (New South Wales)
Taunt	Taunton's Common Pleas Reports
TLR	Times Law Reports
UNCTAD	United Nations Commission on Trade & Development
UN	United Nations
Vern	Vernon's Chancery Reports
Ves Sen	Vesey Senior's Chancery Reports
W&L	Washington & Lee Law Review
WLR	Weekly Law Reports

1.The history and legislative framework of marine insurance

1.1. Historical and policy reasons behind the various English statutes

1.1.1. Early historical background

Marine Insurance, the oldest of the many forms of protection against losses, has a long history which dates back to antiquity and is coeval with maritime commerce itself. The ancient Phoenicians, the Greeks and the Romans - although unacquainted with the art of "*underwriting*" as the latter is being practised nowadays at Lloyd's - were in the habit of guarding themselves against some of the risks of maritime enterprise by various systems of insurance, whether in the shapes of loans or mutual guarantee.[1]

One of the oldest systems is the loan form known under the name of "*Bottomry*". It is defined as the mortgage of a ship[2], in such a manner that if the ship be lost the lender likewise loses the money advanced on her, but if she arrives safely at the port of destination, he would get back the loan and a certain premium previously agreed upon.

The system of insurance arising out of "*Bottomry*", came to be not only amidst the oldest but also amidst the most wide-spread forms of marine insurance. This is principally for two reasons, the first being the extreme simplicity of the transaction and the second being the desire to escape the penalties of the universally prevailing laws against usury, by which was understood the lending of money on interest.

---

1 Although it was probably the Greeks and the Phoenicians who were among the first to have insured against maritime loss, the first existing record of marine insurance appears to have originated from a Roman edict of A533, in the reign of Emperor Justinian.

2 i.e. her bottom or hull.

The form of marine insurance, known as "*Bottomry*", differs from the contemporary one, in that while Bottomry loans are compensations advanced before the actual loss of a ship, modern policies of insurance are promises to pay compensation after the loss has occurred.

Although "*Bottomry*" is said to have formed the commencement of marine insurance at the revival of commerce in the Middle Age, it was, nevertheless, not long before it grew out and developed into the modern system of insurance. Indeed, insurance - as a term - occurs for the first time in an old historical work called "*Chronyk van Vlaendern*", which refers distinctly to the existence of marine insurance as early as the beginning of the 14th century at Bruges, where it is believed that the first "*Chamber of Insurance*" existed.

1.1.2. The Lombards

Over the centuries, various forms of marine insurance have flourished and faded in various parts of Europe. The Hanseatic merchants of northern Europe had an insurance centre based at Bruges, known as the first "*Chamber of Insurance*". In 1432, the city of Barcelona also laid down the first recorded statute for insuring ships. Meanwhile, the first form of marine insurance in Britain had been started by a group of Hanseatic merchants, and was later carried on by some German colonists who were the first known London underwriters to have exercised marine insurance almost exclusively with no apparent sign of competition for many years.

It was only until the late years of their existence that they were faced with competition from another group of foreign immigrants, "*the Lombards*"[3] - who took their name from the name of the street where their businesses and trading firms were established, i.e. Lombard Street and who were the first ones to have seriously engaged in the area of marine insurance. It is believed that from them also originates the word "*polizza*"- i.e. a promise - which is the root of the term "*policy*".[4] The Lombards begun marine insurance by advancing sums on Bottomry loans. Their activity came to an end when England's foreign trade came to the hands of Englishmen; although gone, they, nevertheless, have left something very important in the foundation of a most important branch of finance and commerce, in that they brought marine insurance practice into general use by

3 Brown A (1987) Hazard Unlimited: The Story of Lloyds of London, LLP, pp. 16-17.

4 Brown A (1987) Hazard Unlimited: The Story of Lloyds of London, LLP, pp. 16-17

making it acceptable to the trading community at large, by the introduction of proper rules and regulations.

1.1.3. Early English marine insurance

The commencement of the 17th century formed the starting point of a new period in the history of marine insurance in Great Britain. During the first period, dating back to the beginnings of foreign commerce and ending within the 16th century, marine insurance was carried on chiefly, if not entirely, by foreigners; whilst during the second and subsequent period it fell into the lap of native enterprise.

A distinct line and division between the two periods was formed by the Elizabethan Act of 1601.[5] Being the first statute prepared by the English Government and passed by the Parliament, it was titled *"An Act Concerning Matters of Assurances Amongst Merchants"* and it is highly memorable as the first statute-book regarding marine insurance. The Act of 1601 also established the Court of Insurance, which was unfavourably looked upon both by the mercantile community and the courts of common law, and, as a result of that, only few actions appear to have been brought before it.

1.1.4. The founder of Lloyd's and the rise of the Lloyd's coffee house

Until 1666, the business of underwriting is not known to have been carried in any other specific fixed localities other than at the private offices of bankers, money-lenders and others who also pursued their own avocations besides.

After this period, numerous coffee houses were gradually established in the City of London for the purpose of underwriting.[6] Their establishment had a political importance and at the same time exercised a

5 The reason why marine insurance, so long in existence, did not occupy the attention of English legislators any earlier is believed to lie in its foreign origin and growth.

6 Among the names of known masters of such coffee-houses, gathered from newspaper advertisements are Hains, Garraway and Thomas Good.

marked influence on the business of marine insurance.[7] Within a few years they sprung all over London, and merchants visited them chiefly, if not entirely, for business purposes.

The first London coffee house was opened in 1652, by a Mr. Bowman, in St. Michael's Alley, Cornhill, London.

The *"Lloyd's Coffee House"* originally located in Tower Street, moved to Lombard Street around 1691 or 1692. This, together with the issuing of the weekly newspaper *"Lloyds News"*, furnishing commercial and shipping news, made it the place of resort for persons connected with the shipping business. In 1771, a Committee was elected to represent the underwriters and alongside the payment of a subscription - the first significant movement of underwriters themselves towards assumption of responsibility for the organisation of the market - effectively transformed Lloyd's from a coffee house into an organisation of underwriters. Yet, it was not until the first Lloyd's Act in 1871, that it became a structured organisation regulated by a constitution.

1.1.5. The first marine insurance companies

During the time of the *"South Sea Bubble"* scandal and the manic period following it, more than two thousand company schemes were set afloat mostly in the shape of joint-stock undertakings. Among the schemes brought forward, nearly a hundred of them related to insurance and, furthermore, very few among them were devoted partly or entirely to marine insurance. The bursting of the *"South Sea Bubble"* scandal retarded the development of incorporated companies. Of the companies and projects that found way into the public, only two survived, namely the *"London Assurance Corporation"* and the *"Royal Exchange Assurance Corporation"*.[8] In 1720 an Act was passed, namely *"The Bubble Act"*, giving them the right and monopoly of insuring ships and merchandise. The monopoly granted to them proved to be one of the foundation stones of the greatness and growth of Lloyd's. Thus, at face value, the impact of *"The Bubble Act"* was threefold: firstly, individual underwriting via brokers remained unfettered; secondly, competition was introduced in the form of the *"Royal Exchange Assurance"* and the *"London Assurance"* companies; and

---

[7] They proved very convenient meeting places, for men engaged in a common object not requiring much time, and were as if made entirely for underwriters.

[8] The first idea of starting these two companies, however, arose long before the *"South Sea Bubble"* scandal. These two companies were largely supported by the Government.

thirdly, the marine insurance market was closed absolutely, except to individual underwriters and the two corporations. Thus, the explanation for Lloyd's dominant position in the marine insurance market lies in the combination of corruption, chance and commercial expediency.

1.1.6. The evolution of Lloyd's and other forms of marine insurance companies

The *de facto* monopoly enjoyed by individual underwriters, centred at the premises of Lloyd's, was not to the liking of all shipowners, especially those from provincial ports who found the London underwriters remote and unsympathetic, the Lloyd's premium rates unrestrained by any effective competition and the solvency of any given individual underwriter non predictable.

Thus, shipowners united and constituted unincorporated associations, in order to provide mutual hull insurance. These associations came together to share with each other their hull risks on a mutual basis which is still the basic concept of Protection & Indemnity (P&I) Clubs, despite the fact that they are now incorporated so that in law it is the P&I Club - and not the individual members - providing the insurance. Alhough these unincorporated associations declined due to competition from Lloyd's and the new corporate insurers that entered the market after 1824, the fact that their mechanism was established gave birth to a new generation of mutual insurance associations - which developed into the modern P&I Clubs which cover a variety of third party liabilities - to which shipowners were subject and which the London market and the insurance companies did not cover. Along with the decline of those unincorporated associations came the need to create similar associations, which resulted in the formation of the first protection association - namely the *"Shipowners' Mutual Protection Society"* (predecessor of the *"Britannia P&I Club"*) - in 1855. In 1874, the risk of liability for loss of or damage to cargo carried on board the insured ship was first added to the cover provided by a protection Club. Since then, many Clubs added an indemnity class to provide the necessary cover.[9]

9 Members of the modern P&I Clubs are shipowners and other sea operators, such as charterers. Control of the association is vested in a committee or board of directors elected by the members from among themselves, whereas management is delegated to the club managers, either club employees or independent management companies. (Bennett H(1996) The Law of Marine Insurance, Clarendon Press, Oxford, pp 8-9).

Generally speaking, the categories existing nowadays are the market insurance[10] and the mutual insurance.[11] The function of both categories is that mutual insurance companies provide cover against P & I, war and defence risks; whilst the London market offers marine property insurance together with some collision liability cover. Regarding war risks, the associations offer both property and liability insurance. There is a difference in the ethos that market insurance and mutual insurance share, as the former consists a purely financial bargain, where cover is purchased for a fixed premium from a profit-making entity, and the latter consists of non-profit making organisations permitting pooling of losses over a given period at the cost of a contribution thereto, and where the payable amount is depending on the magnitude of the losses which actually occur.[12]

1.1.7. The growth and evolution of the system and law of marine insurance

Over a hundred years passed after the enactment of the 1601 Act, before any other statute related to marine insurance was adopted.

The Marine Insurance Act of 1745 prohibited the making of policies of marine insurance in the subject matter of which the assured had no interest. This was the first attempt, towards a statutory intervention in marine insurance law, which sought to put an end to the practice of wagering disguised by marine policies, whereby persons without interest in a vessel or its cargo would insure using a marine policy form. The 1745 Act required those procuring marine policies to be interested in the subject-matter, and similarly prohibited the practice of insuring on the basis of "*policy proof of interest*", which had become the standard method of gambling by means of insurance and which rendered enforceable insurances without interest at common law.[13] In 1788, a further Act was passed, which prescribed that all policies made out in blank, were void. It also required the names of all parties interested in a marine policy, to be inserted into the policy. This Act was largely ineffective - as its provisions were satisfied so long as the assured's agent was named in the policy - and it was repealed

10 Incorporating the Lloyd's and the London market.

11 Incorporating the provincial mutual insurance associations – modern protection and indemnity associations or "P & I" Clubs.

12 Bennett H (1996) The Law of Marine Insurance, Clarendon Press, Oxford, pp. 8-9.

13 This Statute was finally repealed by the Marine Insurance Act 1906, the provisions of the earlier Act with regard to *"no interest"* policies being re-enacted in Section 4 of the Marine Insurance Act 1906.

by the Marine Insurance Act 1906, in so far as it applied to marine insurance, however, still operates with regards to non-marine policies on goods.[14]A later statute of 1795, required all policies of marine insurance to be in writing and to be stamped. The subsequent to it Act of 1803, imposed penalties on individuals directing or prosecuting frauds on insurers and was enacted because of the case of *Adventure*.[15] Finally, the Policies of Marine Insurance Act 1868 facilitated the assignment of insurance contracts and was reproduced in sections 50-51 of the Marine Insurance Act 1906.[16] In 1894 *"The Marine Insurance Codification Bill"* was introduced in the House of Lords, and it is the content of this Bill , slightly altered, which provided the basis for the Marine Insurance Act 1906, namely *"An Act to Codify the Law Relating to Marine Insurance"*.

The early marine insurance legislation, in so far as it was concerned with substantive issues, affected only insurable interest, with the market and the courts being left to develop the principles of marine insurance law. Those principles were ultimately codified in the Marine Insurance Act 1906.[17] The Marine Insurance Act 1906 did not seek to change the law but, rather, was a codification of approximately 200 years of judicial decisions. There was, and remains, no equivalent non-marine codification, although at various points the Marine Insurance Act 1906 reflects both marine and non-marine law.

However, the Act has to be viewed with some degree of caution. Much of it is concerned with laying out presumptions which operate only in the absence of any contrary agreement between the parties, whereas in practice, marine insurance contracts, written in England, are governed by the various sets of Standard Marine Clauses published by the International Underwriting Association of London which frequently oust many of the Marine Insurance Acts' presumptions. The Marine Insurance Act 1906 must also be viewed as a snapshot of the law relating to marine insurance practice, as it existed in 1906. Since then, there have been many significant changes in practice, and certain of the Act's concepts relate to superseded forms of dealing. There are also a number of important post-Act decisions, refining the meaning of the Act's wording. Lastly, the Marine Insurance Act 1906 is not fully exhaustive, though most of the important principles of marine insurance law have been enshrined in it.

---

14 Merkin R (2000) Marine Insurance Legislation, LLP, p.xxxvii.

15 The captain of the vessel *Adventure* caused her to be cast away off Brighton. Very heavy insurances-mainly of a fictitious character-had been effected on the vessel and her cargo.

16 Merkin R (2000) Marine Insurance Legislation, LLP, p.xxxvii.

17 An Act drafted by Sir Mackenzie Chalmers.

Because of Marine Insurance Act 1906 section 4,[18] a later statute was enacted, i.e. the *"Marine Insurance (Gambling Policies) Act 1909"*. The statutes are cited as *"The Marine Insurance Acts 1906, 1909"*. The later imposed certain criminal responsibilities on the parties to contracts of marine insurance effected by way of gaming or wagering on loss by maritime perils.[19]

The 1906 Act approved the use of the document known as *Lloyd's SG Form of Policy*. The *Ship and Goods (SG) Policy* was formally adopted by Lloyd's in 1779. It is included in the Schedule to the Marine Insurance Act 1906, and much of the codification contained in the Act concerns cases decided on its wording. The Institute of London Underwriters, took on the responsibility of drafting clauses to deal with aspects of the *SG Policy* thought to be unsatisfactory, and these were appended to policies. Standard form clauses for all aspects of marine insurance were adopted, as annexes to the *SG Policy*, and new ones drafted in 1982 and 1983 broke the link with the *SG Policy* which was scrapped and replaced with a simplified form of wording to be used as a cover sheet for the relative Institute Clauses. The Institute Clauses have been revised many times, lastly in November 2003.[20]

1.1.8. The policy reasons which generated the enactment of the Marine Insurance Act 1906

The sources and policy reasons behind the enactment of the Marine Insurance Act 1906 can only be traced if one carefully examines the Parliamentary Debates that lead to the passing of the Bill[21]. The Bill proposed to state

[18] Which lacked repressing gambling on loss - by maritime perils - and imposed no penalties on those who were parties to such contracts.

[19] Dover V (1957) A Handbook to Marine Insurance, pp. 30-35.

[20] A number of different forms of insurance are required to provide full cover for a marine adventure and these are all available under Institute Clause wording, the three main heads of cover being cargo, hull and freight, (Merkin R (2000) Marine Insurance Legislation, LLP, p.xxxvii).

[21] During its second reading it was stressed, by the Earl of Halsbury, that the Bill was of an extreme importance very seriously affecting an enormous business. Similarly, the Attorney General pointed out that the codifying Bill would constitute a great convenience to the mercantile community which would want to have this branch of law put into a comprehensive and intelligible form, give that the law (as it stood at that time) was primarily found in cases in the law reports and, as a result of that, was not always easily accessible or understood by the ordinary layman.

the whole of the existing law so that the merchantile community would know exactly which liabilities it had. It was a Bill demanded by all involved in the mercantile community and its' passing was the most valuable measure to be appreciated by this community.

It is apparent that the passing of the Bill and the enactment of the Marine Insurance Act 1906 was imposed by the needs and problems of the day and of the mercantile community which desperately sought to codify, in the form of legislation, marine insurance. Commercial needs, usage and customs also imposed the need for the creation of a piece of legislation regulating marine insurance. The mercantile community needed to be reassured that the undertaken risks to be insured were such that they could be legally protected. Also, the flourish of gaming and wagering contracts, during this era, increasingly evoked the need for legal protection and the way to achieve that was through the passing of an Act that would render contracts with illegal content void. In a similar way, other problematic points of the marine insurance practice.[22]

1.2. The history and legislative framework of marine insurance in Greece

The French Commercial Code of 1807 formed the basis of the Greek Commercial Code of 1835.[23] Due to the leading role that maritime affairs played in the Greek economy - even from the very early times - various laws relating to its regulation have been passed through the years and, as a result, there has been a separation from the Commercial Code of the part relating to the regulation of maritime law.[24] Thus, two orders for the crea-

---

22 Such as the lack of good faith and the way to deal with it, valuation and the measure of indemnity, as well as subrogation issues, urged the enactment of the Marine Insurance Act 1906.

23 To this we are being lead by the fact that articles 116-154 of the latter are an identical translation of the relevant ones in the French Commercial Code. These articles were altered, transformed and enriched by Law ΓΨΙΖ/24-04-1910 which in its turn was also based on French Law as well as on the Italian Commercial Code of 1882, the Belgian Commercial Code of 1908 and the German Commercial Code of 1897 and also on various international conventions.

24 This was enacted by various reasons, such as the nature of the work conducted on a vessel, the specific conditions under which maritime affairs are pursued, the specific nature and character of the vessel as a means of maritime transportation and also, in terms of the latter, its navigation into national and international waters.

tion of the relevant laws were formed, i.e. a) Law 3816/1958 *"For the Procurement of the Code of Private Maritime Law"* and b) Law Decree 187/1973 *"Relating to the Code of Public Maritime Law"*. Finally, the two statutes regulating Greek maritime law are: The *"Code of Private Maritime Law (Law 3816/1958) [KINΔ]"*, and *"The Code of Public Maritime Law (Law 187/1973) [KΔNΔ]"*. The legislature resourced to the creation of the two codes, hoping to regulate efficiently all aspects of maritime law.

The main sources that lead to the formation and flourishing of maritime law in Greece are, primarily, maritime custom which is said to be an important source of maritime law and private maritime law, the latter being also substantiated by art. 1 of the Greek Civil Code which states as sources of law the legal rules derived from the context of laws and customs. In Greek law, however, it is accepted that the custom does not render the law void. The former cannot, nevertheless, be a source of law for public maritime law as the latter is governed by the *"principle of legality"* which does not include customs.

In brief, the laws containing maritime features together with the relevant international conventions, ratified in accordance with the Greek Constitution, form the primary sources of maritime law, whereas maritime custom and the general rules of transactions form the secondary sources of maritime law. [25]

Within the context of the Greek Law, until 1997, rules on insurance contracts were incorporated in the Commercial Code. The relevant section in the Commercial Code is today superseded by law 2496/1997.[26] In addition, marine insurance is specifically regulated by the provisions of Chapter XIV of the Code of Private Maritime Law (CPML),[27]articles 257 - 288.[28] According to CPML section 257, sections 189- 225 of the Commercial Code govern also marine insurance. However, given that Law 2496/1997 has superseded the Commercial Code, these sections have been

[25] Marine Insurance owes its appearance to the maritime perils encountered in the process of conduct of maritime affairs. Marine insurance law contains a combination of principles of maritime and insurance law. As a concept it is said to have appeared at the end of the Middle Age, when the concept of perils was initially established. It is the most ancient form of insurance and is considered as part of maritime law (Tsatsos D, Dountas M, Zepos K(1954) Insurance Law Lectures, Sakkoulas Publications, Athens).

[26] Wilhelmsen TL (1998) The Marine Insurance System in Civil Law Countries – Status and Problems, MarIus 242,1, Utgitt Av Sjorettsfondet, Oslo.

[27] Namely, in Greek, Κώδιξ Ιδιωτικού Ναυτικού Δικαίου (ΚΙΝΔ).

[28] Wilhelmsen TL(2001) Issues of Marine Insurance: Duty of Disclosure, Duty of Good Faith, Alteration of Risk and Warranties,MarIus 281, Simply YearBook 2001, 45, Utgitt Av Sjorettsfondet, Oslo.

replaced by articles 1-33 of the Law 2496/1997 while the provisions of the general insurance and commercial law may apply in a supplementary way, i.e. to the extent that they are consistent with provisions relating to marine insurance which are compatible with the nature of marine insurance and not modified by any other special provisions.[29] This is due to the "*lex specialis*" principle in Greek law, as per which where various laws regulate the same issue, the more specialised law prevails over the more general one.[30]

1.3. The history and legislative framework of marine insurance in Norway

In Norway, the codification of maritime law dates back to the 1270's and the reign of the Norwegian King Magnus Hakonson. Christian V's Danish and Norwegian Law of 1687, which included a chapter relating to insurance, was in force until the passage of the Merchant Marine Act 1893. [31]

Marine insurance is regulated by the Insurance Contracts Act 1986 (ICA)[32], with which it is mandatory that all insurance contracts comply with,[33] apart from insurance of commercial activity performed by ships which have to be registered according to the Maritime Code of 1994, or commercial activity dealing with international trade. Thus, for marine insurance, there is complete contractual freedom, limited only by general contractual principles against illegal and unfair contracts.

In the Scandinavian countries, the conditions for marine insurance have traditionally been incorporated into an extensive private codification. In Norway, this codification is published as a Marine Insurance Plan, known as the Norwegian Marine Insurance Plan.[34] The Plan is a kind of private legislation aiming to regulate all practical questions concerning marine insurance, even those questions which are also dealt with in the public legislation which is to be used instead of the governing Insurance

---

29 Spaidiotis K (1999) Marine Insurance Law in Greece, Maritime Advocate, Is. 7.

30 Rokas I (1995) Introduction to the Law of Private Insurance, 4th edn, Oikonomikon Publications, Athens.

31 Derrington S (1998) The Law Relating to non-Disclosure, Misrepresentation and Breach of Warranty in Contracts of Marine Insurance: A Case for Reform, PhD Thesis, University of Queensland, Australia.

32 Dated 16 June 1989.

33 Norwegian Insurance Contracts Act sections 1-3.

34 The Norwegian Marine Insurance Plan.

Contracts Act. In this way private legislation attempts to also regulate issues where the governing Insurance Contracts Acts is not mandatory and to provide other solutions. In addition, mandatory provisions in the governing Insurance Contracts Act are incorporated in the Plan. The provisions, however, are not lifted out of the mandatory regime of the Insurance Contracts Act.[35]

The Plans contains general provisions for all kinds of marine insurance, and special provisions for special interests.[36] In fact the Norwegian Marine Insurance Plans have taken over the ordinary legislative tasks, in the area of marine insurance, at the same time having clear similarities with ordinary legislation. The Plans are also accompanied by extensive commentaries which thoroughly explain the individual provisions. The Commentaries constitute an integral part of the Plans and are as significant as ordinary preparatory works of Acts of Parliament.[37] It can be said that, formally, the Plan constitutes a standard contract which must be incorporated in the individual agreement by way of reference made in the policy. In many ways, however, the Plan bears much resemblance to a piece of legislation, except that its drafting has been carried out by private groups and the Plan as such has not been passed by Parliament.

The first Norwegian Marine Insurance Plan dates from 1871[38] and was introduced in 1876. It was amended in 1894, 1907 and again in 1930. In 1964, there was a new and extensive amendment, caused mainly by the ship-owners' need for a more extensive cover for error in construction and materials.[39] The 1964 Marine Insurance Plan was amended again in 1996,[40]

---

[35] Even if the Plan as such is directory, the parties are obliged to follow the regulation taken from mandatory provisions.

[36] Wilhelmsen TL (1998) The Marine Insurance System in Civil Law Countries-Status and Problems, MarIus No 242, 15.

[37] Bull HJ (1999) The Norwegian Marine Insurance Plan of 1996, In Huybrecht M (ed) Marine Insurance at the Turn of the Millennium, Vol. I, Intersentia, Antwerp.

[38] Derrington S (1998) The Law Relating to non-Disclosure, Misrepresentation and Breach of Warranty in Contracts of Marine Insurance: A Case for Reform, PhD Thesis, University of Queensland, Australia.

[39] The 1964 revision resulted in the cargo clauses being taken out of the Marine Insurance Plan. A separate Plan for Insurance for the Carriage of Goods was established in 1967, which was amended in 1995 and resulted in the Norwegian Cargo Clauses: Conditions relating to Insurance for the Carriage of Goods of 1995, Cefor Form No 252 (Norwegian Cargo Clauses). This amendment was mainly the result of the new Insurance Contracts Act in Norway, which is mandatory concerning national transport of goods. Many clauses, thus, had to be amended to conform to the Insurance Contract Act's requirements. For the

its' form being similar to that of the 1964 one. In terms of content the 1996 Plan is somehow new, if compared to the 1964 Plan. The modus of performing the revision has been based on the pattern of looking at each individual provision of the 1964 Plan and critically evaluating it against the criteria which made its revision necessary. This amendment was caused by changes in the legislative framework and the evolution and contemporary needs of the shipping industry, as well as by the various problems encountered in the marine insurance market. In effect, the Plan was drafted by a Committee consisting of members of all different groups or organisations effecting marine insurance contracts.

Before the introduction of the 1996 Plan, the former Plans had been supplemented by a set of agreed conditions concerning problems where the provisions in the Plan were outdated or insufficient. The 1996 Plan seeks to incorporate such amendments directly into the Plan instead of using separate conditions, and to do so the Drafting Committee has also established a Permanent Revision Committee, to make yearly amendments of the Plan, to the extend needed each time.[41]

1.4. The history and legislative framework of marine insurance in France

In France, marine insurance can be traced back to around 1681, when "*Le Guidon de la Mer*" - which provided for an office of insurance and dealt with the time in which a claim could be admitted and the conditions upon which a ship and its cargo might be insured together - was published.[42] However, marine insurance has evolved, since the Napoleonic "*Code Civil*", through the Law of 13 July 1930, the codification of July 1976 and a series of later laws integrated in the "*Code des Assurances*" consequent upon directives imposed by the European Union.

most parts, these mandatory requirements are also given effect for international carriage of goods, even if the Norwegian Insurance Contract Act is not mandatory for this kind of insurance.

40 Wilhelmsen TL (1998) The Marine Insurance System in Civil Law Countries-Status and Problems, MarIus No 242, 15.

41 Bull H.J (1999) The Norwegian Marine Insurance Plan of 1996, In Huybrecht M (ed) Marine Insurance at the Turn of the Millennium, Vol. I, Intersentia, Antwerp.

42 Derrington S (1998) The Law Relating to non-Disclosure, Misrepresentation and Breach of Warranty in Contracts of Marine Insurance: A Case for Reform, PhD Thesis, University of Queensland, Australia.

The law of 13 July 1930 forms the basis of the insurance contract, its provisions having been integrated into *"Book One"* of the *"Code des Assurances"*. [43] The law addresses the first system of protection for insured parties. Whilst recognising the principle of freedom of contract, it also addresses matters perceived to be prejudicial to the assureds and it has been designed to protect assureds by using provisions of rather an imperative than regulatory nature.

The law of 8 November 1955 foreshadowed the codification of the insurance texts but it was only much later that codification was finally achieved by the Decrees of 16 July 1976, published on 21 July 1976.[44] Finally, reform of marine insurance was achieved by Law No. 522 of 3 July 1967 and the Decree No. 64 of 19 January 1968. Upon entry into force on 26 April 1968, this statute abrogated articles 331-396,431,432 and 435 of the "*Code de Commerce*" and any other provision which was contrary to the new provisions of the Statute. However, the Laws of 1930 and 1967 do not depend on or have pre-eminence over each other. By Law No.92-665 of 16 July 1992, the Law of 1967 was included in the *Code des Assurances* and became Titre[45] VII. The new Titre VII is virtually in identical terms with the law of 1967. Other reforms have consisted principally of the integration into French law of EC Directives. The EC Directive of 18/6/1992, concerning non-life insurance, has been integrated into French Law by Law No 94-5 of 4/1/1994.

Another important source of marine insurance law in France rests in the general professional usages. Some of these professional or local "customs" have been reduced to writing and are known as *"Recommendations of the French and foreign societies established in France (29.2.80)"*, *"Communal regulations concerning marine and transport insurance (29.2.80)"*, *"Customary usages of marine and transport insurance (16.9.82)"* , and *"Rules of moral obligations (20.4.83) and rules of the market (9.7.84)"*.[46]

---

[43] The law of 13 July 1930 forms the basis of French insurance law and, still, even after several revisions, remains its foundation.

[44] The impetus for this ambitious project was the two EU directives of 24 July 1973, relating to the freedom of establishment of insurance business. Codification was effected by two distinct decrees, i.e. the Decree No. 76-666 of 16 July 1976 relating to the codification of the legislative texts concerning insurance, and the Decree No. 76-667 of 16 July 1976 relating to the codification of the regulatory texts concerning insurance.

[45] i.e. title.

[46] Derrington S (1998) The Law Relating to non-Disclosure, Misrepresentation and Breach of Warranty in Contracts of Marine Insurance: A Case for Reform, PhD Thesis, University of Queensland, Australia.

1.5. The history and legislative framework of marine insurance in the USA

1.5.1. Introductory remarks

In the USA, marine insurance underwriting begun in the18th century. The earliest record of marine insurance is a notice by a Mr John Copson, in the American Weekly Mercury of May 25,1721, announcing the opening, at his house in High Street, Philadelphia, of *"an office of public insurances on vessels, goods and merchandises"*.[47]

The American law of marine insurance took its lead and inspiration from English law, as there was no American statute and English legal precedents were frequently cited in American courts. It could, therefore, be said that a unified Anglo-American law of marine insurance existed and in that sense English law was part of the general maritime law of the US.

The importance of having a uniform maritime law was also the legislature's purpose when structuring the Admiralty Clause of the US Constitution[48], which granted jurisdiction to the federal courts as well as a substantive authority to the US Congress to legislate in the field as well as to the federal judiciary to fashion uniform law in the field.

This unity of Anglo-American law was broken in 1955 by the decision of the US Supreme Court in *Wilburn Boat Co v Fireman's Fund Insurance Co*[49] where the Supreme Court ruled that state law should apply to a policy of marine insurance, thus splintering the unity of domestic US law and destroying the relationship between English and American law.[50] Thus, it is difficult to identify a pure US law of marine insurance. Whilst on some issues there is a uniform national rule that could be described as part of the country's marine insurance law, on other issues there is no such national approach and marine insurance disputes are resolved by reference to state law, should the court decide that state law governs. This is complicated further by a wide space of uncertainty, because whilst some courts

---

47 Schoenbaum TJ(2001) Admiralty and Maritime Law, 3rd edn, Hornbook Series,West Group, St.Paul, Minn USA.

48 US Const., art III, para. 2, which states that the judicial power of the US shall attend to all cases of admiralty and maritime jurisdiction.

49 348 US 310, 1955 AMC 467.

50 Schoenbaum TJ (1999) Key Divergences Between English and American Law of Marine Insurance: A Comparative Study, Cornell Maritime Press, pp.12-17.

may look to a theoretically uniform national law of marine insurance, some others may look to state law for answers to the same questions.[51]

1.5.2. The situation prior to and after the *"Wilburn Boat Co v Fireman's Fund Insurance Co"* case

Although the law of marine insurance has never been codified in the United States, the basic substantive law of marine insurance is federal maritime law.[52]

The Supreme Court has stated that United States Courts should look to English Law for the applicable rules.[53] In the *Wilburn Boat*,[54] however, the Supreme Court ruled that in the absence of a controlling federal admiralty law principle to guide the resolution of a particular issue, the courts must apply the applicable state law rule.

The case involved an insurance policy on a small houseboat used for commercial carriage of passengers on Lake Texoma, an inland lake between Oklahoma and Texas. The original owners of the boat, which were also the insured parties under the policy, had conveyed the boat and policy to a corporation in which they were the sole stockholders, and the boat was subsequently mortgaged. The insurance policy issued by the defendant insurance company provided that, without the consent of the underwriter the boat could not be sold, transferred, assigned, or pledged or used for anything other than private pleasure purposes. After the boat was destroyed by fire, the corporate owner brought suit on the policy to recover for the loss. The insurance company denied liability, alleging breach of the warranty

---

51 It was always though that the general maritime law governing marine insurance was largely the same as English law. In *Queens Insurance Co of America v Globe & Rutgers Fire Insurance Co*, [263 US 487,493,44 SCt 175,176,68 LEd 402 (1924)] Justice Holmes declared that : *"...[t]here are special reasons for keeping in harmony with the marine insurance laws of England, the great field of this business"*(Sturley MF (2002)A US Perspective on Marine Insurance Law, Ch. 12 In Thomas R (ed) The Modern Law of Marine Insurance, Vol. 2 , LLP).

52 *Insurance Co v Dunham*, 78 US (11Wall) 1,20 LEd 90 (1870); *DeLovio v Boit*, 7 FCas, 418 (CCD Mass 1815), (No 3776).

53 Due to the *"special reasons for keeping in harmony with the marine insurance laws of England, the great field of this business"* as stated in *Queens Ins Co of America v Globe & Rutgers Fire Ins Co*, 263 US 487, 493, 44 SCt 175, 176, 68 LEd 402 (1924).

54 *Wilburn Boat Co v Fireman's Fund Insurance Co*, 348 US 310, 75 SCt, 368, 99 LEd, 337 (1955).

involving the transfer, pledge and use of the boat. In response, the boat owner contended that under Texas law, the policy provision against pledging was invalid, and that the claim policy breaches were immaterial unless they contributed to the loss.

The District Court and the Court of Appeal denied recovery, holding that federal admiralty law, and not state law, applied and that the established rule required literal fulfillment of every policy warranty.[55] The Supreme Court reversed that ruling, on the grounds that no federal admiralty rule existed to deal with the consequences of warranty breaches in marine insurance policies and that the void should be filled by applying state law.[56]

Wilburn Boat[57]postulated that marine insurance is governed by both federal admiralty and state law and the courts, when interpreting contracts of marine insurance, are now required to struggle with the issue of which to apply. The case creates many problems related to the need for predictability and uniformity in the law governing marine insurance con-

---

55 The District court ruled that federal maritime law governed and that due to the *"literal compliance"* rule, the Wilburns were not entitled to any recovery. The US Court of Appeals (5th Circuit) affirmed (Sturley MF (2002)A US Perspective on Marine Insurance Law, Ch 12 In Thomas R (ed) The Modern Law of Marine Insurance, Vol. 2 , LLP).

56 On 28 February, 1955, the Supreme Court reversed the 5th Circuit's decision. Justice Black, having noted that there was no relevant federal legislation, asked whether there was a judicially established federal admiralty rule governing these warranties and secondly, in the case that there was not, whether they should fashion one. He answered the first question to the negative and did not offer any guidance as to what is required for a rule to become *"judicially established"*, and regarding the second question, the court declined to fashion a "new" admiralty rule firstly because the regulation of insurance had historically been a state matter and the Congress had long accepted and acted upon this division of responsibility, and secondly even if the court decided to fashion a new rule, the latter would prove a difficult task for which the courts might not be the best equipped to perform. Justice Frankfurter accepted the court's judgement but distinguished his position as to the majority's reasoning, and argued for a middle ground, where cases requiring a uniform rule would be governed by general maritime law, whilst those of essentially local interest would be governed by state law. Justice Reed, together with Justice Burton, dissented and argued that the rule, until Congress or court modified it, should apply to all maritime cases so as to preserve uniformity (Sturley MF (2002)A US Perspective on Marine Insurance Law, Ch 12 In Thomas R (ed) The Modern Law of Marine Insurance, Vol. 2 , LLP).

57 *Wilburn Boat Co v Fireman's Fund Insurance Co*, 348 US 310, 75 SCt 368, 99 LEd, 337 (1955) .

tracts. Since this ruling, and with virtually no guidance from the Supreme Court, the lower courts have been divided in their approach to this *"vertical"* choice of law question.[58] There is also the *"horizontal"* choice of law question, i.e. in case state law applies, which state law this may be.[59] Yet, even when a particular state law has been chosen, there is also the problem of applying that insurance state law in the marine insurance context.

Although the situation, following the ruling seems complicated, in practice courts have had little trouble discerning the applicable principles and rules.[60] As a result, courts continue to apply federal law in marine in-

58 The Supreme Court began its vertical choice-of-law analysis by asking whether there was an established federal admiralty rule governing the issue. The court concluded that there was no such rule in the case before it, offering no more guidance on what would be required for a rule to become sufficiently established. The court expected more than two court of appeal rulings so as to accept the literal compliance rule as part of the general admiralty law. However, despite the broad criticism of the *Wilburn Boat*, the judiciary has not uniformly limited or distinguished it. In *Youell v Exxon Corp*, [48 F3d 105 1995 AMC 369] the court – although essentially willing to disregard *Wilburn Boat*- did not declare that the case encompassed a more general impetus justifying the non application of state law. Some courts choose to apply state law simply because the case before them involves marine insurance (Sturley MF (2002)A US Perspective on Marine Insurance Law, Ch 12 In Thomas R (ed) The Modern Law of Marine Insurance, Vol 2 , LLP).

59 When a court has chosen a particular state's law, there is rarely a relevant judicial decision or statute in the maritime context. Many states exclude marine insurance from significant portions of their insurance legislation. Thus, the court is left to resolve a marine insurance dispute with reasoning derived from other areas of insurance such as automobile or homeowner insurance. In identifying which state's law will be applied, federal choice-of-law considerations will govern. In *Advani Enterprises Inc v Underwriters at Lloyd's* [927 F2d. 882 1991 AMC 2211 (5th Circ)] the United States District Court for the Southern District of New York granted summary judgement to a cargo underwriter because of the insured's breach of an express warranty that voided the policy under New York State Law. On appeal, the United States Court of Appeal for the 2nd Circuit found there was no established federal law, under the *Wilburn Boat*, and balancing the contacts under federal choice-of-law rules held that English law applied. The result is that under *Wilburn Boat*, where federal law is not deemed well established, state or foreign law may be applied but federal law may not. (Sturley MF (2002)A US Perspective on Marine Insurance Law, Ch 12 In Thomas R (ed) The Modern Law of Marine Insurance, Vol 2 , LLP).

60 In *Kossick v United Fruit Co*, [365 US 731,81 SCt886,6 LEd 2d 56 (1961)] the Supreme Court explained *Wilburn Boat*, justifying the application of state law due to a lack of any provision of maritime law governing the matter there presented and clarified that *Wilburn Boat* did not require state law to govern in

surance cases, either because they find that there is an established federal admiralty rule, or they conclude they should fashion one. However, courts are not particularly eager to do the latter, as there is a presumption against creating a federal rule law and in favour of applying of state law.[61] Nevertheless, in most instances, there is no difference between state and federal marine insurance principles. The US substantive law of marine insurance has, therefore, become an admixture of English, Federal Admiralty and State law and must be applied to a variety of contracts. In practice, the application of the *Wilburn Boat* doctrine means that marine insurance in the US will be dominated by state law rules. Most federal courts simply recite the rule and apply state law. Another major consequence of the *Wilburn Boat*[62] is that, few maritime cases have arisen, and even when they have arisen they have not been accepted by the Supreme Court. Fortunately, although the *Wilburn Boat*[63] problem affects insurers, it has not driven many out of the US market. The American Institute of Marine Underwriters recognises this ruling as a problem, and has requested the Supreme Court to revisit the issue. In addition, in 1991 the Maritime Law Association of the US proposed that a step towards a Federal Marine Insurance Act be taken, but there was no support from the Congress. The American Institute of Marine Underwriters also objected, fearing that the proposal might draw marine insurance matters to the regulators' attention and result in greater uncertainty.[64] Of the latest developments in this field are the Restatement, proposed and considered by the American Law Institute, and the work of the Comité Maritime Internationale (CMI) on the harmonisation among nations in important areas of law.

---

every admiralty case. *Wilburn Boat* can also be explained on the basis that it would have been inappropriate for the Court to have *"fashioned"* a federal law rule, for insurance on a boat plying the waters of a small inland lake that just happened to be in admiralty jurisdiction.

61 *Big Lift Shipping Co v Bellefonte In. Co*, 594 FSupp 701, 1985 AMC 1201 (SDNY 1984); *Kamani v Port of Houston Authority,* 702 F2d 612,614 (5th Cir.1983); *Elevating Boats Inc v Gulf Coast Marine Inc*, 766 F2d 195 (5th Cir 1985).

62 *Wilburn Boat Co v Fireman's Fund Insurance Co*, 348 US 310, 75 SCt 368, 99 LEd, 337 (1955).

63 *Wilburn Boat Co v Fireman's Fund Insurance Co*, 348 US 310, 75 SCt 368, 99 LEd, 337 (1955).

64 Sturley MF (2002)A US Perspective on Marine Insurance Law, Ch. 12 In Thomas R (ed) The Modern Law of Marine Insurance, Vol. 2 , LLP.

1.6. The history and legislative framework of marine insurance in Canada

Canada is a country following partially the continental law system, in the French speaking area of Québec, and the Common law system in the rest of the territories forming part of the Commonwealth. Before the passing of the Federal Statute dealing with marine insurance, all provinces and territories of Canada had the power to shape insurance contract law extensively. The provincial statutes enacted, deal with the form and the content of insurance contracts. British Columbia, Manitoba, New Brunswick and Ontario have their own Insurance Acts in relation to marine insurance, i.e. the Marine Insurance Act RSBC 1996,[65] the Marine Insurance Act RSM 1987,[66] the Marine Insurance Act RSNB 1973,[67] and lastly the Marine Insurance Act RSO 1990.[68] In the provinces of Nova Scotia and Québec, there is no specific statute regulating separately marine insurance but law on marine insurance is regarded as a separate part of the general body of insurance contract legislation. Since 1993, there also exists a Federal Marine Insurance Act.

Canadian law of marine insurance is derived largely from the English Law. The latter regulates marine insurance via the various statutes passed by the English Parliament, the Marine Insurance Act 1906 being the most significant one, together with the developed by Courts case law. Canadian maritime law includes the body of law which was administered in England by the High Court on its admiralty side, as amended from time to time by the Federal Parliament and as it has developed through judicial precedent to date.

In order to better understand which law governs marine insurance, one must always consider the constitutional division of powers and the constitutional applicability of any particular statute.

Until approximately 1993 it was generally considered that, for constitutional purposes, marine insurance was within the power of the various provinces to legislate under the heading *"Property and Civil Rights"* in the Constitution Act. For this reason, many provinces had passed provincial marine insurance acts and had provided for insurance acts of general application to apply to contracts of marine insurance.

---

[65] for British Columbia.

[66] for Manitoba.

[67] for New Brunswick.

[68] for Ontario.

In *Triglav v Terrasses Jewellers*,[69] the Supreme Court of Canada held that a contract of marine insurance was, first and foremost, a contract of maritime law and that it was within the power of the Federal government to legislate under the heading *"Navigation and Shipping"* in the Constitution Act. The Supreme Court, further, held that the law governing contacts of marine insurance was Canadian maritime law, as enacted by the Federal Court Act. As a consequence of this ruling, it was recognised that there was a need for a Federal Act dealing with marine insurance and the Federal Marine Insurance Act was ultimately passed, modeled on the English Marine Insurance Act 1906. This appears to have been a mistake, in the sense that the Marine Insurance Act 1906 provides an incomplete regulation of marine insurance. In England, as in the provinces prior to this court decision, marine insurance is not regulated solely by the Marine Insurance Act 1906 but, in addition, case law has formulated the way marine insurance contracts and related arising legal issues are interpreted. By simply modeling the Federal Act on the English Marine Insurance Act of 1906, other important aspects of the regulation of marine insurance were ignored. This has not been a problem, as in the absence of specific federal legislation the provincial acts would apply. However, the situation created by the ruling in *Triglav v Terrasses Jewellers*[70] has changed, following *Ordon v Grail*[71] where the Supreme Court of Canada held that it would be very rare that a provincial act of general application would apply to a matter otherwise governed by Canadian maritime law. The importance of this decision, for marine insurance, is that it is now extremely doubtful whether provincial statutes have any application to contracts of marine insurance. This leaves a number of gaps in the law of marine insurance and as a result the possibility of federal legislative reform, to deal with these gaps, is currently under discussion.

1.7. The history and legislative framework of marine insurance in Australia

In Australia, the Act regulating marine insurance is the Australian Marine Insurance Act 1909. It came into effect on 1/7/1909 and it has been frequently supported that it is a replica of the English Marine Insurance Act 1906 because of its similarity to the English statute.

---

69 [1983] 1 SCR 283.
70 [1983] 1 SCR 283.
71 [1998] 3 S.C.R. 437.

The Australian Law Reform Commission (ALRC) was asked on 21/1/2000 to review the Marine Insurance Act 1909. The Commission was asked to report by 30/4/2001 and it has recommended vast changes to the law governing marine insurance in Australia. The threshold question for the Australian Law Reform Commission was whether to maintain the Marine Insurance Act 1909 and amend it, or repeal it and start again. The Australian Law Reform Commission decided not to abandon the Marine Insurance Act 1909 altogether, retaining the division between general and marine insurance by the use of separate Acts. This has the benefit of retaining almost a century of judicial decisions interpreting key phrases in the Marine Insurance Act 1909 and its UK predecessor. Thus, the proposals for reform[72] are to be viewed by way of amendments to the Marine Insurance Act. Despite its recommendation that the traditional Marine Insurance Act 1909 be maintained, the Australian Law Reform Commission seeks to achieve clarity and fairness. The Commission recognised the importance of some international consistency but without excessive subservience to the English Marine Insurance Act 1906. [73]

1.8. General conclusive remarks and comparative discussion

Due to its nature as the most ancient form of insurance, marine insurance law is dealt with separately than other forms of insurance; in some countries it is codified in a separate statute, whilst in others it is codified in a law statute regulating it along side with other forms of insurance, in more general statutes.[74]

In England, the Marine Insurance Act 1906 primarily codified the then existing cases. Many think of it nowadays as obsolete and out of date, nevertheless, it is remarkable the extent to which it has covered various legal issues in connection with marine insurance law and practice. The Marine insurance Act 1906 is supplemented by the Institute Clauses and their interpretation.

In relation to the argument that the Marine Insurance Act 1906 is obsolete and should be abolished in light of a new modern code, it is worth noting that any new codification should render the law more accessible and

---

[72] If accepted.

[73] Australian Law Reform Commission Reform (Report 91) <http://www.austlii.edu.au/au/other/alrc/publications/reports/91/>

[74] Argyriadis A (1986) Elements of Insurance Law, 4th edn, Sakkoulas Publications, Thessaloniki, Greece.

prevent disputes from arising. The primary aim of the Marine Insurance Act 1906 was to achieve certainty[75] and, to a certain extent, this has been achieved at the time of its enactment. Nevertheless, on the assumption that it is neither possible nor permissible for the draftsmen, in a pure codification process to anticipate and provide clear answers to the issues which will subsequently rise, it appears that, both back in 1906 and nowadays, it would have been impossible to come up with a *"perfect"* statute. Thus, to simply render the Marine Insurance Act 1906 invalid, only to replace it by another code with the same amount of imperfection, will make none substantial difference. Moreover, if we consider the actual operation of the Marine Insurance Act 1906 since its inception, we cannot say that it has not worked well, although it retains little relevance in the present market; firstly, because many of the questions raised are factual, thus solved by reference to market evidence; secondly, because important matters that have been left unsaid in the 1906 Act have been clarified by courts; and thirdly, because the evolution and development of the marine market and practices has seen the disappearance of old problems and the creation of new ones. In addition, the role of the judiciary has been crucial in clarifying what the Act may fail to achieve in the modern era and has assisted a lot in eliminating the *"weak"* points of the Act. Since 1906, the courts have spent much of their time seeking to develop and reapply code principles to novel situations, and the code has really been little more than a token starting-point. In effect, the courts have in practice been able to apply the law flexibly, heavily influenced by market practice. Finally, the marine market has constantly revised its standard wording, and in construing such changes it has been necessary for the courts to look at the common law, at the original wordings and at the changes themselves, in order to ascertain the purpose of the new wordings.[76] The introduction of the Institute Clauses and their various amendments, have largely contributed to bringing an air of innovation to the formulation of law by the courts on the basis of their interpretation. Not least, the English courts have demonstrated, over time, that they are capable of reaching results which are user-friendly and embrace flexi-

[75] The business community wanted to see simple and easily expressed statements of principle, and pressed that case in 1906.

[76] The 1906 Act has not removed the need to refer to pre-Act authorities, and that even where the wording of the Act is clear the courts have accepted the need to construe its terms flexibly in order to give the Act a sensible modern application. (Croly C, Merkin R (2001) Doubts About Insurance Codes, J.B.L. 2001, Nov, 587-604).

bility and have achieved to largely modernise law on the face of their rulings.[77]

The rest of the common law jurisdictions discussed, have been largely influenced by the English law in regulating marine insurance. In the USA, marine insurance had been regulated by federal maritime law until the infamous ruling of the Supreme Court in the *Wilburn Boat,*[78]as a consequence of which, in the absence of an established federal admiralty principle, state law should apply.[79] In Canada, marine insurance used to be regulated by provincial statutes, leaving any gaps to be filled in by the application of federal maritime law, until 1993 that the Federal Marine Insurance Act, largely based on the English Marine Insurance Act 1906, was enacted. Similarly, in Australia, the Australian Marine Insurance Act 1909 has been largely founded on the English MIA 1906.

In relation to the regulation of marine insurance in the continental law jurisdictions discussed, we note that the English law influence has been substantial. In Greece, marine insurance law is mainly regulated in two separate statutes[80], whilst the provisions of general insurance and commercial law may also apply, wherever permitted, in accordance with the principle of *lex specialis.* In Norway, marine insurance is regulated through the means of private codification, i.e. the Norwegian Marine Insurance Plans. The pre-eminence of the Plans has in recent years been diminished to some extents, due to the new Insurance Contract Act [81] and the internationalisation of the Norwegian insurance market. Nevertheless, the position enjoyed by the Norwegian Marine insurance Plan is still strong and widely accepted in the market. In France, marine insurance is mainly regulated by the Insurance Code and additionally by national laws communicating the requirements set by the relevant EU directives, as well as by customs and professional usages embodied in the form of recommendations or rules.

---

77 Croly C, Merkin R.(2001) Doubts About Insurance Codes, J.B.L. 2001, Nov: 587-604

78 *Wilburn Boat Co v Fireman's Fund Insurance Co*, 348 US 310, 75 SCt 368, 99 LEd, 337 (1955) .

79 This has had the effect not only to split the unity of Anglo-American maritime law and to create confusion, but also to reduce substantially the number of marine insurance law cases that are adjudicated by the Supreme Court.

80 The Code of Private Maritime Law (CPML) [ΚΙΝΔ] Chapter XIV, Art. 257-288 and Law 2496/1997.

81 It regulates contracts generally and is now mandatory with respect to certain types of marine insurance ; for example it applies to all vessels under 15 meters.

It is apparent that the English law has strongly influenced the continental law regimes in regulating marine insurance although these jurisdictions have ultimately come to create their own statutes, which differ significantly in nature from those of the common law jurisdictions. Hence, amidst the distinctive differences to be noted, is the fact that the continental law regimes have evolved to ultimately regulate separately marine insurance, alongside other general laws. Thus, in the common law countries marine insurance is regulated most of the times in a separate statute[82], whereas in the continental law regimes the trend is to regulate marine insurance in a separate statute and to supplement its regulation with that from other parts of law as well. Notwithstanding the differences in the regulatory framework, in relation to indemnity, there is a general consensus that the assured should receive indemnity for the loss he may have sustained without being over-indemnified.

---

[82] However, in the USA there is no specific statute to regulate marine insurance other than federal maritime law. Moreover, due to the *Wilburn Boat v Fireman's Fund Insurance Co*, 348 US 310, 75 SCt 368, 99 LEd, 337 (1955) ruling, courts will nowadays mostly apply state law. Nevertheless, even in this case the situation is not always that clear-cut, as not all states have a statute to regulate marine insurance law and, subsequently, they will have to resort to either home or automobile insurance law to resolve the issue arisen.

2. Indemnity marine insurance contracts: basic features and cover provided

2.1. Basic features of the marine insurance contracts

2.1.1. Basic features of the marine insurance contracts in England

2.1.1.1. The nature of the marine insurance contract: basic literature review

The basis of insurance is the law of contract. Between the assured and the underwriter, there is a contractual relationship with mutual rights and obligations of both parties within the terms of the specific contract each time.

In theory, the purpose of any form of insurance is to replace that which has been lost. The assured should not profit from the loss or be in a worse position than he was before the loss occurred. In practice, the recompense is of monetary nature and this system of reimbursement is called *"indemnifying"*.[1]

Thus, the insurance policy is a contract of indemnity, the latter forming a basic principle of insurance law in the sense that the assured can only recoup the loss occurred. Before the act of indemnification, the loss has to be primarily identified and then measured or quantified. These are two acts that take place separately. Upon identification of losses and their valuation, the other party may claim that the losses are either misconceived, or wrongly measured and quantified, or that they do not fall into

---

[1] United Nations (1982) UN Conference on Trade & Development: Legal and Documentary Aspects of the Marine Insurance Contract, UN, NY, pp. 1-2.

the defendant's liability due to a specific reason, such as the fact that they might not be covered by the terms of the relevant policy.

Ivamy (1986)[2] states that the relevant type of insurance is each time formed according to the nature of the event. In marine insurance, for example, the sum insured becomes payable on the happening of a marine peril. In the contracts of indemnity, the amount recoverable is measured by the extent of the assured's pecuniary loss, hence a marine insurance contract's characterisation as a contract of indemnity.[3]

Marine insurance forms a category of general insurance. Likewise, marine insurance contracts form a category of general insurance contracts. Templeman (1986)[4] says that the marine insurance contract is special, primarily in that it is an insurance contract. Moreover, it is a special form of insurance contract as it has many unique characteristics. A distinctive feature of marine insurance is that it is very much international in scope. Most cargo insurance is inherently international since coverage of goods usually involves international transportation of them. In addition, hull insurance is international as a result of the risk of loss or damage to the vessel occurring abroad and the tendency to place all or part of the insurance in a country other than that of the ship-owner.[5]

As also stated in Bennett (1986),[6] fundamental to the nature of a contract of marine insurance, is its' characteristic as a contract of indemnity.[7] This means that the law provides the assured with indemnification equal to the loss occurred, i.e. equal either to the amount of the loss sustained or to the actual or agreed value of the insured object. It is in s. 1 of the Marine Insurance Act 1906 that the contract of insurance is defined as a contract of indemnity[8] and indemnification is being expressly mentioned. The section reads: *"...a contract of marine insurance is a contract whereby the insurer*

---

2 Ivamy ERH (1986) General Principles of Insurance Law,5th edn, Butterworths, Ch.3.

3 Ivamy ERH (1986) General Principles of Insurance Law,5th edn, Butterworths, Ch.3.

4 Lambeth RJ (1986) Templeman on Marine Insurance: Its Principles and Practice, 6th edn, Pitman.

5 United Nations (1982) UN Conference on Trade & Development: Legal and Documentary Aspects of the Marine Insurance Contract, UN, NY, pp. 1-5.

6 Bennett H (1986) The Law of Marine Insurance, Clarendon Press, Oxford,Ch.1.

7 Bennett H (1986) The Law of Marine Insurance, Clarendon Press, Oxford, Ch.1.

8 Lambeth RJ (1986) Templeman on Marine Insurance: Its Principles and Practice, 6th edn, Pitman, Ch.1 ; Mustill, MJ & Gilman JCB (1981) Arnould's Law of Marine Insurance And Average, 16th edn, Vol. I, Stevens, Ch. 1.

undertakes to indemnify the assured, in manner and to the extent thereby agreed, against marine losses, that is to say the losses incident to marine adventure".

It is clear that the most operative word in it is the word *"indemnify"*, and it is within the scope of the cardinal principle of indemnity that the whole contract is founded and the rules relating to the right of claim under a policy emanate from. Also, the rights and liabilities of the parties are dictated by this basic concept and the amount recovered by the assured, which is measured by the extent of his pecuniary loss, is also governed by it.[9]

The most incisive comment on the subject of indemnity can be found in Lord Wright's judgement of the House of Lords in *Rickards v Forestal Land, Timber and Railways Co*[10] where he said:

"...the object both of the legislature and of the courts have been to give effect to the idea of indemnity, which is the basic principle of insurance, and to apply in the diverse complications of fact and law in respect of which it has to operate..."

Accordingly, in *Castellain v Preston*[11], Mr Justice Brett remarked:

"...the contract of insurance...is a contract of indemnity, and of indemnity only, and this contract means that the assured, in case of a loss against which the policy has been made, shall be fully indemnified, but shall never be more than fully indemnified..."

It is also the incidents and the legal consequences of the contract, which stem from this great principle. Thus, in *Brotherston v Barber*[12], Lord Ellenborough stated:

"...the great principle of the law of insurance is that it is a contract for indemnity..."[13]

Although indemnity is not always perfectly achieved, nevertheless, it forms the basis of the insurance contracts, whether marine or non marine ones. As also per Arnould (1981),[14] it is of the essence of the contract of marine insurance that it is a contract of indemnity. However, the principle of indemnity may be violated by means of a valued policy; the valuation of the subject of insurance therein being in general conclusive against both parties although it may not in fact reflect the true value.

As a result, indemnity can be based on the values agreed upon in advance. These values might be greater or less than the values actually at risk. It has, therefore, been argued that a policy of insurance is not a perfect contract of indemnity and that it must be taken with this qualification

---

9 However, this should not come as a surprise, for, the very purpose of effecting a policy of insurance- marine or non-marine- is for indemnity for loss.

10 [1941]3 All ER 62, HL.

11 (1883)11 QBD 380.

12 (1816)5 M & S 418.

13 Hodges S (1996) Law of Marine Insurance, Cavendish Publications, Ch.2

14 Mustill MJ, Gilman JCB, (1981) Arnould's Law of Marine Insurance & Average 16th edn, Vol. I, Stevens,Ch.1.

that the parties may agree beforehand in estimating the value of the subject insured, as indeed they may in any other contract to indemnify.

In relation to that Lord Summer noted, in the case of *British & Foreign Insurance Co Ltd v Wilson Shipping Co Ltd*[15]:

"... in practice, contracts of insurance by no means always result in a complete indemnity, but indemnity is always the basis of the contract..."

Similarly, Patteson J. stated, in *Irving v Manning*[16]:

"...a policy of assurance is not a perfect contract of indemnity..."

Thus, ideally, an assured should be compensated only to the extent of his loss, but in practice this is not always easily feasible.

It is also clear, from the study of s. 1 of the Marine Insurance Act 1906, that the marine insurance contract is only one of indemnity. Firstly, the Act indicates that the indemnity offered by the contract is not perfect but *"...in manner and to the extent thereby agreed..."* - nevertheless, it is a real and existent loss that must be sustained and proved before the act of indemnification can take place - secondly, it refers to *"...losses incident to the marine adventure..."*[17]; thirdly, indemnity has also evolved to relate to parties' agreements.[18] The Act sets a barrier in the freedom of a contract of marine insurance through its provision stating that indemnity should not exceed the sum set out in the policy of insurance.[19] In practice, however, the insured is allowed to receive compensation in excess of the actual total loss that he has suffered, as the sum fixed by the policy or the assured may exceed the actual value of the interest.

The conclusion drawn is that indemnification is not always fairly awarded, as the amount may be bigger or smaller than it should be. On the one hand, the Act allows the parties to determine the extent of indemnification, whilst on the other hand the Courts - through their various rulings - have stated that an absolute and perfect indemnification is not always possible under a marine insurance contract. Both the Act and the Courts allow parties - up to an extent - to decide on the indemnity amount that is to be

---

15 [1921]1 AC 188.

16 (1847)1 HLC 287.

17 As this was commented in *Wilson v Owners of the Cargo per Xantho* [(1887) 12 App. Cas. 503], *Rickards v Forestal Land, Timber and Railways Co* [1941]3 All ER, HL.

18 The law is not always clear in setting the extent of indemnity and as a consequence there is much difficulty in the exact measuring of the insurable value of the subject-matter insured, which has resulted to the parties being left free to agree upon the extent of the indemnity.

19 S.67(1) of the Marine Insurance Act 1906 states: *"The sum which the assured can recover in respect of a loss on a policy by which he is insured, in the case of an unvalued policy to the full extent of the insurable value, or in the case of a valued policy to the full extent of the value fixed by the policy, is called "measure of indemnity."*

payable, even if the sum is different when compared with the indemnity corresponding to the loss in fact occurred.

2.1.1.2. The nature of the interest: insurable interest

The concept of insurable interest evolved from the statutory avoidance of wagering contracts.[20] The requirement that the assured must possess an insurable interest in the subject-matter of a marine insurance contract is correlated to the principle that the marine insurance contract is a contract of indemnity.[21]

Although it was before the Marine Insurance Act of 1745 that the contract of marine insurance - being a contract of indemnity - required the assured to have an interest in the thing insured, nevertheless for some period of time the policies issued, expressly waived proof of the assured's interest or admitted the existence of interest and thus came to be called *"interest no interest"* policies. The parties in such a policy agreed to wager regardless of the insurable interest[22] and it was with the passing of the Act of 1745 that such contracts were prohibited so as to stop the fraudulent loss of vessels in furtherance of wagers upon their safe arrival, the endangerment of seamen's lives, the solvency of underwriters and the flourish of illicit trade. However, they were still permitted on ships and cargoes from abroad due to the difficulty of proof of interest in such cases.

Within the terms of the Marine Insurance Act 1906, s.4 renders gaming or wagering contracts void, and states that contracts are considered as such when there is no insurable interest at the time when the contract is entered into, nor any expectation of acquiring it. The Marine Insurance (Gambling Policies) Act 1909, penalises gambling policies, proposes that they are void and in addition makes them criminal. Although the Act does not prohibit them expressly, it does so implicitly.

---

20 Until the Marine Insurance Act 1745 there was no legal requirement that an insured have any connection to the insured adventure.

21 An insurable interest is also required under s.4 of the Marine Insurance Act 1906, so that the contract is not considered a gaming or wagering contract and thus void.

22 And such wagers were called gaming and wagering policies. It is unclear whether courts enforced them at that time but they came to be enforceable 100 years later, probably due to the fact that merchants considered them beneficial, hence they had become very popular (Legh-Jones N (2002) The Elements of Insurable Interest in Marine Insurance Law, In Thomas R (ed) The Modern Law of Marine Insurance Vol. II, LLP).

2.1.1.2.1. Definition and evaluation of the concept of insurable Interest and the requirements set by law for it

In order to obtain coverage there must be a legal or equitable relationship between the person benefiting from insurance and the insured property, i.e. there should exist *"insurable interest"*.[23] Thus, an insurable interest is a basic requirement of a marine insurance contract. In order to be able to request indemnity, the assured must primarily have an insurable interest in the subject-matter insured and secondly also to have it at the time of the loss.

The first requirement, as to the existence of the insurable interest, originates from the indemnity principle. S.5(1) of the Marine Insurance Act 1906 states that:

"...every person has an insurable interest who is interested in a marine adventure..."

The classical definition of insurable interest was given in *Lucena v Craufurd* [24], where Lord Eldon stated:

"...a right in the property or a right derivable out of some contract about the property, which in either case may be lost upon some contingency affecting the possession or enjoyment of the property".[25]

According to this perspective, in order to establish an insurable interest, the assured must stand in a legal or equitable relationship to the subject matter of the insurance and he must also have an economic interest in the subject matter, in the sense that the assured might benefit from the continuing safety of the subject matter or be prejudiced by its loss, damage or detention.[26] If the assured has no insurable interest in the subject-matter insured, he can recover nothing under the policy, no loss is sustained to have been suffered by him, and the insurer has no duty or obligation of indemnification.[27]

S. 5(2) of the Marine Insurance Act 1906, provides that the person involved in a marine adventure must have or expect to have a vested insurable interest[28]. The language of s. 5(2) of the Marine Insurance Act 1906 reflects a technical legal approach to the recognition of insurable interest

---

23 United Nations (1982) UN Conference on Trade & Development: Legal and Documentary Aspects of the Marine Insurance Contract, UN, NY, p. 5.

24 (1806)2 Bos & PNR 269.

25 See also *Macaura v Northern Assurance Co Ltd* [1925] AC 619.

26 In addition, the existence of insurable interest lessens the danger of fraudulent and intentional destruction of the subject-matter insured, and it is in this way that the *"moral-hazard factor"* is introduced.

27 O'May D (1993) Marine Insurance Law and Policy, LLP pp.47-48.

28 *Lucena v Craufurd* (1806)2 B & PNR 269.

and it was confirmed by the House of Lords in *Macaura v Northern Assurance Co Ltd.*[29] In this case, the owner of a timber estate sold all the timber thereon to a timber company in return for 42.000 fully paid shares, of £1 each, which in fact were the only shares that the company issued, and then insured the timber against fire. Whilst the assured was still owed £19.000 by the company, a fire destroyed most of the timber, but it was held[30] that the assured had no insurable interest as either sole shareholder or creditor in the timber that had subsequently been destroyed by fire. As a shareholder he had no right to the property owned by the company - the latter being a separate legal person - even though his shares would fall in value in the event of the destruction of the company's property, nor as creditor - given the fact that *Macaura* had no right to the company's property in the sense of a mortgage or a charge over it or some other proprietary security interest. [31] However, as Birds and Hird (2001) purport[32], this could be considered as too narrow a view, because in both the above capacities the insured did have a real economic interest in the company's property and moreover he could have put matters right by arranging for the company to insure the timber.[33]

English law, however, occasionally recognises an insurable interest, even in the absence of a vested legal or equitable interest in the subject-matter insured. This can be justified firstly from the fact that the interpretation of s. 5(2) of the Marine Insurance Act 1906 is illustrative and not

---

[29] [1925] AC 619.

[30] In the House of Lords.

[31] Birds J, Hird (2001) NJ Bird's Modern Insurance Law, London S&M pp52-53

[32] Birds J, Hird (2001) NJ Bird's Modern Insurance Law, London S&M pp52-53

[33] It should be noted that a shareholder can insure his shares against loss of value due to the failure of an adventure that his company is embarked upon [*Wilson v Jones* (1867) L.R. 2 Ex. 139] and a creditor may insure against his debtor's insolvency [*Waterkeyne v Eagle Star Insurance* (1920) 5 Ll.L.Rep. 12] so that the practical results of the decision in *Macaura v Northern Assurance Co Ltd [1925] AC 619* can be substantially mitigated. The more recent decision of the Court of Appeal in *Glengate-KG Properties Ltd v Norwich Union Fire Insurance Society* [1996]1 Lloyd's Rep. 614 was concerned with the interpretation of the phrase *"the interest of the insured"* in a policy covering the insured owner of a building against consequential loss following a fire or other insured peril. The issue was whether or not the insured could recover for the loss of the architects' plans that were owned by the architects although they might one day have been acquired by the insured. The Court of Appeal held that the insured had an interest in the plans, notwithstanding the lack of a proprietary interest in them, but it is clear that the majority regarded that interest as being to insure in respect of consequential loss and not to insure the plans themselves. (Birds J, Hird NJ (2001) Bird's Modern Insurance Law, London, S&M, p. 53).

exhaustive, for it employs the term *"relation"* and not the term *"interest"*. Secondly, as is observed from the study of the case of *Moran Galloway & Co v Uzielli,*[34] whilst creditors of a single ship company were denied an insurable interest in the vessel by virtue of the debt, it was held that creditors had an insurable interest therein by reason of their right to bring *in rem* proceedings in a Court of Admiralty. Thirdly, according to s.8 of the Marine Insurance Act 1906, a *"partial interest"* of any nature is insurable. Fourthly, in the case of *Sharp v Sphere Drake Insurance p.l.c.("The Moonacre"),*[35] a yacht was acquired for the benefit of the plaintiff and, for tax reasons, ownership was vested in an off-shore company which, by two powers of attorney, granted unlimited and exclusive powers of management and disposal to the plaintiff in whose name the yacht was insured. It was held that the powers of attorney conferred a benefit contingent on the continued safety of the vessel, sufficient to constitute an insurable interest. The *Macaura v Northern Assurance Co Ltd*[36] case was distinguished on the ground that the powers of attorney created a direct relationship between the plaintiff and the yacht.

In cargo insurance, whether a buyer of goods has an insurable interest may depend upon the interpretation of the contract of sale. In *Anderson v Morice,*[37] the assured was the buyer of a cargo of rice which was partially lost after most of its quantity had been loaded. On the basis that the subject-matter of the contract was a complete cargo of rice, the assured was denied recovery for lack of an insurable interest. In *Colonial Insurance Co of New Zealand v Adelaide Marine Insurance Co*[38], the word *"cargo"* referred to the bags of wheat the boat could properly carry, risk passing in each bag being loaded on board as opposed to the indivisible bulk cargo sold and insured in *Anderson v Morice*[39], which came into existence only once the full quantity had been loaded on board. In *Anderson v Morice*[40], moreover, the carrying vessel had been chartered by the sellers who were to receive freight for the carriage of the cargo and therefore the loading did not constitute delivery to the buyers. In *Colonial Insurance Co of New Zealand v Adelaide Marine Insurance Co* [41] the vessel was chartered by the buyer and loading thereon constituted delivery to the buyers

34 [1905]2 KB 555.
35 [1992]2 Lloyd's Rep. 501.
36 [1925] AC 619.
37 (1874) LR 10 CP 58.
38 (1886)12 App.Cas 128.
39 (1874) LR 10 CP 58.
40 (1874) LR 10 CP 58.
41 (1886)12 App.Cas 128.

pursuant to the contract of sale on *"f.o.b."* terms with the master who received the cargo acting as agent of the buyers and issuing bills of lading upon their instructions and the sellers having nothing to do with all that.[42]

Although the Marine Insurance Act 1906, in s. 4(1), states that every gaming or wagering contract is void,[43] nevertheless it does not forbid such contracts. It is remarkable that gaming or wagering marine insurance contracts are used and that the practice of writing marine policies on *"policy proof of interest"* (*"p.p.i."*) terms has continued over the years. This proves that their constant use, serves the scope of meeting a commercial need. These policies are referred to as *"honour"* policies because they are binding in honour only and cannot be used as evidence in court. In general, courts refuse to enforce such a policy if it comes to their attention that there is a *"p.p.i."* provision, even if the defense is not taken by underwriters.[44]

An interesting case, in relation to the requirement and the existence of insurable interest, is *Feasey v Sun Life Assurance Co of Canada*.[45] In this case, a P&I Club sought to recover unpaid sums that it alleged were due to it from the insurance company under a reinsurance contract. The insurers claimed that - as per "The Life Insurance Act 1774", s.1 there was no insurable interest for the P&I Club to protect by the line-slip policy of reinsurance and that, even if there had been, they were still not entitled to recover as this would lead to a recovery of the value in excess of the interest as there were also under reinsurances under which it could claim[46]. At

---

42 Bennett, H (1986) The Law of Marine Insurance, Clarendon Press, Oxford, Ch.1; Mustill, MJ, Gilman, JCB (1981) Arnould's Law of Marine Insurance and Average, 16th edn, vol. I, Stevens, where it is stated that in order to have an insurable interest it is not necessary to have absolute vested ownership or property in the insured thing but it is also sufficient to have a right in the thing insured; or to have a right or be under a liability arising out of some contract relating to the thing insured, of such a nature that the party insuring may have benefit from its preservation or prejudice from its destruction (as per Lawrence J. in *Lucena v Craufurd* (1806)2 B & PNR 302).

43 *Thomas Chesire & Co v Vaughan Bros* [1920]3 KB 240; *John Edwards & Co v Motor Union Insurance Co Ltd* [1922]2 KB 249; *Thames & Mersey Marine Insurance Co Ltd v "Gunford" Ship* Co Ltd [1911] AC 529.

44 *Gedge v Royal Exchange Assurance* (1900)2 QB 214; O'May D (1993) Marine Insurance Law and Policy, LLP pp. 74-76.

45 [2002]2 All.E.R. (Comm) 292.

46 The principal basis of those allegations was that the fixed benefits payable under the master lineslip had been represented to be but were not a realistic estimate of the average sums likely to be paid by the club to its members, and that the club had made a substantial over-recovery as a result of the levels at which the benefits had been set. Section 1 of the 1774 Act provided that: *'no insurance*

First Instance, it was held that s.1 of the Act was intended to prevent gambling in the disguise of insurance. At the time that cover was taken, however, the P&I Club had a legitimate interest in the health of persons aboard the vessels, and in relation to the existence of other contracts, thus the policy was not gaming or wagering. This was immaterial, as the court was only interested in the interest having been insured in a way that did not result to a gamble or a wager at the inception of the contract; thus, the Club should recover the sums owed under the reinsurance policy. Reinsurers appealed against the decision that the P&I Club had an insurable interest under the contract of insurance made between it and a Lloyd's Syndicate[47] and sought to avoid their obligations to the Syndicate by alleging that the Club did not have an insurable interest.[48] Alternatively, the reinsurers submitted that the Club was seeking to claim more than the value of any insurable interest which it had and was not entitled to do so by virtue of s. 3 of the 1774 Act. It was held, dismissing the appeal, that the Club's insurance policy with the syndicate was not contrary to s. 1 of the 1774 Act and the Club was not seeking to claim more than the value of any insurable interest which it had contrary to s. 3 of the 1774 Act. *"Interest"* in the 1774 Act was undefined as it was difficult to arrive at a definition which would apply in all situations. Accordingly, each case depended on the precise terms of the policy under consideration. In the instant case, three questions needed to be asked, i.e. firstly which was - within the true construction of the Club's policy - the subject matter of the insurance; secondly, whether there was an insurable interest which was embraced within that subject matter; and thirdly, whether the insurable interest was capable of valuation in money terms at the date of the contract. In answer to all that, the object of the Club's policy was to cover the Club for the losses that it would suffer as insurer of its members by reference to fixed sums payable on certain events. The Club had a pecuniary interest in covering losses, for which it might be liable, which existed at the time it took out the policy. The sub-

shall be made by any person . . . on the life or lives of any person or persons, or on any other events whatsoever, wherein the person or persons for whose use . . . such policy or policies shall be made, shall have no interest, or by way of gaming or wagering . . .' Section 3 provided that: 'in all cases where the insured hath interest in such life or lives, event or events, no greater sum shall be recovered or received from the insurer or insurers than the amount of value of the interest of the assured in such life or lives, or other event or events'.

47 The Syndicate had insured the Club's liabilities to its members for personal injury or illness of persons occurring on or in relation to vessels or offshore rigs by way of a personal accident and illness master lineslip policy. The reinsurers had then reinsured the Syndicate's liability to the Club.

48 Reinsurers contended that the Club's insurance was illegal by virtue of the Life Assurance Act s.1.

ject matter of the Club's policy was not so specific that it did not embrace that interest.[49] Accordingly the Club's policy did not violate s. 1 of the 1774 Act. The value of a policy had to be assessed at the time that the policy was entered into and the assured was entitled to place such value on his interests as reflected the worse case scenario. Once that was appreciated, it was clear that reinsurers had not even begun to demonstrate that the Club was seeking to recover an amount, in excess of the value of the interest as at the date of the policy.[50]

O' Kane v Jones & Others[51] also deals, *inter alia*, with the requirements for insurable interest. In this case, in late 1999 two vessels owned by a company and managed by two others were insured by a Lloyd's syndicate (WELLINGTON) under a Hull and Machinery (H&M) policy. Due to the fact that the owners were delaying payment of the premiums owed and as a result of that the brokers were threatening to cancel the policy, the main managing company (ABC) sought alternative cover for one of the two vessels (the M/V MARTIN P) and insured the vessel with another syndicate at Lloyd's (JONES). The vessel (MARTIN P) shortly afterwards run aground and became a constructive total loss. The managing company upon receipt of the casualty news found out that the original policy had not been cancelled after all, thus, it cancelled the second policy and claimed for a constructive total loss. The insurers under the first policy initially agreed to pay and reached a settlement; however, upon acknowledging the existence of the second policy, they initially declined to pay the whole sum initially agreed on the basis that the second insurers were liable to contribute to the loss as co-insurers and later on agreed to pay the balance up to the insured value, while maintaining their position that the other insurers were liable to contribute.

In reaching its decision, the court had to answer various questions, one of which was whether ABC, was an assured under both Policies. To answer this question the court had to establish whether ABC had an insurable interest in the vessel MARTIN P. The Court found that ABC had an insurable interest. To support its finding the Court stated that, contrary to the finding of the House of Lords in *Macaura v Northern Assurance Co Ltd*[52], in *Petrofina (UK) Ltd v Magnaload Ltd*[53] it was held by Lloyd J. that all contractors and sub-contractors were insured in respect of loss of or

---

49 *Dalby v India and London Life Assurance Co* (1854) 15 C.B. 364, applied.

50 *Deepak Fertilizers & Petrochemicals Corp Ltd v Davy McKee (London)* [1999] 1 All E.R. (Comm) 69, considered.

51 [2003] All ER (D) 510 (Jul).

52 [1925] AC 619.

53 [1984] 1 QB 127.

damage to the entire contract works and that a sub-contractor was accordingly entitled to recover the whole of the loss insured, holding the excess over his own interest in trust for the others. In *National Oilwell (UK) Ltd v Davy Offshore Ltd*,[54] Colman J. had held that the plaintiff was a co-assured, under a builders' all risks policy taken out by the defendant main contractor, and had an insurable interest in the property involved in the common project not owned by him and not in his possession. The court concluded, from the citation of the above cases, that ownership or possession (or the right to possession) of the property insured is not a necessary requirement of an insurable interest therein and that commercial convenience can be a relevant factor in determining the existence of an insurable interest. The court justified its conclusion that ABC had an insurable interest in the vessel which satisfied the requirements of Marine Insurance Act 1906 s.5(2) as follows: the legal relationship was the one constituted by the Management Agreement, under which ABC contracted to manage the vessel in accordance with the provisions therein set out. Those provisions imposed extensive and ongoing responsibilities upon ABC in relation, among other things, to the maintenance, equipping, repair, survey, classification, crewing, provisioning, operation and navigation of the vessel. Although they did not give ABC possession or the right to possession of the vessel, and although the commercial management of the vessel was in other hands, those provisions gave ABC considerable control over the vessel and over its operation and although this possession or the right to possession is not an essential prerequisite of insurable interest, however, ABC stood to benefit by the safety of the MARTIN P, and might have been prejudiced by its loss, or by damage thereto, or might have incurred liability in respect thereof. In addition, the fact that ABC was entitled to remuneration under the Management Agreement for the services it provided and the Management Agreement automatically terminated if and when the vessel became a total loss - in which event, ABC would be deprived of the opportunity of continuing to earn remuneration there under - was sufficient benefit and corresponding prejudice for the purposes of s. 5(2) of the Marie Insurance Act 1906. In addition the Court stated that, having regard to the close practical relationship between a manager and the vessel under management, there are strong considerations of commercial convenience that support the recognition of an insurable interest in ABC.

In *Murphy v Murphy*[55] - a non marine insurance case - the claimant sought a share of the proceeds of a life insurance policy, and commenced

---

[54] [1993] 2 Lloyd's Rep. 582.

[55] *Murphy v Murphy* [2003] [2004] Lloyd's Rep IR 774.

the present action against the former wife of his father.[56] The claim was brought under the Inheritance (Provision for Family and Dependants) Act 1975. s. 2 of the Act empowers a court to make reasonable financial provision for dependant children out of the estate of a deceased parent. S. 9 is concerned with property jointly owned by the deceased, and provides that such provision can be made out of property of which the deceased was immediately before his death a joint tenant. The question was whether the policy, properly construed, was one under which Mr and Mrs Murphy were joint beneficiaries or whether it was one under which the parties had separate interests, with the survivor taking all. The Court of Appeal held in favour of the latter interpretation and that the claimant had no interest. The policy had distinguished between payments for terminal illness, where joint payment was owed and payments for death where the survivor was entitled absolutely to receive payment of the sum insured.[57]

In *Linelevel Ltd v Powszechny Zaklad Ubezpieczen SA*[58], the insured vessel - the *Nore Challenger* - was chartered by the owners, *Linelevel*, to *NMS* for a year from 29 September 1999, and insured by *NMS* on the Institute Time Clauses Hulls 1983 for loss from perils of the seas and also for loss of hire of US$2,500 per day for any loss of hire exceeding five days. The vessel went into dry dock on 28 September 2000, and the propulsion unit was found to have been damaged. On 5 October 2000 the insurers acknowledged that the vessel's managers, *SMS*, was to be treated as assured from that date. The insurers refused the claim, arguing that *Linelevel* and *SMS* had no title to sue and that the loss was not proximately caused by perils of the sea. On 26 June 2002, in order to facilitate recovery under the policy, *"Nore Maritime Shipping Limited T/A Murray Tugs"* assigned to *Linelevel* all outstanding claims. It was held that *Linelevel* could recover for damage to the vessel and *SMS* could recover for loss of hire. *NMS* had an insurable interest in its capacity as bareboat charterer, given its obligations to repair the vessel and to insure it, and had assigned its right of recovery to *Linelevel* who had title to sue for the hull damage. *SMS* was entitled to recover for loss of hire and had insurable interest in their capacity as managers. In addition, *NMS*'s duty of repair had been broken

56 Mr and Mrs Murphy had taken out a joint lives policy with Royal Insurance for 25 years, for payment of the insured sum to the survivor on the death of either or in respect of either contracting a terminal illness. Though the parties divorced, the policy was kept. Mr Murphy commenced living with Ms Holland and their child was born six days after Mr Murphy's death.

57 Merkin R (2006) Insurance Law Update 2003-2006.

58 *Linelevel Ltd v Powszechny Zaklad Ubezpieczen SA (The Nore Challenger)* [2005] EWHC 421 (Comm).

and *NMS* was liable to *Linelevel* for breach of that obligation and for the loss of hire caused by the need for repair; *NMS* therefore had an insurable interest in the loss of hire, which it had validly assigned to *Linelevel*.[59]

2.1.1.2.2. On the illegality of the insured adventure

S. 3(1) of the Marine Insurance Act 1906 states:

"…every lawful marine adventure may be the subject of a contract of marine insurance".

In addition, s. 4(1) of the Marine Insurance Act 1906 states that it is an implied warranty that the insured adventure has to be lawful and that it has to be conducted in a lawful manner. Where the insured adventure is illegal *-ab initio-* no valid contract of insurance is ever created. However, simply because the performance of the adventure contravenes the law, does not necessarily render the adventure itself unlawful.[60]

All persons have the right to protect their property by insurance, except *alien enemies*[61] as all trading with the enemy becomes illegal, as do the insurances effected in protection of such trade which are consequently void.[62] War does not, however, cease actions brought against any alien enemy who carries on business by representation in the UK, as the latter - having commercial domicile in the UK - can be sued and appear and defend an action against himself although he cannot counterclaim.[63]

2.1.1.2.3. The time when the insurable interest must attach

The time that the interest must attach is stated in s. 6(1),(2) of the Marine Insurance Act 1906. There has to be a genuine interest in prospect at a time an insurance contract is made, and not the mere expectation and hope of an interest. In *Buchanan & Co v Faber*,[64] a mere expectancy or hope of con-

---

59 Merkin R (2006) Insurance Law Update 2003-2006.

60 As Bennett (1996) evaluates in Bennett H (1996) The Law of Marine Insurance, Clarendon Press, Oxford 1996, Ch. 1, in *Archbolds (Freightage) Ltd v S Spanglett Ltd* [1961]1 QB 374], a contract for the carriage of goods was not rendered illegal by the carrier's failure to have a required by statute license, as the statute aimed to regulate the providers of transport and not to prohibit *"carriage of goods"* contracts.

61 i.e. subjects of a foreign state at war with the UK.

62 *Potts v Bell* (1800)8 TR 548.

63 *Robinson & Co v Mannheim Insurance Co* [1914]20 Com. Cas 125; Lambeth RJ (1986): Templeman on Marine Insurance: Its Principles and Practice, 6th edn., Pitman, Ch.1.

64 (1899)4 Com Cas 223.

tinuation of employment as ship managers was held to have been insufficient to constitute an insurable interest in commission and brokerage, there being no contract in existence.[65]

The insurable interest must attach for definite at the time of loss, if not earlier when insurance was effected. In *Piper v Royal Exchange Assurance,*[66] the defendants recovered the amount of claim paid under a mistake of fact, only when they later discovered that the plaintiff had no interest, or had had at most a contingent one which had not attached.

As Templeman (1986)[67] comments, only a mere expectation or hope is not sufficient to constitute an insurable interest - as happened in the *Buchanan* [68] case - but if the expectation is *bona fidae* the contract will not be deemed a gambling one.[69] S. 6(2) of the Marine Insurance Act 1906, states that an assured must be interested in the subject-matter insured at the time of the loss, if not at the time when the insurance was effected. In *Anderson v Morice,*[70] the insurable interest was held not to exist at the time of loss, thus the plaintiff was deemed not to have any insurable interest at all and could not recover under the policy for the loss sustained. However, this is not always the case and there are two exceptions to this general rule relating to a *"lost-not-lost policy"* and to the position of an assignee.

The assured of a *"lost-not-lost policy"* is allowed to recover for a loss, even though he may not have acquired his interest in the subject-matter insured until after the loss. The only condition barring him from recovery would be that, at the time the contract was effected, he would have been aware of the loss whilst the insurer would have not. In such a case, he would have been breaching both the duty to observe utmost good faith and to disclose all material facts and the insurer would be entitled to avoid the contract.

In the second exceptional case,[71] assignment of a policy of insurance may be effected before or after a loss. The assignee has no better right than the assignor and the policy is of benefit to him only if the assignor also has an insurable interest on the subject-matter insured at the time of the loss. The policy may be assigned after the loss, provided that

---

65 O'May D (1993) Marine Insurance Law and Policy, LLP pp 47-48.

66 [1932]44 Ll.L.Rep. 103.

67 Lambeth RJ (1986): Templeman on Marine Insurance: Its Principles and Practice, 6th edn, Pitman, Ch.1

68 (1899) 4 Com Cas 223.

69 Lambeth RJ (1986): Templeman on Marine Insurance: Its Principles and Practice, 6th edn, Pitman, Ch.1

70 (1876)I App.Cas 713.

71 As per s. 51 of the Marine Insurance Act 1906.

the assignor also has an insurable interest at the time of loss.[72] Nevertheless, it is the insurable interest and not the assignor's rights that are assigned.[73] If the policy has terms prohibiting its assignment, it cannot then be assigned by the assured.[74] The policy might be assigned before or after the loss, provided that the assured has not parted with or lost his interest in the subject-matter insured before or at the time of the assignment. The assignee can sue in his name for loss recovery, but the underwriter is entitled to any defense section.[75] The assignee only has the same rights of recovery as those possessed by the assignor. When partial assignment of interest under a policy is effected, it has been held that the assignee can sue underwriters in his own name alone, only if the whole of the beneficial interest has been assigned to him.[76] An assured, who has parted with or lost his interest cannot assign. In *North of England Pure Oil Cake Co v Archangel Maritime Bank & Insurance Co Ltd,*[77] a cargo of linseed was insured with the defendant company from Istanbul to London, including risk of lightering. During the vessel's voyage, the original assured sold the cargo to the plaintiffs with payment to be made in 14 days from being ready for delivery. The cargo was landed in London in public lighters, employed by the plaintiffs, one of which sank. After the loss, the original assured assigned the policy to the plaintiffs who sought loss recovery from the defendants. It was held, that the policy had not passed to the plaintiffs by the contract of sale, that the original assured had lost interest upon delivery of the linseed into the lighter and that the assignment was void; thus, the defendants were not liable for the loss.[78]

2.1.1.2.4. Critique on the existence of the requirement for insurable interest in relation also to over-valuation

The 1745 Act classified agreed value policies with an excessive overvaluation of the subject-matter insured as a species of contracts by way of gaming and wagering. A simple, i.e. non extravagant, over-valuation was not presumed as one breaching the indemnity principle and was not to be re-opened, whereas policies were to be considered as wagers in case the

---

[72] Lambeth RJ (1986): Templeman on Marine Insurance: Its Principles and Practice, 6th edn., Pitman, Ch.1

[73] As per s. 15 of the Marine Insurance Act 1906.

[74] As per s. 50 (1) of the Marine Insurance Act 1906.

[75] As per section 50 (2) of the Marine Insurance Act 1906.

[76] *Williams v Assurance Co Ltd* [1993]42 Ll.L.Rep. 206.

[77] (1875) LR 10 QB 249.

[78] Hodges S (1996) Law of Marine Insurance, Cavendish Publications, Ch. 2.

agreed value significantly exceeded the quantum of the overall loss which the assured could sustain in the event of a casualty.

Nowadays, however, should an insurable interest exist, the contract is not a wager, despite the existence of over-valuation. In *The Maira (No 2)*,[79] the wager point was not appealed. Thus, it can be said that in this way the 1906 and 1909 Acts do not prevent gambling on the loss of maritime property through the medium of excessive over-valuation by those having an interest in it, as long as the policy is not on "*p.p.i.*" terms. If there is over-valuation alongside with insurable interest, the insurer has two courses of action, i.e. either to rely on the defense of the assured's willful misconduct, or - if the assured was not aware of it - to rely on the non disclosure of a fact suggesting the adventure was of a speculative nature or that the subject-matter was fraudulently over-valued with the intention to cheat the insurers. We note, therefore, that the latter Acts differ from that of 1745 in that their approach towards over-valuation is more relaxed, so long as insurable interest exists and the contract has not been written on "*p.p.i*" terms. Still, the legislator did not mean to harm the insurer's interests; therefore the insurer is not trapped because of the existence of insurable interest and has available means of defense in case of over-valuation.

2.1.2. Basic features of the marine insurance contracts in Greece

2.1.2.1. An introduction to the Greek legal system and the interpretation of law in relation to contracts

Within the context of the Greek legal system and law, the judgments of courts are often different, in the sense that the courts are permitted to interpret the same provisions in any chosen way even if such an interpretation is against a previous judgment of another or the same court. For, the role of the courts - through their various rulings- is mainly to interpret and not to create law. Only on rare occasions, if the judgments are the same for a very long period, they might then implicitly create law as per them and

79 [1984]1 Lloyd's Rep. 660.

the content of their rulings, but even in that case it is possible that a court may thereafter decide differently.[80]

Insurance contracts are interpreted according to the general rules on the interpretation of contracts established by articles 173 and 200 of the Commercial Code[81], i.e. by applying the criteria of good faith and established trade practice and by seeking the true intention of the parties, regardless of the wording of the contract.

The courts will not depart easily from the contract's wording. The provisions of the Civil Code on contract interpretation are mandatory and cannot be waived. However, since it is the objective average model of interpretation which is being sought (when dealing with the interpretation of standard printed terms), the fact that there is no negotiation on the contract terms at the time of conclusion of the contract strongly influences the law interpretation which tends to favour the assured, in view of justifying also non existence of abuse of power from the insured who is *a priori* perceived as a stonger party. Thus, the general tendency is that interpretation should not challenge the validity of the contract so that the assured is protected; however to secure the latter, the contract interpretation is ultimately subjected to the Supreme Courts'[82] control for establishment of potential abuse of power and unconstitutionality in the formation of the contract. Other criteria applied by courts to determine the parties' intention are the purpose of the disputed term, the interest to be protected, the legal and factual environment, the pre-contractual negotiations and the nature of the contract. [83]

2.1.2.2. The nature and objective of marine insurance contracts in Greece

The disputes arising from marine insurance law are considered to be maritime law disputes. The objective of marine insurance law is to cover any form of insurable interest exposed to maritime perils and to provide indemnity to the assured for the loss occurred. Thus, marine insurance con-

---

80 It is for this reason that Greek court decisions and their facts have not been explicitly analysed, and, instead it is the results drawn from the study of the various court rulings that have been incorporated in the text and are presented together with all relevant conclusions.

81 See Case *High Court : ΑΠ 1714/1991, ΕΕμπΔ, 1985,301.*

82 Namely Αρειος Πάγος (Areos Pagos).

83 Campbell D (2001) International Insurance Law and Regulation, Vol. I, Oceana Publications, Section GRE, p 6.

tracts are also perceived as indemnity contracts under the Greek law regime, offering cover for losses due to maritime perils.

2.1.2.3. The formation of the marine insurance contract: basic requirements

If combined, article 257 of the CPML [KINΔ] and article 189 of the Commercial Code produce the terminology of the marine insurance contract under Greek law:

> "...it is a contract, whereby, the insurer undertakes to indemnify the assured, in return for the premium paid, for all losses that the assured may suffer, in due time after the occurrence of maritime perils."

The conclusion of a contract in writing is a prerequisite for the existence of marine insurance, not in terms of its validity, but due to the fact that it is required in case it is to be used as evidence of it in court.[84] Evidence by witnesses is only allowed if it can be shown that the policy was lost accidentally.[85] Thus, the issuance of the policy is compulsory for the insurer. It must have a minimum content[86] and have attached its printed general and special terms, binding for the insurer. Practice shows that marine insurance policies on cargo may be issued as negotiable instruments. In this case, the policy must contain the clause *«to order»* and is transferred by endorsement and delivery.[87] The contract should contain:

- the details (name, residence) of the assured.
- the details of the insurer who undertakes to indemnify the assured in case of losses.
- the nature and the object of the insured property to be exposed in maritime perils and the expected profit from it.

Objects of marine insurance can be, amidst others :

- a vessel (art. 263 of the CPML (KINΔ))
- a cargo (art. 264 CPML (KINΔ))
- the premium (art. 194, Commercial Code)
- the freight (art. 266,267 CPML (KINΔ))

---

84 See *Piraeus Court of Appeal ΕφΠειρ 564/1986 ΕΕμπΔ 1989,620.*

85 See *High Court : ΑΠ 1179/1980 ΝοΒ 29,511.*

86 Stating the basic contractual terms that have been agreed.

87 Interim insurance contracts are concluded in the form of cover notes, and are valid for the period between the agreement on coverage and the signing of the policy (Campbell D (2001) International Insurance Law and Regulation, Vol. I, Oceana Publications, Section GRE, p 6).

- the expected profit (art. 259,264,286 CPML (KINΔ) and art. 197 of Commercial Code)
- the risks covered
- the measure of indemnity
- the premium - as per article 265 CPML (KINΔ), the whole premium is owed to the insurer, once his cover against the marine risks has commenced, with the exception of termination of the risk prior to the commencement of the cover under the marine insurance contract.[88] Insurers can pursue judicially the collection of dully owed premiums.[89]
- a valid date, as per art. 192 of the Commercial Code.
- the details of the vessel, i.e. name, classification, capacity, flag.
- the perils insured against and the time period for which they are insured.
- any exemptions.
- explicit reference to any special and specific terms applicable etc.

The cover note[90] is not equal to a simple insurance proposal[91] or to a temporary insurance,[92] but it is a temporary insurance certificate stating that an insurance contract exists. Case law has shown that this is a reversible means of proof, in cases where the insurers prove that there has been no contract concluded from their part or that their agents had no power to do so.[93] The validity of the insurance contract is determined by the general rule of validity of contracts, as stipulated by the Greek Civil Code. Thus, the contracting parties must be adult, sane and capable in law to engage in legally binding transactions at the time of conclusion of the contract, and the insurer's party must have a legal license to operate. Furthermore, there must be an existing risk and insurable interest. Lack of any of the above renders the contract void. Contracts are also void or voidable, under Greek

88 Argyriadis AA (1986) Elements of Insurance Law, 4th edn. Sakkoulas Publications , Thessaloniki, Greece.

89 In addition the International Convention on Arrest of Ships 1999 explicitly allows arrest for premiums including mutual insurance calls (Argyriadis AA (1986) Elements of Insurance Law, 4th edn. Sakkoulas Publications , Thessaloniki, Greece).

90 issued by the insurer's agent according also to English practice.

91 i.e. the slip.

92 i.e. insurance cover.

93 See *Athens Court of First Instance: ΠΠρΑθ 3831/1979 ΕΝΔ 10,30.*

law according also to the Civil Code provisions, in case of fictitious or erroneous declaration of will in terms of a legal transaction.[94]

2.1.2.4. The nature of the interest: insurable interest

Under Greek Law, article 196 of the Commercial Code provides that in order to obtain coverage there must be a legal or equitable relationship between the person benefiting from insurance and the insured property, i.e. an insurable interest has to exist. Moreover, the insurable interest has to be a lawful one.[95] The policy accompanies the insured object, in the sense that its transfer confers to the new owner, the rights and obligations of the previous owner towards the insurer. In case of insurance of a vessel (hull insurance), if the latter is mortgaged the creditor is entitled to the marine benefit as he is deemed to have insurable interest.[96] The requirement under Greek law that a legal or equitable relationship should exist in order to have insurable interest is not a condition strictly imperative, in the sense that a loss occurred due a peril insured against will have to be proven as having existed, before actually indemnification can occur, and it is the party contesting the existence of this insurable interest that will bear the burden of proof. However, it is more the factor of illegality that will render it non insurable and, in effect, the conclusion of such a contract not one justifying indemnification.

2.1.3. Basic features of the marine insurance contracts in Norway

2.1.3.1. General requirements for marine insurance contracts under the Norwegian law regime

Chapter 1 of the Norwegian Marine Insurance Plan 1996 contains introductory provisions in relation to marine insurance contracts.

---

94 Campbell D (2001) International Insurance Law and Regulation, Vol. I, Oceana Publications, Section GRE, p 6.

95 Kiantos BD (1998) Insurance Law, 6th ed. Sakkoulas Publications, Thessaloniki, Greece.

96 Campbell D (2001) International Insurance Law and Regulation, Vol. I, Oceana Publications, Section GRE, p 6.

Norwegian insurance law distinguishes between *"the person effecting the insurance"*, (the person entering into the contract with the insurer) and *"the assured"*, (the person entitled to compensation from the insurer).[97] Although the person effecting the insurance and the assured will often be one and the same, this is not necessarily always the case. The decisive criterion for having status as an *"assured"* under the insurance is that the person in question is in a position where he may have a right to compensation under the policy, not that he does in actual fact have such a right under the relevant agreement. In addition to the distinction between the person effecting the insurance and the assured, a distinction must be made between *"the person effecting the insurance"* and his authorised representative. A broker, agent or intermediary is not the person effecting the insurance, but the authorised representative of the person effecting the insurance. *"Loss"* is defined[98] as a common designation for total loss, physical damage, costs, liability for damages and other loss which the insurer covers according to the Special Conditions. The concept of *"loss"* is consequently a more comprehensive concept than *"damage"* which, according to ordinary usage, must be equated with physical damage.[99] A *"policy"*, according to the Norwegian Marine Insurance Plan, corresponds to an *"insurance certificate"* under the Insurance Contracts Act.[100] However, the term *"policy"* is firmly established in marine insurance, and for this reason it was thought necessary to retain it.

In contrast to the provision contained in the Insurance Contracts Act, the insurer has no obligation to issue a policy, unless the person effecting the insurance requests him to do so. Frequently other documents will have been issued replaces the policy, in which event a policy would be superfluous. The insurer cannot invoke conditions to which no reference is made in the policy. It would not be expedient, however, to prevent the insurer entirely from invoking provisions that do not appear in the policy or the references contained in it. If the insurer can prove that the person effecting the insurance was aware of the relevant condition and that this was to form part of the contract, the agreement of the parties shall prevail over the written contract.[101]

---

97 Ch.1 § 1 letter (c). Norwegian Marine Insurance Plan (1996) Commentary. [http://exchange.dnv.com/nmip/index.htm].

98 *Letter (d)*.

99 Ch.1.para.1of the Norwegian Marine Insurance Plan of 1996 (Commentary). [http://exchange.dnv.com/nmip/index.htm].

100 section 2-2.

101 See Ch.1 § 2 Norwegian Marine Insurance Plan (1996) Commentary. [http://exchange.dnv.com/nmip/index.htm].

Where the person effecting the insurance enters into a contract through a broker, the latter thereby acts as the representative of the person effecting the insurance who under contract law will acquire status as a principal. He is different from the agent who normally acts on behalf of the insurer. The broker will prepare a slip for the insurer and upon reach of full cover, he will issue a cover note sent to the person effecting the insurance; thus, each party retains a different document.

The Norwegian procedure contains an extra stage if compared with the English system, i.e. that of the *"Provisional Insurance Bordeau"* (PIB). It could be said that this constitutes a means of proof for approval by the parties of the terms of the policy to be issued. The PIB is merely a confirmation that a binding insurance contract has been entered into, whereas the *"slip"* - with endorsement - represents the actual contract. Consequently, a PIB does not provide any documentation to the effect that a binding agreement has been entered into, and this may lead to ambiguities as to what the broker and the insurer have in actual fact agreed.

Another common feature which is common to both the Norwegian and English procedures, is that the person effecting the insurance does not get to see the terms of the insurance contract through the cover note until after a binding agreement has been entered into. The person effecting the insurance, therefore, has no possibility of objecting to the content of the insurance contract until the agreement is already binding. In Norwegian practice, a contract is concluded between broker and rating leader and is then sent to the other insurers. Upon their acceptance, the PIB is issued and sent to each individual insurer for his signature, and then it is returned to the broker.

2.1.3.2. Insurable interest under the Norwegian law regime

Under Norwegian marine insurance law, the concept of insurable interest is fundamental and to some extent regulated in mandatory law.

Two main requirements exist in relation to insurable interest and its insurability, i.e. that the interest is a legal one and that it encompasses an economic value. It can be argued that in this respect the Marine Insurance Act 1906 is more restrictive.

The main idea under Norwegian law is that it is sufficient that the assured has some clear possibility of economic loss.[102] A *"gambling insu-*

---

102 One could also conclude, if strictly interpreting the law, that in Norwegian law it is possible to find some objective measure of the money value of the assured's interest at least to the extent of requiring that a court would be pre-

rance", where it has been clear from the outset that no insurable interest existed, is invalid. Likewise, the assured must be precluded from invoking the insurance after the interest is no longer in his hands.[103] This is a point of coincidence with the English law regime. The insurance should also not cover illegal activity. The Norwegian Plan defines illegal activities as an alteration of risk.[104] The regulation leads to a distinction according to how strong the illegal aspect is. If the ship is used primarily for the furtherance of illegal purposes the insurer will not be liable for any loss.[105]

2.1.4. Basic features of the marine insurance contracts in France

2.1.4.1. General requirements and duties of the contractual parties to a marine insurance contract under the French law regime

Art. 8 of the Law of 13/7/1930 and art. L.112-3 of the Insurance Code (*Code des Assurances*), state that the contract of marine insurance has to be formulated in writing. This is required, since the written form serves the means of proof and is not strictly a necessity for the existence of the contract. The commencement of the contract can also be justified by verbal agreement. Thus, it could be said that the written form exists only *ad probationem*.

The slip is prepared and following it a cover note confirming it is being prepared too; however, the latter is not part of modern established practice. The policy is defined formerly in art. 7 of the Law of 13/7/1930, now in art.L.112-2 of the Insurance Code *(Code des Assurances)*, can be

pared to grant damages against a third party who had interfered with the assured's interest.

103 For example, when a ship is definitely condemned in prize or passes to a new owner. Nor will the new owner of the ship normally acquire the position of assured under the insurance contract, to the effect that the assured must be specifically named in the contract, and relating to change of ownership; Ch. 2 para. 1 of the Norwegian Marine Insurance Plan of 1996(Commentary). <http://exchange.dnv.com/nmip/index.htm>

104 Norwegian Marine Insurance Plan (1996) §3-16.

105 Norwegian Marine Insurance Plan (1996) §3-16, third paragraph.

construed in the form of either a public or private document and has to be in writing, as per art. 2 of the Decree of 10/1/1968. The assured can appoint someone else to receive the insurable benefit, whilst remaining liable for the premium payment. The insurer cannot escape from his obligation to indemnify and the assured cannot guarantee to the appointed party the validity of the contract.

There is an obligation to pay the premium, under art. 23 of the Law of 3/7/1967 and more recently art. L.172-19 of the Insurance Code (*Code des Assurances*). Before the law of 3/7/1967, in cases where the premium was not paid, the insurer had the right within 48 hours after the time that the premium was due, either to rescind or suspend the contract. According to art. 24 of the law of 3/7/1967 and now art. L. 172-20 of the Insurance Code, in cases where the insurer elects to suspend, the contract still exists and the premium obligation continues to run, however the insurer's guarantee to indemnify is suspended until the premium is paid. There is a retrospective validation of the insurance contract if the premium is finally paid before nine days have passed since the occurrence of the contracts suspension. If the insurer elects to rescind the contract, then the contract is ended, however, this is not automatic and has to be done judicially.

2.1.4.2. The nature of the interest: insurable interest

Art. 3 of the Law of 3/7/1967, now art. L. 171-3 of the Insurance Code defines insurable interest and the requirement that it has to be legitimate. The French Civil Code in art. 6, prohibits all contracts which are contrary to public policy.

The existence of insurable interest is not necessary at the time of the conclusion of the contract but can also be an expected one. The insurance contract cannot be concluded if the subject-matter insured is already lost before the contract's conclusion, as per articles 1108, 1126 of the Civil Code. This does not apply, however, in relation to a floating policy.

Under French Law, a stipulation that the insurer agrees to dispense with proof of interest, other than production of the policy itself, reverses the burden of proof. This requires the insurer, if he contests the existence of a valid insurable interest, to prove that no such interest exists.[106]

---

106 UNCTAD Report (1978) Legal and Documentary Aspects of the Marine Insurance Contract, UN, NY.

2.1.5. Basic features of the marine insurance contracts in the USA

2.1.5.1. General requirements for the formation of marine insurance contracts in the USA

To effect an insurance agreement, each party must provide to the other consideration in support of the contract, i.e. the insured's promise to pay premiums and the insurer's promise to pay the claims arising under the contract. The contract is concluded in writing and conforms to statutory requirements, administrative regulations or regulatory policies.

An insurance contract may be cancelled in four ways; firstly, it can be rescinded by mutual agreement of the parties; secondly, an insured has an implicit right to cancel a policy unilaterally at the end of the premium period by simply refusing to pay the next premium; thirdly, an insured may also have an explicit right under the contract to terminate the insurance policy unilaterally; fourthly, an insurer often has the right to terminate the policy unilaterally although such a right is sometimes restricted by statute.

With regards to the interpretation of marine insurance contracts, the Courts determine the meaning of policy language by considering the intention of the parties at the time of conclusion of the insurance contract.[107]

2.1.5.2. The nature of the interest: insurable interest

In the USA an insurable interest requirement for all forms of insurance was primarily adopted by the courts and then many states enacted statutes defining the requirement.[108] These statutes are generally written in broad language, leaving room for judicial interpretation.

---

[107] Johnson JF IVth, Brown DR (2001) International Insurance Law and Regula tion: United States, March 2001, Oceana Publications Inc., Dobbs Ferry, NY, USA.

[108] The American authorities, however, differ upon insurable interest in some im portant respects from English law, and must not be presumed to be identical. Thus, American courts have been prepared to treat a *"p.p.i."* policy as ordinary indemnity insurance if interest could in fact be shown and there was no intention to wager, *Brown v Merc.Mar. Ins. Co.* 152 Fed. Rep.411.(C.C.A.

In essence, insurable interest laws require the owner of the policy to have ownership or similar interest in or relationship to the thing or person insured.[109] An insurable interest is a necessary precondition for a valid contract of insurance. If the insured has no interest, he can suffer no loss, the contract is deemed to be a wagering contract and is therefore void. [110] When an interest is insured *"p.p.i"* or *"full interest admitted"* (*"f.i.a."*), the underwriter will simply not raise the defence of lack of insurable interest.[111]

Sometimes marine insurance policies are issued without a clear indication of whose interest is insured. The policy is simply written *"for the account of whom it may concern"*. The general rule in regard to such policies is that if it was the intent of the person taking out the insurance that the interest of the party seeking indemnity be covered, that the party actually had an insurable interest and that indemnity is due by the insurer to that party. The individual covered by the marine insurance policy need not have been known to the one procuring the insurance or the underwriter.[112] Where the underwriter declines to indemnify on the grounds of a lack of insurable interest, the insured has the burden of proving the existence of an insurable interest.[113] Where more than one party asserts a claim for indemnification under the policy, the determination of each party's insurable interest is according to their interests in the policy, not in proportion to their interests in the vessel.[114] To assert a valid claim for indemnification, it is sufficient that the insured possesses an insurable interest at the time of loss.[115] Whether the insured possessed the interest at the time of contracting

9,1907); *Hall v Jefferson Ins. Co.*, 279 F.893 (S.D.N.Y.D.C. 1921) ; *Cabaud v Federal Ins. Co.*, 37F.2d23 (C.C.A. 2,1930) ; *The Hai Hsuan (No. 2),* [1958]2 Lloyd's Rep. 578 (D.C., Md), (Legh-Jones N et al (2002) MacGillivray on Insurance Law, 10th edn, London, S&M, Ch.1).

109 The insurable interest doctrine is simply a means used by the states to preclude insurance in situations where the contract might amount to wagering.

110 The insurable interest must be held at the time of the loss (*Hooper v Robinson* 98 US (8 Otto) 528.25 L.Ed. 219 (1878) ; *Hart v Delaware Ins.Co.*, 11F.Cas 683 (CCDPa. 1869 (No 6150) ; *Chase v Hammond Lumber Co*, 79 F.2d 716 (9th Circ. 1935).

111 *Hall & Co v Jefferson Ins Co*, 279 F.892 (SDNY 1921) ; Such *"honour pol cies"* are used when it is difficult to ascertain if the interest insured is *"insurable"*, even though commercial practice is to insure that interest.

112 *The John Russel* 68 F.2d. 901 (2nd Circ) 1934.

113 *Republic of China v National Union Fire Insurance Co.,*163 F.Supp. 812 (D.MD. 1958).

114 *Eagle Star & British Dominions v Tadlock,*22 F.Supp. 545 (SD Cal. 1938).

115 *The John Russel* 68 F.2d. 901 (2nd Circ) 1934.

is immaterial.[116] Insurance contracts that violate public policy are not enforceable by courts, thus they are void.[117]

2.1.6. Basic features of the marine insurance contracts in Canada

2.1.6.1. General requirements and the objective of marine insurance contracts in Canada

A marine insurance contract, is a contract in which the insurer undertakes to indemnify the assured to the extent provided in the contract, against losses incidental to marine adventures or analogous ones. It has been held that it is a contract of indemnity.[118]A marine insurance contract, under the Canadian law regime, is different from a policy. A marine policy is an instrument evidencing the contract between the insurer and the insured. As a consequence, the general rules of interpretation of contracts apply to insurance policies.

The first rule of interpretation of contracts is that the court will consider the contract as a whole in order to search for an interpretation that is consistent with and promotes the intention of the parties to the contract.[119] The application of this general rule, however, is not always straight forward. In general, courts tend to broadly interpret coverage clauses and narrowly interpret exclusions.[120] Further, if there is any ambiguity in the policy, such ambiguity is almost always resolved in favour of an interpretation that benefits the insured.

This is an application of the doctrine of *contra proferentem*, which means that the words of a contract should be interpreted against the interests of the person who drafted it. There are many cases where the courts seem to have used the doctrine of *contra proferentem* as a tool to avoid the

---

[116] Schoenbaum TJ (2001) Admiralty and Maritime Law, 3rd edn, Hornbook Se ries,West Group, St.Paul, Minn, USA.

[117] Johnson JF4th, Brown DR (2001) International Insurance Law and Regulation: United States, March 2001, Oceana Publications Inc., Dobbs Ferry, NY, USA.

[118] *Kenny v Halifax Marine Insurance Co*, (1840) 1 NSR 141 (NSCA); Braen A (1992) Le Droit Maritime au Quebec, W&L.

[119] *Consolidated Bathhurst v Mutual Boier & Machinery*, [1980] 1 S.C.R. 888.

[120] *Reid Crowther v Simcoe & Erie General Insurance* (1993)13 C.C.L.I. (2d) 16.

plain meaning of the policy and the intention of the parties as disclosed by the words used.

Although we could easily believe that the doctrine of is the first rule of interpretation of insurance contracts, however, this is not the case. In *Consolidated Bathhurst v Mutual Boier & Machinery*,[121] it was clearly stated that the doctrine of *contra proferentem* is nothing else but one tool to determine the true intention of the parties. The approach set out in *Consolidated Bathhurst v Mutual Boier & Machinery* [122] was recently restated by the Supreme Court of Canada in *Brisette v Westbury Life Insurance Co*[123] where the Supreme Court noted that where two or more meanings are possible, the court should select the meaning that promotes the intent of the parties. Furthermore, the Supreme Court specifically said that courts should avoid an interpretation which will give either a windfall to the insurer or an unanticipated recovery to the insured.

2.1.6.2. The nature of the interest : insurable interest

The object of a contract of marine insurance is to indemnify the assured, for loss suffered due to the realisation of a risk covered by the insurance policy. The assured only suffers a loss if he has an insurable interest on the subject-matter insured. If there is no insurable interest, he is not in a position where he has suffered any loss, and therefore he has no right of indemnity. If no insurable interest or expectation of acquiring such an interest exists, then the insurance contract is void and treated as a gaming or wagering insurance contract.[124]

An insurable interest is any interest which would be recognised by a Court of law or equity. In *Clark v Scottish Imperial Marine Insurance Co* [125], where an assured had advanced funds to a shipbuilder on an unfinished vessel which was in the possession of a shipbuilder, the assured was found to have an insurable interest in the vessel.

A party may also insure property *"for whom it may concern"*. In *McGee v Phoenix Insurance Co,* [126] a vessel was owned by a firm consisting of three partners, but was registered in the name of one of them and was insured *"for whom it may concern"*. The court found that any of the

[121] [1980] 1 S.C.R. 888.
[122] *Consolidated Bathhurst v Mutual Boier & Machinery*, [1980] 1 S.C.R. 888.
[123] (1992) 13 C.C.L.I. (2d) 1.
[124] Braen A (1992) Le Droit Maritime au Québec, W&L.
[125] (1879) 4 S.C.R. 192.
[126] (1889) 28 N.B.R. 45 (CA).

three partners had the right to insure the interest of the partnership and any payment made to one would have been a good payment. One partner was obtained to be the agent of the other members of the partnership in obtaining the insurance. Also, a party who has a mortgage on a vessel has an insurable interest in the vessel to the amount of the mortgage.[127] A supplier of goods on a trading voyage has an insurable interest in the property. A vessel owner has an insurable interest in the freight, though the latter must be specifically insured.[128]

In Canada, however, the restrictive approach taken by the House of Lords in *Macaura v Northern Assurance Co Ltd.*[129] was rejected in the non-marine case *Constitution Insurance Co of Canada v Kosmopoulos.*[130] Mr Andreas Kosmopoulos had been in the business of operating a leather goods manufacturing establishment in Toronto since 1972. The business was actually carried out by *"Kosmopoulos Leather Goods Ltd"*, of which Mr A.Kosmopoulos was the sole shareholder and director. The incorporation notwithstanding, Mr Kosmopoulos conducted all his business as though it were a sole proprietorship, whilst the business correspondence and his insurance policies identified the business of Andreas Kosmopoulos operating as *"Spring Leather Goods"*. The insurance company namely *"Constitution Insurance Co"* were subscribers to a subscription policy insuring the business against fire. In May 1977 a fire broke out in adjoining premises and as a consequence the area leased to Mr Kosmopoulos was damaged by fire, smoke and water. The insurance company denied a claim on the policy on the grounds that Mr Kosmopoulos did not have an insurable interest in the assets that were lost. At trial, this argument was rejected. His Honour Holland J. declined to attribute any significance to the incorporation as being a mere fiction. The insurance company appealed and the appeal was dismissed. The Ontario Court of Appeal expressly declined to follow *Macaura.*[131] The submission was made that *Macaura v Northern Assurance Co Ltd* [132] should, therefore, no longer be followed in Canada. The Supreme Court of Canada agreed, finding that there was no basis in public policy for the restrictive approach adopted by Lord Eldon. The Court noted that this approach had been abandoned in many American jurisdictions in favour of the test of any lawful economic interest in the preservation of the property from loss or damage without leading to any

[127] *Crawford v St Lawrence Insurance Co* (1851)8 UCQB 135 (CA).
[128] *Heard & Hall v Marine Insurance Co* (1871)1 PEI 428.
[129] [1925] AC 619.
[130] (1987)34 DLR (4th) 208.
[131] [1925] AC 619.
[132] [1925] AC 619.

difficulties. It was also noted that the commentators in the USA and Canada seemed to be uniformly in favour of the adoption of a test based on whether the insured has a factual expectation of loss.[133]

2.1.7. Basic features of the marine insurance contracts in Australia

2.1.7.1. Basic requirements under the Australian law regime

S. 7-10 of the Marine Insurance Act 1909, define marine insurance. S. 7 of the Marine Insurance Act 1909 defines a marine insurance contract as a contract whereby the insurer undertakes to indemnify the assured, in manner and to the extent thereby agreed, against marine losses, i.e. the losses incident to marine adventure.

2.1.7.2. The nature of the interest: insurable interest

S. 10-21 of the Marine Insurance Act 1909 cover insurable interest. The principle of insurable interest is derived from the fundamental principle of indemnity, namely that the insurer is under an obligation to reimburse the assured for the actual loss from the covered risk and the insured is entitled to be restored, subject to the terms and conditions of the policy, to the financial position enjoyed immediately before the loss. To confirm that the assured suffered a loss, he must show that he had an insurable interest in the subject-matter insured. S.10 of the Marine Insurance Act 1909 provides:

"(1) Every contract of marine insurance by way of gaming or wagering is void.

(2) A contract of marine insurance is deemed to be a gaming or wagering contract:

(a) where the insured has not an insurable interest as defined by this Act, and the contract is entered into with no expectation of acquiring such an interest ; or

(b) where the policy is made *"interest or no interest"*, or *"without further proof of interest than the policy itself"*, or, *"without benefit of salvage to the insurer"*, or subject to any other like term.

---

133 Australian Law Reform Commission (2001) Review of the Marine Insurance Act 1909, Report 91, April 2001, p 237.

Provided that, where there is no possibility of salvage, a policy may be effected without benefit of salvage to the insurer".

S.11 of the Marine Insurance Act 1909 provides:

"(1) Subject to the provisions of this Act, every person has an insurable interest who is interested in the marine adventure.

(2) In particular, a person is interested in a marine adventure where he stands in any legal or equitable relation to the adventure, or to any insurable property at risk therein, in consequence of which he may benefit by the safety or due arrival of insurable property, or may be prejudiced by its loss, or by damage thereto, or by the detention thereof, or may incur liability in respect thereof."

The Marine Insurance Act 1909 does not provide an extensive definition of an insurable interest. [134] In the general law of insurance in Australia, the Insurance Contracts Act, in sections 16 and 17, modified the concept of insurable interest. S. 16 of the Insurance Contracts Act states:

" a contract of general insurance is not void by reason only that the insured did not have, at the time when the contract was entered into, an interest in the subject-matter of the contract."

The Insurance Contracts Act uses an economic loss test to determine whether the insured has a sufficient interest to claim under the policy. S. 17 states that where the insured has suffered a pecuniary or economic loss, the insurer is not relieved of liability by reason only that, at the time of loss, the insured did not have an interest in law or in equity in the property. Since the implementation of these provisions in the Insurance Contracts Act, there appear to have been only three cases dealing with s. 16 or 17. In *Pacific Dunlop Limited v Maxifirm Boilers Pty Limited*,[135] Theaghe J., in the Supreme Court of Victoria, identified uncertainty as to whether section 17 could be relied upon by a non-party insured. In *Howard v Australia Jet Charter Pty Limited*,[136] Hill J., in the Federal Court, held that - by virtue of sections 16 and 17 of the Insurance Contracts Act - a company that had contracted to maintain and crew an aircraft could not be said to have an interest in a contract of insurance covering loss from damage to that aircraft. In *Advance (New South Wales) Insurance Agencies Pty Ltd v Matthews*, [137] Samuels J.A. found that, under s.17, a husband had an eco-

---

[134] It does, however, provide that mortgagees and lessees of insured property have an insurable interest and that an insurable interest may be partial, defeasible or contingent. It also specifically referes to other interests as being insurable such as that of a lender of money on bottomry or *respondentia* , the master or crew members in respect of their wages, a person advancing freight and an insured in costs of insurance which it effects.

[135] (1997) 9 ANZ Insurance Cases 61-357.

[136] (1991) 6 ANZ Insurance Cases 61-054.

[137] (1988) 12 NSWLR 250.

nomic, thus insurable, interest in his wife's clothing and other personal effects. [138]

Although the requirement of insurable interest has been abolished in relation to contracts governed by the Insurance Contracts Act[139] nevertheless, a contract is deemed as gaming or wagering and thus void, unless the insured party has an insurable interest in the insured property at the time of loss. It is not necessary however to have such an interest when the insurance is effected, however the assured must at least have an expectation of acquiring one. As per s. 21 of the Act, the insurable interest may be assigned, although that does not transfer the rights under the contract of insurance, unless that is also part of the agreement. As per s. 56(1) of the Act, a policy is also assignable unless precluded by its express terms. As per s. 57 of the Act, if the policy and the insurable interest are not transferred at the same time, (in case the assured looses or disposes of its insured interest before agreeing to assign the policy) any subsequent purported assignment of the policy is inoperative, although it seems that the actual assignment can occur at a later time. [140]

2.1.7.3. Insurable interest and the requirements for marine insurance contracts under the Australian law regime: the reform proposals

The Australian Law Reform Commission has undertaken the task to reform Australian marine insurance law and has produced a report.[141] Chapter 15, of the Australian Law Reform Commission's Report, covers issues relating to the formalities of the contracts and policies of marine insurance.

S. 28(1) of the Marine Insurance Act 1909, prevents the admission into evidence of any contract of marine insurance, unless a policy has been issued in an action for recovery under a policy. In order to protect stamp

---

138 Derrington S (2002) Australia: Perspectives and Permutations on the Law of Marine Insurance, Ch. 11 In Thomas R (ed) The Modern Law of Marine Insurance, Vol. 2, LLP .

139 Under which the insured may only suffer an economic loss in order to claim.

140 A strict approach on insurable interest was taken in the South Australian Su preme Court case of *Truran Earthmovers Pty Ltd v Norwich Union Fire Insurance [(1976)17 SASR 1],* which involved the purchase of a bulldozer. The purchaser was held to have no insurable interest in the bulldozer even though he had lent the owner money which was to be deduced from the purchase price.

141 "The Australian Law Reform Commission Reform: 91: Report", in http://www.austlii.edu.au/au/other/alrc/publications/reports/91/.

duty revenue, the Australian Law Reform Commission proposes to repeal the relevant part of s.28, since there is no longer any revenue to protect; therefore s.28 has become a formal hindrance to the proof of a contract in legal proceedings for the recovery of a loss under the policy.

In order to clarify the legal status of the *"slip"*, the Discussion Paper, drafted by the Australian Law Reform Commission, suggested that the provisions of the Marine Insurance Act 1909 should be amended to allow a slip or any other document recording or evidencing the contract of marine insurance to be regarded as *prima facie* evidence of the contract in the absence of any other documents. The Australian Law Reform Commission, in allowing this, did not wish to give the slip or any other contractual document any greater status or evidentiary value[142] but to permit the parties[143] to introduce into evidence whatever contractual documents are available to it in the absence of a duly issued policy in order to advance his case.

Chapter 11 of the Australian Law Reform Commission report reviews the requirements under the Marine Insurance Act 1909, that the assured have an insurable interest in the insured property at the time of loss. The Australian Law Reform Commission proposes to remove the requirement that the assured have an insurable interest in the goods insured at the time of the loss. Although this interest is not required when the contract is concluded, the assured must nonetheless have it at that time an expectation of acquiring an insurable interest.

Usually, an assured is taken to have an insurable interest in goods if there is the legal relationship of property, i.e. ownership, or if he bears the risk of damage to the goods. In this respect the Australian Law Reform Commission seeks to replicate the Insurance Contracts Act reforms by substituting a requirement that the insured suffer an economic or pecuniary loss. The proposal aims to overcome a usual problem in cargo insurance when an insured has paid for the goods and arranged insurance cover over the goods but has not yet acquired an insurable interest in the goods under the sales contract at the time the goods are damaged or lost. The requirement for an insurable interest appears to create problems in case the assured purchases goods on *"f.o.b."*, *"c&f"* or *"c.f.r."* terms, where the assured does not have an insured and insurable interest in goods prior to loading aboard a ship, even if he has paid for the goods before that time, unless a policy includes both a *"lost or not lost"* clause and *"warehouse to warehouse"* cover. Also, in case of assignment of a policy, this can be in-

---

142 Than the one it normally bears when used to show the true contractual intention of the parties.

143 Especially the insured.

effective if it is assigned when the assured has already parted with or lost its insurable interest. The insurance industry has strongly resisted to the abolition of the requirement for an insurable interest.[144] Having anticipated some resistance to be faced, the Australian Law Reform Commission has also prepared additional alternative recommendations to resolve the problems.[145]

If the subject-matter of the policy is assured *"lost or not lost"*, the assured may recover although he may not have acquired his interest until after the loss, unless at the time of effecting the contract of insurance, the assured was aware of the loss and the insurer was not so aware.[146] Policies are effected upon a *"lost or not lost"* basis where insurance is taken out in the absence of any information as to the loss or otherwise of the subject matter, be it a vessel or cargo. Thus, without this exception, an assured who is acting in good faith without knowledge of any loss may well have been deprived of recovery merely upon the grounds of ignorance as to the state of affairs. Even under this provision, however, the assured must prove that at the time of the loss the risk had attached to the subject matter.[147] For example, in the case of *Andeann Pty Ltd v South British Insurance Co Ltd* [148] where, in response to an advertisement to ship goods, persons purporting to represent a transport company collected the goods, whilst the owner insured them under a certificate of marine insurance as from the following day and the goods were apparently stolen by the collector. It was held that the plaintiff failed to prove that the loss occurred after the risk attached to the goods and there was no obligation to indemnify the assured under a *"lost or not lost"* provision. Further, the assured cannot call in aid the *"lost or not lost"* clause unless the loss in question has fallen upon him.

A case which is of particular interest in the marine context in relation to the requirement of insurable interest in marine insurance law is *New*

---

[144] Nevertheless, the Commission is not convinced that this requirement is necessary for the preservation of the marine insurers' legitimate rights. The change should make little difference to the legal position of insurers as there is still a requirement for a loss suffered by the insured that falls within the terms of the policy. In any event the insured can only ever recover under the policy its actual loss under the indemnity principle.

[145] The alternative is to provide that buyers of insurable property acquire an insurable interest no later than when the buyer pays for it or is obliged to pay for it, assuming the buyer does ultimately pay for it.

[146] s.12(1) Marine Insurance Act 1909.

[147] Butler DA, Duncan WD (1992) Maritime Law in Australia, Legal Books, p 355.

[148] (1987) 4 ANZ Insurance Cases, 75-029, Supreme Court of Tasmania.

South Wales Leather Co. Pty Ltd v Vanguard Insurance Co Ltd.[149] Between May and July 1998, the appellant agreed to purchase quantities of leather on *"f.o.b."* terms from a number of Brazilian suppliers. The goods were consigned by the sellers to a forwarding agent who arranged for cargo consolidators to pack them into eleven containers. Seals were then attached to the containers. In June, July and August 1998, the containers were loaded on board three vessels for carriage to Sydney. However, prior to loading, ten of the containers were pilfered. Fresh seals had been fraudulently attached, but there was no suggestion that the sellers had been involved in the theft or any fraudulent conduct. The appellant claimed under its open policy with the respondent, which contained *"warehouse to warehouse"* cover. The claim was rejected on the basis that the goods had not been at the appellant's risk when they were stolen.[150] The appellant then claimed against its sellers, hoping to obtain the benefit of their insurance, however the sellers were uninsured. The appellant elected not to pursue any contractual remedies. Thus, the action proceeded against the respondent marine underwriter. The contracts of sale called for the appellant to pay on the goods on a *"cash against documents"* basis (i.e. prior to their arrival in Sydney and before they could be inspected). The trading terms, therefore, entered into by the appellant meant that it ran the risk of paying for goods *after* they had already been stolen. Despite the submissions made by counsel for the appellant that, by virtue of the course of dealing between the parties, they impliedly agreed that the risk of the goods would pass to the appellant prior to loading of the goods onto the ship, the majority judgement held that certainty must prevail. As the appellant gave the court a range of alternatives as to when the risk may have passed, varying from inland warehouses to the time of packaging into the containers, the court was unable to accept that any of those submissions for the purposes of giving the contract of sales business efficacy or added implied terms.

The court held that the open policy issued by the respondent was for *"goods and/or merchandise"* and was limited to such goods *"in which the insured had an insurable interest"*. Subject to the *"lost or not lost"* clause the court, however, held that the open policy did not cover the appellant in respect of the goods prior to their loading onto the ship (i.e. before the risk passed) and did not cover it against the financial risks it in-

[149] (1990) 103 FLR 70 ; [1991] NSWLR 699.

[150] Derrington S (2002) Australia: Perspectives and Permutations on the Law of Marine Insurance, Ch. 11 In Thomas R(ed) The Modern Law of Marine Insurance, Vol. 2, LLP .

curred when it paid cash against documents.[151] At First Instance, Justice Carruthers confirmed the rule that a purchaser *"f.o.b."* does not have an insurable interest in goods during transit form the seller's warehouse to the ship's rails. His Honour held that the transit clause could not operate to extend the cover to an earlier point in time in the absence of an insurable interest. [152] On Appeal, the New South Wales Court of Appeal agreed with the trial judge that the assured did not have an insurable interest in the goods at the time of loss, and therefore could derive no assistance from the transit clause. The pre-loading portion of the warehouse to warehouse clause is, viewed in isolation, worthless to a purchaser on *"f.o.b."* terms and does not in fact provide the cover as its name suggests. The position of an insured buyer *"f.o.b."* or *"c&f"* may be improved by the insertion of a *"lost or not lost"* clause in the policy and, ultimately, it was held in the Court of Appeal that the insured was able to recover relying on the that particular type of clause in combination with warehouse to warehouse cover.[153]There has been extensive criticism regarding the operation of the requirement for insurable interest in this context, amidst other reasons, mainly due to the differences in interpretation reached by Justice Carruthers at First Instance and by the Court of Appeal. [154]

Thus, in Australia, the only appellate decision that has recently considered the issue, namely *New South Wales Leather Co. Pty Ltd v Vanguard Insurance Co Ltd*,[155] appears to be authority for the proposition that

---

151 Taylor M (2000) Is the Requirement of an Insurable Interest in the Marine Insurance Act Still Valid? Insurance Law Journal, 11: 147.

152 Derrington S (2002) Australia: Perspectives and Permutations on the Law of-Marine Insurance, Ch. 11 In Thomas R (ed) The Modern Law of Marine Insurance, Vol. 2, LLP .

153 Derrington S (2002) Australia: Perspectives and Permutations on the Law of Marine Insurance, Ch. 11 In Thomas R (ed) The Modern Law of Marine Insurance, Vol. 2, LLP .

154 At first instance, Justice Carruthers stated that, consistently with the fundamental principle that a contract of insurance is a contract of indemnity, an insured cannot rely on a *"lost or not lost"* clause unless the loss falls on it. He held that the loss in question had clearly not fallen on the insured, even though it had already paid for the goods, who was entitled to recover the purchase price from the sellers. In contrast, the Court of Appeal found that the insured had suffered a loss even though the insured was not at risk when the goods were stolen. It was sufficient that the insured suffered financial loss because of the prior loss of the goods. The fact that it had contractual remedies against its sellers was no barrier to a claim on the insurance (Derrington S (2002) Australia: Perspectives and Permutations on the Law of Marine Insurance, Ch. 11 In Thomas R (ed) The Modern Law of Marine Insurance, Vol. 2, LLP).

155 (1990)103 FLR 70 ; [1991] NSWLR 699.

where an insured suffers a loss prior to obtaining the insurable interest in the goods,[156] and subsequently acquires an insurable interest in those goods, a combination of a *"lost or not lost"* clause and a warehouse to warehouse clause entitles the insured to indemnity.[157]

As a consequence to the current law pertaining to the requirement of an insurable interest in marine insurance, the Australian Law Reform Commission has recommended the abolition of the requirement for an insurable interest and the implementation of provisions in similar terms to s. 16 and 17 of the Insurance Contracts Act., with the aim and purpose to enable purchasers of insured goods to obtain insurance to cover their exposure to the potentiality of loss if they pay for the goods before they acquire an insurable interest in them under the contract of sale.[158] More extensively, the Australian Law Reform Commission report recommends that in relation to insurable interest, s. 10-12 of the Marine Insurance Act 1909 Act should be amended to be consistent with the Insurance Contracts Act s. 16-17 in relation to the requirements for an insurable interest. The Marine Insurance Act 1909 should provide that a contract of marine insurance is not void by reason only that the insured did not have an interest in the subject matter of the contract at the time when the contract was entered into and, secondly, where the insured under a contract of marine insurance has suffered a pecuniary or economic loss by reason of damage to the insured property, the insurer is not relieved of liability under the contact by reason only that the insured did not have an interest at law or in equity in the property. S.13-21, 57 and 90(3)(c) and (d) of the Marine Insurance Act 1909, which rely on the concept of insurable interest, should be repealed as a consequence of the abolition of the requirement for an insurable interest.

The Australian Law Reform Commission - being aware of the sensitivity of the issue of insurable interest[159] - also included in its report some alternative recommendations in case the initial ones would not be adopted, allowing in such a case for a new provision should be inserted into the Marine Insurance Act providing that a purchaser of insurable property acquires an insurable interest in that property by no later than the time when it pays for the property or when it becomes bound to pay for the property

[156] For example by paying cash against documents.

[157] Derrington S (2002) Australia: Perspectives and Permutations on the Law of Marine Insurance, Ch. 11 In Thomas R(ed) The Modern Law of Marine Insurance, Vol. 2, LLP .

[158] "Australian Law Reform Commission Reform: 91: Report" §11.92.

[159] Derrington S (2002) Australia: Perspectives and Permutations on the Law of Marine Insurance, Ch. 11 In Thomas R (ed) The Modern Law of Marine Insurance, Vol. 2, LLP .

provided that it subsequently pays for it. Similarly, if the initial recommendation on insurable interest is not adopted and the requirement for insurable interest is retained, Marine Insurance Act 1909 s. 16 should be amended to cover secured loans over insurable property generally, not just *"bottomry"* and *"respondentia"*.[160] The effect of the alternative recommendations, should they be followed, would be that there would be no legal impediment in principle to the insurance of goods prior to loading aboard a ship or at any other early stage of the transit. A purchaser of goods would be able to seek cover for any loss of the value of the goods or any profit that it might earn from them with the risk attaching as soon as the goods are paid for. It is considered that this would avoid the need for the market to resort to *"f.o.b."* or *"c&f" "Pre-shipment clauses"* which, given the requirements of insurable interest in the Marine Insurance Act 1909, are probably unenforceable. [161]

2.2. The cover offered under marine insurance contracts in the various common law and continental law jurisdictions

2.2.1. The coverage offered under marine insurance contracts in England

Schedule 1 to the Marine Insurance Act 1906 contains the standard form of marine policy perfected in the 18th century, adopted in 1779 and being used until 1983.[162]

In 1983, the Lloyd's SG Policy was scrapped and replaced with two new standard forms one for use by Lloyd's underwriters, and one for use by insurance companies. The broad effect of the old form of the policy was to provide cover for perils of the sea, war risks and all other related perils. It was nevertheless limited; firstly by s. 55 of the Marine Insurance

---

160 "The Australian Law Reform Commission Reform: 91: Report", in < http://www.austlii.edu.au/au/other/alrc/publications/reports/91/ >

161 Derrington S (2002) Australia: Perspectives and Permutations on the Law of Marine Insurance, Ch. 11 In Thomas R (ed) The Modern Law of Marine Insurance, Vol. 2, LLP .

162 When it was replaced by a much simpler common form.

Act 1906, which codifies the position established by common law and excludes from the coverage of marine policies, losses not proximately caused by an insured peril, losses proximately caused by the assured's willful misconduct; and provides that losses proximately caused by delay, ordinary wear and tear, inherent vice and the like are to be regarded as excluded, unless specifically included, and secondly by the established standard terms for different classes of marine insurance agreement to be appended to them, known as Institute Clauses. Most of the basic Institute Clauses exclude liability for loss resulting from war, strikes, malicious acts and nuclear explosions, and coverage is provided for such risks by specific Institute War and Strikes Clauses.[163] The most important feature of the clauses, however, can be said to be that they excluded the war risk cover included in the Lloyd's SG Policy and have also sought to reverse the effect of rulings made by the Court as to the meaning of the Lloyd's SG Policy. The Clauses were revised in a number of respects in 1995 and again in 2002 and in 2003.[164]

More specifically, the latest version of the Clauses, i.e. the International Hull Clauses, provide cover under four heads, i.e. for marine perils covered irrespective of due diligence, for marine perils covered subject to due diligence, for pollution hazards and for collision hazards.

Regarding marine perils covered irrespective of due diligence, the list of the revised clauses provides also, in clause 2, cover for loss or damage caused by accidents in loading, discharging or shifting cargo or fuel. The new element is that this cover has been extended to include stores or

---

163 In addition, the Institute Cargo clauses exclude liability where a loss arises from the unseaworthiness of the vessel.

164 The new International Hull clauses 2002 were published on 1 November 2002 and were revised again on 1 November 2003. Known as International Hull clauses 1/11/02 and International Hull clauses 1/11/03 respectively, they supersede the 1995 Hull clauses with the aim to provide clarity and reduce uncertainty for both the shipowners and the underwriters and to bring the standard wordings up-to-date with current market price. The new clauses update, as opposed to revise, the 1983 and 1995 wordings, and have improved the clarity of previous ones, by simply being closer into line with practice. The new clauses leave more complex areas to be debated at the next revision. A market-wide review of the clauses is under way, as the Joint Hull Committee undertook to make a six month assessment of how the new clauses were working.; (Wall DJ (2003) International Hull clauses 1/11/02: A Commentary, Shipping & Trade Law, Vol.3,No 1) ; Lloyd's List News(2003) Fresh Look at Hull Clauses Under Way).

parts.[165] Clause 2.1.9., extends clause 6.2.5. of the ITC 1995 to include contact with satellites, aircraft, helicopters or similar objects, and no longer is subject to the need of due diligence that was previously essential.

The cost of repairing or replacing burst boilers or broken shafts is excluded from the cover in respect of loss or damage caused by such incidents; loss or damage caused by any latent defect in the machinery or hull continues to be covered, but not any of the costs of correcting the latent defect.

All the perils previously listed in clause 6.2. of ITC 1995 were subject to a proviso whereby loss or damage caused by such perils was not recoverable if it was due to the want of due diligence by the assured, owners, managers or superintendents or any of their onshore managers; whereas now there is no longer any reference to superintendents or onshore managers, in line with the reaction of the market and the people involved in making business within it.[166]

The 2003 revision also offers cover for common costs given at 50% where loss or damage is caused by burst boiler, broken shaft or latent defect and for the correction of the latent defect and the repair of the loss or damage caused thereby. As per Clause 41 of the 2003 revised clauses, subject to the underwriters agreement and in the absence of due diligence, additional peril cover is given, as optional, to include the remaining 50% of the common costs , the costs of repairing the broken boiler/shaft and correcting the latent defect as well as for loss or damage to the vessel caused by accident, negligence, incompetence of error of judgement of any person. Clause 3 is new. Entitled *Leased Equipment* it provides cover in respect of loss or damage by an insured peril to equipment and apparatus installed for use on the vessel which is not owned by the assured, but for which he has assumed contractual liability the value of which is stated to be included in the vessel's insured value. Furthermore, the underwriter's liability is limited to the assured's contractual liability for the loss or damage or the reasonable cost of repair or replacement, whichever is less. Similarly Clause 4 is new, providing cover for loss or damage by an insured peril to parts taken off the vessel. Cover is limited to 60 days, whilst

165 Wall DJ (2003) International Hull Clauses 1/11/02: A Commentary, Shipping & Trade Law, Vol.3,No 1.

166 The fact that superintendents and onshore managers were included under the ITC 1995 regime was one of the major factors why ITC failed to gain widespread acceptance. Still, this deletion will not be helpful to owners in all cases, since it leaves open the question of whether the assured can be personified by a high-ranking marine superintendent with partial or complete autonomy delegated to him, even though he may be below board level.

the parts are not on board the vessel. Periods in excess of 60 days are subject to a held covered proviso. Clause 4.5 limits the underwriters' liability to 5% of the vessel's insured value, with further provisions within cl.4 relating to the measure of indemnity in respect of both leased parts and any parts covered by other insurance. Clause 6 replicates Clause 8 of the ITC 1995, providing cover for 3/4ths collision liability. A significant alteration, however, is that of clause 6.3 whereby underwriters have successfully capped their exposure to such costs by limiting their liability under this clause to 25% of the vessel's insured value. If the extension for 4/4ths collision liability is agreed upon, then, although underwriters will be covering all the costs, the 25% limitation will nevertheless apply.[167]

The Institute Cargo clauses fall into three classes, (A), (B) and (C). The Institute Cargo clauses (A) provide all risks cover, whilst (B) and (C) are narrower and limited to coverage of specific risks, again subject to specific exclusions. The Institute Cargo clauses (A) on *"all risks"* - via clause 1 - cover all risks of loss or damage to the subject-matter insured. *"All risks"* concerns fortuitous events only. The principle also encompasses express exclusions apart from those contained in the policy. Although it involves all forms of losses, it should also encompass physical loss of the insured subject-matter. The major difficulty in relation to all risks policies has been the determination of the burden of proof. The case of *British and Foreign Marine Insurance Co v Gaunt,*[168] which sets the principles, raised a presumption of loss within the policy,[169] as long as the loss is of a nature that would not normally arise in the ordinary course of events.[170]

In more recent cases,[171] a less generous presumption towards the favour of the assured has been taken and the insurer could suggest a number of possible causes of the loss outside the policy and also require the assured to rebut these possibilities so as to prove that the loss was within his cover. [172] In *Tioxide Europe Ltd v CGU International Insurance Plc*[173],

---

[167] This limit is not likely to affect the run-of-the-mill collisions; rather it will very likely only *"bite"* in cases involving very low insured values or substantial collisions (Wall, DJ (2003) International Hull Clauses 1/11/02: A Commentary, Shipping & Trade Law, Vol.3,No 1).

[168] [1921]2 AC 41.

[169] Although previous cause could not be indicated by the assured.

[170] Once this is proved, the onus of proof switches to the insurer to demonstrate that the loss arose as a result of a specific excepted peril (Merkin R (2002) Colinvaux & Merkin's Insurance Contract Law, S&M London, Para. B-0570-B-0591, The Coverage of Marine Policies.)

[171] *Theodorou v. Chester* [1951]1 Lloyd's Rep. 204.

[172] In relation to insurable interest, the Clauses follow the line drawn by the Marine Insurance Act 1906. The Act states that the assured need not have an in-

where claims were made for indemnification for false product supply, the court held, *inter alia*, that the policies provided cover against loss in the form of the award of damages *"on account of"* property damage, defined as including *"physical injury ... to tangible property"*; but that there had been no *"losses"*, as per the policy, as the latter did not contain any provision whereby a large number of small claims could be aggregated into a single loss or accident for the purposes of applying the deductible, and also because there had been no valid notification of the losses to the excess layer insurers. The policy stated that, in order for there to be coverage, the property damage had to be *"neither expected nor intended"* and the Court felt that this had not been met. In *Pilkington United Kingdom Ltd v CGU Insurance Plc*[174] the claim related to the installation of the glass panels in the roof of the Eurostar terminal at Waterloo Station. *Pilkington* was insured by *CGU* under a liability policy, the insuring clause of which applied to all sums which *Pilkington* became legally liable to pay for compensation and claimants' and costs and expenses in respect of any occurrence to which the policy applied, and all costs and expenses of litigation incurred with the written consent of *CGU* in respect of a claim falling within the policy. The Court of Appeal held that as far as the coverage of the policy was concerned, in order to establish cover in respect of the loss claimed, the insured must demonstrate some physical damage caused by the commodity for which purpose a defect or deterioration in the commodity is not itself sufficient and that the loss claimed must be a loss resulting from physical loss or damage to physical property of another (or some personal injury). In *Heesens Yacht Builders BV v Cox Syndicate Management Ltd, (The Red Sapphire)* [175] the Court of Appeal, stated that the policy in ques-

terest at the inception of the policy, but as marine policies are ones of indemnity, the assured must possess an insurable interest at the time of loss (see s.6(1)) The Institute Cargo clauses (A),(B),(C), cl.11.1 are to the same effect. If insurable interest is lost by the date of the occurrence of the peril, then the assured has no claim. Difficulties of communication between distant geographical locations, meant that the assured would seek to insure a cargo or vessel which might have been lost by the time of acquiring his interest, though interest had just been obtained in it, thus the *"lost or not lost"* cover was established, permitting the assured to claim even if the subject-matter had been the subject of a casualty prior to the agreement. The Institute Cargo Clauses (A), (B),(C), deal with that in cl.11.2.

173 *Tioxide Europe Ltd v CGU International Insurance Plc* [2005] Lloyd's Rep IR 114, [2005] EWCA Civ 928.

174 *Pilkington United Kingdom Ltd v CGU Insurance Plc* [2004] Lloyd's Rep IR 891.

175 [2006] EWCA Civ 384.

tion only covered vessels work on which had started during the currency of the policy, and that the intention of the wording was not to indemnify by applying the guarantee risk to vessels work on which had commenced before the inception of the construction risks policy, thus to cover different vessels.In *Talbot Underwriting Ltd v Nausch Hogan & Murray, (The Jascon 5)*[176] the barge Jascon 5, owned by *CPL*, was sent to party *S* in Singapore for repair and refurbishment. The contract stated that *S* would indemnify *CPL* for all claims for damage to the vessel and would insure against those risks and that *CPL* would take out a Builders' All Risks Policy to cover the interests of S but in doing so *CPL* did not inform the insurers that *S* was intended to be a co-assured under the policy. Following the flooding of the vessel *S* made a claim rejected on the basis that they were not assured under the policy. The court held that the policy by its terms did not cover the interests of *S*.[177]

The courts set high criteria to be met in order to ascertain that coverage exists and in that way preserve the insurer's party and aim to avoid over-indemnification.

2.2.2. The coverage offered under marine insurance contracts in Greece

The distinguishing feature of marine insurance contracts is that they cover damages, losses due to the occurrence of marine risks, or otherwise as characteristically stated in the Greek text of law "maritime navigation risks" (as per art. 259, 257 of the CPML (ΚΙΝΔ)).[178]

The insured risks are always maritime perils, as per art. 259 of the CPML (ΚΙΝΔ).[179] Maritime perils are not exhaustively those linked directly to the sea. Thus, the peril of fire to the vessel[180] or cargo, or damage to the vessel's engines or mechanical equipment may be considered.[181] In

176 [2005] EWHC 2359 (Comm).

177 Merkin R(2006) Insurance Law Update 2003-2006.

178 Argyriadis AA (1986) Elements of Insurance Law, 4th edn., Sakkoulas Publications , Thessaloniki, Greece.

179 The principle of universality of insured risks is preserved. The concept includes coverage of all events that may happen in a sea voyage, i.e. it covers maritime perils in the broad sense of the term (Argyriadis A(1979): Marine Insurance: A General Comparative View in the Light of Greek Law, Revue Hélenique de Droit International, 32:28-40).

180 *Piraeus Court of Appeal: 265/1999 ΕφΠειρ ΕεμπΔ 2000,116.*

181 The practical significance of characterising an insurance contract as a marine

principle, every maritime peril is covered by the *"all risks principle"*, which is a traditional feature of the Greek marine insurance law. As Argyriadis (1986)[182] states, this is different to the English law, which follows the *"specified or enumerated perils principle"*.[183] However, the *"all risks principle"* is subject to the opposite agreement of the insurer and the assured, who may even elect to use the English clauses.[184] If the insurer wishes to exempt a specific maritime peril from the insurance policy, it is his duty to describe it in written and clear terms within the policy; otherwise it is deemed by the law that the underwriter shall cover every maritime peril. If the parties do not specify the perils against which insurance is provided, it is accepted that all possible risks are covered apart from war risks and third party liability, for which special cover has to be agreed.[185] Thus, it is common in practice that by special clauses the exact maritime perils are described and thus the list is reduced most of the times. In practice, the modern form of marine insurance policies has eliminated the need for extra clauses and specification of the risks to be included, as these are stipulated and are already contained in the forms used nowadays. There is an exclusion, from insurance coverage, of perils and losses resulting exclusively from a defect of the subject-matter insured, provided that such defect had not been known/made known to the underwriter.[186]

It is important to define apart from the perils insured against also the exact period of the time for which they are insured. As per art. 269, of

---

one rather than a general one (terrestrial) within the Greek law system is a rather procedural one, i.e. in the case of the former the time-barring for legal action is two years whereas in the latter it is three years. (Rokas I (1995) Intro duction to the Law of Private Insurance, 4th edn, Oikonomikon Publications, Athens, p 3)

182 Argyriadis AA (1986) Elements of Insurance Law, 4th edn., Sakkoulas Publications , Thessaloniki, Greece.

183 Argyriadis AA (1986) Elements of Insurance Law, 4th edn., Sakkoulas Publications , Thessaloniki, Greece.

184 Case law has also shown that the parties, may elect to disregard the *"all risks principle"* and instead insert special clauses defining them, in accordance also with articles 173,200,288 of the Greek Civil Code (AK), known also in English practice as Institute Time Clauses. It is therefore accepted, and has also been ruled through various court judgements, that the *"all risks principle"* may not be followed so that the contract will cover only specific maritime perils *(Athens Court of First Instance (ΠΠΑΘ) 3831/1979, 10 ΕΝΔ 30, Athens Court of Appeal (ΕφΑΘ) 6191/1981, 33 ΕΕΔ 263).*

185 However, in cases of collision, the damage caused to the third party is covered, even if no insurance for third party liability has been taken out.

186 Argyriadis A(1979): Marine Insurance: A General Comparative View in the Light of Greek Law, Revue Hellenique de Droit International, 32:28-40.

the Code of Private Maritime Law CPML (ΚΙΝΔ), in the case of a time policy, the insurer is liable for all losses and defects caused by any event during the course of voyage as well as for theft. The time commences as from the date appearing on the contract and it is the local time of the country where the insurance contract was effected. Should the time end during the voyage, then it is automatically renewed until the next day after the first port is reached and the vessel has berthed. In the latter case, however, an additional premium is owed to the insurer.

As per art. 263 CPML (ΚΙΝΔ), in the case of a voyage policy, the insurer is liable from the time of the commencement of loading until the conclusion of its unloading.

As per art. 264 CPML (ΚΙΝΔ), in the case of a policy effected for cargo, the insurer is liable from the time that the cargo is loaded[187] up to the time of their unloading. In any case it is deemed to have concluded thirty days after the arrival at the port of destination. The perils not included in the contracts are most of the time insured separately usually in the English market, via the P& I Clubs. The positive damages (positive-cover) marine insurance[188] comprising insurance on cargo, freight, future profit etc., and the negative damages (negative-cover)[189] marine insurance on comprising insurance of ship-owners' liability towards third parties, insurance of freighter's liability for damage or tortious delay of cargo, insurance on sea

[187] In detail *"when goods seize to be attached to earth"*.

[188] Rokas I (1995) Introduction to the Law of Private Insurance, 4th edn, Oiko nomikon Publications, Athens.

[189] According to the Greek Civil Law, the damages that can be awarded may be listed either as positive damages (positive cover damages) ,(Θετικό Διαφέρον ή Διαφέρον Εκπληρώσεως), comprising those attributed to a person for loss suffered due to the non-fulfilment or non dully fulfilment of a contract term in a legally bind transaction; or as negative damages (negative cover damages), (Αρνητικό Διαφέρον ή Διαφέρον Εμπιστοσύνης), comprising those attributed to a person for loss suffered due to the non-fulfilment or non dully fulfilment of a contract term in a transaction which was originally agreed and never in fact executed or even if executed for some reason rendered void upon its execution. Also, as per the Greek Civil Law, losses leading to either a positive or negative damages award, may be also categorised either as positive losses, (Θετική Ζημία), (caused by the decrease of the revenue / non-increase of the expenditure, as either of these would have been normally expected in the course of ordinary transactions) or as negative losses, (Αποθετική Ζημία ή Διαφυγόν Κέρδος), (caused by the non-increase of the revenue / non-decrease of the expenditure, as either of these would have been normally expected in the course of ordinary transactions) . Both positive and negative damages may be awarded due to either positive or negative losses suffered.

pollution etc., form other categories of insurance that are considered to be of a maritime nature and as such marine ones.[190]

As per art., 205 of the Greek Commercial Code and art. 257 of the CPML (ΚΙΝΔ), the insurer is no longer liable when due to the assured's fault, the maritime perils change in such a way that the insurer, had he known that at the conclusion of the contract, would not have consented to enter it or would have done so on different terms.[191] The same applies when there is alteration of risk, i.e. a change that would have caused the insurer not to have accepted the insurance at all or on the same conditions, had he known about the alteration. The sanctioning degree depends on how much the assured is to blame for not having notified the insurer about the alteration. Thus, if there has been negligence, then there is a reduction of indemnity, whereas in case of intention there is, as a result, complete freedom from liability.

2.2.3. The coverage offered under marine insurance contracts in Norway

Under the umbrella of the Norwegian law, insurance against marine perils is based on the *"all risks principle"*, with the starting point that the insurance will cover all perils to which the interest may be exposed unless there is a provision to the contrary.

Regarding the perils[192] covered by an insurance against marine perils[193] as under the 1964 Norwegian Marine Insurance Plan, the perils are divided into two groups. A distinction is made between perils covered by the insurers against ordinary marine perils and perils covered by the insurers against war perils. The perils covered by the war-risk insurance are specified, while the range of perils covered by the insurance against marine perils is negatively defined, covering any other form of perils to which the interest is exposed. In case of a combination[194] of perils[195], the rule of apportionment is maintained as the causation principle when a loss is

---

190 Velentzas I(1998)The New Law of Private Insurance, Ius Publications Athens

191 *Athens Court of Appeal: ΕφΑθ 6347/1990 ΕΝαυτΔ 1991.82* ; Velentzas I (1998) The New Law of Private Insurance, Ius Publications, Athens.

192 Paragraph 2-8 of Chapter 2.

193 This provision corresponds to § 15 of the 1964 Plan and Cefor I.1 and I.2 and PIC §§5.1 and 5.3.

194 Paragraph 2-13.

195 The paragraph is identical to § 20 of the Norwegian Marine Insurance Plan 1964.

caused by a combination of perils, i.e. when a loss is caused partly by a peril covered by the insurance and partly by a peril which is not covered by the insurance.

2.2.4. The coverage offered under marine insurance contracts in France

The insured risks are defined in art. 51 of the Law of 3/7/1967 and now art. L. 173-16 of the Insurance Code. In general, under French law, the risks covered are perils of the seas and exposed perils to preserve the subject-matter insured. In addition, we could say that the risks covered are negatively defined, i.e. by definition of the excluded risks.[196]

In case of insurance covering a voyage policy or a time policy excluded risks are also ones due to the assured's fault,[197] vice or inherent vice,[198] illegal acts,[199] commercially prejudiced acts like strike or delay, war risks, damage caused by the subject of insurance to other things or persons.[200] The insurance contract is still valid in case of route deviation due to reasons imposed by the security of the maritime operation, or due to events independent to the assured or due to motives imposing it.[201] As per art. 5 of the Law of 3/7/1967 an insurance is not valid if the risks do not attach at the commencement of it.

The insurer is considered to be a professional who owes a duty of pre-contractual information to the assured. Before the conclusion of the contract, he is therefore obliged to furnish information on the price and extent of the coverage, as well as to provide the assured with a draft copy of the contract with annexes or a detailed notice on the coverage. By the proposal, the insurer guarantees for the coverage of the risks described, which will form the basis for the conclusion of the contract later. The insurer

196 Such as damages due to vice/inherent vice, deviation of route, bad conditionning or insufficiency of the subject-matter insured.

197 As per art. 17 of the Law of 3/7/1967 and now art. L.172-13 of the Insurance Code.

198 As per art. 39 of the Law of 3/7/1967 and now art. L. 173-4 of the Insurance Code.

199 As per art. 22 of the Law of 3/7/1967 and now art. L. 172-18 of the Insurance Code.

200 As per art. 20 of the Law of 3/7/1967 and now art. L. 172-16 of the Insurance Code.

201 Art. 19 of the Law of 3/7/1967 and now art. 172-15 of the Insurance Code.

provides the assured with a risk declaration form (Art. L.113-2 of the Insurance Code) to which the assured must respond precisely.[202] Furthermore, the assured has to inform the insurer within fifteen days, of any new occurrence increasing the risks or creating new risks which may render the responses made to the proposal inexact or void.

As per art. 348 of the Commercial Code, the contract is void if the assured, prior to the conclusion of the contract, has not disclosed a material circumstance related to the risk involved or has intentionally misrepresented information. The same applies if he has made a false declaration as per art. 21,22 of the Law of 3/7/1967 and now art. L. 113-8,113-9 of the Code of Insurances. Throughout the duration of the contract, the assured has a duty to inform the insurer on any risk modification as under 6,7 of the Law of 3/7/1967 and now art. 172-3 of the Insurance Code.

Under art. 7 of the Law of 3/7/1967, if the risk aggravation is not owed to the assured's fault, the insurance contract is still valid, whereas if it is due to the assured's fault, the insurer has to decide within three days if he will rescind the contract or increase the premium.

In case of an inexact declaration performed in bad faith, the assured is not able to recover the indemnity, under art. 32 of the Law of 3/7/1967 and now art. L.172-28 of the Insurance Code.[203]

2.2.5. The coverage offered under marine insurance contracts in the USA

In the USA the standard marine insurance policy gives protection against a wide variety of perils. The policy, however, does not protect against every sort of loss that may occur to a vessel or a cargo.

---

202 Thus, exercising the duty of utmost good faith. If general questions are posed the assured bears no liability for imprecise responses that might have been given.

203 The justification of the duty to disclose lies in the risk is the base of the contract and the object of the guarantee given by the assured. Any fault on that is substantial justifying the contract to be void. (Art. 1109 of the Commercial Code).The insurer is discharged from the obligation to indemnify the assured (art. L. 121-12 of the Insurance Code) if the latter -due to his actions- has lost or not preserved the action to suit against the carrier, i.e. when the transport contract is annulated due to a false declaration, when the type of contract used prevents actions against the carrier.

The *"named perils"* clause of the policy sets out the principal risks actually insured against under the policy; typically, the *"perils clause"* is supplemented or restricted by special clauses. Common perils insured include perils of the sea; fire; violent theft; jettison; piracy; arrests by governments and people; barratry; war; salvage; general average; collision and explosions. The burden of proving the loss was caused by a peril insured against is on the assured.[204] A *"peril of the sea"* is not merely an occurrence at sea; the event must be fortuitous in character.[205] The loss must be due to an exceptional event associated with the sea; routine or ordinary occurrences at sea are not covered.[206]

Although at first glance, upon examination of a standard American policy of marine insurance, one sees that the basic maritime perils insured against are described in venerable terms and, therefore, gets the impression that the coverage provided is often an all-embracing one, this is not actually the case, as was demonstrated in *Dwyer v Providence Washington Insurance Corp.*[207] Here the Court actually remarked that the term *"perils of the sea"* did not embrace all losses happening on the seas and that a policy insuring against perils of the sea, covered only extraordinary risks.[208]

2.2.6. The coverage offered under marine insurance contracts in Canada

Canadian law recognises the *"all risks"* principle. It is often assumed by the assured, that an *"all risks"* policy of insurance provides coverage against all risk of damage or loss. In fact, this is not the case. Firstly, most *"all risks"* policies of insurance generally provide such coverage subject to the exclusions specifically enumerated within the policy. To the extent that any loss comes within the exclusions it will, of course, not be covered. Secondly, even if a loss does not come within an exclusion it may still not be covered under an *"all risks"* policy, following the leading English case

[204] Schoenbaum TJ (2001) Admiralty and Maritime Law, 3rd edn, Hornbook Series, West Group, St.Paul, Minn, USA.

[205] *Darien Bank v Travelers Indemnity Co* 654 F2d 1015, AMC 1813 (5th Circ 1981)

[206] *Glover v Pfiladelphia Fire & Marine Ins. Co*, 1956 AMC 1210 (City Ct. Balt. 1956).

[207] 1958 AMC 1488.

[208] *Tropical Marine Products Co v Birmingham Fire Insurance Co*, (1956 AMC 567).

of *British and Foreign Marine Insurance Company Limited v Gaunt*,[209] in which the House of Lords held that the words *"all risks"* do not cover all damage however caused, and specifically held that the words would not cover damage caused by wear and tear, inevitable deterioration or inherent vice. Further, it was held that *"all risks"* policies cover only damage caused by an accident or due to some fortuitous circumstance or casualty.

In order for coverage to exist under an *"all risks"* policy, the loss must have been caused by a fortuity i.e. an accident or casualty. A loss caused by wear and tear, deterioration or inherent vice of the subject matter insured is not covered. The risks covered are maritime perils, i.e. perils of the seas. A marine adventure, is defined as the exposure of insurable property to maritime perils which include perils of the seas, i.e. fortuitous accidents or casualties of the seas but not any ordinary action of the wind or waves.

In the leading Canadian case regarding losses by perils of the seas, *CCR Fishing Ltd v Tomenson Inc.*,[210] the insured's ship sank while it was docked. Seawater had entered the hulls because a valve was left open and unsuitable screws had corroded. It was held, that the loss was fortuitous as it would not have occurred, had the valve not been left open.

2.2.7. The coverage offered under marine insurance contracts in Australia

S. 9(2) of the Marine Insurance Act 1909, defines a marine adventure and refers to the exposure to risk of the insured property itself, or money earned form that property or adventure, and the liability arising for a third party if that property is lost or damaged.

Maritime perils are defined in section 9(2)(c) of the Act, the definition not being exhaustive and allowing also other perils to be defined by the policy as long as they are a consequence of or incidental to the navigation of the sea.

---

209 [1921] A.C. 41.

210 (1990) 43 CCLI 1 (SCC).

2.2.7.1. The coverage offered under marine insurance contracts in the Australian law regime: the reform proposals

This area is covered in Chapter 8 of the Australian Law Reform Commission report.

The Australian Law Reform Commission reforms initially seek to develop a clear dichotomy between commercial and non commercial marine insurance. This is consistent with the overall approach that consumer contracts of insurance should be covered by the Insurance Contracts Act. The Insurance Contracts Act should be amended to cover contracts of insurance for the transportation by water of goods other than those transported for the purposes of business, trade, profession, or occupation carried on or engaged by the insured and such an amendment will in effect remove the insurance of the carriage of goods for non-commercial purposes from the Marine Insurance Act 1909.[211] Secondly, the reform seeks to extend coverage, to include adventures on inland waters. At present, the Act's operation is confined to maritime adventures and incidental non-maritime risks. The expansion would remove some of the uncertainty existing in relation to this matter.

Since the enactment of the reforms contained in the Insurance Contracts Act 1986, the law of general insurance in Australia has been vastly different from marine insurance in many respects. It has, therefore, been critical to determine which Act applies to any particular contract of insurance. Two areas of real difficulty have emerged in practice. One arose out of the exclusion of inland water risks from the Marine Insurance Act. As already noted, the Australian Law Reform Commission proposes to include such risks in the ambit of the Marine Insurance Act. The second, regarding policies covering both marine and non marine transit risks, has proven more difficult to solve.[212]

---

211 "The Australian Law Reform Commission Reform: 91: Report", in < http://www.austlii.edu.au/au/other/alrc/publications/reports/91/>

212 Except where the contract provides for the application of foreign law (where this is permissible) it seems that either the Marine Insurance Act 1909 or the Insurance Contracts Act must apply to the whole of any contract of general insurance not covered by another statutory scheme. Neither Act appears to contemplate the splitting of a contract or policy between them. The Insurance Contracts Act was drafted with clear knowledge of the provisions of the Marine Insurance Act 1909 but there is no provision in the Insurance Contracts Act which anticipates that one or other Act might apply to severable portions of the contract. Therefore, in some circumstances there may be uncertainty as to whether a contract of insurance is one to which the Marine Insurance Act 1909 applies (Derrington S (2002) Australia: Perspectives and Permutations on

Regarding mixed risks, it has been noted that, in cases of policies including a substantial land transit component, there are real problems in deciding which Act applies. The test that has been developed is that the marine risk involved in the transit must be a *"substantial"* part of the risk covered by the contract for the Marine Insurance Act 1909 to apply.[213] The problems become significant with open or annual floating cover for any form of transit risk because the parties will be unable to assess whether the sea transit component is *"substantial"* until the end of the cover period. The parties, therefore, cannot be sure which of the two insurance regimes will apply to the contract until after the contract has expired.[214]

---

the Law of Marine Insurance, Ch. 11 In Thomas R (ed) The Modern Law of Marine Insurance, Vol. 2, LLP).

213 In *Norsworthy & Encel v SGIG*, [Unreported, per Olsen J, Supreme Court of South Australia, Nov. 30,1999.] , the plaintiffs sustained personal injuries and property damage in a boating accident during a diving excursion operated by *"G.D.C. Pty Ltd"* (GDC). GDC was insured by SGIC, the State Government Insurance Corporation, pursuant to a policy described as being one of *"marine insurance"*. GDC went into liquidation and the insurer was sued directly by the plaintiffs. The issue as to which statute governed the policy became then apparent; s.51 of the insurance Contracts Act makes limited provision for a right of direct action by third parties against insurers. There is no equivalent provision in the Marine Insurance Contracts Act 1909. The Insurance Contracts Act does not apply to contracts to which the Marine Insurance Act 1909 applies; and the Marine Insurance Act 1909 does not apply to *"state marine insurance"*. Thus, there seems to exist a hiatus in the law governing contracts of marine insurance written by state insurers. However, being properly construed as a marine policy, the contract of insurance here was held to be governed by the Marine Insurance Act 1909 and there was no prospect of direct action by the third party plaintiff against the insurer (Derrington S (2002) Australia: Perspectives and Permutations on the Law of Marine Insurance, Ch. 11 In Thomas R (ed) The Modern Law of Marine Insurance, Vol. 2, LLP).

214 The uncertainty as to the applicable law also arises in the context of cargo insurance where more than one form of carriage is often involved in the carriage of goods. In *Con Stan Industries of Australia Pty Ltd v Norwich Winterthur (Australia) Limited*, [(1986)160 CLR 226] , was a case involving insurance of stock and trade from a variety of risks, no evidence was lead to illustrate the importance of the carriage of goods by sea, the policy and its term indicated that it was but one part of one section of the cover afforded. The High Court held that it could not be held that the policy, viewed in its entirety, indemnified the insured against losses substantially incidental to a marine adventure. The case shows that a policy covering various modes of transport will be governed by the Insurance Contracts Act if there is no evidence that sea transport predominates (Derrington S (2002) Australia: Perspectives and Permutations on

The Australian Law Reform Commission has concluded that no statutory reformulation of that sort will satisfactorily remove the uncertainty, has already rejected the option of fusing the two regimes and has accordingly recommended that the Marine Insurance Act 1909 remain unaltered in this respect. In relation to the coverage of the Marine Insurance Act 1909, however, the Australian Law Reform Commission has recommended that the Marine Insurance Act 1909 be amended so that, subject to the terms of the contract, marine insurance covers risks on inland waters and the sea, stating that the seas should be read as including inland waters. This recommendation arises out of the importance of the distinction between inland waters and the sea in determining the respective coverage of the Marine Insurance Act 1909 and the Insurance Contracts Act.[215]

It has also been recommended that the insurance for the carriage of goods for non-commercial purposes be removed from the Marine Insurance Act 1909, that the Marine Insurance Act 1909 refer expressly to losses arising from any air risk incidental to a sea voyage and that the Marine Insurance Act 1909 be amended to refer expressly to losses arising from the repair of the ship.[216]

2.3. General conclusive remarks and comparative discussion

Under the auspices of the English law regime, insurable interest may be described as the insured's pecuniary interest in the subject-matter of the insurance arising from a relationship with it recognised in law.[217]

---

the Law of Marine Insurance, Ch. 11 In Thomas R (ed) The Modern Law of Marine Insurance, Vol. 2, LLP).

215 Whilst in practice the need to make this distinction is limited, there are instances in which commercial navigation may occur on inland waters whether incidental to a sea voyage or not. Of course, most inland waters in Australia are used for pleasure craft, the insurance of which is expressly covered by the Insurance Contracts Act (Derrington S (2002) Australia: Perspectives and Permutations on the Law of Marine Insurance, Ch. 11 In Thomas R (ed) The Modern Law of Marine Insurance, Vol. 2, LLP).

216 Derrington S (2002) Australia: Perspectives and Permutations on the Law of Marine Insurance, Ch. 11 In Thomas R (ed) The Modern Law of Marine Insurance, Vol. 2, LLP.

217 Until the legislature intervened, gambling and wagering contracts were not prohibited by English law, so that a wager as such was not an illegal agreement and was justifiable in a court. The same principle was also applied to wagers

Under US law, an insurance contract which violates public policy is void and not enforceable by Courts, and the existence of insurable interest at the time of loss, is a necessary precondition for a valid contract of marine insurance. In Canada, the assured can only claim for indemnity when he has suffered a loss, and to qualify as such, he must have had an insurable interest in the subject-matter insured or -at the conclusion of the contract- an expectation of acquiring such an interest. In Australia the Australian Law Reform Commission has proposed to remove the requirement that the insured have an insurable interest in the goods insured at the time of the loss. The Australian Law Reform Commission is oriented towards the approach that the only needed requirement for an insurable interest is that it entails an economic interest.

Contrary to the approach followed in the common law jurisdictions, in the continental law countries the main requirements is that the insurable interest is lawful and that it encompasses an economic relationship. Under Greek law, insurable interest is a prerequisite for the obtaining of coverage and the most important factor for acquiring insurable interest is that the latter is lawful and is conducted in a lawful manner. Under Norwegian law, the two main requirements for insurable interest to exist is firstly that it be lawful - since illegal activities are defined under the Plan as an alteration of risk- and secondly that it be of an economic value, the most significant prerequisite being the latter.[218] In France, the main requirement for insurable interest is that it be legitimate.

concerning marine insurance, namely if the parties chose to make a wager in the form of a marine policy, the court enforced the contract. It is shown in a few early cases that the courts had the tendency to cancel policies on proof of no interest (*Martin v Sitwell* (1691) 1 Shaw. 156 ; *Goddart v Garrett* (1692)2 Vern.269 ; *Le Pypre v Farr* (1716)2 Vern.716 ; *Whittingham v Thornburgh* (1690)2 Vern. 206) It is clear, however, from later decisions that wager policies were recognised as valid if it was clear that both parties really intended to wager and not to conclude an insurance contract to indemnify the assured for a real loss [*Lucena v Craufurd* (1802) 3 Bos. & Pul. 75,101]. In the modern era, the Marine Insurance Act 1906 defines in section 4(1) that wagering contracts are void and in section 4(2) which contracts are to be defines as wagers, i.e. those made without interest and without expectation of acquiring interest in the subject-matter, as well as *"p.p.i."* policies. The Act does not prohibit such contracts and thus does not make them illegal as void (Legh-Jones N et al (2002) MacGillivray on Insurance Law, 10th edn, London, S&M, Ch 1).

218 However, due to the existence of the Plan and the fact that here has been no real case law on insurable interest for many years, no real rules apply in relation to insurable interest and the most common practice nowadays is that the parts decide themselves primarily on the marine insurance contract rules and their content, thus taking *ab initio* the risk on them.

The concept of insurable interest developed, not merely to distinguish indemnity insurance from wager policies, but also to satisfy the requirement of the indemnity principle itself that the assured should suffer a loss against which he can be indemnified.[219] The test of legal relationship cannot, however, guaranty that the assured would certainly have benefited if the subject-matter had not been lost. Nevertheless, it has been widely accepted that the present concept of a principle of insurable interest has worked quite well in marine insurance, making it difficult to support a case for radical reform of s.5 of the Marine Insurance Act 1906.[220]

It has been submitted, however, that the courts are free to develop a new sub-head of insurable interest in a marine adventure within the scope of s.5(1) of the Marine Insurance Act 1906, by which a valid insurable interest is held to exist in cases where the gain of a property right or other benefit - to which the assured is entitled in law or in equity - is dependent upon the successful outcome of a marine adventure, albeit the assured possesses no legal or equitable right to, or in, insurable property prior to its conclusion.[221] Such a development would not be of a highly beneficial character, as it would jeopardize the interests of the assured, in the sense that he would not be able to claim for his loss in the case of a non successful outcome of a marine adventure since he would be deemed as not to have gained insurable interest and therefore not to have a right in law to claim for the loss sustained.

It is normal at this point to raise questions such as: *"Can we really waive the requirement for an insurable interest which would entail a legal or equitable relation to the subject-matter of the insurance?"* or *"If there is no need for insurable interest, why has there been no serious adjudication on the issue?"*

In relation to the first question, i.e. whether one can seek legitimately the insurance of goods with no insurable interest, it has been suggested that, due to the fact that there is no real big market demand, there is no reason to provide the insurers with a technical defence to claims where the risk is no different that what the insurer perceived it to be, especially

[219] That in turn, as Lawrence J. recognised in *Lucena v Craufurd*, (1806)2 Bos & Pul (NR) 269 involves a satisfactory degree of certainty that, had the insured property not been lost or damaged, the assured would have benefited, and English law has adopted the requirement of a legal relationship between the assured and the insured subject-matter as the criterion for that degree of certainty.

[220] Legh-Jones N et al (2002) MacGillivray on Insurance Law, 10th edn, London, S&M, Ch 1.

[221] Legh-Jones N et al (2002) MacGillivray on Insurance Law, 10th edn, London, S&M, Ch 4.

because there is also no general rule requiring the insured to specify the nature of his interest in the property insured. In a commercial context, English law should permit the broader economic loss test and leave the insurers to enquire on the nature of insurable interest so as to safeguard themselves against fraud, although this seems more difficult to embrace in an individual consumer context. The requirement for insurable interest should not be abolished, but instead be relaxed, for various reasons, in light also of the evolution of modern market circumstances in relation to transportation and marine insurance law. This is further supported, on the one hand by the fact that not a feasible option to abolish *"p.p.i."* polices, for they are very popular and continue to be effected - by and large because they meet commercial need and practicality amidst other reasons - and because it is surprising the number of professionals in the market opting for them, without actually knowing that such contracts are unenforceable and cannot be used as evidence in courts; and even where such knowledge exists, these policies are still widespread and to simply expect the market to stop using them is not a pragmatic aspiration. On the other hand, it would seem a good proposal to relax the requirement for insurable interest and to mainly expect an interest which is lawful in its nature and the modus of its exercise and which also entails an economic benefit, firstly because the danger of wagering policies is rare nowadays; secondly, due to the precondition that the assured must have actually suffered a loss covered for in the policy, in order to get indemnified, and for him to be able to claim for such a loss he must have a justified economic interest either directly in the subject-matter insured, or as a consequence of its loss. In relation to the second question, it is indeed true that there has been no substantial amount of litigation on the issue of insurable interest. Having said that, it is worth mentioning that the Courts in Canada have abandoned the narrow view adopted by English Courts in *Macaura v Northern Assurance Co Ltd* [222] in the case of *Constitution Insurance Co of Canada v Kosmopoulos*[223] where Judge Wilson J. embraced Lord Eldon's view in *Lucena v Craufurd*[224] - that there is no justification in adopting the narrower definition of insurable interest[225]- just because the broader definition[226] is not the right one. Her Honour stated the importance of the necessity to examine the policy requirements underlying the insurable interest requirements and

---

222 *Macaura v Northern Assurance Co Ltd* [1925] AC 619.

223 *Constitution Insurance Co of Canada v Kosmopoulos* (1987)34 DLR (4th) 208.

224 (1806)2 Bos & PNR 267.

225 i.e. one requiring a legal or equitable relation to the subject-matter insured.

226 Which encompasses the adequacy of only an economic interest in the subject-matter insured.

whether they have necessitated the adoption of the narrow view, and she further went on saying that a policy is not wagering if the insurer can demonstrate pecuniary interest irrespective of whether it was based on strict proprietary interest. In addition, she referred to the prevailing view in USA which also provides for the wider test for the insurable interest, and concluded that there was no reason to follow *Macaura v Northern Assurance Co Ltd* [227] and the earlier Canadian cases. It is true that, until recently, there had been no substantial litigation on the issue which would enable us to treat the approach followed in *Constitution Insurance Co of Canada v Kosmopoulos* [228] as a general new trend, mainly because the matter has dominantly been governed by the House of Lords authority in *Macaura v Northern Assurance Co Ltd* [229], and also because there are ways to go around the *Macaura v Northern Assurance Co Ltd*[230]strict rule, such as the fact that a shareholder can insure his shares against loss of value owing to failure of an adventure of the company[231] and the fact that courts recognise that there can be lack of insurable interest if the assured can prove that the insurable interest requirement has been properly waived.[232] Recent litigation, however, has started to reveal the move towards a different approach to be followed by the courts.

Thus, it is highly probable that *Macaura v Northern Assurance Co Ltd* [233] would not have been followed nowadays, in light of *Feasey v Sun Life Assurance Co of Canada* [234] - where the Court of Appeal held that a Club had actually a pecuniary interest in covering losses for which it might be liable and that interest existed at the time the policy was issued - and *O'Kane v Jones & others* [235] - where the court held that possession or the right to possession is not an essential prerequisite of insurable interest and that commercial convenience is enough to support the existence of insurable interest from a managing company in a vessel. The court, in *Feasey v Sun Life Assurance Co of Canada* [236], based its decision on the fact that the interest had been insured in a way that it did not result to a gamble or wager at the inception of the contract. Although there was also a legitimate

227 [1925] AC 619.
228 *Constitution Insurance Co of Canada v Kosmopoulos* (1987)34 DLR (4th) 208.
229 [1925] AC 619.
230 [1925] AC 619.
231 Which has evolved to be a widespread type of insurance.
232 In the sense that the true policy construction was for the insurer to pay notwithstanding insured with no insurable interest.
233 [1925] AC 619.
234 *Feasy v Sun Life Assurance Co of Canada* [2002]2 All E.R. (Comm) 292.
235 *O' Kane v Jones & Others* [2003] All ER (D) 510 (Jul).
236 *Feasy v Sun Life Assurance Co of Canada* [2002]2 All E.R. (Comm) 292.

interest entailed, the latter was an immaterial fact for the court, so long as there was no gaming or wagering in the policy issued. This seems to be the first recognition by the judiciary that insurable interest can be justified in cases where it is founded on an economic basis. Also in *O'Kane v Jones & others,*[237] the court seemed to be willing to disregard the importance of possession or the right to possession as an essential requirement for insurable interest. The fact that the managing company of the vessel was entitled to remuneration under the Management Agreement for the services it provided and the fact that the Management Agreement automatically terminated if and when the vessel became a total loss, was sufficient evidence for the purposes of s.5(2) of the Marine Insurance Act 1906. In addition the court recognised that strong considerations of commercial convenience - relating to the close practical relationship between a manager and the vessel under management - supported the existence of an insurable interest in the managing company. More recently, in *Linelevel Ltd v Zaklad Ubezpieczen SA*[238], the court held that the justification of commercial convenience and economic relationships such as the loss of hire owed due to the breach of a duty of repair were enough to support the existence of insurable interest. However, in the non marine case of *Murphy v Murphy*[239] the court, following he traditional approach towards the requirement for insurable interest, held that proper construction of the policy purported that the parties had separate interests, as - in case of death of one of the parties - the survivor was the only person entitled to receive payment of the sum insured, and that the claimant, who was the son of the deceased, could not share the profits with the former wife of the deceased who was the other party in the life insurance policy.

It follows, from the study of related litigation that, to a certain extent, English law is beginning to move towards a wider definition of insurable interest. Chances are that, today, the assured in *Macaura v Northern Assurance Co Ltd*[240], would have been able to recover for the loss of the timber by the fire, as it would have been enough to demonstrate the existence of real economic interest in the company's property. All that purports to the support of the proposal that there should no longer have to exist strict requirements for the justification of the existence of insurable interest. So long as the interest is economic and lawful in nature, also lawfully exercised, there is no reason for stricter requirements; the assured

237 *O' Kane v Jones & others* [2003] All ER (D) 510 (Jul).
238 *Linelevel Ltd v Powszechny Zaklad Ubezpieczen SA (The Nore Challenger)* [2005] EWHC 421 (Comm).
239 *Murphy v Murphy* [2003] [2004] Lloyd's Rep IR 774.
240 [1925] AC 619.

should be able to claim for indemnity where he possesses a pecuniary interest in the subject-matter insured, and the insurer should be given the option to contest the existence of a wager policy provided he also asserts the burden of proof in such a case. This approach is justified not only by the necessities and practical needs of the modern market[241], but also by the fact that there no longer exists such an imminent danger[242] for wagers, as well as by the realisation that many jurisdictions have either legislated *ab initio* or have felt the need to propose reforms in their law towards this direction.

With regards to the cover offered under marine insurance contracts, in contrast to English marine insurance law - which recognises the *"enumerated risks principle"* - Greek law adopts the *"all risks principle"* and perceives in a wider context the concept of marine risks and perils, so that -unless otherwise stated- all possible risks are covered under a Greek marine insurance contract, with the exception of war risks and third party liability for which special insurance cover has to be agreed. This shows, at a first glance, that the insured is more widely protected in the Greek legal order. However, this legal difference is not significantly substantial as in most cases the risks covered are eliminated by specific mention of those included and also because some of the ship-owners will inevitably choose to effect the insurance required within the London market.[243]

In Norway, the *"all risks principle"*, with the insurance covering all perils to which the interest may be exposed unless there is a provision to the contrary; and in France, although the "all risks" principle applies, it is nevertheless subject to exclusions stipulated by the contract.

In the USA the *"named perils"* clause, which sets out the principal risks actually insured against under the policy, is often supplemented or restricted by special clauses. In Canada, although the law may recognise the *"all risks"* principle, however the cover does not include risks such as ordinary wear and tear and most *"all risks"* policies eliminate this cover to the risks specifically enumerated within the policy. In Australia, the Australian Law Reform Commission seeks to develop a clear dichotomy between commercial and non commercial marine insurance, and also to extend coverage, to include adventures on inland waters.

All jurisdictions examined, but England, initially entail the *"all risks"* principle, but eventually narrow its scope by special clauses enu-

---

[241] For example cases where goods insured are sold F.O.B. and there is the need to provide a basis for an indemnity claim in the case of their loss even before ownership passes to the claimant.

[242] The way it used to exist in the past in relation to the effecting of wagering contracts.

[243] Papapolitis NI (1957) Insurance of the Liability of Shipowner , Athens,p.106.

merating the risks covered or the ones excluded. Thus, the tendency is to approach the English law's position, although the parties are left with the contractual freedom to stipulate themselves the exact extent of the cover and this is clearly an advantage when one compares the position of law in the various jurisdictions examined.

3. Types of losses in marine insurance contracts

3.1. Types of losses in marine insurance contracts under the English law regime

3.1.1. Indemnity and losses

A marine policy entitles the assured to indemnification in respect of several types of losses.[1] Calculation of the measure of indemnity is determined by two factors: the nature of the policy and the classification of the loss as total or partial loss. A marine insurance policy provides the assured or his assignees with an indemnity for total and partial loss of the subject-matter insured. A distinction is drawn by the Marine Insurance Act 1906 between actual total loss, constructive total loss and partial loss. Any loss which does not fall within the first two categories falls into the residual category of partial loss.[2] A total loss can either be an actual or a constructive total loss. Unless the policy states differently, insurance will include both types of total loss[3].

---

1 In general, first there is the extent of damage or loss of the subject-matter insured caused directly by a covered peril, which triggers the award of indemnification. Also, the insured may recover losses, charges or expenditure incurred voluntarily or as a matter of law in order to avert or minimise a loss and thus, may also thereby incur *"suing and labouring"* costs as a separate measure.

2 S.56(1) Marine Insurance Act 1906; Bennett, H (1986) The Law of Marine Insurance, Clarendon Press, Oxford, Ch 18.

3 S.56(3) Marine Insurance Act 1906.

All claims for loss, either partial or total, are subject to the *"Notice of claims"* clause within the International Hulls clauses. This clause[4] specifies that notice must be given to the leading underwriter.[5] It requires the assured to notify underwriters as soon as possible of any occurrence which may result in a claim. The difference between this clause and its predecessor, i.e. cl. 13 of the ITCH (95), is that the latter stated that notice had to be given to underwriters in general, whereas now the requirement for such a course of action arises only where the assured feels that there is a strong possibility for a claim to arise. In the absence of any agreement, underwriters are discharged from liability for the claim if they are not notified within 180 days of the assured becoming aware of the occurrence. This is similar to the 1995 version which gave the assured 12 months.[6]

3.1.1.1. Total losses: actual total loss

The Marine Insurance Act 1906 classifies two types of losses, i.e. partial loss and total loss,[7] the latter being further on subdivided into actual total loss and constructive total loss.[8]

A total loss is one on account of which the assured is entitled to recover from the underwriter the whole amount of his subscription.[9] With respect to actual total loss, section 57(1) of the Marine Insurance Act 1906 applies to any subject-matter insured within a policy of marine insurance, and this might include amongst others, ship, goods, freight, profits and commissions, as well as wages and disbursements. Furthermore, subject to its definition, actual total loss may be construed in three distinct ways, i.e. primarily when the subject-matter is totally destroyed, secondly when the

---

4 i.e.clause 46 of the IHC 1/11/2003.

5 In part 3 of the new 1/11/2002 clauses, clause 45 authorises the leading underwriters designated in the slip or policy to deal with a range of claims-related matters on behalf of all underwriters subscribing to the insurance. This clause is a development of reforms set out in the Lloyd's Market Principles. (Wall DJ (2003) International Hull Clauses 1/11/02: A Commentary, Shipping & Trade Law, Vol.3,No 1).

6 Wall DJ (2003) International Hull Clauses 1/11/02: A Commentary, Shipping & Trade Law, Vol 3, No 1.

7 In section 56(1).

8 As per section 56(2). Hodges S (1999) Cases and Materials on Marine Insurance Law, Cavendish Publications, p 15.

9 Mustill MJ & Gilman JCB (1981) Arnould's Law of Marine Insurance and Average, 16th edn, Vol I, Stevens, p 963.

subject-matter is so damaged as to cease to be a thing of the kind insured, and thirdly when the assured is irretrievably deprived thereof.

S. 57(1) of the Marine Insurance Act 1906 has codified the facts and ruling of an early case, which is widely considered as the *locus classicus* on the topic of actual total loss,[10] i.e. *Roux v Salvador* [11] where the plaintiff shipped a cargo of hides - aboard the vessel *Roxalane* from Valparaiso to Bordeaux - which was insured with the defendants under a voyage policy of insurance covering usual perils and being warranted free of particular average unless the ship be stranded. Due to severe weather, the ship had to be put to Rio de Janeiro where it was found, upon landing of cargo, that the hides were so wetted that if they would have been carried further on they would have lost their character as such; thus, they were sold there for a quarter of their true value. The plaintiff claimed upon his policy for a total loss, due to damage and eventual sale of the hides at the port of repairs of the carrying vessel. It was held that the plaintiff could recover for a total loss, as the goods in question were both perishable and out of control of the assured.[12] The principle establishing the kind of casualty that may amount to a case of total loss is the impossibility, owing to the perils insured against, of ever procuring the arrival of the thing insured. [13]

---

10 O'May D (1993) Marine Insurance Law and Policy, LLP p 411

11 (1836) 3 Bing NC 266.

12 Hodges S (1999) Cases and Materials on Marine Insurance Law, Cavendish-Publications, p 15; Also, Lord Abinger stated in this case:
"...if the goods, once damaged by the perils of the sea and necessarily landed before termination of the voyage, are in such a state, that they ...cannot be re-shipped with safety to any vessel...if it be sure that before termination of the original voyage they would disappear and assume a new form losing all their original character, ...the loss is in its nature total to him who cannot recover them due to either their annihilation or any other insuperable obstacle........the underwriter engages that the assured object will arrive safely in its' destined termination. If, in the progress of the voyage it becomes totally destroyed or annihilated..... he is bound by the very letter of his contract to pay the sum insured."

13 If the assured , by reason of those perils, is irretrievably and permanently deprived of present possession and control over it, as well as of any reasonable hope or possibility on future recovery of possession or further prosecution of the adventure upon it, that is then the case of an actual total loss - irrespectively of the assured electing or not to treat it as such - and notice of abandonment is not needed in accordance also with the leading legal principle of *"lex non cogit ad absurdum"*. However, if there is any doubt as to whether the assured has been *"irretrievably deprived"* of the subject-matter insured, the assured should in practice give notice of abandonment to underwriters, leaving it to be decided later whether the loss was an actual total loss or not; as in giving this notice, the assured forfeits nothing, should the notice prove to be unnecessary, for, then the total loss proves to be actual. In the past, if any remains

3.1.1.1.a. Where the subject-matter is totally destroyed: actual total loss of a ship – a "total wreck"

To qualify as an actual total loss the vessel has to be so severely damaged as to become a total wreck. In *Cambridge v Anderton,*[14] where a vessel was badly damaged in the St. Lawrence and later sold, she was considered a total wreck and, as a result of that, an actual total loss. Also in *Bell v Nixon*[15], the Court again had to consider the degree of damage required to determine whether the vessel was a total loss, and, where also the significance of a notice of abandonment was raised too. Although *Sailing Ship Blairmore Co Ltd v Macredie*[16] is a case concerned with constructive total loss, the issue of what constituted an actual total loss was also raised. The opinion voiced by Lord Halsbury, that a vessel need only be sank so as to be a total loss, was later averted and clarified in the case of *Captain JA Cates Tag and Wharfage Co Ltd v Franklin Insurance Co.*[17] More recently, in the case of *Fraser Shipping Ltd v Colton and Others (The Shakir III)*[18] , the vessel *Shakir III* was insured for actual total loss only for a voyage under tow from Jebil Ali to either Shanghai or Huang Pu. The brokers of the plaintiff did not inform the underwriters of a change of destination. The vessel was damaged and in the event had to be towed to Huang Pu, where a typhoon was encountered, and as a result the vessel was driven aground and stranded and the costs of its salvage were considered prohibitive. The plaintiff owners of the vessel claimed under their own policy, on the basis that the vessel was an actual total loss in that it was a wreck.[19] The issue arose whether the vessel was an actual total loss. The insurers refused to

---

of the thing insured or money corresponding to profit from it were to be retrieved, they were considered as a salvage entitled to the underwriters after the payment of total loss, and that is why in the past an absolute total loss in insurance law was treated and termed as a *'salvage loss without abandonment'* (Mustill MJ & Gilman JCB (1981) Arnould's Law of Marine Insurance and Average, 16th edn, Vol I, Stevens, p 963).

14 (1824) 2 B & C 691.

15 (1816) Holt NP 423.

16 (1898) AC 593.

17 (1927) AC 698.

18 [1997] 1 Lloyds Rep 586; Hodges S (1999) Cases and Materials on Marine Insurance Law, Cavendish Publications, p 15.

19 And also in that it had *"ceased to be a thing of the kind insured"* as per s. 57(1) of the Marine Insurance Act 1906.

indemnify the owners contending, *inter alia*, that *Shakir III* was not an actual loss.[20]

What counts as the actual total loss of a ship as per s. 56(1),(2),(3),(4) together with s. 57 of the Marine Insurance Act 1906,[21] is also applicable to any subject-matter insured, whether ship, cargo or freight.[22]

3.1.1.1.b. Actual total loss of a ship: a missing ship

According to s. 58 of the Marine Insurance Act 1906, a missing ship, with no news received from it after lapse of reasonable time, is presumed as an actual total loss. No particular time period is stipulated by law, but what s. 58 of the Marine Insurance Act 1906 means by the use of the term *"reasonable time"* is a question of fact, mostly. It is crucial, however, to confirm that the vessel actually sailed on the voyage insured.[23] The assured has to show that the presumed loss of the missing ship, which is considered as an actual total loss, has been caused by perils insured under the policy.[24]

3.1.1.1.c. Actual total loss: where the subject-matter insured ceases to be "a thing of the kind insured"

No problem seems to arise relating to the nature of loss, where the subject-matter insured against a peril is physically destroyed. However, this is not the case where the damage of the thing is of such a degree, that the subject-matter cannot be said to have been physically destroyed; instead it continues to exist, but has ceased to be *"a thing of the kind insured"*, and for that reason there is a right of recovery for the damaged thing. The di-

20 Held, that the issue was whether the plaintiffs were irretrievably deprived of the vessel. While the costs of recovery would outweigh the insured value of the vessel this went only to demonstrate constructive total loss. The vessel was not an actual total loss within the period of the policy. The underwriters had not waived their rights in respect of late notification of change of destination in that they had no knowledge of the change. The underwriters demonstrated that, on these facts, they had been induced to enter into the contract on the basis of material non-disclosure.

21 O'May D (1993) Marine Insurance Law and Policy, LLP ,Ch.14

22 Hodges S (1999) Cases and Materials on Marine Insurance Law, Cavendish Publications, Ch 15.

23 *Koster v Reed* (1826) 6 B & C, 19 ; *Cohen v Hinckley* (1809)2 Camp 51.

24 O'May D (1993) Marine Insurance Law and Policy, LLP ,Ch 14.

rect effect is that, as a result of the damage of the thing, its commercial value is significantly impaired, sometimes may be rendering it almost obsolete; therefore, the claim has to be one for actual total loss. A ship destroyed so much so as to become a total wreck would also *"cease to be a thing of the kind insured"*, although this category of loss mostly applies to cargo than to ship or freight.[25] In *Asfar v Blundell,*[26] a consignment of dates was recovered after having been sunk, but it was so contaminated by sewage that it was fit for use only as fertiliser. It was held to be an actual total loss and on payment thereof the underwriters were entitled to the salvage.

However, in case the damaged goods can be reconditioned after the damage, even if not suitable for commercial use while in damaged condition before restitution , the loss is considered as one that does not render the goods anymore not *" a thing of the kind insured"*. Thus, the loss cannot be deemed to be a total loss and will be characterised as a partial loss.[27] In *Berger & Light Diffusers Pty Ltd v Pollock*[28] steel injection moulds were found on arrival to have been damaged by rust, due to immersion in water after a fracture of a pipe of the ship's hold. As the effect of rust could not be eliminated, even after an attempt of cleaning it, it was held that the goods had suffered an actual total loss since they could only be used as scrap metal. In *Francis v Boulton*[29], however, a cargo of rice was insured for £450, and, after the barge in which it was carried sank, the rice was so damaged that the assured refused to accept it and claimed for a total loss. As the rice was dried and sold for £110, it was considered to have remained *in specie* and was held to be only a partial loss.[30] When the forced sale of goods is arranged,[31] to prevent a total loss of the insured goods, the assured retains the net proceeds of the sale and the underwriter has to pay the *"salvage loss"* which corresponds to the difference between the insured value of the goods sold and the net price realised.[32]

An owner of cargo may also sustain a loss because it has become unidentifiable, due to obliteration of marks.[33] In *Spence v Union Marine*

---

25 Hodges S (1999) Cases and Materials on Marine Insurance Law, Cavendish Publications, Ch 15.

26 (1895)2 QB 196.

27 See *Francis v Boulton* (1895) 65 QB.

28 [1973] 2 Lloyds Rep 442.

29 (1895) 1 Com Cas 217.

30 In some certain circumstances , when there is a total loss of an apportionable part there will be a total loss for this part.

31 As happened in the case of *Roux v Salvador* (1836)3 Bing NC 266.

32 O'May D (1993) Marine Insurance Law and Policy, LLP ,Ch 14.

33 S. 56 (5) of the Marine Insurance Act 1906.

Insurance Co Ltd,[34] cotton belonging to different owners was shipped in specifically marked bales. In the course of the voyage the cotton bales were so damaged that even those which were not lost had to be sold short of destination. The marks on them were obliterated, and only two of them were identifiable. It was held that, in respect of the cotton lost, there was a total loss of a part of each owner's cotton and all owners were tenants of the cotton that arrived at the port of destination with another vessel. It was also held that there was no total loss[35] of the bales that arrived *in specie*, the property in the obliterated cotton did not cease to belong to the respective owners, the proceeds of the sale were apportioned and that the losses were treated as partial ones.[36]

3.1.1.1.d. Actual total toss: where the assured is "irretrievably deprived" of the subject-matter insured

Actual total loss also occurs where the assured is "*irretrievably deprived*" of the subject-matter insured by way of it not being by any means retrievable, as well as in the case where the latter is taken out of control or possession of the insured by ways like capture or sale of vessel by the master. The insured, is required to show a complete absence of control over the retrieval. However, a mere sale does not always sustain actual total loss.[37] The subject-matter need not be destroyed, but it need remain *in specie* and in the hands of a third party which is irretrievably depriving it from its owner.

In the case of *George Cohen, Sons v Standard Marine Insurance*[38] an almost obsolete battleship was insured while being towed from one port to a second port (in Germany) where she was to be dismantled. On her way she went ashore a Dutch coast. It was evidenced that the vessel could "*get-off*" at a rather high cost, but the Dutch authorities in fear of damage of the sea defences existing there were not willing to allow her move.[39] It was

---

34 (1868) LR 3.

35 Actual or constructive.

36 O'May D (1993) Marine Insurance Law and Policy, LLP, Ch 14.

37 O'May D (1993) Marine Insurance Law and Policy, LLP, Ch 14; Willes J remarked in *Barker v. Janson* [(1868)LR 3CP.303] :

"...if a ship is so injured that it cannot sail without repairs and cannot be taken to a port at which the necessary repairs can be executed, there is an actual total loss, for that has ceased to be a ship which ever can be used for the purposes of a ship".

38 (1925) 21 Ll L Rep 30 KBD.

39 Their decision being also subject to appeal to a higher tribunal.

held that, in terms of the context of s. 57 (1) of the Marine Insurance Act 1906, the vessel was not to be considered as an actual total loss as the assured had not been *"irretrievably deprived of"* her.[40] In the case of *Captain FA Cates Tug and Warfage Co Ltd v Franklin Insurance,*[41] a tug sank in shallow waters as a result of a collision and was afterwards, within a short period of time, raised. It was held that she was not an actual total loss. In addition, in the case of *Marstrand Fishing v Beer* [42] it was held that just the taking of a vessel by barters does not constitute enough evidence so as to support an actual total loss, since there exists a possibility for the vessel to be recovered.[43] Even in the case where the insurer is left with a *"broken"* value of a deteriorated ship, a claim for actual total loss may not be successful if there is a possibility for the ship to be restored in the condition it were when it was damaged.[44]

3.1.1.1.e. Actual total loss of freight : actual total loss of freight caused by a total loss of ship and/or goods

Payment of freight and delivery of goods tend to be, though not always, concurrent conditions. Thus, if freight is not delivered at its proper destination, it is not payable. A total loss of goods, caused by an insured peril, might naturally result in a total loss of freight. However, if the cargo arrives, even damaged, at its proper destination or is short delivered, the agreed freight is nevertheless payable in full and the charterer or consignee may claim for damages for the damaged goods or the short delivery. In *Iredale v China Traders Insurance Co,*[45] it was ruled that freight was recoverable because the cargo became an actual total loss when it overheated and had to be off loaded and sold. The insurers argued that the loss was not a total one, but a general average loss. In *Denoon v The Home And Colo-*

---

40 For, under the Marine Insurance Act, the cost of repairing a damaged vessel is immaterial, unless it has proven to have exceeded the value of the vessel after the repairs have taken place.

41 (1927)137 L.T. 709, P. C.

42 (1936) 56 Ll. L . Rep. 163 KBD.

43 As J. Porter has stated: *"....no one could say that the vessel was irretrievably lost to the owners.....loss by barratry is not necessarily an actual total loss......and in this case......there was no actual total loss".*

44 *St. Margaret's Trust Ltd v Navigators And General Insurance Co Ltd* (1949)82 Ll L Rep 752 KBD.

45 (1900)2 QB 519 CA.

nian Assurance, [46] the ship in which the cargo of rice was carried was wrecked resulting in total loss of the rice and consequently total loss of freight of the rice.[47]

If non-delivery of the cargo is caused by a peril insured against, the assured of freight should be able to claim for a total loss of freight.[48] This was made clear in *Rankin v Potter,*[49] by Prett J., who observed:

" There may be an actual total loss of freight under a general policy if there be.....an actual total loss of the cargo...".

In this case, it was ruled that there was a total loss of freight occasioned by peril of the seas.[50]

Freight need not be payable if the cargo is so severely damaged so as not to be in a merchantable condition, as in the previously described case of *Asfar v Blundell*[51] where a cargo of water impregnated dates was held as a total loss for which freight was not payable on delivery.[52] However, there can also be an actual total loss of freight caused by a loss of voyage or of the adventure. In *Jackson v Union Marine Insurance Co,* [53] it was held that where the payment of freight is conditional upon the delivery of the cargo, then a loss of the voyage concerned through delay or frustration will also result in an actual total loss of the freight.

3.1.1.1.f. Recovery for a partial loss

According to s. 56(4) of the Marine Insurance Act 1906, the assured may recover for a partial loss instead of a total one, if as per the evidence it only proves to be such,[54] unless the policy *"otherwise provides"* , e.g. it con-

---

[46] (1872) LR 7 CP 341.

[47] See *Iredale And Another v China Traders Insurance Co* (1900)2 QB 519 CA.

[48] See *Price And Another v Maritime Insurance Co Ltd* (1900)5 Com Cas 332 (1901) 2 KB 412 CA.

[49] (1837) LR 6 HL 83.

[50] And also that in case there has been a constructive total loss of the vessel concerned, there is no requirement for a notice of abandonment to be given in respect of the total loss of freight (Hodges S (1999) Cases and Materials on Marine Insurance Law, Cavendish Publications, Ch 15).

[51] (1896)1 QB 123; Hodges S (1999) Cases and Materials on Marine Insurance Law, Cavendish Publications, Ch 15.

[52] Hodges S (1999) Cases and Materials on Marine Insurance Law, Cavendish Publications, Ch.15.

[53] (1873)2 Asp MLC 435.

[54] i.e. partial loss.

tains a *"free from particular average"* warranty.[55] In *Boon & Cheah Steel Pipes Sdn Bhd v Asia Ins Co,* [56] the plaintiff, made a claim for a total loss as the policy was warranted free from particular average, thus, barring him to recover for a partial loss instead of a total loss.[57]

3.1.1.2. Constructive total loss

The doctrine of constructive total loss is closely connected with marine insurance.[58] It can be said that constructive total loss is a device serving the indemnity concept, in the sense that it enables the assured[59] to dispense[60] from the danger and pass the burden on to the insurers.[61]

The concept of constructive total loss is outlined in s. 60(1) of the Marine Insurance Act 1906, whereby it is stated:

"..subject to any express provision in the policy, there is constructive total loss where the subject-matter insured is reasonably abandoned on account of its actual total loss appearing to be unavoidable or because it could not be preserved from actual total loss without an expenditure which could exceed its value when the expenditure had been incurred."

To recover for a loss under this section, the assured has to show that the subject-matter insured was *"reasonably abandoned"* either *"on account of its actual total loss appearing to be unavoidable"* or *"because it could not be preserved from actual total loss without an expenditure which would exceed its value when the expenditure had been incurred"*.[62]

Also in s. 60(2) of the Marine Insurance Act 1906, it is stated:

"...In particular, there is a constructive total loss:

(i) Where the assured is deprived of the possession of his ship or goods by a peril insured against, and

(a) it is unlikely that he can recover the ship or goods, as the case may be, or

---

55 Hodges S (1999) Cases and Materials on Marine Insurance Law, Cavendish Publications, Ch 15.

56 [1975]1 Lloyd's Rep. 452.

57 Hodges S (1999) Cases and Materials on Marine Insurance Law, Cavendish Publications, Ch 15.

58 *Moore v Evans* [1918] AC 185 HL.

59 In cases where due to insured perils the postulated danger of loss or deprivation is caused.

60 Subject to definite limits and conditions.

61 Ivamy ERH (1986) General Principles of Insurance Law, 5th edn, Butterworths, p 362.

62 Hodges S (1999) Cases and Materials on Marine Insurance Law, Cavendish Publications pp 362-365.

(b) the cost of recovering the ship or goods, as the case may be, would exceed their value when recovered; or

(ii) In the case of damage to a ship, where she is so damaged by a peril insured against that the cost of repairing the damage would exceed the value of the ship when repaired. In estimating the cost of repairs, no deduction is to be made in respect of general average contributions to those repairs payable by other interests, but account is to be taken of the expense of future salvage operations and of any future general average contributions to which the ship would be liable if repaired; or

(iii) In the case of damage to goods, where the cost of repairing the damage and forwarding the goods to their destination would exceed their value on arrival."

To recover for a loss under this section, the assured has to show that he has been deprived of the possession of his ship or goods due to the occurrence of an insured peril and that *"it is unlikely that he can recover the ship or goods"*, or that the cost of recovering *"would exceed their value when recovered"*. It may also be that he has to show, in the case of damage to the ship, that the ship has been so damaged by a peril that the cost of repairs *"..would exceed the value of the ship when repaired"*, or in the case of goods damaged, that the cost of repairing the damage and forwarding the goods to their destination would *"exceed their value on arrival"*.

It has become apparent, via the various cases' rulings, that the two subsections within s. 60 of the Marine Insurance Act 1906 contain two separate definitions which may be applied to different conditions of fact.

In *Robertson v Petros Nomikos Ltd,*[63] the plaintiffs were the owners of a chartered tanker, and the chartered freight was insured with the defendants. Prior to arriving to the port of loading the tanker suffered an explosion and subsequent fire. As a result of the conditions laid down in the policy, the owners did not claim for a constructive total loss although they could have done so, but claimed for a partial loss on that policy and did not abandon. Then, on the policy covering the chartered freight, they claimed for a total loss but the underwriters refused payment as there was a term in the freight policy stating that such a claim was invalid unless the vessel was a constructive total loss. The House of Lords, ruled that the vessel had been a constructive total loss and that a notice of abandonment, with respect to a hull policy, was more to show that the assured intended to claim for such a loss. Thus, no such notice was required to claim for a total loss of freight and therefore the plaintiffs could recover under their policy on chartered freight. In *Rickards v Forestal, Land Timber and Railways Co,*[64] a German vessel was scuttled, by the master and crew, off the Faroe Islands so as to avoid capture by a British warship. The cargo owners successfully claimed for a constructive total loss, caused by the actions of the German Government in taking over control of all German shipping. Yet in

63 [1939]AC 371 HL.

64 [1941]3 All ER 62, HL.

Irving v Hine,[65] the claim for constructive total loss was based on the proposition that the complete definition of s. 60 of the Marine Insurance Act 1906 did not preclude other claims which were valid under common law.[66] It was in *Rodocanachi v Elliot*[67] and later in *British and Foreign Marine Insurance Co v Samuel Sanday and Co ("The Sanday"),*[68] that it was established that another form of constructive total loss also existed under common law, even before the passing of the Marine Insurance Act 1906, stating that in case of hostilities goods may also be lost due to the existence of the hostile conditions themselves leading to the premature termination of the adventure or voyage; thereinafter having been established that a claim for constructive total loss of goods could be brought when the voyage or adventure be abandoned or frustrated.[69]

3.1.1.2.a. Types of constructive total loss: reasonable abandonment of the subject- matter insured

The first category of constructive total loss, as envisaged by s. 60(1) of the Marine Insurance Act 1906, contains reasonable abandonment of the insured property because actual total loss appears unavoidable. In *Court Line*

---

65 [1949]1 KB 555.

66 Hodges S (1999) Cases and Materials on Marine Insurance Law, Cavendish Publications, pp 623-671; The case of *Irving v Hine* [1949]1 KB 555] involves a trawler which was being towed to a dry dock, during WWII. She stranded and as a result was severely damaged. At all material times the assured would have been unlikely to obtain a license to repair her or to place her in a dry dock within reasonable time. The assured claimed she was a constructive total loss. It was held that, since the type of loss did not fall within any of the heads of loss stated in s.60 of the Marine Insurance Act 1906, there was no constructive total loss. Thus, the assured could only claim for a partial loss (Ivamy ERH (1986) General Principles of Insurance Law,5th edn, Butterworths, p 363).

67 (1874) LR 9.

68 (1916)1 AC 650.

69 Following that, the Frustration Clause was introduced in cl. 3.7 of the Institute War clauses (cargo) (IWC(C) (82)), and in cl.3.8 of the Institute Strikes clauses (cargo) (ISC(C) (82)) ; however, it does not appear in the ICC (A),(B), or (C); thus, this principle of loss of voyage or adventure no longer applies during conditions of strife, and the only case that it would still be applicable, is for a planned adventure under normal trade circumstances, being frustrated by a vessel no longer capable of prosecuting the voyage and not existing any alternative method of continuing the venture.

Ltd v R "The Lavington Court", [70] the Court of Appeal had to decide whether the vessel was *"abandoned"* within the meaning of s. 60(1) of the Marine Insurance Act 1906.[71] According to *"The Lavington Court"*, to constitute abandonment the physical act of leaving the ship must also be accompanied with the intention of never returning. The court held that since the master had no intention of abandoning the ship in this sense, there was no constructive total loss.[72]

Constructive total loss also exists when the ship has to be abandoned by reason of an *"actual total loss appearing to be unavoidable"*. In *Lind v Mitchell*, [73] the master abandoned the vessel after she was damaged by ice and was leaking rather badly. Expecting a gale in which he thought she would be lost, he decided to abandon her and set fire to her to prevent her from being a danger to navigation before he and the crew left her. One of the issues that have concerned the Court of Appeal was whether the abandonment was *"unreasonable"*. The court concluded that her abandonment could not be justified as having been made *"on account of its actual total loss appearing to be unavoidable"*.[74]

In s. 60(1) of Marine Insurance Act 1906, however, another category of constructive total loss is introduced, namely the reasonable abandonment of the insured property due to the fact that the cost of preservation from actual total loss would exceed its preserved value.[75]

---

70 [1945]2 All ER 357, CA.

71 The dispute was in relation to a charterparty under which there was a clause providing that : *"Should the vessel become a constructive loss, such loss shall be deemed to have occurred and the hire under this contract shall cease"* . The court had, therefore, first to determine whether the vessel was a constructive total loss as understood in the law of marine insurance.

72 The vessel was not *"given up for lost"* as the master was mainly concerned with saving the lives of the crew and property.

73 [1928]45 TLR 54 CA.

74 *Lind v Mitchell* [1928]45 TLR 54 CA, *Read v Bonham* (1821)3 Brod & B 147, *Court Line Ltd v "Lavington Court"* [1945]78 LlL Rep 390, CA.

75 Thus, abandonment, in s. 60(1) of the Marine Insurance Act 1906 means, in the context of a ship, either leaving the ship or giving it up for lost, the former being the physical act of vacating the property and the latter a decision based on economics and business expediency (Bennett, H (1986) The Law of Marine Insurance, Clarendon Press, Oxford, p 367).

3.1.1.2.b. Types of constructive total loss: deprivation of possession of ship or goods

S. 60(2) of the Marine Insurance Act 1906, states:

"...there is a constructive total loss : i/ where the assured is deprived of the possession of his ship or goods by a peril insured against and (a) it is unlikely that he can recover the ship or goods, as the case may be, or (b) the cost of recovering the ship or goods, as the case may be, would exceed their value when recovered ii/ in the case of damage to a ship, where she is so damaged by a peril insured against that the cost of repairing the damage would exceed the value of the ship when repaired iii/ in the case of damage to goods where the cost of repairing the damage and forwarding the goods to their destination would exceed their value on arrival".

Constructive total loss as expressed in section 60(2)(i), is restricted to cargo and hull insurance and occurs where the insured peril deprives the assured of possession of the insured property and either recovery is unlikely, or the cost of it would exceed the recovered value[76]. The original base of the whole doctrine of constructive total loss on the effects of capture and seizure, was clearly illustrated in *Moore v Evans,* [77] whereby Lord Atkinson, in his summation, explained the concept, origin and purpose of constructive total loss. In *Polurrian Steamship Co Ltd v Young,*[78] war having broken out between Greece and Turkey, a Greek warship seized a neutral vessel for carrying contraband. The assured gave notice of abandonment but six weeks later the vessel was released. The relevant date for determining whether the vessel had been a constructive total loss was that of commencement of the action, deemed also to be the date notice of abandonment was given; but the claim failed as it was not proved that at this time recovery of possession, within a reasonable time, was unlikely albeit that it was uncertain.

However, in *Roura & Forgas v Townend* [79], the vessel namely "*Igor Mendi*", having sailed on 4 Nov. 1917, was not heard of again until 27 Feb. 1918 when it was abandoned by the prize crew which had manned it after capture by a German warship on 10 Nov., until subsequently stranded and considerably damaged. Having been refloated in March by a salvage company hired by the shipowners, the vessel was under repair until September. It was held that the vessel had been a constructive total loss, within s. 60(2)(i) of the Marine Insurance Act 1906.[80] In the arbitration

76 *"Possession"* here refers to free use and disposal of the ship or goods.

77 [1918] AC 185 HL.

78 [1915]1 KB 922.

79 [1919]1 KB 189.

80 Bennett, H (1986) The Law of Marine Insurance, Clarendon Press, Oxford, p 368.

award *The Bamburi*[81] the ruling clearly showed a case which , amidst other issues, deals with the situation where the owner of a vessel is deprived of possession of her as a consequence of the deprivation of its free use and disposal. In this case, a specialised cement carrier, carried a cargo to Iraq in September 1980. The vessel was insured under Lloyd's War Risk Policy with Institute War & Strikes clauses attached. By reason of War Risk Trading warranties, the specific area in the Persian Gulf where the vessel was to be berthed was an excluded area subject to payment of an additional premium to reinstate cover. Because of fighting in the vicinity of the port where the vessel had berthed, the authorities forbade all movements of merchant shipping. A skeleton crew was kept thereon until the date of award. The question whether the vessel was a constructive total loss by reason of an insured peril when C gave notice of abandonment to R on September 30 and October 14, 1981 was arbitrated as a test case on various hypotheses; it was held that the order of the Iraqi government was a restraint of princes; C had been deprived of possession, by losing free use and disposal; on September 30 and October 14, 1981 it was unlikely that C would recover possession within a reasonable period, namely 12 months.

3.1.1.2.b.1. Types of constructive total loss: deprivation of possession of ship or goods: damage to ship

Damage to a ship such that the cost of repair exceeds the repaired value, constitutes another category of constructive total loss.[82]

In *Angel v Merchants' Marine Insurance Co,*[83] the Court of Appeal held that the unrepaired value should be excluded, which is a view which represented the common law at the time the Marine Insurance Act 1906 was being drafted and enacted. S. 60(2)(ii) of the Marine Insurance Act 1906 has been held to enact *Angel*[84] and thus exclude the unrepaired value of the vessel from the equation.[85] In the absence of a market value, the test is what the vessel was fairly worth to the owners from a business point of

---

[81] *Owners of the Bamburi v Compton (The Bamburi)* [1982]1 Lloyd's Rep 312.

[82] See s. 60(2)(ii) of the Marine Insurance Act 1906 & cases: *Allen v Sugrue* (1828)8 B&C 561, *Phillips v Nairne* (1847)4CB 343, *Irving v Manning* (1847)1 HL Cas 287, *Moss v Smith* (1850) 19 LJCP 225. The Marine Insurance Act 1906 requires the value of the wreck to de disregarded when determining the cost of repairs (*Hall v Haymann* [1912]2 KB 5).

[83] [1903]1 KB 811.

[84] [1903]1 KB 811.

[85] Bennett H (1986) The Law of Marine Insurance, Clarendon Press, Oxford, pp 368-370.

view. In *Compania Geval de Seguros v Lloyd Continental Insurance Co Ltd,* [86] an insurance company claimed from the defendants under a reinsurance policy in respect of a sailing lugger lost off the coast whilst on voyage. As to the evidence the vessel had to be beached, for it had experienced bad weather. The amount of damage to her hull was one of 84.9%. It was held that the assured were entitled to claim for a constructive total loss. The general rule is that in estimating the value for the purpose of determining whether or not there is a constructive total loss, any agreed value in the policy is to be ignored. Accordingly, s. 27(4) of the Marine insurance Act 1906 states:

"...Unless the policy otherwise provides, the value fixed by the policy is not conclusive for the purpose of determining whether there has been a constructive total loss".

Usually, there is also a clause in the policy relating to this matter. The effect of s. 27(4) of the Marine Insurance Act 1906 is to require market value rather than the agreed value to be used as the basis of the calculation.[87] It is worth mentioning here that, as per the new Hull Clauses 1/11/2003, clause 21, dealing with constructive total loss, significantly alters the previous wording under ITC 1995. Under clause 21, in order to ascertain whether the vessel is a constructive total loss, 80% of the insured value is to be taken as its repaired value, as opposed to the 100% provided in previous Hull clauses.

3.1.1.2.b.2. Types of constructive total loss: deprivation of possession of ship or goods: damage to goods

Insurance on goods entails a contract to indemnify the assured for any loss he may suffer by his goods being prevented from arriving safely at their destination.[88] Where goods are insured for a specific voyage, the insurance is on the adventure, i.e. the voyage, as well as on the goods themselves.

S. 60(2) (iii) of the Marine Insurance Act 1906, refers to goods.[89] According to it, a constructive total loss also exists where the repair and forwarding of damaged goods to their intended destination exceeds their value on arrival. In that case, the mode of computation to be adopted in order to decide whether or not there is a constructive total loss, is to take the whole cost of getting them to their destination which will have to be in-

---

[86] [1992]13 Ll L Rep 26 KBD.

[87] However, the Institute clauses reverse the statutory rule and provide that the agreed value is the relevant measure.

[88] *Rodocanachi v Elliot* (1873)LR 9 CP 518.

[89] O'May D (1993) Marine Insurance Law and Policy, LLP pp 415-436.

curred by reason of their position and condition.[90] Thus, in *Boon and Cheah Steel Pipes Sdn Bhd v Asia Insurance Co Ltd* [91] the claim for constructive total loss of some steel pipes failed because the assured had not notified the insurers or obtained a survey report from them, and without detailed examination the actual damage suffered could not be known for certain. In *Farnworth v Hyde,* [92] it was held that credit must be given for the freight payable on delivery under the original bill of lading.[93]

3.1.1.2.3. Effects of constructive total loss: abandonment of the subject-matter insured – the meaning of "the notice of abandonment"

The requirement of a valid abandonment is a prerequisite to a claim for constructive total loss. Abandonment is intimated to an insurer by means of a 'notice of abandonment' which must be given with reasonable diligence after receipt of reliable information about the loss. If the information is of a doubtful character, further time is allowed for better particulars to be received by the assured. If the assured fails to give a notice of abandonment, the loss can only be treated as a partial loss. It is only the assured, or his authorised agent or servant, who is entitled to abandon. Notice of abandonment is generally needed, though in some cases it is not necessary. The notice need not be in any special form, but what is important is must be given to the insurers or their agents. In addition, it should be unmistakable in its terms, absolute and unconditional.[94] The assured is entitled to wait a reasonable time so as to acquire a full knowledge of the damage, before he elects to abandon or not,[95] but he must act with reasonable diligence as delay from his part may prevent him from recovering

---

90 This will include such charges as landing, drying, warehousing, re-shipping , and carriage to their port of destination.

91 (1975)1 Ll L Rep 452.

92 (1866) LR 2 CP 204.

93 *Rosetto v Gurney* (1851)11 CB 176, *Reimer v Ringrose* (1851)6 Exch. 263.

94 In *Russian Bank For Foreign Trade v Excess Insurance Company Limited* [1918]2 KB 123, the assured offered to release his underwriters from all liability, if they agreed to pay the insured value of a shipment of barley, less its' value at the port of loading, from which the vessel was prevented from sailing owing to the closure of the Dardanelles in 1914. It was held that the offer to the underwriters suggesting a compromise was not a good notice of abandonment because the offer was conditional.

95 *Gernon v Royal Exchange Assurance* [1815]6 Taunt 383.

for more than a partial loss. The question of what is a reasonable time is a question of fact.[96] However, he is not allowed to wait and watch the turn of events to his benefit before making up his mind. The timing of a notice of abandonment is an important consideration in practice, as it may be given too early or too late.

The notice, though useful to both parties, imposes no obligation on the insurer. A notice of abandonment may be waived by underwriters[97], however in practice waiver is not express but is often implied. Where notice is waived, the assured can claim to fix the date of the notice at any time which suits him[98]. The waive of the notice of abandonment will not avail the assured to enable him to turn a partial loss into a constructive one, if the thing insured has been abandoned in circumstances which cannot be justified. The purpose of giving notice of abandonment was alluded to by Atkin L.S. in *Vacuum Oil Co v Union Insurance Society of Canton*,[99] in the following words:

> "...Nevertheless it is a requisite to give notice of abandonment and in many cases it is a very necessary part of the contract, because the principle of it is that the assured is – as soon as he is aware of the circumstances that make it a constructive total loss – to give notice to the underwriters that the property is to be theirs and that he abandons the property to them, and that from thenceforward, whatever dealings take place with the property, take place for the benefit of and for the account the underwriters."

The notice of abandonment is a matter of great importance in practice.[100] The requirement of giving such a notice is justified by the need for the underwriter to be entitled, should he wish to do so, to take over whatever remains of the subject-matter insured and to take steps to protect their interests. Mere silence on the underwriters' part is not an acceptance of an abandonment.[101] The acceptance of an abandonment need not be express, but can be implied from the conduct of the insurer.[102] By the acceptance of a notice of abandonment by the assured, the underwriter not only acknowledges the sufficiency of the notice but also admits his liability for a total

---

[96] *Currie & Company v Bombay Native Insurance Company* (1869)LR 3PC.

[97] For, it is only inserted so as to ascertain the amount due to the assured in the event of loss and for no other purpose (See s. 62(8) of Marine Insurance Act 1906).

[98] As per Lord Wright in *Middows v Robertson & Other Test Cases* [1941]70 Ll L R 173.

[99] [1926]25 Ll L Rep 546 CA.

[100] S. 62(9) of Marine Insurance Act 1906 ; *Uzzielli v Boston Marine Insurance Co* (1884)15 QBD.

[101] See s. 62(5) of the Marine Insurance Act 1906.

[102] *Hudson v Harrison* [1921]3 Brod. & Bing 97 contrasted with *Captain JA Cates Tug and Wharfage Co Ltd v Franklin Insurance Co* [1927]137 L.T. 709.

loss by perils insured. Where notice of abandonment is accepted, the abandonment is irrevocable.[103] However, irrevocability is tempered where notice of abandonment was given and accepted under a fundamental mistake of fact.[104] By giving notice of abandonment, the assured merely makes an offer which remains executory, unless and until it is accepted.[105] The abandonment also constitutes an offer to transfer the subject-matter insured from the assured to the insurer, in return for a full indemnity. Such an abandonment, was raised in *Rankin v Potter*[106] where a vessel was so damaged in Calcutta that the charterer withdrew and there was a total loss of freight. However, under certain circumstances lack of giving notice of abandonment may be justified. In *Kaltenbach v Mackenzie*[107] where a vessel was abandoned in Saigon as a constructive total loss but no notice of abandonment was given, the court deliberated on the meaning and significance of abandonment.[108] The case of *The Kastor Too*,[109] is the only modern adjudicated case in which the Court held that there existed a constructive total loss despite the lack of a notice of abandonment. *Kastor Too* was a steel built four hold geared motor bulker.[110] On Feb. 29, 2000 the vessel

---

103 S. 62(6) of the Marine Insurance Act 1906.

104 See the case of *Norwich Union Fire Insurance Society Limited v William H. Price Ltd* [1934] AC 455, in which the true facts were neither known to the assured nor to the underwriters at the time the assured gave notice of abandonment .

105 See s. 62(6) of the Marine Insurance Act 1906 ;. O'May D (1993) Marine Insurance Law and Policy, LLP, pp 415-436; As also per J.Atkinson in *Pesquerias y Secaderos de Bacalao De Espana SA v Beer* [1946]79 Ll L Rep 417.

106 (1873) LR 6 HL 83.

107 (1873)3 CPD 467.

108 No notice of abandonment is required, and still, there can be a claim for a constructive total loss of ship or goods, provided that the ship or goods are of no benefit to the insurer; (s. 62(7) of the Marine Insurance Act 1906). Also, in the case of *Black King Shipping Corporation v Massie, ("The Litsion Pride")* [1985]1 Lloyd's Rep 437] where a vessel was sunk by a missile during the war between Iraq and Iran and part of the defence was that a notice of abandonment was not given, Hirst J. stated that a notice of abandonment was immaterial in the circumstances, as there was no possibility of benefit to the underwriters in that they could not salvage the wreck because of the hostilities which were still taking place.

109 *Kastor Navigation Co Ltd v AGF MAT ("The Kastor Too")* [2003]1 Lloyd's Rep, 296.

110 The first claimant was the registered owner of the vessel. The defendants subscribed to insurance of his interest in the hull and machinery of the vessel

sailed from Aqaba bound for Vizagapatnam laden with a cargo of rock phosphate in all four holds. When the vessel was in a position between the island of Socotra and the coast of South Yemen, a fire was discovered at the purifier flat level in the engine room. Attempts to extinguish the fire were unsuccessful. On Mar. 10, the vessel sank stern first. The vessel was abandoned. The ship would not have sunk with the engine room alone flooded. In order for her to sink, at least two compartments must have been flooded. The claimants originally claimed for an actual total loss. In the event, claimants' primary claim was for a constructive total loss caused by fire and/or explosion. In the alternative, the claimants claimed for an actual total loss also caused by fire and/or explosion. Underwriters denied that the claimants could recover for a constructive total loss. As to the actual total loss they asserted that a fire in the engine room and consequent explosions would not have caused and did not cause the flooding of the hold in question or any double bottom tanks or any other spaces of the vessel than the engine room, or the sinking of the vessel.

The court stated that if the vessel had not sunk it would be axiomatic that the claimants could recover for her constructive total loss. The premise therefore upon which the issue arose, whether the claim for a constructive total loss was not maintainable, was that the vessel sank other than by reason of the fire, or, to put it another way, that the fire and the sinking are unconnected coincidences. The court expressed the view that the argument, stating that cause of action cannot be pursued in the absence of service of notice of abandonment and that notice of abandonment cannot effectively be given once the vessel has become an actual total loss, could not be valid in the present case because service of notice of abandonment is not an essential ingredient of the cause of action; rather it is the notification of an election between payment for a partial or a total loss. The court, further on, stated that neither authority nor reason would seem to support the proposition that where a constructive total loss, caused by an insured peril of which loss the insured is unaware, is followed (before he acquires such knowledge) by a total loss caused by an uninsured peril or even by an excepted peril, the insured cannot recover for the constructive total loss. The court also stated that in such a case like the present, cession or transfer of the ship while the vessel is and remains a constructive total loss is not just impossible but of no conceivable benefit to underwriters, simply because in case the underwriters subsequently pay the insured's claim for a total loss cession or transfer will in any event take place by operation of law ; and to allow the assured to recover for a constructive total

against marine risks for the period of 24 months at Dec. 30, 1999, at 80% of the risk. The insured perils included fire, explosion and perils of the sea.

loss does not involve that the assured is unilaterally throwing onto underwriters the risk of market fluctuation, or taking to himself the advantage of a favourable market. Thus, the court concluded that the proper analysis is that abandonment of the subject-matter insured will take place by operation of law when the underwriters settle the claim; s. 61 of the Marine Insurance Act 1906 had been satisfied; the insured had been deprived of his right of choice as this is envisaged by s. 61 of the Marine Insurance Act 1906 and he had no option but to treat the vessel as a total loss. In addition, the court concluded that s. 62(7) of the Marine Insurance Act 1906 stipulates that notice of abandonment is unnecessary where, when the insured receives information of the loss, there would be no possibility of benefit to the insurer if notice were given to him and for all these reasons held that the claimants could recover for a constructive total loss. The court also held that had it been necessary to consider the claimants' claim for an actual total loss it would have been concluded that such a claim would have failed, thus the claimants should recover from the defendant underwriters in respect of the constructive total loss of the vessel.[111]

---

[111] In *Kaltenbach v Mackenzie* [1878] 3 CPD 467 at 471-475, Brett L.J. described the origin of the necessity of giving a notice of abandonment and explained its function . He said :"*With regard to the notice of abandonment, ...in [no] contract of indemnity, except in the case of contracts of marine insurance, a notice of abandonment is required....but in the case of a constructive total loss it is necessary, unless it be excused. It seems to me to have been introduced into contracts of marine insurance -- as many other stipulations have been introduced -- by the consent of shipowner and underwriter, and so to have become part of the contract, and a condition precedent to the validity of a claim for a constructive total loss. The reason why it was introduced is on account of the peculiarity of marine losses. These losses do not occur under the immediate notice of all the parties concerned. A loss may occur in any part of the world. It may occur under such circumstances that the underwriter can have no opportunity of ascertaining whether the information he received from the assured is correct or incorrect. The assured, if not present, would receive notice of the disaster from his agent, the master of the ship. The underwriter in general can receive no notice of what has occurred, unless from the assured, who is the owner of the ship or the owner of the goods, and there would therefore be great danger if the owner of a ship or of goods -- that is the assured -- might take any time that he pleased to consider whether he would claim as for a constructive total loss or not -- there would be great danger that he would be taking time to consider what the state of the market might be, or many other circumstances, and would throw upon the underwriter a loss if the market were unfavourable, or take to himself the advantage if the market were favourable. ... I think that it should be a part of the contract and a condition precedent that, where the claim is for a constructive total loss, there must be notice of abandonment, unless there were circumstances excusing it.*" None of the reasons which Brett L.J. thought had informed agreement of the condition precedent would lead to the conclusion that an insured in such circumstances ought not to be permitted to recover for a constructive total loss, at any rate not simply on account of failure to serve notice

Although constructive total loss is a device intended to serve indemnity by enabling the assured to discharge himself, through the notice of abandonment, and throw the burden on the insurers, practice has shown that insurers are in fact very hesitative in accepting the notice of abandonment. For, it encompasses not only the assignment and passing of rights but also all obligations and implications accompanying the property abandoned.

3.1.1.2. Indemnity and partial losses

The term *"partial loss"* is a general expression, used to embrace any loss which is not a total loss. It can be said that partial losses are divided, primarily into losses arising when the subject-matter insured sustains direct physical damage caused by a peril insured against, which may be described as *"true particular average losses"*; and secondly into losses engendered by extraordinary expenses incurred after the casualty had arisen for rescue operations undertaken to prevent further losses from taking place. *"Particular average loss"* covers all types of partial loss, except a general average loss and a particular charge.[112]

3.1.1.2.1. Indemnity and particular average losses

Particular average is defined by the Marine Insurance Act 1906 in s.64(1) whereby it is stated:

> "...A particular average loss is a partial loss of the subject- matter insured, caused by a peril insured against, and which is not a general average loss."

The expression *"particular average"* means a partial loss caused by a peril insured against, in contradiction to general average and total loss.[113] Particular average losses may occur to ships, cargoes or freights. It must be accidentally and fortuitously caused by a peril insured against, and

---

of abandonment before the vessel becomes an actual total loss by operation of a peril other than that which has caused the constructive total loss (Andrewartha J & Riley N (1993) English Maritime Law Update, 33 (3)JMLC 329).

[112] Hodges S (1999) Cases and Materials on Marine Insurance Law, Cavendish Publications Ch 16.

[113] Lambeth RJ (1986) Templeman on Marine Insurance: Its Principles and Practice, 6th edn, Pitman, p 253.

it solely concerns the person interested in the subject-matter of the insurance and his underwriter. [114]

Particular average may also be defined as a partial loss by a peril insured against, which is not distributed over the whole of the interests at risk in the common adventure as is general average. It may happen that a policy may be expressed not to cover partial loss, but only total loss, but even then reference relating to payment of particular average must be made.[115]

3.1.1.2.2. General average losses

The essential concept of general average is that losses sustained or expenditure occurred in time of peril and for the common good should be shared between those interested in the adventure in proportion, according to their shares in the adventure.[116]

According to the definition embodied in the Marine Insurance Act 1906, a general average loss is a loss caused by or directly consequential to an extraordinary sacrifice or expenditure voluntarily and reasonably made or incurred in time of danger, for the purpose of preserving the interests imperiled in the common adventure.[117]

---

114 Particular average claims on ship are dealt with in s. 69 of the Marine Insurance Act 1906, under the heading *"measure of indemnity"*. S. 70 of the Marine Insurance Act 1906, provides for the measure of indemnity in cases of particular average on freight. S. 71 of the Marine Insurance Act 1906, provides for the measure of indemnity in cases of particular average on goods, the first part dealing with cases of valued policies and the other part dealing with unvalued policies. S. 72 of the Marine Insurance Act 1906 deals in its first subsection with cases where different species of property are insured under one valuation, whereas the second subsection provides for cases where there is no means of arriving at the insurable value of the part lost and thus stipulates that in order to apportion the insured value, the net arrived sound values of the different species of goods may be utilised (Lambeth RJ (1986) Templeman on Marine Insurance: Its Principles and Practice, 6th edn, Pitman, p 253).

115 Bennett, H (1986) The Law of Marine Insurance, Clarendon Press, Oxford, Ch 18.

116 Bennett, H (1986) The Law of Marine Insurance, Clarendon Press, Oxford, Ch 18.

117 S.66 (1),(2) of the Marine Insurance Act 1906 ; The whole foundation of general average is contribution. All persons benefiting from such a loss must make a *"general average contribution"*, i.e. they must contribute according to the

Before a loss can be classified as to be by way of general average, the sacrifice or expenditure need satisfy the following requirements: i.e. primarily the sacrifice must be voluntary and it has to be the intentional act on the part of man as opposed to an accidental loss by maritime peril.[118] Also, the sacrifice or expenditure, as the case may be, must be reasonably made. In case of a sacrifice the act has to be done prudently, whereas in case of expenditure it must be fair and reasonable.[119] Also it has to be extraordinary in its nature, and not one which is necessarily involved in performance of the contract of affreightment. Its object must be nothing other or less than the preservation of the property imperiled in the common adventure.[120] Lastly, the loss must be the direct result, or the reasonable consequence, of a general average act.[121]

---

value of their benefited interests to the amount of the loss (s.66(3) of the Marine Insurance Act 1906).The owner of the interest which has been saved, has to make a contribution to the party who has sacrificed his property or expended money to save the whole venture. The liability of the interested parties to make a contribution is declared in s.66(3) of the Marine Insurance Act 1906 ; whereas the liability of the insurer is embodied in s.66(4) and 66(5) of the Marine Insurance Act 1906 ; In *Watson v Firemen's Fund Insurance* [(1927)127 LT 754] during the course of a voyage, the master saw smoke and thought the vessel's hold was on fire so he caused high-pressure steam to be turned into the hold so as to put out the supposed fire and as a result the insured cargo was damaged by the steam. The assured claimed an indemnity on the ground that a general average loss had been incurred. It was held that such a loss did not exist as the danger was not a real one but, instead, the master was merely mistaken. In the case of *Societe Nouvelle d' Armement v Spillers & Bakers Ltd,* [[1917]1 KB 865] an action was brought by the owners of a sailing vessel, to recover from the charterers who were the owners of the cargo a contribution towards the cost of hiring a tug to tow the vessel owing to the presence of enemy submarines in the area. It was claimed, by the owners of the vessel, that the sum paid for the hire of the tug was a general average expense. The claim failed on the ground that there was no clear evidence that the vessel and her cargo were being exposed to any extra and abnormal peril.

118 *Austin Friars Steamship Co Ltd v Spillers & Bakers Ltd* [1915]1 KB 833.

119 And is only allowable in general average so far as these essentials are complied with ; See *Anderson, Tritton & Co v Ocean SS Co* (1884)5 Asp MLC 401.

120 It must not be for the safety of the ship alone, or of the cargo alone, nor merely for the completion of the adventure.

121 For instance, in the case of jettison , if water gets into the hold during the act of jettison, the damage caused to cargo by the water is allowable in general average equal with the value of the cargo jettisoned, the reason being that the risk of incurring such damage or the likelihood of its happening would have been

3.1.1.2.3. Indemnity and the "sue & labour" clause

The *"duty of assured (sue & labour)"* clause's provisions apply when by the operation of some peril insured against, there is a danger that the subject-matter insured may suffer loss or damage.[122]

S. 78(4) of the Marine Insurance Act 1906 states:

"...it is the duty of the assured and his agents in all cases to take such measures as may be reasonable for the purpose of averting or minimising a loss."

The test relating to reasonableness seems to be an objective one. The whole concept of the *"sue & labour"* clause is to *"avert"* a loss, i.e. prevent it from happening or *"minimise"* it, i.e. prevent a partial loss that has already occurred from turning into a total loss. In either event the subject-matter has to be in danger of loss. Such an illustration is provided in *Kidston v The Empire Marine Insurance Co Ltd*[123] where goods became wet in a storm and, had they not been dried out when the damage was slight, they would have decayed and have become even more damaged. Unlike general average, it is not carried out for the benefit of a common adventure but for the benefit of the subject-matter insured.[124]

3.2. Types of losses in marine insurance contracts under the Greek law regime

Losses, under the Greek law of marine insurance, fall into two large categories. They are primarily treated as total losses, and if they fail to fulfil the criteria to be categorised as total losses, they might be treated as partial

present in the mind of those who resolved to make the primary sacrifice ; General average losses and contributions are only recoverable where an insured peril has led to the general average act. If the assured mistakenly believes that there is a peril in operation, and a sacrifice is made accordingly, the insurers are not liable. In the case of *Joseph Watson & Son Ltd v Firemen's Fund Insurance Co of San Fransisco*, (1922)2 KB 355, an imagined peril was afterwards found not to have existed and the loss was not recoverable as a general average loss but only in connection with avoidance of a peril insured against.

122 Lambeth RJ (1986) Templeman on Marine Insurance: Its Principles and Practice, 6th edn, Pitman, Ch 12.

123 (1866) LR 1 CP 535.

124 Same, the duty of *"sue and labour"* is applicable to cargo insurance where it is usually accompanied by a similar clause known as the forwarding charges clause (Hodges S (1999) Cases and Materials on Marine Insurance Law, Cavendish Publications, Ch 18).

losses. A loss is total if the subject-matter insured is totally lost, or it has been so damaged that it has ceased to be *"a thing of the kind insured"* and cannot be repaired to such an extent as to be able to be considered, upon the completion of the repair, as *"a thing of the kind insured"*. There is also total loss in case where a vessel has been seiged or captured by a foreign state in a state of war.[125] There is also presumed total loss if the vessel is a missing ship, with no news received from it for either three or five months[126] upon receipt of last notice. Any loss other than that is a partial loss. There is no such concept as actual or constructive total loss under the Greek law on marine insurance.[127]

3.2.1. Total loss and abandonment under the Greek law regime

In case of total loss of a ship, the assured has the right to request full indemnification from the insurer, without first having to exercise his right of abandonment.[128] He may, however, choose to exercise the right of abandonment. As per art. 280-288 CPML (ΚΙΝΔ), the assured has the right to abandon to the insurer the objects of marine insurance (whether it be vessel, cargo or freight) and to claim that the measure of indemnity corresponding to total loss is awarded to him.

This may occur under the following circumstances:

- The vessel is a total loss, more specifically it has either been totally destroyed or it has been so damaged that it has ceased to be *"a thing of the kind insured"* and as a result can neither be repaired, nor is it in a position to navigate through sea waters.
- Where the thing continues to exist but has ceased to be *"a thing of the kind insured"* and the repair costs exceed 3/4 of its insurable value, or the repair cannot be conducted at the place of the accident nor can the vessel be transported at a place to be repaired.

---

125 provided the insurance covers also war risks.

126 The period required by law is three months from last notification for motorship vessels and five months for yachts and pleasure crafts.

127 See art. 281-285 CPML (ΚΙΝΔ).

128 *Athens Court of First Instance: ΠΠρΑθ 1803/81 ΕΕμπΔ 33,257*; Kalantzis AK (1998) Private Insurance Law-Cases and Materials, Nomiki Vivliothiki Edn, Athens, 1998.

- The vessel is a missing ship, with no news received from it for either three months upon receipt of last notice (for motorship vessels) or five months (for yachts) and is presumed a total loss. The accident or maritime peril is considered to have occurred, in such a case, the following day after receipt of last notification.
- The vessel has been seiged or captured by a foreign state in a state of war, provided the insurance covers also war risks. In this case, the right to abandon can be exercised only after three months upon receipt of notification for seizure or capture.

The right to abandon can be exercised within three months, the period starting the one day after the accident or maritime peril is known to have occurred, or when the time period required, since receipt of last notification is reached or three months after notification of its seizure or capture.

As per art. 284 CPML (ΚΙΝΔ), the right to abandon is exercised by a written notice to the insurer. Should the insurer not waive the notice of abandonment within thirty days, or in the case that the right is judicially recognised within this period, then the abandoned property and the rights and obligations following it are transferred to the insurer. The assured has to disclose to the insurer all relevant information of which he might be aware and hand all relevant documentation that might also be used as a means of evidence. The insurer, as per art. 287 CPML (ΚΙΝΔ), might reject, by written notice to the assured, ownership of the abandoned property and instead offer to indemnify the assured to the full extent of the insured value. In addition, as per section 288 CPML (ΚΙΝΔ), the insurer has the right to invite the assured to abandon the insured property within reasonable time that is specified. Should the assured not do so, he then loses the right to abandon. A prerequisite for abandonment is the liability of the insurer under the marine insurance contract. Thus, the insurer may waive the notice if he can prove that he is not liable under the marine insurance contract.[129]

In the case of damage to the vessel due to a maritime peril that has occurred, if the repair costs exceed the ¾ of its insurable value or repair is impossible, should the assured wish to do so , he may give to the insurer a notice of abandonment which cannot be waived. As a result the assured can claim the agreed indemnification, due to total loss of the subject-matter insured and the insurer bears all the rights and obligations on it as from the time of abandonment. Should the insurer waive the right of the assured to abandon, the latter can seek the judicial recognition - through a

[129] Rokas I (1995) Introduction to the Law of Private Insurance, 4th edn, Oikonomikon Publications, Athens.

court judgment - of his right to abandon and that he be awarded the sum corresponding to full indemnification. Case law has shown that the report of the Council of Maritime Accident, on the causes that lead to the maritime accident, is a full proof and no further evidence need be provided in court.[130]

The basic difference from English law that can be noted, is that under the scope of the Greek law relating to marine insurance, abandonment is a concept linked to total loss in general and not only to constructive total loss as per the English law regime. It can be said that within this respect, the scope of abandonment is wider under the Greek regime.

3.3. Types of losses in marine insurance contracts under the Norwegian law regime

3.3.1. The cover offered under the Norwegian marine insurance contracts

It is customary in marine insurance law to distinguish between ship-owners insurance -which is associated with vessels- and cargo insurance. The main idea behind the concept of ship-owners marine insurance is insurance for the ship or vessel. The main insurance in this group is hull insurance for ocean going ships. Hull insurance provides indemnity for the ship owner for loss or damage to the ship.

The distinction between total loss or damage, is made through a more or less detailed definition of circumstances giving the ship-owner a right to claim for total loss.[131] Damage to the ship that does not fulfil the conditions of being a total loss will be indemnified as damage or partial

[130] *Athens Court of First Instance: ΠΠρΑθ 11070/1981 ΑρχΝ 35,33.*

[131] See Norwegian Marine Insurance Plan 1996 § 11-1, § 11-3, §11-7. The main distinction between total loss and partial damage is that a total loss results in the insurer being liable for the sum insured, limited to the insured value of the ship, whereas for partial damage the measure of indemnity is limited to the cost of repairing the ship, added to which are some connected costs, but less general deductibles and deductibles for ice-damage and machinery damage (Norwegian Marine Insurance Plan 1996 § 4-1 & Chapter 12). Hull insurance in Norway is effected with full coverage, on the so-called *"Full Conditions"* (Norwegian Marine Insurance Plan 1996 § 10-4).

damage.[132] Hence, one could successfully argue at this point that Norwegian Law is more restrictive than the English law, in determining what losses will fall into the category of total ones. In addition to the indemnification for the reduction of the value of the ship, hull insurance traditionally covers collision liability.[133] A general exception in the different hull covers is one with regard to general financial loss and loss resulting from delay.[134] However, some hull conditions include an element of cover for loss of time in the regulation for partial damage.[135]

Objects that can be insured under the category of hull insurance, under Norwegian Law,[136] distinguish between *"ship"*, *"equipment"* and *"spare parts"*. The *"ship"* comprises the hull as well as the engines. *"Equipment"* is a collective term for loose objects that accompany the ship in its trade, but which cannot be deemed to be part of it. The prerequisite for covering equipment and spare parts under the ship's hull insurance is that they are normally on board, which indicates that the object in question shall be on board for an indefinite or prolonged period of time.[137]

Hull interest insurance covers in principle the value of the ship that is not already included in the hull valuation. As the interest covered is the added value of the ship, this insurance is only triggered when there is a to-

---

132 See Norwegian Marine Insurance Plan 1996 § 12-1 ff.

133 See Norwegian Marine Insurance Plan 1996 § 4-1 & Ch 12. The original reason for this extension of the hull insurance was the absence of general liability insurance cover for the ship-owners. Today P&I insurance has become just as common as hull insurance and an international trend is also seen in the direction of the P&I insurer assuming the entire collision liability.

134 See Norwegian Marine Insurance Plan 1996 § 4-2.

135 The starting point is that the insurer is only liable for the costs following from the cheapest repair alternative, which states that liability for temporary repairs should be limited to necessary temporary repairs, and that he should not be liable for costs incurred in expediting repairs. However, to protect the assured's interest in reducing loss of time, some hull conditions state that the insurer will also have a limited liability for added costs due to the choice of a more expensive repair yard, for temporary repairs that are not necessary and for expediting costs (See Norwegian Marine Insurance Plan 1996 § 12-7, §12-8, §12-12.).

136 They are dealt with in paragraph 10-1.This paragraph corresponds to § 148 of the 1964 Norwegian Marine Insurance Plan.

137 Objects brought on board while the ship is in port and taken ashore when the ship is leaving, such as a fork-lift truck to be used during loading and discharging, are therefore not covered whilst on board (ND 1972.302 *"NV Balblom"*) notwithstanding the fact that the object is used only on board this one particular ship.

tal loss and will not be paid when the ship is damaged.[138] The ship owner's income is protected in a loss of hire or freight insurance.[139] This basically covers loss due to the vessel being wholly or partially deprived of income as a consequence of damage to the vessel.[140] This type of insurance is connected to the hull cover and will only arise if the ship has suffered a casualty as covered under the hull conditions.

3.3.2. Types of losses under the Norwegian marine insurance law

Losses are classified either as total losses or as damages/partial damages. The assured has a right to total loss compensation when the ship is in actual total loss, when it is a constructive total loss (condemnation)[141] and when it is presumed a total loss. In hull insurance, indemnity is provided for the shipowner for loss or damage to the ship. The framework of the Norwegian Law stipulates as damage or partial damage whichever loss cannot be identified as a total one. To this extent, there is a departure from UK law, where total loss that has not resulted in the vanishing of the vessel, is classified as a constructive total loss.

In English law, the significance of the distinction between actual total loss and constructive total loss is, that where there has been a constructive total loss the assured's right to claim for a total loss is dependent on his having given notice of abandonment[142]. Thus, actual and constructive total loss are always treated separately. In Norwegian law, the main division of total losses is between cases of *"condemnation"* and all the rest and this undoubtedly reflects the relative practical importance of the various types of total losses.

The insurer, in case of constructive total loss under the Norwegian Law, is in some respects in a stronger position than his English counterpart. The assured must not only give notice to the insurer that a casualty has occurred, but, before he takes any action to prevent or minimise further loss, he must, if possible, consult the insurer and take any action which the insurer requires him to take. Secondly, the insurer has a right, at any time after the casualty has occurred, to give the assured notice that he will pay

[138] See Norwegian Marine Insurance Plan 1996 Ch. 13 for conditions on Hull Insurance.

[139] See Norwegian Marine Insurance Plan 1996 Ch. 16.

[140] Which is recoverable under the Norwegian Hull Conditions.

[141] See § 11-3 of the Norwegian Marine Insurance Plan 1996.

[142] See Marine Insurance Act 1906 s.62(1) subject to the provision in s.62(7).

for a total loss and thereby prevent himself from being liable for any future expenses. Thirdly,[143] the insurer has the right to attempt to salvage the insured ship at his own expense and risk. The real difference, however, is to state that so long as the insurance is not limited to total loss only, the differences between English and Norwegian rules will not be of great practical consequence.

3.4. Type of losses in marine insurance contracts under the French law regime

3.4.1. Losses under French marine insurance contracts

Losses are classified as total and partial losses. A loss which is not total, is thus characterised as a partial one. The only situation where the law would perceive total loss as an actual total loss, is in the case of occurrence of the concept of abandonment.[144]

3.4.2. French marine insurance contracts and abandonment

In French marine insurance law, abandonment is dealt with under art. 48 of the Law of 3/7/1967 and now art. L. 173-13 of the Insurance Code. It occurs in case of a loss which is total, when the repairs of the subject-matter insured exceed ¾ of the insurable value, or when it is not possible for the vessel to navigate due to risks occurred which are covered by the policy, i.e. when it is not possible to repair the vessel or the vessel is missing with no news received from her after the lapse of a reasonable period of time.

In the case of abandonment, the subject-matter insured is regarded as totally lost and the loss is treated as an actual total loss. The insurer has the option to refuse the transfer of proprietary rights if he wishes to do so, since the enactment of the Law of 3/7/1967. The assured looses all rights on the subject-matter insured regardless of whether the insured accepts the transfer of proprietary rights or not. Abandonment constitutes a means of

---

143 In contrast to the rule in *Sailing Ship "Blairmore"* (1898) AC 593 HL.
144 Art. L173-13 of the Code of Insurances.

stipulating and arranging the indemnity which arises from the contract of insurance, it is therefore only possible when it is due to a loss that happens because of the occurrence of a risk which is covered by the policy of insurance.[145] Abandonment is not an option where the loss has occurred due to an unauthorised voyage,[146] or because of the inherent vice or fault of the assured.[147] The abandonment can neither be partial nor conditional, under art. 31 of the Law of 3/7/1967 and now art. L. 172-27 of the Insurance Code. The assured has to give a notice of abandonment to the insurer, either in the form of a letter or judicially. By the act of notification, the assured accepts that he wants to be indemnified, as if there was a total loss.

In the case of hull insurance, abandonment occurs when there is total loss,[148] or the repairs needed exceed the agreed value of the vessel, when there is lack of news for more than three months, or where it is impossible to repair.[149] In the case of cargo insurance, abandonment is exercised when transportation of the cargo is not possible, i.e. due to the vessel's incapacity to navigate, because the vessel is missing with no news received of her after the lapse of a reasonable period of time, when there is a total loss of the cargo, when there is loss or deterioration of the ¾ of the insurable value of the cargo, or when the cargo is sold whilst afloat due to an average cause from a risk encountered. Under articles 4, 5 of the Decree of 1968, abandonment has to be notified to the insurer.[150]

---

[145] Tassel Y(2001) Assurance Maritime: Contrat, Editions du Juris- Classeur 611 :11 ; See Cases Cass Req ,27 Oct 1926:Dor 1927 p 6. ; Cass.Com,11 Oct. 1977: DMF 1978,p 328, note Latron ; CA Aix-en-Provence,24 Oct 1929:Dor 1930, p 28.

[146] CA Marseille, 13 Juin 1913: Autran t30, p 78 ; Tassel Y (2001) Assurance Maritime: Contrat, Editions du Juris- Classeur 611 :11.

[147] Cass Req.10 Janv.1939:JCPG 1939,II,1011, Droit maritime ; CA Rennes, 21 Juin 1969:D.1970 jurispr. P 296 ; Tassel Y (2001) Assurance Maritime: Contrat, Editions du Juris- Classeur 611 :11.

[148] CA Rabat, 12 Juin 1957: DMF 1958,p.747 ; T Com Seine,7 Janv.1963:DMF 1963 p 415 ; Tassel Y (2001) Assurance Maritime: Contrat, Editions du Juris- Classeur 611 :11.

[149] Cass. Req, 17 Aout 1859:DP 1859, 1 p.356 ; CA Rouen, 19 juin 1876:DP 1878,2 p. 205 ; Cass Req, 14 Aout 1876:DP 1877, p 314 ; Cass Req 16 Dec 1889: Autran t5, p472 ; Tassel Y (2001) Assurance Maritime: Contrat, Editions du Juris- Classeur 611 :11.

[150] T Com Seine, 7 Janv 1963:DMF 1963 p 425 ; Tassel Y (2001) Assurance Maritime: Contrat Editions du Juris- Classeur 611:11.

3.5. Types of losses in marine insurance contracts under the US law regime

In the US, in marine insurance, the main categories of losses are total loss and partial loss.[151] Any loss which is not total loss is considered as partial loss. In a total loss, the assured is entitled to recover from the underwriter, the whole amount insured by the policy on the subject so lost. The meaning of the term *"actual total loss"* came before an American Court in the case of *Edinburgh Assurance v RL Burns Corporation*[152] American Law and Courts, in interpreting actual total loss, have accepted not only physical annihilation or destruction of the subject-matter insured but also loss of specie or of value to the assured. Many early cases found actual total losses when the estimated cost of repairs exceeded the sound value of the subject-matter insured. The reason for this is that under American Law[153] there is a constructive total loss when the cost of repairing the vessel exceeds one half of her repaired value. In *Soelburg v Western Assurance Corporation*,[154] the Court said:

> "There is an actual total loss when the subject-matter of the insurance is wholly destroyed or lost to the insured or where there remains nothing of value to be abandoned to the insurer."

Thus, even though something may remain of the subject-matter insured, if there is nothing of value to abandon to underwriters, an actual total loss has occurred.

In American Law, there is constructive total loss if ship or goods insured are damaged to more than one half of the value, by any peril insured against, or more than half of the freight is lost. When a vessel is incapable of recovery or repairs within foreseeable time, the assured is justified in abandoning her to his underwriters as a constructive total loss.[155] The assured has to give notice of abandonment to the underwriter within reasonable time after receipt of reliable information of the loss. Even in cases where no formal notice of abandonment has been given, it has been held by American courts, however, that any actions of the assured specifically implying the intention to abandon, will be deemed to be sufficient notice.[156] It is customary for underwriters to decline to accept abandonment

---

151 A partial loss is any loss other than total loss. A total loss can either be an actual total loss or a constructive total loss.

152 479 Fed Supp 138.

153 *Bradlie v Maryland Ins Co*, 7US 378.

154 119 F23,1902.

155 *The Portmar,Calmar, Steamship Corp v Sydney Scott et al* 1954 AMC 558.

156 *Patapsko Ins Co v Southgate*, 30US 604 (1831).

when it is tendered to them. In the US the validity of the abandonment is subsequently tested by the circumstances existing at the time of abandonment and not at the time of bringing suit, as is the case in the UK where it is accepted that only the expenses subsequent to tendering notice of abandonment are taken into account in determining whether or not a vessel is a constructive total loss; in the US however, it was held, in the case of *Northern Barge Line Co v Royal Insurance Co Ltd*,[157] that where a marine policy precluded recovery for constructive total loss unless the expense of recovering and repairing the vessel exceeds the insured value, the assured may defer tendering abandonment of the vessel to underwriters until she is raised and repair costs are determined. In addition, the insured can include recovery expenses prior to tender of abandonment, for determining the existence and proof of a constructive total loss. Also the width of the scope of constructive total loss is larger than that under English law and a constructive total loss exists already when the cost of repairing a vessel exceeds one half of her repaired value. This is also the main reason why many early cases found actual total losses when the estimated cost of repairs exceeded the sound value of the subject-matter insured. Notice of abandonment is also required, however the American courts have held that even in the absence of a formal notice of abandonment, where the assured has by his actions specifically implied the intention to abandon, this will be deemed to be sufficient notice.

3.6. Types of losses in marine insurance contracts under the Canadian law regime

The categorisation of losses is similar to that under the English Law regime. A total loss can be either an actual or a constructive total loss. Actual total loss occurs firstly when the subject-matter insured is either totally destroyed or ruined to the point of it not being any more of the species and quality assured, and secondly when the assured is definitely deprived of it. Where insurance on goods has been declared in the policy to be against *"total loss"* a constructive total loss is within the terms of the policy unless specifically excluded.[158] Constructive total loss occurs when the subject-matter insured is reasonably abandoned because its actual total loss seems inevitable or because it could not be preserved without the cost of its preservation exceeding its value. In case of constructive total loss, the assured

[157] 1974 AMC 136.

[158] *O'Leary v Stymest* (1865) 11NBR 289 (C.A.).

may consider the loss as a partial one or abandon the subject-matter insured to the insurer and consider the loss as an actual total loss. In the latter case the assured has to issue to the insurer a notice of abandonment. This can be in either written or verbal form and transmitted with due diligence within a reasonable lapse of time from receipt of the news regarding the loss occurred. Failure to do so will result in the loss being eligible to be classified and treated only as a partial loss and not as a constructive total loss. Should the insurer accept the notice of abandonment, he acquires not only the rights (such as ownership) but also the obligations deriving for the subject-matter which has been insured and abandoned. Should he refuse to accept the notice of abandonment, the assured continues to owe the subject-matter insured which is treated as *res nullius* from that point onwards. Once accepted, either expressly or implicitly, the abandonment cannot be revoked and encompasses the recognition by the insurer of his obligation to indemnify the assured for the loss occurred.[159]As per s. 57(1) of the Federal Act:

"..A loss may be either total or partial and any loss, other than a total loss as hereinafter defined is a partial loss".

All losses which are not total ones – either as per the law regulating marine insurance contracts or as per the clauses of the contract – are partial ones.

As to the difference between total losses and partial losses, Justice Graham stated in *Hart v Boston Marine Insurance Co*[160]:

" As to its being a total loss or a partial loss that is a question more applicable to the quantity of the damages than to the ground of the action. The ground of the action is the same whether the loss be partial or total, both are perils within the policy."

It is clear that an assured claiming for a total loss may recover for a partial loss if the policy permits it.[161]

3.7. Types of losses in marine insurance contracts under the Australian law regime

In Australia, marine insurance losses are categorised either as partial or total ones.

The Australian Marine Insurance Act 1909 deals with losses in s. 62-72 and s. 62 of the Marine Insurance Act 1909 states that any loss

[159] Braen A(1992) Le Droit Maritime au Québec, W&L.
[160] (1894) 26 NSR 427, at 448-49 (CA).
[161] See *Troop v Union Insurance Co* (1894) 26 NSR 427, at 448-49, (CA).

which is not a total loss, is a partial loss and continues to classify total losses. In general the law follows the English pattern and the provisions are mostly identical to those of the English Marine Insurance Act 1906. For example, total losses are either actual or constructive total losses. The same requirements, as in English law, also apply in relation to the notice of abandonment. The same provisions also apply in relation to particular average losses, salvage charges and general average losses.

3.8. General conclusive remarks and comparative discussion

In relation to losses and their classification within marine insurance, we note the following:

From the common law countries examined, English law offers a wide scope of categorisation of losses that might occur under a contract of marine insurance. The distinctive feature in relation to losses is the classification of a total loss as a constructive total loss, a concept invented within marine insurance law to better serve the interests of the assured in relation to the indemnity he may be entitled to receive. Thus, the assured may recover the amount corresponding to an actual total loss, even when he has not suffered such a total loss, provided his loss fulfils certain criteria and he has given the insurer notice of abandonment.

Recent case law[162], however, has shown that the tender of a notice may not be an essential component for a claim for constructive total loss, if it is a case where the insurer could not have possibly benefited from such a notice. In the USA the concept of actual total loss is more restricted, in that any loss where the repair cost exceeds ½ of the repaired value is classified as a constructive total loss. Another difference is that the law has been *ab initio* more relaxed in relation to the requirements that constitute tender of the notice of abandonment. In effect, the requirement for a valid tender is satisfied even in cases where the latter has not been expressly performed but is deduced by the conduct of the assured. There is nothing worth mentioning in relation to the classification of losses under the Canadian and Australian law regimes, for they have largely based their law provisions to the English law pattern.

---

162 *Kastor Navigation Co Ltd v AGF MAT (The Kastor Too),* [2003]1 Lloyd's Rep, 296.

The study of the continental law countries permits us to remark the following in relation to the types of losses in marine insurance: In Greek law, the scope of the notion of abandonment is wider, for it is linked to total losses in general. In Norway, the scope of categorisation of losses is narrower than that of English law and any loss which is not a total loss will be classified either as damage or as partial damage. Constructive total loss also exists as a notion, though it is termed somehow different.[163] In addition, the insurer is in that case in a stronger position than under the English law, as he may opt at any stage to pay for a total loss and disentangle himself from future liabilities or he may elect to proceed and salvage the insured vessel. In addition, the assured, on top of giving notice of abandonment, must consult the insurer as to any future action to prevent or minimise any further loss. There is nothing peculiar to note, in relation to the classification of losses in marine insurance in the French law. It appears that all legal systems have been influenced by English law, more or less, in regulating types of losses and their categorisation in marine insurance. Lately, however, English law has relaxed the criteria relating to tender of notice of abandonment thus imitating the position under US law. Other than that, it is worth noting as a conclusive remark the fact that in some jurisdictions there is a wider scope in relation to the criteria and applicability of constructive total loss and abandonment[164], whilst in others the insurer enjoys a much stronger position in case of a constructive total loss.

[163] i.e. it is termed as condemnation or unrepairability.

[164] Such as the US where constructive total loss encompasses a wider scope of losses. Also in Greece, notice of abandonment is related in general to cases of total loss.

4. Valuation and the measure of indemnity in marine insurance contracts

4.1. Valuation and the measure of indemnity

4.1.1. Valuation and the measure of indemnity in England

A marine policy entitles the assured to indemnification for damage to or loss of the subject-matter insured caused directly by a covered peril and secondly for losses, charges or expenditure incurred voluntarily or as a matter of law in order to avert or minimise a loss. The sum recoverable by the assured, in connection therewith, is being termed as the measure of indemnity.[1] Calculation of the measure of indemnity is determined fundamentally by the classification of the loss and the nature of the policy.[2]

---

1 Marine Insurance Act 1906 S. 67(1).

2 Bennett, H (1986) The Law of Marine Insurance, Clarendon Press, Oxford, pp 344-362; Basically, the term *"measure of indemnity"* means *"the extent of the liability of the insurer for loss"*, i.e. the maximum amount which the insurer must pay in event of a claim under the policy. Within the Marine Insurance Act 1906, the term *"measure of indemnity"* is to be found in s. 67 - 78 thereof. S. 67(1), mostly defines the term, while s. 67(2) of the MIA 1906 precisely states the recoverable proportion of the measure of indemnity and the remaining sections give the basis on which the measure of indemnity is to be calculated each time, according to the case involved. The measure of indemnity laid down in these sections is exhaustive. Losses falling outside these sections are irrecoverable. S. 75(1) of the Marine Insurance Act 1906 extends the principles of indemnity set out in the Act to forms of cover that are marine in nature but, nevertheless, are not dealt with by the Act, i.e. double insurance, want of insurable interest or the fact that the subject-matter was not at risk due to any factual or legal reason when the loss occurred. Equally if part of the matter was not at risk, the insurer's liability is reduced proportionately, as in the case of

The precise amount which the assured is entitled to recover depends upon whether the policy is valued or unvalued, whether the loss is total or partial, and whether the policy is marine or terrestrial.[3]

The definition of the term *"measure of indemnity"*, as stated in s.67(1) of the Marine Insurance Act 1906, is subject to the distinction between valued and unvalued policies.

4.1.1.1. Valued and unvalued policies

All marine insurance policies are either valued or unvalued. A valued policy is a policy which specifies the agreed value of the subject-matter insured.[4] A policy is not valued merely because the assured is required to state the value of the insured subject-matter.[5] The extent of the indemnity provided by the policy must depend upon the value of the insured interest.

The measure of indemnity is calculated in case of a valued policy by reference to the agreed value, whereas in case of an unvalued policy by reference to the insurable value, as the latter is calculated in s. 16 of the Marine Insurance Act 1906. The insurable value takes the value of the subject-matter when the risk attaches and not[6] immediately before the occurrence of the event causing the loss.[7]

S. 27 of the Marine Insurance Act 1906 permits the parties to agree a valuation of the interest insured in the policy and such valuation is de-

---

share certificates - which are not within the definition of cargo - dispatched by sea (*Baring Brothers & Co v Marine Insurance Co* (1894)10 TLR 276; *Forbes v Aspinall* (1811)13 East 323 ; *Rickman v Carstairs* (1833)5 B&Ad 651; *Tobin v Harford* (1864)34 LJCP 37). S. 75(2) of the Marine Insurance Act 1906, draws the obvious point that the measure of indemnity may be subject to other provisions of the Act which may operate to reduce the insurer's liability (*Forbes v Aspinall* (1811)13 East 323; *Rickman v Carstairs* (1833)5 B&Ad 651 ; *Tobin v Harford* (1864)34 LJCP 37).

3 Merkin R (ed) (1997) Colinvaux's Law of Insurance, 7th edn, S&M, London 1997, pp 169-172.

4 It is upon that value that the premium is calculated (Merkin R (2000) Marine insurance Legislation, LLP, London, annotated s. 27-30 of the Marine Insurance Act 1906; *Bousfield v Barnes* (1815)4 Camp 228).

5 *Wilson v. Nelson* (1864)33 LJQB 220 ; Merkin R (2000) Marine insurance Legislation, LLP, London, annotated s. 27-30 of the Marine Insurance Act 1906.

6 As in the case of non-marine insurance.

7 Although the presumption ,that this is the appropriate date, is rebuttable, where the evidence demonstrates that the assured's loss is properly felt at the time and place of the casualty (*The Captain Panagos* [1985] 1 Lloyd's Rep 625).

clared to be conclusive between the parties to the policy for all purposes except deciding whether there has been a constructive total loss.[8] The valuation is, as per s. 27(3) of the Marine Insurance Act 1906, binding only as between the insurer and the assured.[9] Valued policies, though common in the case of insurance on ships and profits, are rare in the case of goods.[10]

Once the insurer has accepted the premium based on the agreed value, it is not open to the insurer to contest the valuation for any reason[11] unless the assured has been guilty of fraud in presenting the valuation,[12] or the assured has over-valued the subject-matter in a material fashion and has failed to disclose or has misrepresented the valuation, or in the case of a floating policy the value of each declaration has not been honestly stated.[13] The purpose of fixing in advance the amount of compensation to be paid to the assured is to avoid disputes as to the value of the subject-matter insured.

The validity of such a policy - regardless of the fact that it may offend the principle of indemnity - was first raised in *Lewis v Rucker*[14] and then in *Irving v Manning*[15] where upon initially admitting that a policy of insurance is not a perfect contract of indemnity, a valued policy was identified as an example of its imperfection. The agreed valuation cannot ope-

---

8 No allowance is made for market appreciation, expected profit on cargoes at the destination, or replacement cost of a capital asset (Grime R (1991) Shipping Law, S&M, London, pp 370-371; *Irving v Manning* (1847)1 HL Cas 287, *Woodside v Globe Marine Insurance Co* (1896)1 QB 105, *Helmville Ltd v Yorkshire Insurance Co Ltd (The Medina Princess)* [1965]1 Lloyd's Rep 361; Merkin R (2000) Marine insurance Legislation, LLP, London, annotated s. 27-30 of the Marine Insurance Act 1906).

9 *North of England Iron SS Insurance Association v Armstrong* (1870 LR 5 QB 224, *SS Balmoral v Marten* (1902) AC 511 HL ; Hodges S (1996) Law of Marine Insurance, Cavendish Publications, Ch 5.

10 Merkin R (ed) (1997) Colinvaux's Law of Insurance, 7th edn, S&M, London 1997, pp 169-172.

11 *Barker v Janson* (1868) LR 3 CP 303 ; *Herring v Janson* (1895)1 ComCas 177; *Muirhead v Forth & North Sea Steamboat Mutual Insurance Association* (1889)2 AC 72; *The Main* (1894) P 320 .

12 See *Lewis v Rucker* (1761)2 Burr 1167, *Haig v De la Cour* (1812)3 Camp 319, despite the fact that over valuation is not enough to prove that, as also shown in *General Shipping & Forwarding Co v British General Insurance Co Ltd* [1923]15 Ll LR 175, *Papadimitriou v Henderson* [1939]64 LlLR 345.

13 *Steamship Balmoral Co v Marten* [1902]AC 511.

14 (1761)2 Burr 1167.

15 (1847)1 HL Cas 287.

rate where the valued risk has not attached.[16] The case of *Irving v Manning*[17] also held that an agreed value is conclusive, and this was later on embodied in s. 27(3) of the Marine Insurance Act 1906.[18]

An over valuation provides no ground to defeat a claim.[19] In the absence of fraud, the agreed valuation is binding upon the insurer even where considerably inflated through erroneous assumption. In *Barker v Janson*[20] the court refused to open a ship's valuation agreed on an non-damaged basis, despite the fact that - unknown to the parties - the vessel had been so severely damaged by a storm as to be rendered a constructive total loss. The case of *The Main*[21] concerned insurance on a return freight from New Orleans reasonably valued. On the outward voyage, the vessel sustained damage requiring repairs and resulting in delay. During this time, the freight market from New Orleans declined considerably but the court refused to open the valuation when the vessel and most of the freight were lost on the delayed return voyage.[22]

---

16 In *Denoon v Home & Colonial Assurance Co* (1872) LR CP 341 a ship carrying both passengers and rice was wrecked, resulting in a total loss of the rice and its freight. Nearly all the passengers survived and their passage money was paid. The assured claimed for a total loss on a policy on chartered freight valued at £2,000 and insured for £1,000. Although freight in the policy in question did not include passage money, it was held that a valuation of freight in a valued policy refers, in the absence of contrary intention, to a full cargo which there had never been. Consequently, in calculating the measure of indemnity, the policy was to be treated as unvalued insurance of half the lost freight, not exceeding £1,000 (Bennett H (1986) The Law of Marine Insurance, Clarendon Press, Oxford, pp 344-362).

17 (1847)1 HL Cas 287.

18 The section itself, provides two exceptions to the general rule encapsulated in the phrases *"...subject to the provisions of this Act"* , and *"...in the absence of fraud"*.

19 *Herring v Janson* (1895)1 Com Cas 177.

20 (1868) LR 3CP 303.

21 (1894) P 320.

22 To the extent of such a discrepancy between an agreed valuation and the true loss, marine insurance law departs from a perfect indemnity principle (*Irving v Manning* (1847)1 H.L.C. 287) and such a departure is sanctioned on the ground of commercial convenience (*Lidgett v Secretan* (1871) LR 6 CP 616) and is not viewed as infringing prohibitions on wagering. The significance of the agreed valuation is not, however, confined to the measure of indemnity. In determining whether the assured has broken a warranty to maintain uninsured a specified proportion of the value of the property, the court will have regard to the agreed rather than the real value.

Another case illustrating the conclusive nature of the agreed value is *North of England Iron Steamship Association v Armstrong & Others*[23]. In this case, a policy of insurance was effected for £6,000 on the vessel *"Hetton"* valued at £6,000. The *Hetton* was hit by another ship and sank, and the underwriters paid the owners the £6,000 with regards to a total loss. Afterwards, £5,000 was recovered in the Court of Admiralty for the *Hetton* against the owners of the other ship. The real value of the *Hetton* was £9,000 and there was no other insurance upon her. It was held that because the underwriters and the assured agreed £6,000 as the value of the *Hetton* for all purposes, the damages recovered, which were in the nature of salvage, belonged entirely to the underwriters.[24] In reality, however, what may amount to over-valuation is merely a question of fact,[25] and there is no fixed rule as to what constitutes such an excess in valuation so that it may necessitate disclosure,[26] or add to the transaction fraud.[27]

Policies may also contain clauses permitting the opening of valuation in other circumstances, for example in the case of part insurance. In practice, marine insurance policies on ship cargo and freight are invariably

---

23 (1870)LR 5 QB 244.

24 In this Case Cockburn CJ, stated: "... *where the value of a thing insured is stated in the policy in a manner to be conclusive between the two parties, the insurer and the insured, as regards the value, ...the parties are estopped between one another from disputing the value of the thing insured as stated in the policy" and further on "...if parties will enter into such policies they must take the consequences"*. Also Mellor J, stated : "... *the basis of the contract is the agreed value... and ..all... rights...must be governed by the agreed value"*.

25 Hodges, S (1996) Law of Marine Insurance, Cavendish Publications, Ch. 5.

26 An assured failing to disclose to the insurer that the agreed valuation in a single policy or the total sum of the agreed valuations of more than one policy is excessive, is guilty of a breach of a duty of disclosure. The case of *Ionides v Pender* (1874)LR 9 QB 531 was the first to consider non-disclosure of an excessive over-valuation as a ground for avoidance of a policy, and was followed by the cases of *Gooding v White* [1913]29 TLR 312, *Piper v Royal Exchange* [1932]44 Lloyd's Rep 103 and *Berger and Light Diffusers Pty Ltd v Pollock* [1973]2 Lloyd's Rep 442.

27 A valuation considerably exceeding the selling value of a ship is not necessarily fraudulent or so excessive as to require disclosure. If a policy is tainted with fraud, however, then the agreed valuation and the whole policy are at risk. The question of fraud was initially considered in the *Haig v de la Cour* [(1812)3 Camp 319] and later on in *Loders and Nucoline Ltd v the Bank of New Zealand* [1929]33 Ll L Rep 70] and *The Gunford* (*Thames & Mersey Marine Insurance Co v The Gunford Ship Co)* [1911]AC 529]. Gross over-valuation could also be evidence of a gaming or wagering policy, thus a void one as per s. 4 of the Marine Insurance Act 1906 (*Ionides v Pender* (1874)LR 9 QB 531).

valued. This enables the assured to cover losses that are not within the statutory valuation in s.16 of the Marine Insurance Act 1906 or which are difficult to assess.[28]

In light of the above, two cases encapsulate the significance of the proper ascertaining and characterisation of a policy as a valued one or not. The first one is *Kyzuna Investments Ltd v Ocean Marine Mutual Insurance Association (Europe)*[29], concerning a marine insurance for a yacht, where the proposal for insurance stating the sum to be insured - accompanied by a certificate of valuation - was accepted by the insurers as the sum to be insured and in accordance they had a policy issued for the sum proposed as well as for its renewal. The question that arose was whether the policy was a valued or an unvalued one, and whether the sum insured was different from the *"agreed value"* within the meaning of s. 27(2) of the Marine Insurance Act 1906, or only constituted the *"sum insured"*. It was stated that, in compliance also with s. 27(2) of the Marine Insurance Act 1906, the standard form of marine policy allowed for agreement as to the value, by making only specific reference to the value as an agreed value. [30]

The second case is *Quorum SA v Schramm (No1)*, [31] where Thomas J. had to determine whether a policy was valued or unvalued and then, having concluded the latter, he had to calculate the measure of indemnity for unique subject-matter under an unvalued policy. Mayfair Fine Art owned and stored the famous painting of Degas namely *"La Danse Grec-*

---

[28] Overvaluation is as binding as if it were accurate or under-valued, except in extreme cases where gross overvaluation may be misleading thus constituting material misrepresentation. However, valuation must be sharply distinguished from the extent of the cover (Grime R (1991) Shipping Law, S&M, London, pp.370-371).

[29] [2000]3 QBD.

[30] In *Wilson v Nelson* [(1864)33 LJ QB 220] a careful distinction had been drawn between the sum insured and what was required if there was to be a valued policy. It was common for a policy of marine insurance to be a valued one as agreement on valuation avoided disputes over valuation in the event of loss, (*Barker v Janson* (1864 LR 3 CP)) and also because although the agreed value was not conclusive for determining whether there had been a constructive total loss, nevertheless, the Institute clauses had for many years provided that the insured value was to be taken as the repaired value, making it often more difficult for there to be a constructive total loss. In the present case the words *"value to be insured"* contained in the proposal, were not indicating that the value so stated would be agreed as the insured value by underwriters, as nothing pointed to the intention that the sums stated in the schedule were to be the agreed value of the yacht and her equipment. The words *"sum insured"* ordinarily indicated a ceiling on recovery in an unvalued policy.

[31] [2002] Lloyd's Rep I R].

que". During a fire that occurred in the warehouse, caused by a change of humidity and temperature in the room where the painting was stored, the painting suffered minor damages; in effect, it was repaired, valued and later sold for US$3.275 million. The stated basis of valuation under which the painting had been insured was prescribed as "*...original cost price to the assured plus 20% or market value at loss/damage time, whichever of the two the greater*". The final sum insured was US$ 5.3 million. After the fire had occurred the parties negotiated a fresh endorsement, stating that in the event of partial loss or damage, the amount of loss shall be the cost and expense of restoration plus any depreciation in value, and that the underwriters will be liable for the proportion of loss or damage that the sum insured bears to the market value immediately prior to loss, and in no case more than its insured value.

The issues that arose were whether the policy was valued or unvalued, and if it were to be unvalued, then the effect of the endorsement, the degree of damage suffered and the valuation of the painting before and after the fire. Thomas J. concluded that the painting was insured under an unvalued policy. He drew the familiar distinction between insured value and a sum insured, where the former constitutes an agreed value and forms the basis of recovery, and the latter simply provides a ceiling upon the amount recoverable by the assured, leaving him the onus of proof of the loss, by the demonstration of a difference between the market value before and immediately after the occurrence of the peril. This was also based on his ruling in *Kyzuna*.[32] He concluded that the wording "*sum insured*" merely provided a ceiling on recovery and that other forms of wording were required to render it an agreed valued policy.[33] Regarding the extent of the damage, it was ruled that there had been direct physical damage caused by a peril, since the fire had caused sub-molecular damage to the pastel.[34] Regarding pre-loss and post-loss valuation it was considered to be US$3.6 million before the fire and US$2.2 million after the fire, giving the assured a recovery of US$1.4 million.[35] The Court assessed the damage

---

32 [2000]3 QBD.

33 The endorsement was considered by Thomas J. as ambiguous. The purpose of the endorsement was to avoid any party's dispute as to the amount of recovery, however Thomas J., treated it more as an average clause stipulating what would happen if the insured value was less than the market one in case of partial loss.

34 It was immaterial that the damage was invisible and unascertainable in its extent.

35 Valuation had to be in the relevant market and the private dealers' was chosen as this guaranteed the likelihood of obtaining a higher price. The amount reco-

not immediately after the fire, but in light of later developments. As there was no fixed value for the subject-matter the court was forced to be based on expert evidence.[36]

The issue of valued or unvalued policies has re-surfaced more recently. In *Thor Navigation Inc v Ingosstrakh Insurance*,[37] the assured was insured under two fleet policies of hull and machinery insurance. The policies stated that the *"sum insured"* in respect of each vessel was US$1.5 million. An insured vessel became a constructive total loss in September 2002. The key issue was whether the policies were valued or unvalued. It was held that that the policies were unvalued: there was no statement of an agreed value, but merely a maximum sum insured; the phrase *"sum insured"* was generally recognised as referring to a policy ceiling and not a valuation; and the incorporation of the Institute Hulls clauses made no difference as there was nothing in English custom and practice[38] which led to the conclusion that policies on vessels were to be valued, and nor was there anything in the clauses themselves which required policies to be valued. It was also found that there was no implied term to that effect and therefore no basis for rectifying the policy and no estoppel against the insurers preventing them from denying that the policy was valued. Regarding the final issue which was the measure of indemnity, the court held that the measure of indemnity laid down in s.68 of the Marine Insurance Act 1906, which is based on the value of the vessel at the date the policy was taken out[39], had no application. S.16 of the Marine Insurance Act was found to be archaic and in any event was subject to the terms of the policy: the policy in the present case provided for indemnity, and that was to be calculated at the time and place of the loss. The significance of this decision is that s.16 of the Marine Insurance Act has been held to have no application where the policy is governed by the Institute Hulls clauses.[40]

verable was not to be reduced by the amount of commission that may have been payable.

36 This case shows that the insurance under an unvalued policy of unique property or of property which due to its nature is difficult to be valuated, will inevitably give rise to market valuation problems which are incapable of objective determination, thus the only sensible thing would appear to be the use of a valued policy.

37 [2005] EWHC 19 (Comm)

38 Referred to in the clauses.

39 So specified by s 16 of the 1906 Act.

40 Merkin R: Insurance Law Update 2003-2006.

4.1.1.2. The mode of calculation and the finality of losses

The mode of estimating the insurable value of the interest at risk, has to be done with a view to procuring indemnity for the assured in case of loss.

Thus, the object of such a valuation ought to be to place the assured, in case of loss, in exactly the same situation as he would have been if no loss had taken place.[41] Although this idea ought to underlie the mode of estimating the value of the interest at risk,[42] instead, the result in practice is to put the assured in the same position as the one in which he was at the commencement of the risk, and not in a position as he would have been in if no loss had been incurred.

The difference between a valued and an unvalued policy, in terms of form and practicality, is that in a valued policy the space corresponding to the sum at which the parties agree to fix the amount of the insurable interest is filled in, whereas in an unvalued policy it is left blank. The real difference, however, is that under an unvalued policy the value of the interest at risk is not fixed in the policy but is estimated by a certain standard and in the case of a loss, the assured must prove the actual value of the subject of the insurance[43] ; whereas under a valued policy he need not do so, as the valuation between the parties is conclusive.

---

41 On the principle of valuation and for the purposes of insurance, the ship ought to be estimated at her value, after deducting the wear and tear of the voyage, for, that is what the ship would have been worth to her owner on arrival, but for the loss against which the insurance is intended to indemnify him. In the same way, with regard to freight, the true mode of estimating its value, for the purpose of insurance on the above principle, would be to take it at that sum which the shipowner might calculate on receiving on the safe arrival of the ship. With regard to goods, in order to put the merchant in the same situation as if no loss on his goods had taken place, i.e. to try to procure him a complete indemnity, it is clear that the value of the goods should be estimated for the purpose of insurance, at the price which they would actually have produced, had they arrived undamaged at their port of destination.

42 By which complete and absolute indemnity can in all cases be procured for the assured.

43 The amount of insurable interest in such cases being the sum measuring its worth to the assured at the commencement of the risk plus the charges of the insurance.

4.1.2. Valuation and the measure of indemnity in Greece

Under Greek law, the amount insured is determined on the basis of the value of the insured object, and the parties are bound by the agreed valuation.[44]

Valuation of the subject-matter insured, resulting in the determination of the insurable value, as per art. 268 CPML (ΚΙΝΔ), is calculated according to the true value, i.e the market value of the insured property at the commencement of the effect of the insurance.[45] The measure of indemnity is based on the extent of the damage occurred and it can be no higher than the insurable value, as per art. 268 CPML (ΚΙΝΔ)[46] and as established by various court rulings.[47] Once accepted by the insurer, the insurable value is binding.[48] Case law has shown that the use of the collision liability clause[49], also described as the *"running down clause"*, effectively reduces the insurer's liability to indemnify the ship-owner for all (100%) of the damages occurred to the insured vessel, as well as up to the limit of 75%,[50] for the damages incurred to the other vessel and/or the cargo.[51]

Due to the fact that a maritime accident does not have the benefit of being a generally approved concept and because of the *"all risks principle"* that has been adopted, the maritime accident is not a prerequisite *per se* for the award of indemnification, but, more specifically, it is the total

44 Spaidiotis K (1999) Marine Insurance Law in Greece, Maritime Advocate, Iss.7.

45 Should the insured property be cargo, then costs of loading and unloading as well as freight and premium are added

46 Skouloudis Z (1998) Private Insurance Law, 3rd edn, PN Sakkoulas Publications, Athens, Greece. It must be noted that in the Greek marine insurance law, the measure of indemnity is governed by the clauses of general law, as various case law has also elaborated (*Athens Court of First Instance: ΠΠρΑθ 14133/1984 ΕΝΔ, Piraeus Court of First Instance : 904/1985 ΕΕμπΔ 36,698 Athens Court of Appeal: ΕφΑθ 10200/1984 ΕΣυγκΔ 13,473*).

47 See Cases: *High Court: ΑΠ 1357 /1994 Δ/ΝΗ 196,624, ΑΠ 1156/1988 ΕΕΝ 1989,553.*

48 See Velentzas I (1998) The New Law of Private Insurance, Ius Publications, Athens.

49 Cl. 6 of the International Hull clauses 01/11/02 (on collision liability).

50 What is meant by the 75% maximum liability, is that the insurer , as far as the damages incurred to the other vessel/cargo from the collision with the insured vessel are concerned, is obliged to reimburse for a sum – of up to a maximum of 75% - corresponding to the 75% of the insurable value of the assured's vessel.

51 *Athens Court of Appeal ΕφΑθ 6191/81 ΕεμπΔ 33,263* ; Kalantzis AK (1998) Private Insurance Law- Cases and Materials, Nomiki Vivliothiki Edn, Athens.

loss of the vessel or its incapacity to navigate that are considered as such (art. 269,281 (CPML) (ΚΙΝΔ)). If, however, the marine insurance contract specifies that it also covers risks resulting from a maritime accident, then the latter is also considered as a prerequisite (art. 173, 200 Greek Civil Code (AK)) as also shown by case law.[52] According to article 269(2) of the Code of Private Maritime Law (ΚΙΝΔ), if no special agreement is present in the policy, the underwriter is legally bound to cover the damages paid by the assured to the third parties.[53] Due to the *"all risks principle*", shipowner's liability insurance is automatically included in the insurance of the vessel effected; thus, the insurer is liable to cover the full extent of the costs incurred by the assured, also including damages and legal costs.[54] Although no precise wording exists, it is presumed by the interpretation of the text of law that only damages in tort are recoverable from the underwriters.[55] Article 269(2) of the CPML (ΚΙΝΔ) states:

"...the insurer is liable for all damages that the ship is obliged to pay to third parties".

There is no express distinction between damages arising in tort or in contract. However, damages arising in contract are not, in principle, recoverable from the underwriter under article 269(2) of the CPML (ΚΙΝΔ). In terms of Greek law *"responsibility"* (which is the term used) mainly refers to liability arising in tort. Should this term also be used to describe liability arising in contract, it should always be expressly referred to. Thus, both the wording and the substance of article 269(2) of the CPML (ΚΙΝΔ) point towards the direction that only damages in tort are recoverable. However, such an interpretation operates in favour of the insurer who already finds himself in a difficult position as he must cover all damages.

---

52 See case: *Athens Court of Appeal ΕφΑθ 1760/81 ΕλΔ 22,637.*

53 Skouloudis Z(1995) The Law of Private Insurance, 2nd edn, P Sakkoulas Publications, Santaroza 1d, Athens, p 384.

54 Papapolitis NI(1957) Insurance of the Liability of the Shipowner, Athens, p.127.

55 Article 269(2) of the CPML (ΚΙΝΔ) provides that the insurer is not obliged to indemnify the assured owner of the vessel for collision damages paid to third parties relating to harm in body or health. However, an expressed opposite agreement is permitted. (Skouloudis Z(1995) The Law of Private Insurance, 2nd edn, P Sakkoulas Publications, Santaroza 1d, Athens, p 384.) The reason for this exclusion is that the insurance of the vessel cannot include life insurance which is the object of general, private insurance (Kiantos DV (1998) Insurance Law, 6th edn, Sakkoulas Publications, Thessaloniki, p 108). Life insurance is compulsory to passengers of vessels operating between Greek ports and the price of the ticket embraces the respective premium(Art. 1-3, Presidential Decree 91/1979).

The damages for which indemnity is granted, under article 269(2) of the Code of Private Maritime Law (ΚΙΝΔ), are all damages that the vessel is responsible to pay for[56], i.e.:

- loss of or damage to any other vessel or property;
- delay to or loss of use of any other vessel or property thereon;
- salvage of any other vessel or property thereon, irrespective of the salvage result;[57]
- removal or disposal of obstructions and wrecks;
- any real or personal property on the insured vessel (in tort);
- the cargo or other property on the insured vessel (in tort);

Special clauses which exclude the liability of the underwriters are permitted under article 269(2) of the CPML (ΚΙΝΔ), usually in relation to cargo on the insured vessel, because the article does not establish *ius cogens*. Articles 173,200,281,288 of the Greek Civil Code (AK) operate in such a way that the courts may decide whether a specific exclusion is unfair, thus, illegal and void.[58] The insurer is obliged to restore only the damages that the assured has actually paid for. This is a legal principle based on the interpretation of the wording of article 269(2) of the CPML (ΚΙΝΔ).[59] If the shipowner becomes bankrupt, the insurer is not liable against third parties.[60]

In connection with the insurance of third party liabilities, indemnity claims cannot be brought directly against insurers by third parties, with the exception of claims for pollution damage in line with the International Convention on Civil Liability for Oil Pollution Damage. [61]A special feature of the law is that the insurer is released from coverage and from subsequent liability, if damage was caused by personal fault of the shipowner, but not if this was done due to the fault of the master, crew or

---

56 Papapolitis NI (1957) Insurance of the Liability of the Shipowner, Athens, pp. 224,271,272.

57 Skantzakis (1970) Insurance Lessons, Athens, p. 200.

58 Argyriadis A (1986) Elements of Insurance Law, 4th edn., Sakkoulas Publications, Thessaloniki p 117.

59 Papapolitis NI (1957) Insurance of the Liability of the Shipowner, Athens, p 207.

60 In Greek Law, there is no equivalent to the English "Third Parties(Rights Against Insurers) Act 1930.

61 Spaidiotis K (1999) Marine Insurance Law in Greece, Maritime Advocate, Iss.7.

other persons. It is also important to note that in case of multiple marine insurances, all insurers are jointly and severally liable, irrespective of the time of conclusion of each contract; whereas in general Greek insurance law only the first one is liable and the rest are called to contribute only for the part of damages remaining uncovered by the first insurer.

4.1.3. Valuation and the measure of indemnity in Norway

It is accepted that the sum insured acts as the limit of the liability of the insurer.[62] The principle established is that the insurer is liable up to the sum insured for each individual casualty and shall apply in all branches where a sum insured is agreed.[63]

The assured also gets an additional sum, as compensation for the loss of time whilst the vessel is undergoing repairs in the repair yard.[64] The assured, in addition to the cover which the insurance affords him within the limits of the sum insured, is entitled to separate cover of a number of accessory expenses and other losses which the casualty has caused him. The expenses that are to be covered, in addition to the sum insured, include: costs of providing security, costs of filing suit against or defending a suit filed by a third party, costs in connection with the claims settlement, costs of necessary measures to preserve the object insured and interest on the compensation.[65]

The insurer's liability is, however, reduced in various cases. Damage and replacement costs of certain parts of equipment are not recoverable, unless caused in a particular way, and some parts are not covered in certain circumstances. In the case of ND 1972.302 *"Balblom"* a fork lift truck, owned by a firm of stevedores, was to be used in the insured ship's hold. While being lifted into the hold, the truck fell and was totally destroyed. The ship's P&I insurers claimed that the truck was part of the ship's equipment and therefore recoverable. The arbitrator rejected that ar-

---

62 Chapter 4, section 4.

63 Ch. 4§18 of the Norwegian Marine Insurance Plan (1996) Commentary. <http://exchange.dnv.com/nmip/index.htm>

64 In light of the conflicting interests between him and the insurer, regarding the choice of repair yard, since the latter would prefer the cheapest yard whilst the assured's interests would be best served if he could use a fast albeit expensive yard to effect repairs.

65 Ch. 4§19 of the Norwegian Marine Insurance Plan (1996) Commentary. <http://exchange.dnv.com/nmip/index.htm>

gument stating that what was meant by *"equipment"* was equipment on board following the ship from place to place.[66] Where loss is caused by a combination of perils,[67] the assured should in no case render himself, through the compensation based on a combination of perils, in a more advantageous position than the one he would have been if there had not been a combination of perils.[68]

4.1.4. Valuation and the measure of indemnity in France

Although it is perceived[69], under French law, that the insurable value is equal to the agreed value, in reality, the insurable value is fixed in relation to the real value, i.e. increased real value,[70] or destination value, even if it surpasses the increased real value.[71] In general, the indemnity sum is not more than the agreed insurable value. Under French law, [72] however, an increased value insurance is not a quoted part of the insurable value of the initial insurance, but it is considered as an independent additional insurance which does not mix with the initial one. Indemnity is owed for all legitimate interests, including expected profits, as per art. 3 of the Law of 3/7/1967 and now art. L. 172-7 of the Insurance Code.

---

66 Wilmot N (1975) The Contract of Marine Insurance in English and Norwegian Law: Part I and II, Oslo, p 5/20.

67 As per paragraph 4-20.

68 Ch. 4§20 of the Norwegian Marine Insurance Plan (1996) Commentary. <http://exchange.dnv.com/nmip/index.htm>. The provision is based on ND 1956.323 NH *"Pan"*, where the question was how the limitation up to the sum insured was to be applied in the event of a casualty with a *"mixed cause"*. Liability for the damage to the ship was apportioned, with the marine insurer covering 40% and the war-risks insurer 60%. The costs of repairs, etc. exceeded the hull valuation, but the assured demanded full compensation, alleging that each of the insurers was liable for his share of damage to the ship up to his sum insured. The Supreme Court rejected the claim on the grounds that the assured shall not *"in a case of a combination of different perils, be in an economically more advantageous position than if there had been no combination of different perils"*.

69 Art. 13 of the French policy.

70 i.e. the real value plus a 20%.

71 Also, in case of insurance per each kind or ballot of merchandise, the indemnity owed cannot exceed the insurable value of each of these kinds or ballots of merchandise.

72 Art. 359 of the Insurance Code.

The liability of the insurer is limited in that no enrichment of the assured exists upon indemnification. Payment has to be made within thirty days after the submission of all required justifying documents. Whatever it may be, the insurable value has to be justified by an insurable interest as per art. 10,11 of the Law of 3/7/1967 and now art. L. 172-6,172-7 of the Insurance Code. The exception to this rule is the agreed value which is binding and by itself justified by the parties' agreement.

4.1.5. Valuation and the measure of indemnity in the USA

It is usual for policies of marine insurance to be valued, but unvalued policies are written from time to time.[73]

Generally speaking, the insurable value is the value of the vessel at the commencement of the risk, including fuel, provisions and stores. In the case of a vessel engaged in a special trade, the value of any equipment required for that trade should also be included.The purpose of a valued policy here is also to stipulate indemnity in advance.[74] As in English law, also as per the American rule, an agreed value in a marine policy, in the absence of fraud or of breach of the duty of utmost good faith, is binding and conclusive.[75]

---

73 *Lenfest v Coldwell* 525F2d 717,1975 AMC 2489(2d Circuit 1975); *NY & Cuba Mail SS Co v Royal Exchange Assn*, 154 Fed Rep. 315.(Schoenbaum TJ (1999) Key Divergences Between English and American Law of Marine Insurance, Cornell Maritime Press, p 27).

74 *Purofied Down Prods Corp* 278F2d 442 ; In the United States also, the parties' determination in this regard will be accepted in the absence of fraud, or breach of the duty of utmost good faith. (Schoenbaum TJ (1999) Key Divergences Between English and American Law of Marine Insurance: A Comparative Study, Cornell Maritime Press) Also, the valuation clause in the American Institute Hull Clauses makes it clear that all leased equipment is to be considered part of the subject-matter insured and included in the agreed value.

75 Fraud is a recognized exception, under American Law, to the rule that valuation is conclusive (*Lenfest v Coldwell* 525F2d 717,1975 AMC 2489(2d Circuit 1975); *NY & Cuba Mail SS Co v Royal Exchange Assn*, 154 Fed Rep 315; *Disrude v Commercial Fishermen's Inter-Ins Exch* 570 P2d 963, 1978 AMC 261 (Or. 1978) and Schoenbaum TJ (1999) Key Divergences Between English and American Law of Marine Insurance: A Comparative Study, Cornell Maritime Press, p 72).

4.1.6. Valuation and the measure of indemnity in Canada

The rule on valuation is similar to that under the English law (as per the Marine Insurance Act 1906). Agreed valuation is binding and conclusive, unless there has been fraud or such an overvaluation that the insurer would not have taken the risk, had he known it. In *Biggin v British Marine Mutual Insurance Association Ltd,*[76] a boat was valued at a price in excess of the purchase price which had been misrepresented to the insurer. The court noted that the agreed-upon value is often higher than the purchase price or the market value, and that there was no fraud. It was, however, held that the insurer was bound by the valuation in the policy.

4.1.7. Valuation and the measure of indemnity in Australia

In Australia, the law regulates valuation and the measure of indemnity in as much the same wording as in the English Marine Insurance Act 1906.

If there is nothing provided in relation to valuation and the measure of indemnity, s. 81 of the Marine Insurance Act 1909 provides that the measure of indemnity shall be ascertained, as nearly as may be, in accordance with the provisions in relation to the measure of indemnity, in so far as they are applicable to the particular case. In s. 22 it is stated that the insurable value of the subject-matter insured is in case of insurance on a ship, the value of the ship, at the commencement of the risk, including her outfit, provisions and stores for the officers and crew, money advanced for seamen's wages, and other disbursements -if any- incurred to make it fit for the voyage or adventure, plus the charges of insurance upon the whole. The insurable value, in the case of a steam-ship insured, includes also the machinery, boilers, and coals and engine stores if owned by the assured, and, in the case of a ship insured which is engaged in a special trade, includes also the ordinary fittings requisite for that trade.

In insurance on freight, whether paid in advance or otherwise, the insurable value is the gross amount of the freight at the risk of the assured, plus the charges of insurance, and in insurance on goods or merchandise, the insurable value is the prime cost of the property insured, plus the expenses of and incidental to shipping and the charges of insurance upon the whole. In insurance on any other subject-matter, the insurable value is the amount at the risk of the assured when the policy attaches, plus the charges of insurance.

---

[76] (1992)14 CCLI (2d) (Nfld TD).

The Australian Marine Insurance Act 1909, states in s. 33 that a policy is valued when it specifies the agreed value of the subject-matter insured. The value fixed by the policy is, as between the insurer and assured, conclusive of the insurable value of the subject intended to be insured, whether the loss be total or partial, but for the purpose of determining the case of a constructive total loss. As per s. 34 of the Marine Insurance Act 1909, a policy is unvalued when it does not specify the value of the subject-matter insured, but, subject to the limit of the sum insured, leaves the insurable value to be subsequently ascertained, in the manner specified by the Act.

4.2. Total losses and the measure of indemnity

4.2.1. Total losses and the measure of indemnity in England

In the event of a total loss, the assured recovers the full value of the subject-matter insured, subject to policy limits.[77] It should be noted that the valuation agreed on in the policy does not determine the question of whether there has been a constructive total loss of goods; [78] the latter being solely determined by the fact that the costs of repair and forwarding exceeds the goods' value on arrival.

The repaired value of the ship, when a loss occurs, determines the actions of the assured, in relation to repair expenses, that are to be undertaken and also in relation to the decision to be adjudicated by the relevant court. If part of the damages sustained are non-repaired, the whole amount of valuation, to be calculated for the award of indemnification, is depreciated accordingly. In calculating the depreciation arising from non repaired damage,[79] it is the value fixed by the policy which must be taken into account and not the true undamaged value.

In *Irvin v Hine*,[80] by an all risks policy of marine insurance, the value of a steam trawler was agreed at £9,000. The ship stranded in January 1942, and in February 1942 the owner gave the underwriters notice of

[77] Hodges S (1996) The Law of Marine Insurance, Cavendish Publications, Ch 5.

[78] *Irving v Manning* (1874)6 CB 391.

[79] For which the assured is entitled to be indemnified.

[80] [1950]1 KB 555.

abandonment which was not accepted. In June 1942, the ship was salvaged by the Admiralty and beached, but the assured refused to interest himself in her and in November 1942, an inspector of the Ministry of Transport concluded that her repair was not an economical proposition. The assured claimed for constructive total loss on the grounds that it was unlikely that a license would be obtained to repair the ship, alternatively for a partial loss. It was held that the claim for constructive total loss could not be based under s.60 of the Marine Insurance Act 1906, and thus was not accepted. The assured had however suffered a partial loss and was entitled to be indemnified under s. 69(3) of the Marine Insurance Act 1906 for the depreciation arising from the damage, and not exceeding the cost of repair (£4,620).

There can be a change in the valuation by reduction of the risk. If the entirety of the insured subject-matter is not at risk, its total agreed value is inappropriate and the insurer is liable only for the relevant proportion. S.75(2) of the Marine Insurance Act 1906, states that the insurer is entitled to plead that the whole or part of the subject-matter insured was not at risk under the policy at the date of the loss. If the only change in the risk between the date of the insurance and the date of the loss is the actual value of the insured subject-matter, as opposed to a change in the proportion of the subject matter coming on risk, the agreed value stands and it is open to the insurer to plead change in the circumstances.[81]

By virtue of the indemnity principle, an assured may recover only for the loss sustained but the initial impact of a casualty may be reversed or reduced by subsequent events. Thus, a captured vessel may be redeemed by re-capture or ransom or a casualty may result in an initial prognosis which proves unduly pessimistic. The question arises as to the point in time, for insurance purposes, by which to judge definitively whether the assured has suffered a loss[82] and if so, the measure thereof.[83] However, the indemnity principle and the doctrine of ademption of loss cannot be overstretched, so as to permit intervention of the underwriters change of a total loss into a partial loss and subsequent reduction of the measure of indemnity accordingly.

---

[81] In *Woodside v Globe Marine Insurance Co* (1896)1 QB 105 the insurer was held liable for an amount based on the agreed value of a vessel following its actual total loss, even though the vessel had become a constructive total loss, before the date of the actual total loss, and therefore was worthless, by operation of an uninsured peril.

[82] Commonly referred to as the *"doctrine of ademption of loss"*.

[83] *Hamilton v Mendes* (1761)2 Burr. 1198; *Goss v Withers* (1758)2 Burr 683; *Falkner v Ritchie* (1814)2 M&S; *Bainbridge v Neilson* (1808)10 East 329.

In *Sailing Ship "Blairmore" Co Ltd v Macredie*[84] the assured served a notice of abandonment in respect of the insured vessel which had sunk in the harbour. The cost of raising and repairing the vessel, compared to its repaired value, rendered it a constructive total loss, whereas the cost of repairs on their own amounted only to a partial loss. The House of Lords held the insurers liable for a total loss, since they had undertaken a contractual obligation to pay as on a total loss in circumstances constituting a constructive total loss, and when such a loss occurred they could not defeat that obligation by their own act.[85] Similarly, any loss which fails to satisfy the criteria specified in the Marine Insurance Act 1906 for a total loss, whether actual or constructive, can only constitute a partial loss and the assured cannot treat it as, or convert it into, a total loss.[86]

Later cases reveal the tendency to define valuation, the inconsistent court rulings produced as a result of doing so and the complexity involved. In *Ramco (UK) Ltd v International Insurance Co of Hannover Ltd*[87] the claimant bailees were insured under a combined risks policy which insured *"...stock and materials in trade therein or thereon the property of the insured or held by the insured in trust for which the insured is responsible"*. Following a disastrous fire, the question arose as to the exact amount recoverable under the policy. The First Instance Court held that the policy was a goods policy which covered the full value of the goods in the claimants' possession, but only in respect of those goods for which the claimants bore a legal liability to the owners in the event of the loss of the goods and that the word *"responsible"* referred to goods in respect of which the claimants bore a legal liability. The Court of Appeal upheld this reasoning, and ruled that the word *"responsible"* had in both *North British and Mercantile Insurance Co v Moffatt*[88] and in *Engel v Lancashire & General Assurance Co Ltd*[89] acquired the meaning of legal liability. The Court of Appeal held that it would be wrong for these cases to be overruled and thereby to introduce a change which underlined the market's understanding of the position. The Court of Appeal could not easily reconcile the pre-

---

84 (1898)AC 593.

85 Otherwise, all insurers could avoid paying on many total losses on the simple expedient of effecting some minor repairs, although there can be no objection to insurers effecting a complete reversal of a loss, for example by procuring the release of a detained vessel ; See *Pollurian Steamship Co Ltd v Young* [1915]1 KB 922.

86 *Navone v Haddon* (1850)9 CB 30; Bennett, H (1986) The Law of Marine Insurance, Clarendon Press, Oxford, pp 344-362.

87 [2004] EWCA Civ 675.

88 (1871) LR 7 CP 25.

89 (1925) 21 Ll L R 327.

viously expressed views - in the First Instance Court - that while the insurers were liable only for goods for which the assured bore a legal liability, the insurers were liable for the full value of those goods even though the amount of the assured's liability might be less.

The quantum of indemnity was also addressed in the non marine case of *Horbury Building Systems Ltd v Hampden Insurance NV*[90]. AMC wanted to convert a warehouse into a multiplex consisting of 16 cinemas. GN was head contractor and HB was the sub-contractor for the provision of partition walls and suspended ceilings. Whilst the work was carried out the ceiling of one of the auditoriums collapsed. HB - being insured against products liability - brought a claim for a declaration that the insurers would be liable for any claims which might be brought by GN for loss of revenue for the period during which the complex was closed, the costs of making good the defects in the ceilings, and additional marketing and advertising costs. It was common ground that HB was entitled to an indemnity from the insurers for physical damage caused by the falling ceiling[91] and economic loss directly flowing from physical damage, but the dispute related primarily to the HB's liability for the economic losses flowing from the closure of the complex and the court held that the insurers were not liable for any such claim as the policy aimed to provide indemnity for physical loss, otherwise it would have been a general and not a products liability policy.[92]

As the insurer's obligation is to hold the assured harmless,[93] the date on which the loss occurs is the date on which damages become payable and on which the limitation period begins to run,[94] although the policy may provide that the insurer's duty to make payment arises at some later date.[95] Late payment by the insurer cannot, as a matter of principle, amount to a further breach of contract, for it is not possible to be in breach of an obligation to pay damages[96] and the appropriate remedy is interest which will generally be imposed by the court from the date on which the insurer could reasonably have been expected to make payment. In this respect, it

---

[90] [2004] EWCA Civ 418.

[91] For example, damage to seats, carpets and walls.

[92] Merkin R Insurance :Law Update 2003-2006.

[93] *Luckie v Bushby* (1853)13 CB 864; *Edmunds v Lloyd's Italico* [1986]2 All ER 249.

[94] *Chandris v Argo Insurance* [1963]2 Lloyd's Rep. 65; *Catle Insurance v Hong Kong Islands Shipping* [1983]2 Lloyd's Rep 276; *Hong Kong Borneo Services v Pilcher* [1992]2 Lloyd's Rep 593; *Bank of America v Chrismas [The Kyriaki]*, [1993]1 Lloyd's Rep 137.

[95] *Transthene Packaging v Royal Insurance* [1996]LRLR 32.

[96] *Ventouris v Mountain, The Italia Express* [1992]2 Lloyd's Rep 281.

was suggested by the Court of Appeal in *Sprung v Royal Insurance*[97] that the insurer is under an implied contractual duty to make payment within a reasonable time,[98] that the insurer is liable in damages for failure to do so, and that such damages might in principle be awardable for loss of business.[99]

Sprung[100] is supported by earlier *dicta* to the effect that a refusal by the insurer to make due payment is a distinct repudiation of the policy.[101]

In *The Italia Express*[102], the plaintiffs vessel was sunk by explosives attached to it while undergoing repairs and refurbishment near Piraeus. The plaintiff's insurance claim was resisted on the ground of wilful misconduct, until the 37th day of the trial when the Lloyd's underwriters withdrew that defence. The plaintiff in addition to indemnity and interest, claimed damages,[103] not only for the income that would have been earned if the insurance money had been paid on time, but also for hardship inconvenience and mental distress. The judge decided for the underwriters mainly on the basis that s. 67, 68[104] of the Marine Insurance Act 1906 are conclusively definite of the extent of the liability of the insurer for a vessel under a valued policy.[105]

---

[97] [1997] CLC 70.

[98] The insurer is liable to indemnify the assured as soon as he sustains loss no withstanding the accepted customary period for investigation and processing of the claim before payment is actually made.

[99] Although apparently not for distress, as a contract of insurance is not one which has as its specific objective the assured's piece of mind. In that case the assured's loss was held to be caused by his own inpecuniosity and not the insurer's failure to pay in due time (*Ventouris v Mountain, The Italia Express* [1991]1 Lloyd's Rep.441).

[100] [1997] CLC 70.

[101] *Lefevre v White* [1990]1 Lloyd's Rep. 569, *Transthene Packaging v Royal Insurance* [1996]LRLR 32 ;Merkin (1997) (ed) Colinvaux's Law of Insurance, 7th edn, S&M, London, pp 169-172.

[102] [1992]2 Lloyd's Rep 281.

[103] As he was unable to exercise his right of 8,5 days of counteraction in the High Court of England.

[104] Which provide that the measure of indemnity shall be *"...the sum fixed by them"*.

[105] In the *Italia Express* the judge took the view that the insurer's obligation was to prevent the insured from suffering the loss in question and this was broken the very moment the insured did suffer loss. As soon as this happened (by the sinking of the ship) the primary obligation gave rise to the secondary obligation to pay damages. The insured had an immediate right of action the moment the loss occurred, no prior demand was necessary and no subsequent breach was constituted by the underwriter's failure to respond immediately to the de-

The cases of the *Italia Express* [106]and *Sprung*[107] rest, in part, on flawed reasoning. The nature of the insured's remedy tell us little about the nature of the insurer's obligation to indemnify. The English law adopts a conception of the insurer's obligation, indemnity as prevention of loss, which is consistent with having a remedy in damages, but also, equally consistent to conceive of the insurer's obligation as being to indemnify by way of compensation in the event of loss. In the *Italia Express*,[108] Hirst J. thought that s. 67-68 of the Marine Insurance Act 1906 limit the insurer's secondary obligation to pay damages to the assured, rejecting the insured's argument that the sections merely quantified the insured's primary obligation to indemnify.[109]

---

mand for payment. However it would be commercially inconceivable, in a large total loss case like this, as the judge pointed out, that the underwriter would pay in full by post without further investigation. Indeed in case of liability insurance, the insurer is not obliged to pay until the insured's liability is ascertained and determined, even though the insured may suffer measurable economic loss at an earlier time. The insurer has to pay damages and in the *Italia Express* it was stated that this was not referring to non liquidated damages but damages just like any other. The plaintiff was not awarded damages for late payment as there was no separate subsequent breach by the writer's failure to respond immediately to the demand for payment. Damages for distress were not also awarded because although it was well settled that damages in contracts for distress are recoverable *"where the contract which has been broken was itself a contract to provide peace of mind or freedom from distress"*, and this could not apply to a marine insurance contract *"because of the very nature of the contract itself"* , i.e. which is to provide financial indemnity for a commercial loss damage liability and expense, but also because in the majority of marine insurance contracts the assured is not an individual but an insurance company which could never invoke the *"peace of mind"* test.

106 [1992]2 Lloyd's Rep. 281.

107 [1997] CLC 70.

108 [1992]2 Lloyd's Rep. 281.

109 In the US, such conduct of the insurer is called "*the reverse moral hazard*", and for that reason some courts have made them liable for damages, contractual or tortuous, for late payment. In France, the insurer is liable not for damages as such, but for interest , on an escalating scale, i.e. the slower he is the more he pays. (Clarke M (1992) The Nature of the Insurer's Liability, LMCLQ 287).

4.2.2. Total losses and the measure of indemnity in Greece

The insurance of a vessel, i.e. hull insurance, is a positive damages insurance and as such it covers any damage to the vessel or loss of it, as well as liability to third parties due to collision. The measure of indemnity reflects most often the commercial or market value of the ship, as this is dictated by the international trade practice standards and trends. The determining of the value, via the acceptance of the commercial value as per trade usage, has come to be widely accepted within the Greek marine insurance law and practice. Thus, the obstacle of determining the exact true value of the vessel, which changes from time to time, and the consequent over-insurance or under-insurance of the vessel are overcome in this way.[110]

If, due to the assured, the vessel is changed or it deviates from its route, the insurer is not liable thereafter and, as per article 273§1 CPML (ΚΙΝΔ), may keep the premium. However, he is liable for the period up to the change or deviation of route.[111] It has also been accepted by case law that in case of insurance of a vessel, i.e. hull insurance, it can be agreed between the parties that the indemnity will be awarded in Greece, albeit in a foreign currency.[112]

In cargo marine insurance, the measure of indemnity reflects the value of the cargo at the time of loading, costs for loading and unloading, freight costs and the premium. The insurer is also liable for any existing fault even if this has not been disclosed. In case of damage occurred to the insured cargo and not included within the cover provided by the contract, the insurer is obliged to pay full indemnification. Upon occurrence of the peril, the insurer is obliged to indemnify the assured for the damage caused for the period from the loading of the cargo up to the point of its' unloading at the port of destination. Should the assured, upon occurrence of the maritime peril, omit any act towards the interest of the insurer, the latter may seek damages; however, there can be no deduction to the indemnification awarded.[113]

Thus, the measure of indemnity to be awarded is the difference between the value of the subject-matter insured at the time of the accident

---

110 Rokas I (1995) Introduction to the Law of Private Insurance, 4th edn, Oiko nomikon Publications, Athens.

111 Velentzas I (1998) The New Law of Private Insurance, Ius Publ, Athens.

112 *High Court: ΑΠ 1683/84 ΕλΔ 26,650;* Kalantzis AK (1998) Private Insurance Law-Cases and Materials, Nomiki Vivliothiki Edn, Athens 1998.

113 *Piraeus Court of First Instance: ΠΠρΠειρ 1545/1980 ΕΝΔ 9,124.*

and their value at the port of destination.[114] The insurance is held to also include every loss or damage due to an extraordinary event linked to the maritime voyage.[115] Therefore, the omission of the carrier to transport the cargo and the insolvency of the cargo owner are not included within the scope of cover of maritime perils. However, the omission of declaration of a fault at cargo, during loading, does not render the assured liable to the insurer.[116] Moreover, as case law has shown, the assured who sues a petition against the insurer runs the risk of his petition being dismissed as *"non defined"* if he does not clearly enumerate within it the perils covered by the contract, but instead afterwards state the peril occurred and seek whether the latter is covered by the contract.[117]

Marine insurance on freight, covers the loss of freight or part of it due to a maritime accident or event that occurs as a result of exposure to a maritime peril.[118] If the person offering the freight is liable for the freight, i.e. if he bears the risk of safe arrival of vessel and cargo, then the regulations on vessel insurance are applied in case of loss or damage; whereas if the person owing the freight is liable for it, then the regulations on cargo insurance are applied in case of loss or damage. Insurance on future expected freight is also possible to exist.[119]

4.2.3. Total losses and the measure of indemnity in Norway

The assured has a right to a total loss compensation when the ship is in actual total loss, when it is a constructive total loss (i.e. condemnation) and

---

[114] *Salonica Court of Appeal: ΕφΘεσ 250/1984 Αρμ 38,640;* Velentzas I (1998) The New Law of Private Insurance, Ius Publ, Athens.

[115] *Piraeus Court of Appeal: ΕφΠειρ 801/1992 ΕΕμπΔ 1992,462.*

[116] *Athens Court of Appeal: ΕφΑθ 9449/1987 ΕΕμπΔ 1988,310.*

[117] *Athens Court of Appeal: ΕφΑθ 10128/1983 ΕΕμπΔ 35,465; Athens Court of First Instance: ΠΠρΑθ: 10128/1983 ΕΕμπΔ 1984,465;* Velentzas I (1998) The New Law of Private Insurance, Ius Publ, Athens; Apart from cargo insurance, there also exists another type of marine insurance on future profit from the cargo upon its safe arrival at the port of destination and the extra valuation that the cargo gets once having reached its destination. This insurance covers the risk of not achieving the expected profit as an indirect result of exposure to maritime perils (Velentzas I (1998) The New Law of Private Insurance, Ius Publ, Athens)

[118] Rokas I(1995) Introduction to the Law of Private Insurance, 4th edn, Oikonomikon Publications, Athens.

[119] Velentzas I (1998) The New Law of Private Insurance, Ius Publ, Athens.

when it is presumed a total loss. There will be a gradual transition from an absolute loss (i.e. when the ship has foundered in such deep waters that it cannot be reached) to cases where it is a question of economic assessment whether or not to undertake salvage and repair work.[120]

In the Norwegian Marine Insurance Plan, Chapter 4 deals with the insurer's liability. Paragraph 4-1, deals with total loss.[121] The provision establishes the traditional principle in insurance law that the assured, in the event of a total loss, is entitled to claim the sum insured but not in excess of the insurable value. Thus, in the event of a total loss, the insurer's liability is subject to a double limitation: it can neither exceed the sum insured nor the insurable value. The insurable value is set at the full value of the interest at the inception of the insurance, or by agreement between the parties about the assessed insurable value. Normally, the insurable value will have been assessed and be identical to the sum insured. In that case the insurer will, in the event of a total loss, pay the valuation amount. It is, however, important to keep the concepts of sum insured and insurable value apart in the policy, and the policy should therefore specify both the insurable value and the sum insured. In hull insurance for ocean-going vessels, it is presumed that where only one value is given in the policy, the intention is to state both the assessed insurable value and the sum insured.[122]

---

120 No deductions shall be made in the total-loss compensation for unrepaired damage sustained by the ship in connection with an earlier casualty. However, the assured may not in addition claim separate compensation for such damage; this would give him an unjustified gain at the insurer's expense. If the ship is not to be considered a total loss but is repairable, the assured can only claim losses associated with the asset value of the ship as a starting point, and not others such as loss of earnings. This creates problems, as the hull insurer will be interested in choosing the cheapest yard to repair, and the assured will be interested in the quickest possible repair yard. The Norwegian Marine Insurance Plan has considered this and imposes a duty of the insurer to compensate the assured for part of the loss of time he would have avoided by selecting a more efficient repair yard than the most inexpensive. The loss of time is assessed to 20% per annum of the hull valuation. Even where damage is found to be within the scope of the insurer's liability, pursuant to the Norwegian Marine Insurance Plan Paragraph 12, rules regarding ice damage deductions, machinery damage deductions, and a deductible, will cause the assured to bear part of or even the whole of the damage incurred.

121 This paragraph is identical to § 62 of the 1964 Norwegian Marine Insurance Plan.

122 Total losses only occur in those types of insurance that cover an asset belonging to the assured (hull insurance, freight insurance). In a situation where the insurer covers the assured's future obligations (cover of collision liability under the hull insurance), it will merely be a question of the liability of the in-

The insurer is not liable for loss consequent to the ship not being in a seaworthy condition,[123] provided the assured knew or ought to have known of the circumstances. In ND 1973.450 NSC *"Ramfløy"*, the vessel Ramfløy, on a voyage from Lødingen to Raftsund, grounded and suffered significant damage. The insurer refused to pay any compensation on the basis that the ship was unseaworthy, in part because no-one on board had a master's license which was required, and in part because the master had not been mustered and had not undertaken the required health checks and also because the chart onboard was not up to date. The majority of the Supreme Court concluded that the ship was unseaworthy.

In broad terms, a ship is unseaworthy in relation to marine insurance law rules, when it is not in the condition, crewed and equipped, as it should be - in accordance with prudent seamanship - for the voyage to be performed.[124] One must evaluate whether the deficiencies expose the vessel to a greater than normal risk for total loss, or significant damage in relation to the voyage to be performed. Even if the ship is unseaworthy, the insurer is free from liability to the extent that there is a causative link between the unseaworthiness and the loss in question. In the case of Rt 1964.916 *M/S "Havsulens"*, the vessel *M/S "Havsulens"* was lost due to unseaworthiness. As there had been no valid and up to date classification society certificate, the owner was held liable and no insurance claim against the insurer was valid. However, in the case of ND 1967.69 *M/K "Proceed"*, the vessel *"M/K Proceed"* had a leak and eventually sunk. The insurer refused to pay due to unseaworthiness of the vessel owed to the assured, which subsequently lead it to sink. It was held that the leak did not constitute unseaworthiness and even if there had been such a case of unseaworthiness, the assured was not liable as he had acted in good faith.

Performance of repairs is a concept unique and special in the regulation of marine insurance law in Norway. According to their conduct, the assured will be able to recover, as much as this may be possible, a full indemnity covering all aspects of losses he may have incurred. Performance of repairs is necessary, when the ship has sustained damage for which the

---

surer being limited to the sum insured, and only if a sum insured has been agreed. (See Ch. 4§1 Norwegian Marine Insurance Plan (1996) Commentary <http://exchange.dnv.com/nmip/index.htm>.

[123] As per the Norwegian Marine Insurance Plan 1996 § 3-33.

[124] It is a condition for the termination of cover that the assured knew or ought to have known about the defects causing the ship to be unseaworthy, thus the assured must be culpable in this connection. The knowledge must exist at such a time to make it possible for him to intervene, i.e. usually the time that the ship leaves port.

insurer is liable without the rules relating to total loss being applicable The main rule is that the ship be restored into the condition it was prior to the occurrence of the damage.[125] Damage will normally be surveyed by the assured and the insurer as quickly as possible. Since hull insurance only covers the assured's interest in the asset value of the ship, the assured can only claim losses associated with this asset value as a starting point, and not others such as loss of earnings. In reconciling the different interests involved, i.e. that of the hull insurer and the assured, in the choice of repair yard[126] the NMIP has imposed a duty on the insurer to compensate the assured for part of the loss of time he would have avoided by selecting a more efficient repair yard, rather than the most inexpensive, i.e the assured gets a sum corresponding to 20% per annum of the hull valuation. In case of condemnation the assured entitled to claim for a total loss if the cost of repairing the ship will amount to at least 80% of the insurable value. If the ship is undervalued, so that its real value in repaired condition is higher than the assessed insurable value, the *de facto* value shall be taken for a basis. However, even where damage is found to be within the scope of the insurer's liability,[127] rules regarding ice damage deductions, machinery damage deductions, and a deductible, will cause the assured to bear part of or even the whole of the damage incurred.[128]

---

125 Para.12-1, the Norwegian Marine Insurance Plan, Ch.12

126 The insurer will be interested in choosing the cheapest yard to repair, and the assured will be interested in the quickest possible repair yard.

127 Pursuant to the Norwegian Marine Insurance Plan, Ch 12.

128 In ND 1974.103 NSC *"SunVictor"* the insurance policy referred to the Norwegian Marine Insurance Plan but also had a separate deduction clause incorporated establishing a separate deduction of $100.000 calculated for damage arising out of each separate accident, i.e. meaning that a sequence of damages consequent to the same accident shall be treated as due to that accident. The vessel *"SunVictor"* drifted aground in the St. Laurence Canal and in addition to grounding damage when removed, it suffered ice damage whilst grounded and towed to a port of refuge, plus a series of ice damages when transported the next day to Québec to be docked. The insurer maintained that the ice damage maintained after the port of refuge was a new casualty subject to a new deductible. The Supreme Court held that there should be only one deductible as there was causation between the individual accidents of damage and circumstances made it natural to consider the damage as a *"sequence of damages"*.

4.2.4. Total losses and the measure of indemnity in France

In case of hull or machinery insurance, if the insurable value is more than the actual value of the subject-matter insured, a sanction applies. This means that a separate policy has to exist for the excess value, considered as a complementary policy, each of the policies being cumulative for the whole of the amount of insurable value, although the policies in total might exceed the insurable value.

The sanction is also elaborated in that the indemnity character is re-established and the assured -in case of no existing fraud- is only indemnified for any loss occurred reduced to the capital sum of the insurance, according to the rule that indemnity should not be more than the actual or agreed value.

Alternatively, in case of fraud in the initiative of drafting of the excess insurance, the insurance contract is void.[129] If the insurable value is the same as the actual value, then, where the former is lower than the latter the assured is self-insured for the difference. As per art. 10 of the Law of 3/7/1967 and now art. 172-6 of the Insurance Code, if there is overvaluation in the subject-matter insured as a result of fraud, the insurance is void. If overvaluation is not attributed to fraud, the insurance is valid up to the insurable value of the subject-matter insured.[130]

Another type of insurance is insurance upon safe arrival (*assurance sur bonne arrivée*) which is insurance pending on the good and safe arrival of the subject-matter insured.[131] As per art. 42 of the law of 3/7/1967 and now art. L. 173-7 of the Insurance Code, in case of insurance upon safe and good arrival on the subject-matter insured (*assurance sur bonne arrivée*) , the insurable value can be more than the actual value of the subject-matter insured. With null penalty pending, no same insurance can be effected without the insurer's approval. This type of insurance (*assurance sur bonne arrivée)* can only be effected in case of total loss or abandonment, even if the risk is covered by the policy. Insurable interest also has to exist. No abandonment automatically comes within this type of

[129] Art. 10,12 of the Law of 3/7/1967, now art. L.172-6,172-8 of the Insurance Code.

[130] De Smet R (1960) Traité Théorique et Pratique des Assurances Maritimes, Paris, pp 410-424.

[131] Art. 42 of the Law of 3/7/1967 now art. L. 173-7 of the Insurance Code.

insurance neither can the insurer claim abandonment and the rights deriving from it.[132]

4.2.5. Total losses and the measure of indemnity in the USA

Under American Law, in a total loss, the assured is entitled to recover from the underwriter, the whole amount insured by the policy on the subject so lost. The meaning of the term "actual total loss" came before an American Court in the case of *Edinburgh Assurance v. R.L. Burns Corp.*[133]

In relation always to the measure of indemnity, under US law, a plaintiff may be awarded punitive damages under certain circumstances.[134] The rational behind the reasoning for punitive or exemplary damages is not reparative but punishing and preventive, intended to deter potential tortfeasors from continuous misconduct. The punitive or exemplary damages are awarded in addition to compensatory damages. Although not directly related to contractual liability, quasi-contractual terms may include them. The basis of liability is connected with some kind of grossness conduct.[135] Historically, admiralty courts have been reluctant to impose punitive damages and this is reflected in the paucity of case law dealing with the subject. More recently, there has been an increased willingness by the courts, to permit a plaintiff to seek punitive damages. The *Amiable Nancy* [136] involved the tort of a marine trespass, and it is the case that marked the first time that a court recognised the availability of awarding punitive damages in the area of admiralty law. However, the general consensus of a reluc-

[132] Particular average expenses and general average contributions are covered by the insurer (Art. 15 of the Law of 3/7/1967 now art. L.172-11 of the Insurance Code). General Average is dealt with in art. 29 of the law of 3/7/1967 now art. L. 172-25 of the Insurance Code.

[133] 479 Fed Supp 138.

[134] Basically if he establishes that the defendant was "*guilty of gross negligence, or actual malice, or criminal indifference which is the equivalent of reckless and wanton misconduct*". The purpose of imposing punitive damages is to deter and punish wrongful misconduct.

[135] In some states, such as California, malice is required. In others, such as NY, more than gross negligence is required, even if there is no malice. In other States (Florida and Texas) gross negligence will suffice. In Louisiana and Massachusetts, punitive damages are awarded only on the basis of conditions set in state legislation.

[136] 16 US (3 Wheat) 564 (1818)

tance of courts to impose punitive damages is reflected in the following cases. In *William H. Bailey*,[137] an award of punitive damages was sought for damage to an ocean telegraph cable. The court stated that no jurisprudence supported an award of punitive damages for *in rem* actions, and denied punitive damages on the basis that a tort creates a maritime lien or privilege, i.e. a *jus in re*.[138] It also stated that punitive damages would be available, had the suit been *in personam* and had the vessel owner ratified the malicious acts. In the *Seven Brothers*,[139] the availability of punitive damages *in rem* proceedings was recognised , but no such award was made as the *in rem* action was against the owner of the vessel who was not proved to have had any share in or knowledge of the malicious acts. Had he ratified the malicious acts, then, arguably, he would have been liable for punitive damages.[140]

However, representative examples of cases where the Court has held that the insurer is liable for punitive damages, in relation to issues such as bad faith - amidst other issues - are the following: In the case of *State Farm Mut. Auto. Ins. Co. v Campbell*,[141] the insureds brought an action against the automobile liability insurer to recover for bad faith failure to settle within the policy limits, fraud, and intentional infliction of emotional distress. Following remand from the Court of Appeals of Utah,[142] the Third District Court, Salt Lake County, William B. Bohling, J., entered a judgment, based on the jury verdict, in favour of the insureds, but remitted punitive and compensatory damages. Appeal and cross-appeal were taken. The Supreme Court of Utah,[143] Durham, J., reinstated jury's punitive damage award. In the case of *Pacific Mutual Life Insurance Co. v Haslip*,[144] the insureds brought action against a life insurer and the agent for fraud, alleging that the agent continued to accept premium payments from the insureds even though the policy had been cancelled without notice to the insureds. The Circuit Court, Jefferson County, No. CV-82-2453, Charles Crowder, J., entered judgment for the insureds, and the insurer appealed. The Alabama Supreme Court,[145]affirmed. In the Supreme Court, Justice

137 103 F 799 (D Conn 1900).

138 This lien is only as security for actual damages for the wrong done for which the ship herself is bound to compensate.

139 170 F 126 (DRI 1909).

140 Maslanka MP(1980) Punitive Damages in the Admiralty, The Maritime Lawyer Vol V, 21.

141 123 S Ct 1513 , US ,2003.

142 840 P 2d 130.

143 65 P 3d 1134.

144 111 S Ct 1032 , US Ala, 1991.

145 553 So 2d 537.

Blackmun, held that: (1) imposing liability on the insurer under the respondeat superior doctrine was not fundamentally unfair; (2) the common-law method for assessing punitive damages is not *per se* unconstitutional; and (3) the punitive damages assessed against the insurer, although large in proportion to the insured's compensatory damages and out-of-pocket expenses, did not violate due process. In the case of *Aetna Life Ins Co v Lavoie,*[146] *an a*ction was brought charging a health insurer with a bad faith refusal to pay claim. After two remands,[147] the court rendered a judgment, based on the jury verdict, for the insured for compensatory and punitive damages and the insurer appealed. The Alabama Supreme Court,[148] also affirmed.

4.2.6. Total losses and the measure of indemnity in Canada

Regarding the measure of indemnity, a marine insurance contract is one in which the degree of indemnity is agreed upon between the parties or mandated by Statute. In an unvalued policy, it is the amount not exceeding the value of the subject-matter specified in the policy.

4.3. Partial losses and the measure of indemnity

4.3.1. Partial losses and the measure of indemnity in England

In the event of a partial loss, the insured recovers the proportion of the agreed value representing the degree of loss.[149]

---

146 106 S.Ct. 1580 , U.S.Ala.,1986.

147 374 So.2d 310, 405 So.2d 17.

148 470 So.2d 1060.

149 Merkin R (2000)Marine insurance Legislation, LLP, London, annotated s. 27-30 of the Marine Insurance Act 1906.

4.3.1.1. Partial loss of a ship and the measure of indemnity

Where a vessel is damaged but not totally lost, s. 69 of the Marine Insurance Act 1906 envisages three eventualities: firstly, where the vessel is repaired s. 69(1) provides that the measure of indemnity is *"the reasonable cost of the repairs, less the customary deductions, but not exceeding the sum insured in respect of any one casualty"*, thus the assured obtains the reasonable cost or repairs,[150] subject to customary deductions[151]; secondly, if the vessel is only partially repaired, by virtue of s. 69(2) of the Marine Insurance Act 1906, the measure of indemnity is the reasonable cost of such repairs, calculated as in s. 69(1) of the Marine Insurance Act 1906 and it also includes indemnification *"for the reasonable depreciation, if any, arising from the non repaired damage"*, where the assured obtains the reasonable cost of repairs plus depreciation flowing from the unrepaired value subject to a maximum recovery as calculated in the previous subsection. Thus, the assured may not profit from effecting only partial repairs.

It is unclear however, how, in the case of a valued policy, depreciation is to be calculated. In *The Catariba*[152] it was held that depreciation is the reduced value of the damaged vessel as against the insured value. In *Pitman v Universal Marine Insurance Co* [153] it was held that the assured was entitled to depreciation, in the value of the vessel occasioned by the damage, not to the estimated cost of the repairs had they been carried out. The insurer's liability, in respect of depreciation, was to be calculated by determining the proportion of the sound value of the vessel prior to the casualty lost by reason thereof, and by then applying that proportion to the agreed value or to the insurable value.[154] However, under Clause 20 - on non repaired damages - of the International Hull clauses 01/11/2003, the measure of indemnity shall be the reasonable depreciation in the market value of the vessel at the time of termination of the insurance, arising from such non repaired value but not exceeding the reasonable cost of repairs (cl. 20.1.). The underwriter is by no means liable for non repaired damage, in the event of a subsequent total loss of the vessel (cl. 20.2.). Finally, the underwriter is not liable, in respect of non repaired damages, for more than

150 Including docking and surveyor costs.

151 *Ruabon SS Co v London Assurance* [1900] AC 6; *The Medina Princess* [1965]1 Lloyd's Rep. 361.

152 [1997]2 Lloyd's Rep. 749.

153 (1882) 9 QBD 192.

154 Accordingly, the actual total loss should first be determined by subtracting the actual damaged value from the sound value of the vessel, and then be ex pressed as a proportion of the sound value.

the insured value of the vessel at the time of termination of the insurance (cl. 20.3.).

Where the assured elects not to repair and the vessel is not sold as non repaired during the risk, s. 69(3) of the Marine Insurance Act 1906 entitles the assured to indemnification as in s. 69(2) of the Marine Insurance Act 1906. The measure of indemnity recoverable under subsections (2) and (3) cannot exceed the measure recoverable under subsection (1), in case the assured elected for full repairs. Should the assured sell the ship in a non repaired status during the risk, s. 69 of the Marine Insurance Act 1906 is silent, with respect to the measure of indemnity.

4.3.1.2. Partial loss of goods and the measure of indemnity

Where a partial loss of goods occurs, if the policy is unvalued, the measure of indemnity is the insurable value of the part lost as per s. 71(2) of the Marine Insurance Act 1906. Where the policy is valued, s. 71(1) of the Marine Insurance Act 1906 provides for the assured to receive an appropriate proportion of the agreed value.[155] According to s. 56(5) of the Marine Insurance Act 1906 :

"...Where goods reach their destination in specie, but by reason of obliteration of marks or otherwise they are incapable of identification , the loss if any is partial and not total."

This provision codifies the decision in *Spence v Union Marine Insurance Co Ltd,* [156] whereby it was held that while the loss and sale of bales constituted a total loss, the various owners should be treated as tenants in common of the unidentifiable delivered cotton, which could be regarded as subject only to a partial loss. [157] Where goods are delivered in a damaged condition as opposed to a part of the goods being totally lost, depending on whether the policy issued is a valued or an unvalued one, accordingly, the

---

155 Namely the proportion the insurable value of the part lost bears to the insurable value of the whole .

156 (1868) LR 3 CP 427, in which a cargo of cotton was shipped in bales specifically marked to indicate the ownership of each bale. In the course of the voyage, as a result of the wreck of the ship , some bales were lost or so damaged as to require sale and the remainder - all damaged - conveyed to the destination in another vessel. The marks on many of them, were obliterated by sea water, and thus ownership was not identifiable.

157 Each owner was held entitled to a proportion of the value of the cotton lost and of the damage to the unidentifiable cotton. The share of each owner to this compensation was determined by the proportion of the undelivered quantity shipped by him to the whole quantity shipped but not delivered.

measure of indemnity is the proportion of either the sum fixed or of the insurable value, which corresponds to the sum representing the difference which is born, of the gross sound and damaged values at the place of arrival to the gross sound value.[158]

Where there is partial loss of goods and part of it is necessarily sold at an intermediate port, because of unfitness to continue to the destination by virtue of a casualty caused by a covered peril, the Marine Insurance Act 1906 remains silent. It could be estimated that, the insurer should pay for total loss of a part, less the proceeds of sale, whilst expenses occurred in the sale should be recoverable as *"suing & labouring"* charges.[159]

4.3.1.3. Partial loss of freight and the measure of indemnity

In case of a partial loss of freight, the measure of indemnity is such proportion of the agreed or insurable value, as the proportion that the freight lost by the assured bears to the total freight at the risk of the assured under the policy.

The case of *The Main* [160] concerned a policy on returned freight with an agreed value of £5,500. A casualty on the outward voyage delayed the return voyage, the freight rates fell and the vessel ultimately sailed with a total freight of £3,250 of which £925 was paid in advance and earned on shipment. The vessel subsequently being a total loss, the measure of indemnity reflected a reduction in the agreed valuation, so as to take account also of the advance freight not at risk.[161]

---

158 By virtue of s. 71(3) of the Marine Insurance Act 1906: *"Where the whole or any part of the goods or merchandise insured has been delivered damaged, the measure of indemnity is such proportion of the sum fixed by the policy in the case of a valued policy, or of the insurable value in the case of an unvalued policy, as the difference between the gross sound and damaged values at the place of arrival bears to the gross sound value."* The gross damaged value does not include the cost of any necessary conditioning of the goods prior to sale in their damaged state, for, such expenses are recoverable separately as *"suing & labouring*" charges.

159 Bennett H (1986) The Law of Marine Insurance, Clarendon Press, Oxford, pp 378-379.

160 (1894) P 320 .

161 Bennett H (1986) The Law of Marine Insurance, Clarendon Press, Oxford, p 380.

4.3.1.4. General average losses and the measure of indemnity

The essential concept of general average is that losses sustained or expenditure occurred in time of peril and for the common good, should be shared between those interested in the adventure in proportion, according to their shares in the adventure.[162]

From the perspective of the parties to a contract of marine insurance, general average may be divided into two classes. First the assured himself may have directly borne the sacrifice or expenditure, in which case he is entitled not only to the general average contributions from the other interests in the adventure but he can also claim in respect of the loss from his insurer [163] and the insurer can then, if necessary, exercise his rights of subrogation in respect of any outstanding contributions due. Second, if the assured is the beneficiary of another person's sacrifice or expenditure, so as to have become liable to pay a general average contribution, he may recover the amount due from his insurer. [164]

4.3.2. General average losses and the measure of indemnity in Norway

In cases of general average,[165] the insurer will often be liable for losses incurred by measures to avert or minimise loss, in the sense that he is liable to cover the general average contribution imposed on the assured. The insurer[166] is liable for the contributions which according to the rules of general average fall on the interest insured, even if the assured is precluded from claiming contributions from the other participants in the general average adjustment.[167]

---

[162] Bennett H (1986) The Law of Marine Insurance, Clarendon Press, Oxford, Ch 18.

[163] S.66 (4) of the Marine Insurance Act 1906.

[164] See s.66 (5) of the Marine Insurance Act 1906.

[165] §4-8 covers general average. It corresponds to § 70 of the Norwegian Marine Insurance Plan 1964.

[166] Subparagraph 2.

[167] The rule is concordant with the solution in the Norwegian Marine Insurance Plan 1964. The insurance contract has often been taken one step further and what is known as a *"GA-absorption clause"* has been included in the contract. This entails that the hull insurer is liable for losses which would have been recoverable in general average up to an agreed maximum amount in all cases where the assured chooses not to claim contributions from the other interested

In ND 1993.163 NSC *"Faste Jarl"*, the vessel *"Faste Jarl"* went aground because the chief mate was drunk and fell asleep while on duty. The expenses incurred were distributed between ship and cargo under a general average adjustment. Some of the cargo owners refused to pay their share of the contribution allocated to the cargo, maintaining that they had an indemnity claim against the shipowner under the rules of the Maritime Code. The Supreme Court agreed that in accordance to the Maritime Code rules on transport liability, the ship was unseaworthy due to the chief mate's drunkenness and the cargo owners had a claim for an indemnity against the shipowner for their contribution under the general average adjustment.

Using the facts of this case as an example, it follows that the cargo owners, and subsequently cargo insurers, would not have to cover the general average contributions, as these would be set off against the cargo owners' claim for damages. The ship's general average contribution would still be compensated by the hull insurer, unless the assured was guilty of such a blameworthy behaviour that breach of duty of disclosure and care might apply. The loss suffered by the shipowner, as a result of the fact that he could not recover a general average contribution from the cargo owner, was not recoverable by the hull insurer, but only from the ship's P&I insurer.

The main rule should be that once there is a general average situation, the entire settlement shall be effected according to the general ave-

---

parties. This is a clear simplification seen from the assured's point of view, and an explicit clause to that effect has now been included in *subparagraph 3,* see letter (a). This means that the principle will apply regardless of whether an individual agreement has been entered into concerning this question. The application of the rule is, however, subject to the condition that the policy contains a maximum amount for such settlement. As an alternative to cover under the *"GA-absorption"* clause in letter (a), letter (b) instead entitles the assured to claim compensation for the ship's general average contribution, as this appears in a simplified general average adjustment. In that event, the assured will recover the general average contribution that would have been apportioned on the ship, but without any contribution being claimed from the cargo-owner side. However, the assured must choose between a settlement based on the rules in letter (a) or in letter (b). He cannot combine the solutions, e.g., by first claiming compensation within the agreed sum under item (a) for losses incurred, and subsequently the ship's general average contribution under item (b). When deciding whether and to what extent loss, expenses etc. are recoverable under subparagraph 3, it follows from subparagraph 3, second sentence, that the provisions in the York-Antwerp Rules 1994 shall be used as a basis, regardless of what rules the contract of affreightment might contain relating to general average.

rage rules. Exceptions should only be made where there is either an explicit different regulation in the separate insurance conditions, or where the other interests insured have the predominant interest in the relevant measure taken to avert or minimise loss.[168]

4.3.3. Successive losses and the measure of indemnity in England

Where the assured suffers a sequence of partial losses within a policy period, the assured is permitted to recover for each of those losses even if their total exceeds the sum insured under the policy.

This principle, of successive losses, is of general application and is codified in s. 77(1) of the Marine Insurance Act 1906. It is subject, though, to any policy ceiling on aggregate liability in the period or on the number of admissible claims within the period. However, the ambit of s. 77(1) of the Marine Insurance Act 1906, has apparently been restricted in the context of damage to a vessel, by Colman J. in *Kusel v Atkins, The Catariba.*[169] In this case, Colman J., finding for the insurers, stated that their liability was capped at the insured value of the vessel. It was held, primarily, regarding measure under s. 69(3) of the Marine Insurance Act 1906, that in the case of a valued policy the term *"depreciation"* refers to the actual reduced value of the vessel from the agreed value, at the date of termination of the cover and not at the date of the casualty; thus, the assured was restricted to recover either the reasonable cost of repairs or the amount by

168 Ch. 4§12 Norwegian Marine Insurance Plan (1996) Commentary <http://exchange.dnv.com/nmip/index.htm>.

169 [1997] 2 Lloyd's Rep. 749. The insured vessel ran aground in August 1995 and remained beached awaiting repair when in September 1995 she was further damaged by a hurricane. The cumulative cost of repairs from the two separate losses sustained by the assured's vessel, exceeded the insurance value although the separate costs of repairing each loss did not. Although the assured wrote to the insurers asking them to treat the loss as a constructive one rather than two partial losses (due to the fact that the letter was not unequivocal) regardless of the insurers' response the measure of indemnity had to be determined on the basis of two successive losses. The assured based his claim on the principle expressed in s. 77(1) of the Marine Insurance Act 1906 and demanded to recover for the aggregate of those losses, which if taken separately were for a sum less than the policy limits The underwriters relied upon s. 69(3) of the Marine Insurance Act 1906 and argued that the depreciation had to be determined in relation to the insured value of the vessel and that this provided a ceiling on recovery irrespective of s. 77(1) of the Marine Insurance Act 1906.

which the insured value exceeded the actual value of the vessel when the cover terminated, whichever was less.

Secondly, regarding the relationship between s. 69(3) and s. 77(1) of the Marine Insurance Act 1906, that s. 77(1) had an impact only where successive losses were repaired. Thus, if the assured had suffered a loss and had effected repairs and had then suffered another loss, under s.77(1) of the Marine Insurance Act 1906, he would be allowed to recover for both, even if their aggregate exceeded policy limits.

By contrast, as here, where the first loss was not repaired s. 77(1) of the Marine Insurance Act 1906 had no application and the assured was restricted to the measure of indemnity under s.69(3) of the Marine Insurance Act 1906. In *British Foreign Insurance v Wilson Shipping Co*[170], a vessel was insured against marine perils with one underwriter and against war risk under a Special Admiralty Form. It suffered damage that was not repaired and was then torpedoed and finally lost. It was held that the assured could not recover under the marine policy. However, where the partial unrepaired loss is followed by a total loss which occurs after the termination of a risk set in the policy, the assured may recover in respect of the partial unrepaired loss.[171]

4.3.4. *"Sue & labour"* and the measure of indemnity in England

Section 78(4) of the Marine Insurance Act 1906 states that the measures taken by the assured for the purpose of *"suing & labouring"* must be *"reasonable"*. Thus, the assured would have to take into account all the circumstances of the case, when assessing not only whether he ought to take any action but also the course of action - if any is to be taken - for the purpose of averting or minimising a loss. [172] For a claim for *"suing & labouring"* expenses to qualify as such, it need not be quantified on a *quantum meruit* basis.[173]

It has frequently been argued that where a policy of marine insurance does not contain a *"suing and labouring"* clause, the assured should

170 [1921]AC 188.

171 *Lidgett v Secretan* (1871)LR 6 CP 616 ; s. 69(3) of the Marine Insurance Act 1906.

172 *Meyer v Ralli* (1876) CPD 358.

173 As per Lord Justice Stuart-Smith in the case of *Royal Boskalis* [1997]2 All E.R. 929.

still be able to recover for particular charges.[174] In the case of the *Mammoth Pine*,[175] the Privy Council did not go so far as to accept as a general proposition that the mere fact that an obligation is imposed on one party to a contract for the benefit of others, carries with it an implied term that the latter shall reimburse the former for his costs incurred in performance of the obligation. [176]

Finally, even though there has been no relevant case law or any such discussion, it is worth commenting that where the assured, with his actions in case of general average, instead of preserving or not deteriorating the loss of the subject-matter insured actually worsens its condition and in that sense also worsens his position, and also where, in the case of *"sue and labour"*, the extraordinary expenditure instead of resulting into averting or minimising any loss or damage to the subject-matter insured actually has the opposite effect, in those cases, the assured should not be able to claim and recover the amount corresponding to the general average expenditure or sacrifice or to the *"sue and labour"* expenditure, if he acted in bad faith when actually deteriorating the condition of the subject-matter insured. If, however, the assured acted in good faith and as a result of neg-

---

174 *Emperor Goldmining Co Ltd v Switzerland General Insurance Co Ltd,* Sup.Ct (NSW)[1964]1 Lloyd's Rep. 348.

175 [1986]3 All ER 767 (Privy Council).

176 In the context of marine insurance there is a strong argument that without a suing and labouring clause there should be no recovery for minimisation expenses carried out by the insured even though these are considered to be obligatory. The main reason for coming to this view is the difference in wording between s. 78(1) and s. 78(4) of the Marine Insurance Act 1906. Whereas s. 78(1) is conditional in relation to its applicability on there being a suing and labouring clause, s. 78(4) imposes the duty to *"sue and labour"* in all cases, i.e. whether there is a suing and labouring clause or not. However, there may still be room for the implication of a term allowing recovery within the limited ambit of *The Mammoth Pine* or if there is a trade usage or custom to that effect. This view was also reiterated by Millett L.J. in the case of *Baker v Black Sea and Baltic General Insurance Co Ltd* [1996]L.R.L.R. 353 and in the case of *Yorkshire Water v Sun Alliance & London Insurance Ltd* [1997]1 Lloyd's Rep.1. The issue of abandonment and its effects in the law of marine insurance may raise the issue whether the obligation to *"sue and labour"* survives the abandoning of the subject-matter insured. It is clear from s. 63(1) of the Marine Insurance Act 1906 that the insurer has no obligation to take over the interests of the assured upon the giving of the notice of abandonment. There is a strong argument that the subject-matter of the insurance does not become *res nullius* when the underwriter declines to take over the interests of the insured. (Gauci G (2000) The Obligation to Sue & Labour in the Law of Marine Insurance- Time to Amend the Statutory Provisions? IJOSL 2.)

ligence failed to preserve or not deteriorate the condition of the subject-matter insured or not to avert or minimise the loss, he should be able to get indemnified, if he can prove that his actions were based on good faith.

The insurer should be able to be totally disentangled from indemnifying the assured for the sums corresponding to the general average expenditure or sacrifice or *"sue and labour"* expenditure, in case the assured has acted in bad faith. In case the assured has acted with negligence , the insurer's liability should be limited, according to the degree of negligence owed. The assured should bear the burden of proof on that.

4.3.5. *"Sue & labour"* and the measure of indemnity in Norway

Particular measures are taken to avert or minimise loss[177] in case preventive measures are taken and the general average rules are inapplicable.[178]

The situation to justify such measures is a casualty, or a threatened casualty and the measures must be extraordinary corresponding to the nature of the risk. Preventive measures to avoid the loss are also falling under this category and are covered by the insurance. There is no requirement that the person should understand that the measures taken will bring about expenses. In the case of ND 1947.122 D/S *"Justis"*, the vessel D/S *"Justis"* , a fishing steamship, cut its' fishing net during a storm, in order to avert or minimise a loss, so as to prevent the fishing boats from colliding with the ship and to prevent damage to the propeller, making the steamship immoveable. The owner claimed the damages suffered as costs in order to avert or minimise a loss. It was held that the danger existing was not imminent and even as a threatening one, it was nevertheless only to the boats and not actually to the fishing steamship itself, thus, the cutting of the net was not to be considered as a sacrifice and there was no obligation for the hull insurer to pay.The main rule should be that once there is a general average situation, the entire settlement shall be effected according to the general average rules. Exceptions should only be made where there is either an explicit different regulation in the separate insurance conditions or where the other interests insured have the predominant interest in the relevant measure taken to avert or minimise loss. Where a measure to avert or minimise loss is aimed at saving several interests, without the general average rules becoming applicable, there shall be a proportional apportion-

[177] It corresponds to § 68, 69 of the Norwegian Marine Insurance Plan 1964.

[178] § 4-12.

ment of the loss among all of those who have benefited from the measures in accordance with the principles on which the general average is based.[179]

4.3.6. *"Sue & Labour"* and the measure of indemnity in Canada

In Canada, the *"sue and labour"* clauses recognise the principle that an insured must minimise the loss in order to receive an indemnity. While the statutory provision provides that the insured can recover expenses incurred to preserve the subject-matter insured, case law indicates that the assured has a duty to minimise the loss. In *Fudge v Charter Marine Insurance Co*, [180] a fire started on a fishing vessel while at sea. The owner and his brother abandoned the ship and the vessel was carried to shore where it broke up at the base of a cliff. The vessel was a total loss and the owner sued to recover the amount due under a marine hull insurance contract. The insurer denied liability on the basis of material non-disclosure and the failure of the insured to take reasonable steps to avert or minimise the loss.

4.4. Over-insurance and the re-opening of valuation

4.4.1. Over-insurance, under-insurance and the re-opening of valuation in England

The valuation agreed between the underwriter and assured is primarily inviolate, conclusive and cannot be re-opened.

It was in the case of *Loders & Nucoline v Bank of New Zealand*[181] that it was clarified the qualifications set by s. 27(3) of the Marine Insurance Act 1906, under which valuation might be re-opened, i.e. *"subject to the provisions of this Act"* and *"in the absence of fraud"*. Thus, it was suggested that the former qualification referred to s. 29(4), 75(2) of the Marine Insurance Act 1906, whereas the latter formed a warning shot that in case of fraud, not only the valuation but the whole policy may be re-opened and be avoided. S. 29(4) of the Marine Insurance Act 1906 deals

---

179 Ch. 4§12 Norwegian Marine Insurance Plan (1996) Commentary <http://exchange.dnv.com/nmip/index.htm>.

180 (1992)8 CCLI (2d) 252 (Nfld) TD.

181 [1929]33 LL.Rep. 70.

with a floating policy where no declaration of value is made until notice of loss or arrival of the ship or ships. When this is the case, the policy must be treated as an unvalued one. However, in *Union Insurance Society of Canton Ltd v George Wills and Co*[182], the policy did *"otherwise provide"*, with dire results for the assured.[183] The Privy Council ruled that the failure to declare the interest as soon as possible after sail of vessel, was a breach of a promissory warranty, thus the insurers were not liable with respect to the loss.[184] The value agreed between the assured and the underwriters can only be attacked and re-opened in circumstances where the policy itself is under attack as being void or voidable because the subject-matter has been either fraudulently over-valued to cheat the underwriter; it amounts to a gambling policy; or the nature of the risk has become one of speculation, not an ordinary business risk, a fact which should have been, but was not, disclosed.[185]

Although the mere fact that the agreed value in a valued policy exceeds the assured's true loss is no ground for re-opening the valuation, an over-valuation may be fraudulent.

An over-valuation, however, is not necessarily fraudulent. In *Barker v Janson*[186] it was stated:

"... an exorbitant valuation may be evidence of fraud, but when the transaction is 'bona fidae', the valuation agreed upon is binding".

In *Ionides v Pender*[187], in an action on a policy of marine insurance it appeared that the plaintiffs had insured the goods at a value greatly over their real value without disclosing the over-valuation to the underwriter; it was proved in evidence that underwriters do, in practice, act on the principle that it is material to take into consideration whether the over-valuation is so great as to make the risk speculative. It was held that this practice was

---

182 [1915]AC 281.

183 The respondents, G Wills & Co, were merchants with businesses in London and Australia. In February 1911, the respondents effected a floating policy with the appellants, covering all shipment of merchandise up to February 1912. The policy contained a clause which stated that declarations of interest had to be made as soon as possible after the sailing of the vessel to which the interest attaches. As declaration of interest was forwarded by respondents to the insurers only on the day after the loss of the vessel and goods, the insurers refused to indemnify the respondents on the basis that they had failed to comply with what amounted to a promissory warranty.

184 Hodges S (1999) Cases and Material on Marine Insurance Law, Cavendish Publications, pp 203-204.

185 O' May D (1993) Marine Insurance Law and Policy, LLP pp 64-66.

186 (1868) LR 3CP 303.

187 (1874) LR 9 QB 531.

rational; and that it was proper to leave the issue of whether the valuation was so excessive and whether it was material to the underwriter to know of such over-valuation to the jury. The Court of Appeal affirmed the decision of the trial judge and ruled that the plaintiffs could not recover under the policies, because they had failed to disclose the fact that there was an excessive over-valuation.

Blackburn J, characteristically stated:

"... It would be too much to put on the assured the duty of disclosing everything which might influence the mind of an underwriter....but the rule laid down in "Parsons on Insurance, Vol. I, p. 494", that all should be disclosed which would effect the judgement of a rational underwriter... seems to us a sound one...and applying it to the present case, there was distinct and uncontradicted evidence that underwriters do... act on the principle that it is material to take into consideration whether the over-valuation is so great as to make the risk speculative."

In *The Dora*[188], the law as expressed in *Ionides v Pender*[189] was confirmed as not having been altered by the Marine Insurance Act 1906, so that s. 27(3) of the Marine Insurance Act 1906 should be read as subject to the duty of utmost good faith. However, it was held that where an assured insures a yacht for a sum equal to its purchase price, a discrepancy between the insured value and the market value is immaterial.[190]

In *North Star Shipping Ltd and others v Sphere Drake Insurance Plc*[191] the insurers denied indemnity on the ground that the loss was the result of deliberate misconduct by the assured, and it was held in the Court of Appeal that the vessel had been overvalued the agreed value was US$4 million - whereas the actual market value was no more than US$1.4 million - and the disparity could not be explained on ordinary commercial grounds. This was found to be material, as the difference between the insured value and the market value was not consistent with prudent ship management, however the Court of Appeal commented that it may be prudent that the underwriter takes the extra premium rather than investigate whether the good management reasons establish $4 million as opposed to some lesser figure. Fraud in valuation was also addressed in fairly recent cases, marine and non-marine ones. In *Eagle Star Insurance Co Ltd v Games Video Co SA, (The Game Boy)*[192] the finding in *Agapitos v*

188 *Inversiones Manria SA v Sphere Drake Insurance Co Plc (The Dora)* [1989]1 Lloyd's Rep 69.

189 (1874) LR 9 QB 531.

190 In contrast, in *Piper v Royal Exchange Assurance* [1932]44 Ll.L.Rep. 103, it was held that an assured, who failed to disclose that the insured yacht was worth at most half of the value for which it was insured, had broken the duty of utmost good faith.

191 [2006] EWCA Civ 378.

192 [2004] Lloyd's Rep IR 867.

Agnew[193], that a perfectly genuine claim can be lost if it is supported by fraudulent means and devices, was applied. The assured's vessel was lost by what was conceded to be a genuine accident. The assured had stated in the application that its true value was about US$1,800,000, although the true value appears to have been around US$100,000 for scrap. This was of itself enough to allow the policy to be avoided for material misrepresentation, but the effect of a series of documents prepared by the assured after the loss and submitted to the insurers revealed that the true value had been the originally stated US$1,800,000 and that the documents were forged and false. In *Interpart Comerciao e Gestao SA v Lexington Insurance Co*,[194] a cargo of sugar was loaded in Brazil and carried to Turkey, where it was sold contrary to the wishes of its then owners. The cargo owners and their immediate purchasers claimed against the insurers. Cover had been granted by insurers under an open cover, following presentation of a certificate of inspection which had a false shipping date included in it in order to ensure compliance with the contract of sale. The certificate was again shown to insurers as part of the claim. The insurers denied liability on the basis of breach of the duty of good faith by a false document which was presented and also fraud in the claims process by the presentation of a false certificate of inspection. The court refused to give summary judgment to the insurers in respect of either defence.[195] In *AXA General Insurance Ltd v Gottlieb*,[196] the defendants, husband and wife, were insured under a buildings policy. They made four claims in the policy year beginning 31 August 1993, and the insurers made payments in respect of repairs and the cost of finding alternative accommodation while repairs were being effected. Subsequently the insurers discovered that there had been fraud in respect of two of the claims: no costs had been incurred in respect of alternative accommodation; and an invoice in respect of electrical work had been forged. The insurers sought repayment of the sums paid by them in respect of all four claims, and not just the sums paid in respect of the two fraudulent claims. As to the claims tainted by fraud, the Court of Appeal confirmed the principle that if any significant part of a claim was fraudulent, then the entire claim was undermined. On that basis, the entire sum

[193] [2002] Lloyd's Rep IR 573.

[194] [2004] Lloyd's Rep IR 690.

[195] As to the argument that the claim had been promoted by fraudulent means, the judge's view was that there remained uncertainty as to the degree of nexus between the fraudulent conduct and the claim itself, although it was further held that there was no need for the insurers to show reliance on the fraud as the policy of the law was to discourage fraud.

[196] [2005] EWCA Civ 112.

paid in respect of the fraudulent claims was recoverable. In so deciding, the Court of Appeal held that sums paid by to the assured in respect of these claims on an interim basis, and before the fraud had occurred, were themselves recoverable. The rule was that the insurers' liability arose as soon as the loss occurred, and the effect of a fraudulent claim was retrospectively to remove the assured's cause of action from the date of the occurrence of the insured peril. The Court of Appeal noted that if a later fraud tainted a claim in respect of a genuine loss, the entire claim was forfeited. It made no difference that interim payment had been made before the fraud was committed. In *Danepoint Ltd v Allied Underwriting Insurance Ltd,*[197] the assured suffered a fire at its premises, and claimed against its insurers for the cost of repair and also for lost rent. The insurers accepted liability for the repairs, and it was agreed that these would be carried out by a third party at a cost of £83,000 - subject to inspection by the insurers' loss adjusters - but were instead carried out by a different contractor, who submitted interim invoices for £60,000 when work to the value of only £7,500 had been carried out. As regards the rent, the assured asserted that the flats had been vacated immediately after the fire: this was untrue, but the loss adjuster was not given any information to explain why some of the flats appeared to be occupied. Subsequently the insurers denied liability on the basis that the claims were fraudulent. The court held that the insurers were entitled to refuse to pay. As regards the cost of repairs, the court held that there had not been a fraudulent claim: while there had been deceit, misrepresentation and ineptitude this was not enough to treat the claim as fraudulent because the loss adjuster was to inspect the work periodically and accordingly what was said could not be material to the insurers.[198] However, the entire claim was lost by reason of the fraud in relation to the rent.[199]

---

[197] TCC, 20 October 2005

[198] Merkin R Insurance Law Update 2003-2006.

[199] See *Tonkin v UK Insurance Ltd* [2006] EWHC 1120 (TCC) where the court held that fraud in respect of an insubstantial part of the entire claim would not vitiate the entire claim, and that a claim for an excessive sum for the purposes of negotiation was not in any event necessarily fraudulent.

4.4.2. Over-insurance and the re-opening of valuation in Greece

If the object has been overvalued, either of the parties can ask for a reduction of the insured amount to the market value. If the overvaluation was caused intentionally by the insured, the policy is null and void.[200]

The Courts have found that the agreed valuation cannot be substantially higher than the market value of the insured object, otherwise the insurance contract would become a lottery. Article 201 of the Greek Commercial Code, forbidding over-insurance is also applicable to marine insurance for maritime perils.[201]

4.4.3. Over-insurance and the re-opening of valuation in Norway

The insurer may challenge the valuation, even if the person effecting the insurance has given his information in good faith. If misleading information has been given about the properties which are material to the valuation, the valuation will be *"set aside"*. This means that the agreed valuation ceases to be in effect in its entirety, so that the value of the object insured must be determined according to the full value of the interest at the inception of the contract.[202]

Examples of an insurance company attacking the valuation in the policy are to be found in ND 1925.113 and in ND 1960.68. In ND 1925.113 *"Activ"*, the ship *"Activ"* was insured for NOK 60.000. It was damaged by fire and its damage was estimated as NOK 2.500 and the undamaged value at NOK 20.000. The Court, having based its decision on the difference between the real value and the value in the policy, held that this was such a great difference that the insurer could reject the policy value. In ND 1960.68 *"Dyrstad"*, the policy value was NOK 75.000. The

---

200 Spaidiotis K (1999) Marine Insurance Law in Greece, Maritime Advocate, Issue 7.

201 *Supreme Court: ΑΠ (Ολ) 6/1990 NoB 1990.1321*; Velentzas I (1998) The New Law of Private Insurance, Ius Publications, Athens.

202 § 2-2 in the Norwegian Marine Insurance Plan 1996.

ship was damaged by fire alleged by the company to have been caused by unseaworthiness. The Court held that the company had failed to prove unseaworthiness. On the second argument that the true value of the ship was only NOK 25.000, the Court held that it was NOK 48.000 making it such a large difference from the policy value to entitle the company to reject it and pay the lesser sum.

One cannot help noticing the similarity here with that in the English law regime, where the initial valuation is re-opened or else said set aside, in cases of extreme over-valuation of the subject-matter insured or fraud from the part of the assured, when disclosing information regarding the determination of the valuation and the assessment of the risk to be undertaken by the insurer.

The provision regarding cases when the assessed value can be reduced, applies to all types of insurance. The term *"the subject-matter insured"* must therefore be interpreted, in this context, to be synonymous with *"the interest insured"*. Under this provision, the insurer may challenge the valuation even if the person effecting the insurance has given his information in good faith. If misleading information has been given about the properties which are material to the valuation, the valuation will be *"set aside"*. This means that the agreed valuation ceases to be in effect in its entirety, so that the value of the object insured must be determined according to the rule relating to open insurance value in § 2-2 of the Norwegian Marine Insurance Plan 1996, i.e. the full value of the interest at the inception of the contract. In the case of under-insurance, para. § 2-2 of the Norwegian Marine Insurance Plan 1996, maintains the principle of under-insurance if the sum insured is less than the insurable value, which means that the insurer shall merely compensate the part of the loss that corresponds to the proportion that the sum insured has to the insurable value.[203] In case of over-insurance[204], the insurer will only compensate the loss up to the insurable value if the sum insured exceeds the insurable value.

---

[203] Ch.2 § 4 of the Norwegian Marine Insurance Plan (1996) Commentary. <http://exchange.dnv.com/nmip/index.htm>.

[204] Paragraph 2-5 of the Norwegian Marine Insurance Plan (1996).

4.5. Floating policies and open-cover insurance

4.5.1. Floating, open-cover policies and the measure of indemnity in England

Where a series of similar subjects are to be exposed to the same adventure, there is evident administrative advantage in being able to conclude one contract to cover the series.

In consequence, there evolved the *"floating policy"*defined in s. 29(1) of the Marine Insurance Plan 1906 as :

"...a policy which describes the insurance in general terms, and leaves the terms, and leaves the name of the ship or ships and other particulars to be defined by subsequent declaration".

The policy therefore provides cover up to a specified limit which attaches to risks declared by the assured.

A floating policy is a framework agreement under which the insurer agrees to insure subject-matter of a given description which is subsequently at the assured's risk. The cover under such a policy is exhausted when the financial limits are reached and it is common for the assured to arrange a further policy covering excess risks. The assured merely has to declare each risk and when it incepts, the insurer is liable for any loss following declaration. In the absence of any declaration, the insurer is not in risk in respect of that particular subject-matter.[205] The assured has the obligation to declare all eligible cargoes and the insurer has no option to decline a declaration. It follows from this obligatory character of a floating policy, that it constitutes an immediate contract of insurance. The individual declarations do not give rise to separate contracts but merely apply the contracts to particular risks. A floating policy normally insures cargoes up to a specified maximum aggregate value and its capacity is finalised once the aggregate has been attained. The existence of an obligation on the assured to declare all cargoes, within the terms of the cover, prevents the selective declaration of only those cargoes in peril or already the subject of a casualty.[206] Where under the terms of the cover, the insurer has the right to decline a declaration, the agreement may be termed *"facultative"*. In such a case, each declaration the insurer accepts constitutes a separate contract of insurance

[205] *Union Insurance Society of Canton Ltd v Wills & Co* [1916]1 AC 281; Merkin R (2000) Marine insurance Legislation, LLP, London, annotated s. 27-30 of the Marine Insurance Act 1906.

[206] *Rivaz v Gerusi Bros & Co* (1880) 6 QBD 222.

which is concluded at the time of the insurer's acceptance. Declarations under floating policies on cargo, after notice of loss or arrival at destination, must be regarded as having been made under an unvalued policy and the insurance value calculated accordingly as provided in s. 29(4) of the Marine Insurance Plan 1906. In practice, in open covers and floating policies, it is usual to have a clause stipulating the basis on which the value of declarations shall be arrived at.[207]

In *The Beursgracht*,[208] the underwriters, appealed against a decision on a preliminary issue that was liable under a policy providing the party G with open insurance cover against charters' liability. The open coverage was operated by the making of monthly declarations some six weeks after the month to which the declaration referred. A claim had arisen against G in relation to a charterparty which had not been included in any declarations. G had settled the claim and sought from the underwriters the sum paid as well as certain related costs. The trial judge concluded that the underwriter was automatically on risk upon party G chartering a vessel and that the underwriter was not only bound when a declaration had been made by G of the risk to the cover.[209] It was held, dismissing the appeal, that (1) having regard to the contract terms, there was nothing in the wording either expressly or impliedly binding R only in circumstances in which they had received a declaration; the policy was comparable to a floating policy; while the making of declarations was an essential element of the contractual machinery, it was apparent that the purpose of the declarations was for premium calculation; and (2) that there was an implied obligation to make declarations within a reasonable time - but that obligation was not a warranty or condition, rather it amounted to an innominate term which G had breached.[210]

Similarly, in *BP p.l.c. v Frankonova Reinsurance Ltd*,[211] the claimant (BP) claimed on its own behalf and on behalf of 37 co-insureds.[212] The

---

207 O' May D (1993) Marine Insurance Law and Policy, LLP pp 64-66.

208 *Glencore International AG v Ryan (The Beursgracht)* [2002]1 Lloyd's Rep 274.

209 The underwriters argued that (1) the making of a declaration was a condition precedent to liability, and (2) in the alternative, G's failure to make a timely declaration amounted to a breach of warranty or innominate term such as to entitle them to avoid liability.

210 While the judge might have erred in his assessment of the seriousness of the breach, it could not be said that the breach had been sufficient so as to entitle the underwriters to avoid liability. The failure to make a declaration had been due to a good faith mistake.

211 [2003] EWHC 344 (Comm) [2003]1 Lloyd's Rep 537.

nine defendants were either insurance companies[213] or Lloyd's syndicates,[214] each of whom subscribed a slip later superseded by a binder Global Construction Policy[215] led by AIG and SR International Business Insurance Co. Ltd. (SWISS RE).[216] The open cover was a facultative contract in the form of a standing offer whereby the defendants agreed to accept liability in respect of any declarations made within the terms of the cover. BP was free to choose in its own interest which projects to insure under other arrangements (or not at all) and which projects to declare to the open cover. The defendants were bound to accept liability in respect of all BP's declarations which fell within the terms of the cover. The binder/global construction policy was *"scratched"* by AIG and Swiss Re on May 18, 1999 and July 19, 1999 respectively. For offshore projects the period of the open cover (within which declarations could be made) was between Jan. 1, 1999 and June 30, 2000. The claimants contended that 26 declarations were made during this period. BP sought a declaration that the contracts of insurance the subject of the 26 declarations, made under the open cover were valid and subsisting contracts of insurance. The defendants were therefore obliged to indemnify BP and its co-insureds in respect of claims thereunder, and the defendants counterclaimed a number of declarations.[217] On Mar. 15, 2002 Mr. Justice Colman ordered a trial of preliminary issues relating to the meaning of the open cover and the effect of declarations made under it [218] and it was held that (1) with regards to iden-

[212] The co-insureds were various oil and gas entities including some foreign government owned entities.

[213] First to third defendants.

[214] Fourth to ninth defendants.

[215] i.e. the open cover.

[216] The first to seventh defendants subscribed directly. The eight and ninth defendants were bound to it under a broker's cover issued by them to BP's brokers Aon Ltd. (Aon). The defendants represented 41.66 per cent. of the following market subscribing the open cover in respect of offshore project risks.

[217] Including declarations (1) that the defendants were entitled and had validly avoided the open cover and/or each of the declarations 8-26 and/or that upon its true construction declarations 1-26 did not fall within the terms of the open cover and/or were non-contractual and ineffective; and/or the claimants were estopped by convention from contending that each or any of declarations 8 to 26 gave rise to a binding contract of insurance.

[218] The preliminary issues provided *inter alia*: a) on a true construction of the open cover in order for a project to be declared thereunder (i) whether it was necessary for the project to commence during the period of the open cover; (ii) alternatively whether the commencement of the project was irrelevant to the operation of the open cover and whether the declared date of inception of the project risk selected at the claimant's discretion determined the start of the pe-

tifying at what stage of a project could declarations be made to the open cover, this depended on the express terms of the policy and on the basic principles of insurance law; a declaration had to be made during the period of the open cover i.e. in the case of offshore risks between Jan. 1, 1999 and June 30, 2000 [219] ; (2) that at the time of the declaration, the insureds must have had an insurable interest at risk or must have had a reasonable expectation of acquiring such an interest; and the declaration had to be made for an inception date selected at the option of the claimant within the period of the open cover; in addition, that the insurance attached from inception - as declared - in respect of each part, item or portion of the subject matter of the insurance from the time of becoming at risk of the insured; (3) when a declaration was made by the claimant, under the open cover within the terms of the cover to a particular defendant, a contractually binding obligation was created; there was no need for any specific acceptance by the underwriters, but no underwriter was bound until receipt of a declaration by June 30, 2000 ; a declaration under the open cover had to contain certain minimum information including the projects declared and the inception date; (4) if the risk declared was within the terms of the cover there was no need for any specific acceptance by the underwriter; the open cover was a standing offer whereby the defendants agreed to accept liability in respect of any declarations made within the terms of the cover and whenever an

riod of insurance for each project; (iii) whether it was necessary for the declaration to be made (a) no later than 30 days after the project commencement date and/or (b) within the period of the open cover; (iv) whether it was necessary for the declaration to be presented by the claimants or its agent Aon to each of the first to ninth defendants during the period of the open cover or presented to the leader alone during the period of the open cover or whether it was not necessary for it to be presented to any of the defendants during the period of the open cover; b)if the project commencement date was relevant in the context of answers to issues 2(i) to 2(iii) then on a true construction of the open cover when the question was whether a project had commenced for the purposes of insurance, in particular (i) whether a project could commence prior to physical construction of the project commencing and/or any parts or material coming at risk of an insured; (ii) if the answer to 3(i) was negative, whether plans and/or documents and/or blueprints and or renderings and/or specifications and/or contract documents and/or models in connection with a project constitute parts and/or materials for this purpose.

219 Insurance was available under the standing offer contained in the open cover in respect of projects of whatsoever nature; there must therefore have been an identifiable project in existence at the time of the declaration i.e. a project which had reached one or more of the stages/phases including engineering design, manufacture procurement, storage prefabrication, fabrication assembly and construction.

individual declaration was made thereunder, a contractually binding obligation was created between the principal insured and where applicable other insured and the defendants to whom it was declared; (5) the leading underwriters clause was concerned with defining the leader's authority to bind the following market to the policy terms and settlements which the leaders agreed; the leading underwriter's clause was not concerned with declarations to the open cover ; (6) there was no difficulty in practice for a broker to deliver declarations to the whole market; all it required was anticipation of the needs involved and ensuring that the declarations were made in a timely way; there was no need for any specific acceptance by the underwriter of a declaration, but he was not bound until receipt of a declaration within the terms of the cover and declarations could not be made after June 30, 2000 ; (7) there was no market practice or market procedure as alleged by the claimants ; (8) BP was not party to the contract between defendants eight and nine; defendants eight and nine were in the same position as the other defendants and were not bound unless they received a declaration within the terms of the cover by June 30, 2000 ; following agreement by defendants eight and nine to the declaration of the open cover to the London cover - which was a broker's open cover known as Aon Energy Risks cover - the eighth and ninth defendants were in the same position as the other defendants and were not bound by the open cover unless they received a declaration within the terms of the cover by June 30, 2000; (9) Aon was acting on behalf of BP in relation to declarations to the open cover; Aon knew, or should have known, that declarations by BP under the London cover had to be made to all the defendants; (10) the project commencement date was not relevant to the context of the answers to issues 2(i) to 2(iii) ; and (11) the *King Field* project, i.e. declaration 5, had reached the stage at which declarations could be made to the open cover and no valid declaration was received by any of the defendants by June 30, 2000 in the case of the other three projects .

In *Glencore International A.G. v Alpina Insurance Company Limited* [220] the questions of avoidance of the open cover on the grounds of fraud, non-disclosure, and misrepresentation were raised in the Court of Appeal. The dispute arose out of the collapse of Metro Trading International Inc. (MTI) and Metro Oil Corporation (MOC), collectively known as the Metro Group. For some years prior to their collapse, on the one hand MTI had operated a floating oil storage facility and bunker supply business using a number of vessels anchored in the waters off Fujairah. The centre of these operations was the *Metrotank*, a ULCC that had been specially modified for the purposes of fuel oil blending operations. On the other

[220] QB, 20 Nov 2003.

hand, MOC operated a refinery and oil storage facilities at Fujairah for the processing of crude oil and the handling of the resulting products. A number of different oil companies entered into contracts with MTI for the storage of various grades of oil at Fujairah and in some cases they also sold oil held in store to MTI for use in its bunker supply business. Of these by far the largest depositor in terms of the quantities of oil delivered into storage was Glencore International A.G. (GLENCORE). GLENCORE and other companies also entered into agreements with MOC for the processing of crude oil under which they were entitled to receive refined products in return for the feedstocks they supplied. MTI supplied bunkers to ships calling at Fujairah and from time to time also sold cargoes of bunker fuel, mainly for export to the Far East. When the Metro Group collapsed GLENCORE and the other depositors discovered that the quantity of oil held in the floating storage facility was far smaller than ought to have been the case.

The litigation in this case was so complex that it was divided in five phases. GLENCORE made a claim against its insurers in respect of the loss of oil that had been delivered to MTI for storage but was no longer in its possession and could not be accounted for and a similar claim in respect of refined products that MOC had produced under the processing agreement between them but were likewise no longer in its possession and could not be accounted for. Phase 5 of the litigation, concerns the claim of GLENCORE against its insurers, Alpina Insurance Co. Ltd (ALPINA) and certain other insurers in the Swiss market, in respect of oil misappropriated by MTI from the floating storage facility at Fujairah and refined products derived from feedstock delivered under its processing agreement with MOC which are said to have been misappropriated by MOC. The insurances were open cover insurances. For many years GLENCORE had made use of open covers in connection with its commodity trading activities, for the purposes of insuring goods in transit, because of the flexibility entailed in such an insurance as per which goods in transit falling within the terms of the cover are automatically insured as soon as the policyholder acquires an interest in them.[221] From the early 1980's GLENCORE's open cover in respect of oil and oil products was placed in the London

[221] Open cover provides the flexibility and continuity of cover which are essential to enable a large trading organisation to carry on business in the modern world. Commerce could not function efficiently if traders handling any significant volume of business had to negotiate separate terms for each individual shipment. Open covers also provide benefits for underwriters because they enable large numbers of similar risks to be underwritten without the need for individual presentations.

market through the brokers Lloyd Thompson. Over the years the policy wording developed in response to changes in the nature of GLENCORE 's business but the underlying philosophy throughout was to procure a broad and flexible contract providing cover against all risks of loss and damage to oil in which GLENCORE acquired an interest wherever it was situated. As the insurers were aware, GLENCORE's involvement in the purchase and sale of crude oil and products was solely as a trader; it did not participate either in the production of crude oil or in the final distribution of products. As might be expected in these circumstances, the contract was worded in very broad terms, i.e. in the form of a marine open cover in favour of GLENCORE and its associated and subsidiary companies and other interested parties for whom they might receive orders to insure. It provided cover on four different bases at the insured's option, that which was most commonly used being based on the American Institute Cargo Clauses. To these basic conditions was added a large number of general conditions dealing with various aspects of the business insured. Subject to the insured's right to choose the basis of cover, the contract was obligatory on both sides as regards transit risks. The policy ran for 12 months from 1st April each year and two conditions which formed part of the 1993-1994 London market cover retained as part of the cover in subsequent years, thus having assumed particular importance in the present case.[222] In December 1993 GLENCORE entered into arrangements with MTI for the purchase and storage at Fujairah of four or five parcels of Iranian fuel oil. The vessel *Mount Athos* was chartered by MTI specifically for the purpose of holding these cargoes, but although the arrangements were made in December 1993, it was not until March 1994 that GLENCORE approached Lloyd Thompson for confirmation that the oil held on board the *Mount Athos* was insured under the open cover. Rate was to be agreed. One of the other leading underwriters agreed to hold GLENCORE covered subject to receiving information about the vessel's mooring arrangements. In the event MTI stopped using the *Mount Athos* to store oil before any rate had been agreed and the vessel left Fujairah on 16th May 1994. On 7th June un-

[222] They are as follows:
"1.15 Cover to attach from the time the Assured becomes at risk or assumes interest and continues in transit and/or store (other than as below) or wherever located and until finally delivered to final destination as required...
1.18 Including, if required, storage and blending prior to shipment or after final discharge in Land Tanks, Refineries, and storage in barge(s), irrespective of whether transit covered hereunder subject to Policy terms and conditions but excluding loss and/or damage caused by faulty blending on amount at risk at particular location involved at Additional premium of 0.015% each 30 days or pro-rata in excess of first 30 days if transit covered hereunder, otherwise, 0.015% each 15 days or part thereof."

derwriters scratched another indorsement by which they noted that GLENCORE would be using the *Metrotank* as floating storage for oil to the value of approximately US$80 million per annum and agreed to provide cover at a flat annual premium of US $20,000. The information provided to the underwriters at the time and noted on the indorsement indicated that GLENCORE expected a total volume of 1 million tonnes of oil to be put into storage at Fujairah with a throughput of approximately 85-90,000 metric tons a month. No further reference to floating storage at Fujairah appears to have been made until the end of February 1995 when there was an advising that the *Mount Athos* was again being used to store a quantity of fuel oil and asked that she be added as a named vessel to the addendum covering the *Metrotank*. Underwriters scratched an indorsement dated 1st March giving effect to that request. ALPINA's underwriter received an approach from the broker responsible for GLENCORE's account, who enquired whether ALPINA would be interested in writing the GLENCORE oil open cover. On 26th January the general terms on which ALPINA would be willing to consider writing the cover were indicated and attention was drawn to the fact that ALPINA would wish to delete certain clauses from the existing terms. The negotiations were ultimately successful and the ALPINA open cover came into force with effect from 1st April 1995. The policy was written on the same terms as the expiring Lloyd's and London market cover, including clauses 1.15 and 1.18 but it made no express provision, however, for oil held in the floating storage facility at Fujairah. On 3rd April there was notification that the *Metrotank* and the *Mount Athos* were again being used to store fuel oil. GLENCORE calculated that there would be a combined throughput of approximately 1.75 million metric tons a year with an insured value of US$125 per ton. They suggested flat annual premium say USD 50,000 and awaited confirmation to this effect. By an indorsement dated 7th April 1995[223] ALPINA agreed to extend cover to oil on board the *Metrotank* and *Mount Athos* in accordance with condition 1.18 at an 'in full' premium of US$50,000 and the matter rested there until 14th September 1995 when ALPINA signed a further indorsement noting that GLENCORE occasionally made use of one or two storage tanks at Fujairah terminal when the storage vessels were nearing capacity or for other operational reasons. Two further endorsements, dealing with floating storage at Fujairah, followed in January 1996. In the first, ALPINA noted that, where it was not possible for logistical reasons for GLENCORE to use land tanks for additional storage, cargoes might remain on board the carrying vessel pending delivery into dedicated floating storage and agreed that cover for that period would be deemed in-

---

[223] Subsequently reissued in identical terms on 18th October 1995.

cluded in the marine rate in accordance with clause 1.18. When the policy was renewed for the year beginning 1st April 1996 the endorsements relating to oil in store at Fujairah were replaced by a new clause, condition 1.29, which was in fact a new provision which, although it was following quite closely the language of the endorsements, in some respects differed from them and extended the scope of the cover. When it came to renewing the cover for the year beginning 1st April 1996 GLENCORE failed to provide any estimate of throughput for the coming year and did not provide any information about the quantity of oil that had passed through the facility during the expiring year or the year before that. The policy for the 1996-97 year was extended by agreement to 30th June 1997. Negotiations for the next renewal therefore took place rather later than in previous years, during which no information was given about the actual throughput in 1996-97 or any previous year. The open cover was renewed on substantially the same terms, including condition 1.29.

Although there remains a dispute as to the precise extent of GLENCORE's losses, it is clear that during 1997 and the early weeks of 1998 MTI misappropriated large quantities of oil that it was holding in store for GLENCORE. It is also clear that during the same period some cargoes carried under bills of lading made out to the order of GLENCORE were diverted by MTI to other destinations after the carrying vessel had reached Fujairah, sometimes without any part of the cargo being discharged. GLENCORE contended that MTI and MOC together have misappropriated various quantities and grades of oil with a total value in excess of US$250 million and sought to recover that loss from ALPINA under the open cover. ALPINA declined liability for the losses claimed by GLENCORE on a number of different grounds, such as ' fraud', 'misrepresentation and non-disclosure'.

The Court, in reaching it decision felt the need to address those issues. In relation to fraud, the Court noted the following: GLENCORE first notified ALPINA of a claim under the open cover on 9th February 1998, and a little over two months later, GLENCORE submitted its formal claim under the open cover. The claim proceeded on the footing that the quantities and grades of oil that had been lost were represented by the difference between the quantities that GLENCORE had discharged into storage and the quantities that it had sold to MTI or withdrawn for its own purposes. From an early stage in their relationship GLENCORE sold parcels of oil held in storage at Fujairah to MTI by what became known as *"ITT contracts"*. Such contracts provided for payment by letter of credit against the issue of a stock transfer certificate evidencing the passing of title to the oil in question. However, the course of dealing between GLENCORE and MTI was such that oil sold to MTI under an ITT contract was released to

MTI on the *"ITT date"*, i.e. the deemed stock transfer date for payment purposes, which was some time ahead of the date on which GLENCORE actually received security for the payment of the price in the form of a letter of credit. Furthermore, in the course of the litigation, it became apparent that a few parcels of bunkers and one parcel of naphtha had left Fujairah after the collapse of the Metro Group during a period in which GLENCORE was controlling MTI's operations at Fujairah. They included a parcel of fuel oil shipped on the *Horizon XII* which is the subject of a dispute between GLENCORE and ALPINA. ALPINA took the view that those at GLENCORE who had been responsible for formulating the claim must have been aware of the way in which GLENCORE had done business with MTI and could not honestly have believed that oil released to it pursuant to ITT contracts had been wrongfully taken. It also took the view that they must have known that the parcels of fuel oil and naphtha that were shipped out during the period in which GLENCORE was controlling the Metro Group's activities in February 1998 had been disposed of with its authority and had not been wrongfully taken. Accordingly, in July 2002 ALPINA amended its particulars of defence to allege that GLENCORE had dishonestly exaggerated its losses or had dishonestly sought to enhance the prospects of obtaining a recovery under the policy. However, at the close of GLENCORE 's case, during which all those who were directly concerned in the formulation of the claim under the open cover had given evidence, ALPINA informed the court that they did not wish to pursue the allegations of fraud made against GLENCORE and abandoned that part of its defense.

In relation to the issues of misrepresentation and non-disclosure, ALPINA has purported to avoid the policies for both the 1996-97 and 1997- 98 policy years on the grounds that GLENCORE failed to disclose, or misrepresented, the throughput at Fujairah, failed to disclose various aspects of its relationship with MTI, failed to disclose that MTI was conducting blending operations at Fujairah and indeed made a positive misrepresentation that no blending of its oil was taking place there. More particularly, in relation to the duty of disclosure, the Court noted that the insured is bound to disclose all matters known to him that are material to the risk the insurer is being asked to accept and it follows, therefore, that the scope of his duty of disclosure is to be determined by reference to the subject matter of the proposed insurance. The primary risk that ALPINA was being asked to assume was that of loss of or damage to goods in transit, but, as is common in insurances of this kind, the policy also extended to goods in store, both prior to shipment and after discharge at their final destination. Moreover, since in the present case the policy also extended to goods in store which had not been, and were not intended to be, the subject of an insured transit, the range of risks that the insurers were being asked to assume included the risk of loss of and damage to goods in store generally. Two aspects of the risk that was presented to ALPINA were particularly significant, i.e. the extremely broad scope of the proposed cover which extends to transit by land, water, air and pipeline from any place in the world to any place in the world and the nature of the insured's business. GLENCORE is, and was known by ALPINA to be, one of the largest independent traders in crude oil and products with interests all over the world. A successful commodity trader must take advantage of market opportunities as and when they arise; he must also be prepared to be innovative in the ways he does business. An insurer who is asked by a commodity trader to provide an open cover on goods must be taken to know that. ALPINA submitted that even though the insurer may have agreed to accept a very wide range of risks which on the face of it would allow the insured to conduct his business in a variety of ways, some less hazardous, some more so, the insured was under a duty to disclose any specific plans he might have to conduct his business in one of the more hazardous ways. GLENCORE submitted, on the other hand, that an insurer who has agreed to provide cover to a trader in terms as broad as those of the present policy must be taken to be aware of the whole range of different ways in which such a person may ordinarily be expected to conduct his business. The insured need not, therefore, disclose the fact that he plans to trade in a way that will expose the insurer to greater risk, provided that what he intends to do does not fall outside the range of possibilities that the insurer ought to have in mind. ALPINA also submitted that even where the insurer accepts a range of risks, the insured must still disclose the fact, if it be the case, that he intends to act in a manner that will expose the insurer to a risk at the more hazardous end of the range that he is being asked to undertake.

However, following also *Harrower v Hutchinson,*[224] *Cheshire v Thompson*[225] and *Property Insurance Co Ltd v National Protector Insurance Co Ltd*[226], it is right to say that when an insurer is asked to write an open cover in favour of a commodity trader he must be taken to be aware of the whole range of circumstances that may arise in the course of carrying on a business of that kind. In the context of worldwide trading the range of circumstances likely to be encountered is inevitably very wide. That does not mean that the insured is under no duty of disclosure, of course, but it does mean that the range of circumstances that the prudent underwriter can be presumed to have in mind is very broad and that the in-

---

224 (1870) LR QB 584.

225 (1918) 29 Com Cas 114.

226 (1913) 108 LT 104.

sured's duty of disclosure, which extends only to matters which are unusual in the sense that they fall outside the contemplation of the reasonable underwriter familiar with the business of oil trading, is correspondingly limited. It also means that the insured is not bound to disclose matters which tend to increase the risk unless they are unusual in the sense just described. These are important considerations to bear in mind when considering condition 1.29 and the storage of oil at Fujairah because there is a natural temptation in the light of what subsequently occurred to approach the question of disclosure as if oil in store there had been the subject of a separate policy. GLENCORE accepted that none of the vessels making up the floating storage facility could properly be described as *"barges"* and that condition 1.18 was therefore not apt to cover oil held there.

It follows, therefore, that oil held in the facility was covered during the 1995-96 year only under the endorsements and during subsequent years only under condition 1.29 and to that extent it can be said that that condition provided separate cover in respect of a specific risk.

However, it would be wrong to view those provisions in isolation from the remainder of the cover. As their wording indicated, condition 1.29 and the endorsements that preceded it merely extended the cover provided under condition 1.18 to oil held in floating storage at Fujairah and must be understood in that light. As such it represented a small part of the risks covered by the open cover as a whole.

The primary ground on which ALPINA purported to avoid the open cover was that GLENCORE failed to provide proper information relating to throughput at Fujairah, both as to the volume expected to pass through the facility during the coming year (*"estimated throughput"*) and the volume of oil that had passed through it in previous years (*"historic throughput"*). ALPINA submitted that both were material matters which ought to have been disclosed at the time of the original presentation in April 1995 and at the time of renewal in 1996 and 1997 and that in the light of the circumstances surrounding the renewal in March 1996 GLENCORE had impliedly represented that the estimate given almost a year earlier remained good for the coming year. In fact, however, no one appears to have given any thought to the question, but the volume of oil being shipped into Fujairah by that time suggests that if a fair estimate of throughput had been given the figure would have been greatly in excess of that given the year before. The most significant feature of the cover on oil in store at Fujairah in the present case is that insurers were content to charge an 'in full' premium based on an estimate of annual throughput. That meant that the premium was fixed once and for all by reference to the insured's estimate of throughput and that the insurers were precluded from charging a premium proportionate to the actual risk if the throughput turned out to be significantly higher than the estimate they had been given. Equally, of course, the insured ran the risk of paying an inflated premium if throughput fell significantly below his estimate.[227]

Given the inherent variability of the market and of the nature of an oil trader's business, the Court concluded that it was not possible to draw any conclusion from the fact that the estimate given at the beginning of the year does or does not prove to have been accurate by the time the year reaches its end. An underwriter prepared to write a risk of this kind for an *"in full"* premium based on the insured's estimate of throughput is taking a gamble which cannot be justified in ordinary underwriting terms but may be justifiable on purely commercial grounds as part of a much larger contract. In the present circumstances historic throughput is immaterial to an underwriter considering accepting a risk of this kind on these terms.

ALPINA must be presumed in the present case to have had sufficient knowledge of historic throughput from the information contained in the declarations bordereaux. The declarations bordereaux were sent to ALPINA for underwriting purposes and were reviewed on a regular basis, albeit briefly, by members of the underwriting department. ALPINA must be presumed to have been aware of the individual items of information contained in them. However, it does not necessarily follow that it is to be presumed to have had the kind of information that would be gained only from an extended analysis of the bordereaux over the whole of the previous seven months. Storage risks at Fujairah were just one aspect of the contract and at that time were not regarded as of particular importance. It is not fair to accept that an underwriter of an open cover like this could reasonably be expected in the ordinary course of business to carry out an investigation of that kind into one particular area of the cover or that the

[227] Due to the nature of an oil trader's business, the market value of most, if not all, traded commodities fluctuates over the course of time, and may sometimes change quite rapidly in the space of a few days. Even if the insured were able to estimate with a high degree of accuracy the quantity of goods likely to pass through a given storage location during the policy year, any estimate of throughput in terms of value would be liable to falsification by movements in the market. In the case of a commodity trader, however, any estimate of throughput in purely quantitative terms is inevitably prone to unreliability because the nature of trading is essentially opportunistic. Although the nature of the business may be broadly predictable at a certain level, it is highly unpredictable at the level of individual contracts which are made in response to specific opportunities. An underwriter familiar with this kind of trade ought to be aware that the unpredictable nature of the business would render any estimate of throughput at any given storage location prone to unreliability, as Alpina's underwriters in fact were.

insured is entitled to assume that he has done so. Therefore, in this case ALPINA is not to be presumed to have been aware from the declarations bordereaux that the level of throughput in the 1995-96 policy year was significantly higher than the estimate it had been given or that if GLENCORE would otherwise have been under an obligation to disclose historic throughput ALPINA had waived such disclosure. However, even if the historic throughput was material after all, if the actual throughput for 1995-96 had been disclosed ALPINA would have declined to renew on the same terms. In accordance with the practice of the Swiss insurance market the co-insurers were content to follow ALPINA in relation to the underwriting of this part of the cover without expecting to be separately consulted. Same in 1997 ALPINA most probably would not have declined to renew the cover on the same terms if there had been disclosure of throughput in earlier years.

In relation to the issue of non-disclosure, if ALPINA was to be invited to renew cover on oil in floating storage at Fujairah at an *"in full"* premium, GLENCORE's estimate of throughput for the coming year was material and should have been disclosed. GLENCORE's current estimate of throughput at Fujairah for the coming year was plainly a matter that would influence the judgment of a prudent underwriter in deciding whether to accept the proposed premium or demand a higher one.

In relation to the issue of misrepresentation, by proposing that cover be renewed at the same premium as under the expiring policy GLENCORE was impliedly representing that its estimate of throughput was substantially the same as that which had been given the previous year. This representation was false.[228]

In relation to the issue of inducement, the evidence does not suggest that ALPINA's underwriters understood that GLENCORE was saying that its estimate of throughput at Fujairah in the coming year was the same as the estimate it had given in 1995, much less that the decision to renew was affected by any understanding to that effect. In those circumstances there is no basis for concluding that the misrepresentation induced ALPINA to enter into the contract. The fact that ALPINA was willing to write the Fujairah risk for an *"in full"* premium based on estimated throughput in the first place suggests that it was willing to treat it as a commercial concession and a sum of that amount would not have been regarded as sufficiently important in the ultimate analysis. Thus, it is not

---

228 Because no one at Glencore had turned his mind to the question of throughput for the coming year. If anyone had been asked to give such an estimate it is likely that it would have exceeded that given in April 1995 by a substantial margin.

possible to accept that GLENCORE's failure to provide an estimate of throughput for the coming year entitles ALPINA to avoid the cover for the 1996-97 policy year.

In relation to the renewal of the policy for the 1997-98 year ALPINA's case was that there was once again no mention of throughput and they proceeded on the basis that the estimate given in April 1995 continued to hold good for the coming year. GLENCORE accepted that nothing was said in the course of the renewal negotiations about historic throughput, but maintained that in the course of the meeting ALPINA was told that GLENCORE's estimate of throughput for the 1997-98 policy year was 7 million tons with a value of US$840 million. The duty of disclosure requires the insured to place all material information fairly before the underwriter, but the underwriter must also play his part by listening carefully to what is said to him and cannot hold the insured responsible if by failing to do so he does not grasp the full implications of what he has been told. Although ALPINA's underwriters say that it was a matter of importance to them to charge a premium for cover at Fujairah at a rate appropriate to the risk, it is not hard to believe that they viewed it in that way at the time, because if they had it would be unlikely that they would ever have agreed to write the cover for an 'in full' premium based on an estimate of throughput. Thus, the figure of US$840 million was expressly stated, albeit may be in an indirect manner amidst other things. However, that does not imply that the figure was not put fairly before ALPINA.

In relation to the nature of GLENCORE's relationship with MTI, none of the individual matters of which ALPINA complain were so unusual that they fell outside the range of possibilities that a prudent underwriter writing this policy could be expected to have taken into account.

In relation to the issue of inducement, ALPINA contended that GLENCORE failed to disclose that oil to which it had title or which was at its risk might be blended while in storage with MTI and positively misrepresented that cargoes discharged into the custody of MTI at Fujairah were not subject to any risk from blending. In the event, when ALPINA agreed to extend cover to oil in floating storage at Fujairah it did so expressly in accordance with condition 1.18, as Lloyd's underwriters had done before it. Condition 1.18 covers physical loss of or damage to oil in the course of storage and blending, although losses caused by faulty blending are expressly excluded. GLENCORE submitted that since ALPINA agreed to accept the risks of blending, GLENCORE was under no duty to disclose the fact that blending might take place. For that reason alone, the case based on non-disclosure must fail. The argument based on misrepresentation raises different issues, however, because if a positive statement was made that there was no blending of GLENCORE's oil, that might make an underwriter less concerned about extending the relatively broad form of cover provided under condition 1.18 to that particular location. GLENCORE submitted that even if there was a misrepresentation in relation to blending, it was not material in the light of the fact that ALPINA did actually agree to cover losses sustained in the course of blending. Because ALPINA's complaint relates only to the blending of oil in which GLENCORE retained an interest, the question, therefore, is whether a statement that none of GLENCORE's oil was expected to be blended at Fujairah was material. The test of materiality in relation to misrepresentation is the same as for non-disclosure, namely, whether the statement in question would influence the judgment of a prudent underwriter in fixing the premium or deciding whether to accept the risk. The court expressed no view in whether the prudent underwriter would have entirely disregarded a statement of this kind when deciding whether to extend the cover, because it is possible that the increased handling involved in the blending process might be seen as enhancing the risk of physical loss. Always in relation to the question of inducement, although neither of the underwriters had reminded themselves in any detail of the correspondence passing between ALPINA and the brokers (in March and April 1995) nevertheless, the fact is that there was a clear willingness to follow Lloyd's underwriters by extending cover on the terms of condition 1.18 at a commensurate premium, regardless of the fact that there was no statement; thus, the insurers are not entitled to avoid the contract on this ground. For all the above given reasons, the court ruled that none of the grounds on which ALPINA sought to avoid the open cover have been established. It follows, therefore, that ALPINA and its co-insurers were not entitled to avoid the open cover for either the 1996-97 or the 1997-98 year. We note that the courts have shown the tendency to be flexible and assert no responsibility for indemnification in cases where there has been actual fraud, non disclosure or misrepresentation; nevertheless, the criteria employed by courts in order to establish such a case or not in favour of the insurance companies remain strict and rigid, especially in case of open cover floating policies which – by their nature – offer more grounds to the insurers for avoidance of indemnification.

A distinction between oblige contracts (*Beursgracht*)[229] and facultative or oblige contracts (*Alpina*)[230] should be made at this point. In *The*

229 *Glencore International AG v Ryan (The Beursgracht)* [2002]1 Lloyd's Rep 274.

230 *Glencore International AG v Alpina Insurance Company Limited*, QB, 20 Nov 2003.

Beursgracht,[231] the insurers contended that the declaration required had not been made within a reasonable time as it had been made five years after the event giving rise to the claim, and they asserted that the need for declarations to be made timeously was an implied term of the contract having the status of a warranty and that the delay in making the declaration was due to bad faith on the assured's part entitling the insurers to consider that they had never come on risk. The court held that the cover note did not expressly provide that time was of the essence for the giving of notices and that the continuing and existing obligation to correct errors and omissions in declarations was not a condition precedent to the contract, hence there was no requirement for declarations to be made within a reasonable time. Similarly in the Court of Appeal, the trial judge concluded that the underwriter was automatically on risk upon the chartering of a vessel and his liability was not limited to cases where a declaration of the risk to the cover had been made.

Nothing in the contract wording was limiting the insurers liability only in circumstances in which they had received a declaration and although declarations were essential their main purpose was held to be that of serving as an aid to premium calculation and that the implied obligation to make declarations within a reasonable time was not a warranty or condition upon which the insurer could rely and avoid indemnification liability.

In *Alpina*,[232] GLENCORE had used for years open cover policies in connection with its commodity trading activities, because of their flexibility and the hidden in them philosophy to procure a broad and flexible contract with cover against all risks of loss and damage to oil in which GLENCORE acquired an interest, wherever it was situated. Although the contract was worded in very broad terms, these were justified by the nature of the trade involved and the insurers were bound to know and accept the flexibility and broadness entailed in such a contract for the specific business concerned. The claim that GLENCORE had dishonestly exaggerated its losses or had dishonestly sought to enhance the prospects of obtaining a recovery under the policy was not valid because although the primary risk under this policy was that of loss of or damage to goods in transit, moreover the policy also extended to goods in store both prior to shipment and after discharge at their final destination. Since the policy also extended to goods in store which had not been the subject of an insured transit, the range of risks assumed to be included in the insurance also involved the

231 *Glencore International AG v Ryan (The Beursgracht)* [2002]1 Lloyd's Rep 274.

232 *Glencore International AG v Alpina Insurance Company Limited*, QB, 20 Nov 2003.

risk of loss of and damage to goods in store generally. The insurers were bound to know that in this situation the scope of the proposed cover was extremely broad and the peculiarity of the nature of the insured's business. Even if there had been a statement that none of GLENCORE's oil was expected to be blended at Fujairah , ALPINA would still have taken the loss and the court felt that this could not have been taken as material in accepting the risk. Because of the nature of the specific trade and in relation always to the practice followed by GLENCORE throughout the years and the broadness of the construction of the terms of the specific policy, there was no specific duty to declare the possibility of a greater risk through a certain operation – such as blending – the risk had attached and GLENCORE was not liable for declaring the hazardous operation of blending after the loss had occurred.

In the case of oblige contracts (such as the case of *The Beursgracht* [233]) the risk attaches automatically so that there is no need for declaration or disclosure. In *The Beursgracht*,[234] the open coverage was operated by the making of monthly declarations some six weeks after the month to which the declaration referred. Nevertheless, time was held to be immaterial , there was no need for declaration for the risk to attach, hence the latter was considered to attach automatically although time considerations were important for amending purposes in relation to the cover offered. In the case of facultative or oblige contracts (such as the case of *Alpina*[235]) the risk does not attach automatically and there has to be some conduct on the part of the assured to make it attach. One of the key issues in *Alpina*[236] was whether this could be done after loss; however, factors such as the nature of the specific trade, the practice followed by GLENCORE throughout the years and the broadness of the construction of the terms of the specific policy meant that no specific conduct was in this case expected and GLENCORE had done nothing wrong in not obviously declaring the greater risk entailed in the operation of blending. The nature and extent of the cover provided was interpreted to include such a basis that the risk would attach even after the actual loss.

---

[233] *Glencore International AG v Ryan (The Beursgracht)* [2002]1 Lloyd's Rep 274.

[234] *Glencore International AG v Ryan (The Beursgracht)* [2002]1 Lloyd's Rep 274.

[235] *Glencore International AG v Alpina Insurance Company Limited*, QB, 20 Nov 2003.

[236] *Glencore International AG v Alpina Insurance Company Limited*, QB, 20 Nov 2003.

4.5.2. Floating, open-cover policies and the measure of indemnity in Greece

Under the Greek law regime, as well, *"open cover"* insurance covers the insurance of cargo up to a limit, for a certain time period.

No other details are required to be given as it is an insurance contract covering future interest. As soon as the assured becomes aware of the full details needed, he has to disclose them to the insurer so that the premium can then be calculated. Should the assured not do so, the insurer is entitled to claim damages. If the parties agree, the duty to disclose may be agreed as not one of compulsory nature, or that the contract will be deemed as void in case of non disclosure.

4.5.3. Floating, open-cover policies and the measure of indemnity in France

In relation to cargo insurance, in the case of a floating policy, the basis of the insurable value is agreed initially and the assured is then required to make subsequent declarations within the time fixed by the policy.

Usually the *"all risks"* principle applies; however, the excluded risks are those due to illegal actions, delays, commercial nature losses, damages of nuclear origin, damages due to the assured's fault, damages due to the vice by the subject-matter of insurance, damages due to delay on expedition or arrival of the insured objects, war risks, thefts, and disappearance. The cover is extended to also include unexpected risks that arise, as long as they are declared within 48 hours after their occurrence. The insurable value is determined by factors such as the market value, the value at the destination, and the value at the time of bought or selling of the cargo.

In a floating policy, the insurable value taken as a basis for the calculation is not more than the value usually undertaken from the insurer in similar situations.

4.5.4. Floating, open-cover policies and the measure of indemnity in the USA

Cargo policies may be on a single lot or may be *"open"* to cover all cargo that is shipped by the insured.

Although a full form policy is not usually issued for each shipment under an open cargo policy, the net effect is that each lot of cargo is insured for the particular voyage as though a separate contract and policy existed. Anyone having an insurable interest in a cargo shipment has need for an ocean cargo policy. The cargo insurance policy indemnifies the exporter or importer in the event of loss or damage to goods due to a peril insured against while at risk under the policy.[237]

4.5.5. Floating, open-cover policies and the measure of indemnity in Canada

In Canada, overvaluation may lead to the underwriter putting aside the agreed valuation where the former is such an overvaluation that the insurer would not have taken the risk, had he known it.

In *Biggin v British Marine Mutual Insurance Association Ltd*,[238] a boat was valued at a price in excess of the purchase price which had been misrepresented to the insurer. The Court noted that the agreed-upon value is often higher than the purchase price or the market value, and that there was no fraud. It was, however, held that the insurer was bound by the valuation in the policy. In the case of floating policies, if a declaration is made after the arrival at a destination, the contract is avoided. This is so, even in the absence of fraud.[239]

[237] See Schoenbaum TJ Admiralty and Maritime Law, 3rd edn, Hornbook Series, West Group, St.Paul, Minn. USA, 2001.

[238] (1992)14 CCLI (2d) (Nfld TD).

[239] See Case: *Fudge v Charter Marine Insurance Co* (1992)8 CCLI (2d) 252 (Nfld) TD.

4.6. Critical discussion on valuation and the measure of indemnity

Under English law, calculation of the measure of indemnity is determined by the classification of the loss and the nature of the policy, the precise amount of recovery for the assured depending upon the type of loss being either total or partial and upon the type of policy effected each time being either valued or unvalued.

Section 27 of the Marine Insurance Act 1906 - in view of avoiding disputes on the value of the subject-matter insured - permits the parties to agree a valuation of the interest insured in the policy, such valuation being conclusive and binding between the parties and the insurer being only permitted to contest it if the assured has been guilty of fraud in presenting it, or if he has over-valued the subject-matter in a material fashion and has failed to disclose the valuation, or has misrepresented the valuation, and in the case of floating policies where the value of each declaration has not been honestly stated.

The mere fact that the agreed value in a valued policy exceeds the assured's true loss is no ground for re-opening the valuation; nevertheless, an over-valuation may be fraudulent. Early case law[240] has shown that the courts have been eager to implement the instrument of valuation, despite the fact that its bare existence is offending towards the principle of indemnity whilst also serving as proof and practical example of its imperfection.

Recent case law[241] has permitted conclusions showing, firstly that courts place great importance to the exact wording used - in deciding whether to classify a policy as valued or not[242] - to avoid cases of abuse of the term, and secondly that the law permits the use of valued policies despite the entailed dangers of overvaluation, probably because of the complexity of the issues involved in ascertaining the exact value of the subject-matter insured in cases where there has been no agreed valuation.[243]

Nowadays, however, should an insurable interest exist, and regardless of the existence of over-valuation, the contract is not a wager

240 *Lewis v Rucker* (1761)2 Burr 1167; *Irving v Manning* (1847)1 HL Cas 287; *Barker v Janson* (1868)LR 3CP 303; *The Main* (1894) P 320; *North of England Iron Steamship Association v Armstrong & Others* (1870)LR 5 QB 244.

241 *Kyzuna Investments Ltd v Ocean Marine Mutual Insurance Association(Europe)*[2000] 3 QBD ; *Quorum SA v Schramm(No 1)* [2002] Lloyd's Rep IR].

242 *Kyzuna Investments Ltd v Ocean Marine Mutual Insurance Association (Europe)* [2000]3 QBD.

243 *Quorum SA v Schramm (No 1)* [2002] Lloyd's Rep IR].

since the Marine Insurance Act 1906 does not prevent gambling on the loss of maritime property through the medium of excessive over-valuation, by those having an interest in it, so long as the policy is not underwritten on *"p.p.i."* terms. Thus, in case of over-valuation alongside with insurable interest, the insurer has the choice to rely on the defense of the assured's willful misconduct, or - if the assured was not aware of it - on the non disclosure of a fact which suggests that the adventure was of speculative nature, or on the fact that the subject-matter was fraudulently over-valued with the intention to cheat the insurers.

It is notable that the approach of the Marine Insurance Act 1906 towards over-valuation is rather relaxed, so long as the prerequisite of the existence of insurable interest is complied with and the contract is not effected on *"p.p.i"* terms. However, the legislator had no intention to harm the insurer's interests, thus the insurer is by no means trapped - because of the existence of insurable interest - and has means of defense in case of over-valuation.

In Greece, the amount insured is determined on the basis of the value of the insured object, and the parties are bound by the agreed valuation.[244] Valuation of the subject-matter insured, resulting in the determination of what is termed "the insurable value", is calculated on the basis of the true market value of the subject-matter insured at the commencement of the insurance. In hull insurance, the commercial or market value of the ship is dictated by international trade practice trends and standards and this is something that has also been accepted within Greek marine insurance law and practice in view of overcoming the obstacle of inevitable over-insurance or under-insurance of the vessel due to the fluctuations in the true value[245] ; whereas in cargo insurance, the measure of indemnity reflects the value of the cargo at the time of loading. Both the interpretation of law and case law, have shown that the measure of indemnity is based on the figure representing the damage occurred and can be no higher than the insurable value, whereas the latter is binding once accepted by the insurer.

In case of overvaluation, reduction to the market value occurs and if such overvaluation was intentional, then the policy is null and void. [246]

---

244 Spaidiotis K (1999) Marine Insurance Law in Greece, Maritime Advocate, Issue 7.

245 Rokas I (1995) Introduction to the Law of Private Insurance, 4th edn, Oikonomikon Publications, Athens.

246 Spaidiotis K (1999) Marine Insurance Law in Greece, Maritime Advocate, Issue 7.

There is no specific rule covering the case of fraud in terms of valuation and the subsequent calculation of the measure of indemnity but the insurer can separately sue for damages on the basis that the assured, upon occurrence of the maritime peril, omitted any act towards the interest of the insurer, those damages not effecting any deduction to the indemnification awarded. Moreover, fraud is tackled by means of law suits which may be brought before national courts, based on the general principles of civil law which prohibit fraudulent actions, unlawful richness and give rise to damages for restitution of the unlawful richness and voiding of the contract.[247] The law safeguards the insurer, by applying huge sanctions on the fraudulent overvaluation.

In Norway the sum insured is accepted as the limit of the insurer's liability, whilst the assured is entitled to separate cover of a number of accessory expenses and other losses due to the casualty, subject to exclusions aimed to reduce also the insurer's liability; and he also receives an additional sum as compensation for the loss of time occurred in the repair yard.[248] In total loss cases, the insurer's liability can neither exceed the sum insured nor the insurable value. The insurable value has, in most cases, been assessed and is identical to the sum insured so that the insurer pays the valuation amount. If the assured has acted fraudulently in giving information in relation to the valuation, the valuation is not simply set aside and replaced by open insurance value, as in the case of misleading information, but in accordance also with the general rules of contract law, the agreement is void.[249] Again, fraud is a serious offence and accordingly is severely sanctioned.

Under French law although insurable value is said to be equal to the agreed value, in reality it is fixed in relation to the real value which represents either the increased real value or the destination value.[250] In general, the indemnity sum is not more than the agreed insurable value. An increased value insurance, however, is considered as an independent additional insurance which does not mix with the initial one. This provision is elaborated in that the indemnity character is re-established and the assured, in case of no existing fraud, is only indemnified for the loss occurred re-

---

[247] Articles 904,914,154 AK (Greek Civil Code).

[248] In light of the conflicting interests between him and the insurer, regarding the choice of repair yard, since the latter would prefer the cheapest yard whilst the assured's interests would be best served if he could use a fast albeit expensive yard to effect repairs.

[249] Ch.2 § 2 Norwegian Marine Insurance Plan (1996) Commentary <http://exchange.dnv.com/nmip/index.htm>.

[250] Even if it surpasses the increased real value.

duced to the capital sum of the insurance. Alternatively, in case of fraud in the initiative of drafting of the excess insurance, the insurance contract is void. If there is over-valuation of the subject-matter insured, the insurance is void in case of fraud, and in the absence of fraud it is valid up to the insurable value of the subject-matter insured.[251] Thus, we note yet another jurisdiction which seeks to prohibit acts of fraud through strict stipulations in the legislation, as a response to it.

Under US law, it is usual for policies of marine insurance to be valued and in the absence of fraud or breach of the duty of utmost good faith, this valuation is binding and conclusive. Should fraud exist in valuation, the insurance is void. In relation always to the measure of indemnity, under US law, a plaintiff may be awarded punitive damages under certain circumstances,[252] in addition to compensatory damages. Historically, admiralty courts have been reluctant to impose them but lately they have shown a tendency to permit them. The latest tendencies of the judiciary here, in relation to the consequences of fraudulent overvaluation, show the importance that law sets in assuring that the insured does not get over-indemnified and gets severely punished for doing so.

There is not much novelty on valuation under Canadian and Australian law, given the influence they have had from English law. In Canada, agreed valuation is binding and conclusive, unless there has been fraud or such an overvaluation that the insurer would not have taken the risk, had he known it; and again in Australia, the value fixed by the policy is, as between the insurer and assured, conclusive of the insurable value of the subject intended to be insured, whether the loss be total or partial.

4.7. Salvage and the measure of indemnity

Salvage is directly linked to the concept of indemnity as it enhances the safety of the subject-matter insured and the prevention of its loss. *"Salvage"* is the remuneration paid or payable to a person who, acting as a third party, independently of contract, voluntarily renders a successful ser-

---

[251] De Smet R (1960) Traité Théorique et Pratique des Assurances Maritimes, Paris, pp 410-424.

[252] Basically if he establishes that the defendant was *" guilty of gross negligence, or actual malice, or criminal indifference which is the equivalent of reckless and wanton misconduct"*. The purpose of imposing punitive damages is to deter and punish wrongful misconduct.

vice in preserving from peril property involved in a maritime adventure. The remedy of salvage is of great antiquity.[253]

The origin of salvage was stated in *Aitchison v Lohre*[254]. However, there exists no statutory definition of salvage. To establish a case for pure salvage, the salvor must act voluntarily without entering into any form of contract with the owner of the property and on the strict that he receives no reward if his services are unsuccessful. This is also known as the principle *"no cure - no pay"*.

If the salvor is successful, his award will be based on the degree of skill used, combined with the expense of the operation, the hazards involved, and the value of the property saved. No salvor is entitled to an award, when he is responsible for the circumstances which led to the need for the salvage act. The salvage services must have been of material assistance in salving the property. As an exception to this, where services are performed in response to a specific request, then, and provided that property is saved, those engaged services should be rewarded even though the eventual saving of the property may have resulted from some other cause.

Salvors may also be entitled to compensation, if their engaged services to complete the salvage are unjustifiably discarded and other assistance is taken.[255] In order to differentiate the term from the use that it has when it concerns remuneration, the Marine Insurance Act 1906 refers to remuneration as *"salvage charges"*. The measure of indemnity in respect of *"salvage charges"* , is set out in s. 73(2) of the Marine Insurance Act 1906 as follows:

"...Where the insurer is liable for salvage charges, the extent of liability must be determined in the like principle".

The measure of indemnity of the insurer's liability to third parties, is dealt with in s. 74 of the Marine Insurance Act 1906, whereby it is stated:

"...Where the assured has effected an insurance in express terms against any liability to a third party, the measure of indemnity - subject to any express provision in the policy - is the amount paid or payable by him to such third party in respect of such liability."

The purpose of a salvage award is not merely to compensate the salvor for the benefit received by the salvage, but also, in terms of its origin from public policy, to provide a positive incentive. The amount of the salvage award may be fixed by agreement. Such an agreement may how-

---

253 An expression of the policy underlying salvage rewards was reported almost 165 years ago in the decision of the English Court of Admiralty in *The Industry* (1835)3 Hag.Adm. 203,204 (Brice G(2000) Salvage And The Role of The Insurer LMCLQ 2000(1):26-41).

254 (1879)4 App Cas 755.

255 *The Loch Tulla* [1950]84 Ll. L.Rep. 62.

ever be set aside on the ground that it is inequitable, and it may be inequitable either because the agreed sum is exorbitantly high or because it is inadequate. Nevertheless, the agreement, unless inequitable or liable to be avoided, will be enforced.[256]

A salvor's usual and most effective remedy is his maritime lien on the property salved, including freight if this has been saved. The lien arises as soon as the salvage services have been rendered and ranks before all previous liens on the property salved. In furtherance of this lien, the court has power to arrest the property and, if necessary, sell it to raise the funds needed to satisfy the award; but often an arrest is avoided by an undertaking by those interested in the property to give security.

In addition to his lien, a salvor has the right to proceed *in personam*, which he may wish to do if the salved property has not been available for arrest within the jurisdiction. A salvor may also seek a *"Mareva injunction"* against the assets within the jurisdiction of the owner of the salved property.

4.8. Consequential, future profit loss and the measure of indemnity

Many businesses wish to insure against the possibility of a catastrophe, giving rise to a loss of profits or additional expense during the period after the occurrence of the peril insured against.

It is accepted law that an ordinary insurance policy against, for example fire, does not cover loss of profits[257] and it has even been held that a loss of market caused by a delay, arising from a peril insured against, is not covered by a standard form policy.[258]Any type of consequential loss can be insured, but loss of profits or additional expenditure are the most

[256] The fact that the court might have awarded a rather different sum (higher or lower) than the sum agreed will not prevent the court from upholding the agreement. Like the amount of the award, the apportionment of it among the salvors can be regulated by agreement, though such an agreement may be set aside if inequitable. If, however, no valid agreement regulating apportionment has been entered into, the court has power to apportion the award.

[257] *Re Wright and Pole* (1834)1 Ad & E. 621, *Cator v Great Western Insurance Co of New York* (1873)LR 8 CP 552, *Maurice v Goldsborough, Mort & Co* [1939]AC 452.

[258] *Lewis Emanuel & Son Ltd v Hepburn* [1960]1 Lloyd's Rep. 304.

usual subjects of insurance, and for this reason this type of insurance is often referred to as a loss of profits insurance. This type of insurance was initially introduced and used in the 19th century as a type of insurance against fire, the cover of it comprising the asset of subject-matter insured and the articles contained in it (e.g. house and its contents), but did not extend to the loss of trade consequential to the fire. Thus, it can be said that in this way the cover was restricted to what emanated from the use of the subject-matter insured in terms of private reasons and purposes solely and did not extend so as to cover loss due to its use for trade reasons as well. It was in the 1890s, however, that it expanded and evolved so that nowadays it also comprises loss of present and future profits as well.

Loss of profits and other forms of consequential loss must be described in the policy and insured as such[259]. The purpose of this insurance is to put the assured into the position he would be in, if the profits had been earned (subject to the conditions of the policy) and he will therefore be liable to tax on the indemnity received.[260] In marine insurance, consequential loss is a term used to describe a loss following and consequent on a loss proximately caused by a peril insured against. The actual loss ascertained is calculated by applying to the sum representing the reduction in the turnover, after the occurrence of the catastrophe, the ratio which standing charges and net profit together normally bear to turnover. This is the basis of most of the consequential loss insurance transacted in the United Kingdom.[261] In order to avoid complex calculations of loss of profit and additional expenditure, the parties sometimes agree that the loss of profit shall be a certain definite amount. Thus, there are examples of policies which provided for the indemnity to be a certain percentage of the amount by

---

259 *Maurice v Goldsborough, Mort & Co* [1939]AC 452, *Mackenzie v Whitworth* (1875)1 Ex D 36.

260 *R. v Fir & Cedar Lumber Co Ltd* [1932]AC 441, *London and Thames Haven Oil Wharves Ltd v Attwood* [1967]Ch 772.; Jones NL (1997) MacGillivray on Insurance Law, 9th edn, London S&M, pp 856-860.

261 From the inception of this form of insurance, the accepted method of determining and defining insurable gross profit was by the addition of the amount of the standing charges to the net profit. But in the 1950s a simpler method was introduced in which the total of the variable expenses is deducted from the turnover. This innovation necessitated a new definition of insurable gross profit, being in a sense a reversal of the traditional one. The latter started at the end of the accounts, with net profit, and added back the insurable standing charges. The new one starts at the head of the accounts, with turnover, and then deducts the total of the variable charges, the difference between these amounts being the insurable gross profit (Riley D (1967) Consequential Loss Insurances and Claims, 3rd edn, S&M, London, pp 1-4).

which the turnover in each month after the fire/catastrophe should be less than the turnover for the corresponding month of the year preceding the fire, with provision for the insured's auditors to assess the amount of the loss[262]; alternatively, the policy might provide for payment of a percentage of the *"ultimate net loss"* as paid on some other policy.[263] On the other hand, an agreement to pay the *"same percentage of the sum insured as the total sum paid on fire policies bears to total sum insured there under"* does not make the policy a valued policy as such, but merely obliges the insurer to pay an amount so calculated, subject to other provisions of the policy.[264]

A consequential loss policy, undertakes to provide an indemnity for the loss during a period of interruption after the incident caused by a peril insured for. Such interruption of trading generally involves additional expenditure so as to quickly minimise the loss of turnover and restore normal conditions. Any insurance which is intended to give an indemnity for loss consequent upon such damage must, therefore, provide compensation for additional expenditure undertaken to reduce the prospective loss of turnover during a period of interruption. In practice, such additional expenditure is generally considerable and, because of its effectiveness, frequently exceeds the loss arising from reduction in turnover. Consequently, provision is made in the policy for the payment of increase in cost of working.

Under Greek law, there exists the concept of marine insurance covering future profit from cargo, which in a way resembles the modern form of consequential loss insurance policies issued nowadays, covering amidst others also future trade profits.

In Norway, there exists the *"loss of hire"* insurance, which is a *"new"* insurance in the marine insurance context and could be compared to the concept of the consequential loss insurance in the English market. The first insurances of this type appeared after the second world war, and it is only during the last 20-30 years they have become commonly used. Initially, the insurance was primarily effected for ships on time charter in order to protect the owner against loss of income if the ship went off-hire.[265] With the current formulation of these insurance conditions,

---

262 *Recher & Co v North British & Mercantile Ins* [1915]3 KB 277, where it was held that the auditor's assessment was conclusive unless it could be shown he went wrong in law or omitted to take into account some material fact, such as for example the possibility that some of the damage might have been caused by something other than the peril insured against.

263 *Bailliere, Tindal & Cox v Drysdale* (1948)82 LlLR 736.

264 *Brunton v Marshall* (1922)10 Ll.L.R. 689 ; Jones NL (1997) MacGillivray on Insurance Law, 9th edn, London S&M, pp 856-860.

265 Thus the term *"off-hire insurance"*.

however, there is nothing preventing the effecting of such insurance for ships employed under other types of contracts of affreightment[266], or for vessels without such contracts.[267] Traditionally, the loss of hire insurance is considered a relatively costly form of insurance.[268] The main rule for the liability of the insurer,[269] requires damage to the ship that is covered by the Norwegian Marine Insurance Plan and the standard Norwegian Hull Conditions. Loss of hire insurance does not therefore cover loss of time arising from causes other than damage to the ship. There is an extension of the cover provided by loss-of-hire insurance in that loss of time is covered in certain cases even though the ship has not been physically damaged.[270]

In relation to total and compromised total loss,[271] a basic principle in loss-of-hire insurance is that the insurance does not cover loss of time which results from total loss of the vessel.[272] Under the second alternative in the rule, a compromised payment of 75% of the hull value without the insurer taking over the vessel or requiring the assured to carry out repairs is regarded as equivalent to an actual total loss.

The rule is designed for compromised cases of total losses. This type of settlement can be used where the vessel is so severely damaged, that it is not economic to repair it, but where - because of a high insurable value - the conditions for condemnation do not apply. In this situation the insurer is liable for the cost of repairs, but only if repairs are actually carried out. However, neither the insurer nor the assured have any interest in carrying out expensive and unprofitable repairs.[273] The main rule for calculating the liability of the insurer,[274] provides that the compensation is to be calculated on the basis of the time during which the ship is deprived of income and the loss of income per day. This method must be used even if the loss of income can be established more directly. The insurer is not liable

---

266 For example voyage charter parties or charters for consecutive voyages.

267 For example cruise vessels or liner vessels.

268 Falkanger T, Bull HJ, Brautaset L (1998) Introduction to Maritime Law: The Skandinavian Perspective,Tano Ashehoug, Oslo, Ch 22.

269 As in the 1972/93 conditions.

270 Ch. 16§1 Norwegian Marine Insurance Plan (1996) Commentary <http://exchange.dnv.com/nmip/index.htm>.

271 § 16-2 deals with total and compromised total loss. The § corresponds to § 3 No. 2 of the 1972 and 1993 Conditions.

272 The wording is identical to that in the 1972 and 1993 conditions but the heading has been changed to *"Total and Compromised Total Loss"*.

273 Ch. 16§2 Norwegian Marine Insurance Plan (1996) Commentary <http://exchange.dnv.com/nmip/index.htm>.

274 The § corresponds to § 2, subparagraph 2, and § 3, No. 3 in the 1972 and 1993 conditions.

for loss of time arising from the cancellation of any contract of affreightment.[275]

Regarding the choice of repair yard,[276] if the insurer has knowledge of the casualty, he must make it clear to the assured whether he requires tenders to be taken. If he fails to do so, the insurer must cover the time actually lost. The loss-of-hire insurer's liability is limited to the loss of time under the shortest repair alternative the costs of which are recoverable in full from the vessel's hull insurer. Naturally the assured is not bound to choose this alternative. He is free to determine which repair alternative is to be used, but the scope of his recovery from the loss-of-hire insurer is determined by reference to the alternative which gives the best total result in the way described above.

Once the assured chooses this alternative, however, he is covered even if it turns out that the tender was too optimistic about the time required to complete repairs. It follows that the assured will, in such cases, be entitled to recover under the loss-of-hire settlement for the time actually taken to complete the repairs.

Regarding regulation in law on the issue of removal to the repair yard[277], removal time is to be allocated to the class of repairs that *"necessitated the removal"*. The rule applies correspondingly to time lost after the completion of repairs. Where removal to the repair yard was made necessary by more than one class of work, the removal time is to be apportioned according to the time that each class of work would have taken if carried out separately. The rule stating that removal time occurring during the deductible period shall not be apportioned, is only of significance in those cases where removal time is to be apportioned; if the removal time falls in its entirety on the insurer, the deductible period will run during the removal in the normal way. The consequence is that the deductible period runs in the normal way, each day counting in full during the removal time even in those cases where the time is to be apportioned.

The liability of the insurer when the vessel is transferred to a new owner,[278] is attributed as follows: where the ship is repaired in connection with a sale, the starting point is that the normal loss-of-hire cover applies up to the time the ship is delivered; where the ship is delivered with unre-

---

[275] This applies both to time lost before the casualty and to time lost after completion of repairs.

[276] Dealt with in § 16-9, which corresponds to § 6 of the 1972 and 1993 conditions.

[277] The § corresponds to § 8, No. 4 of the 1972 and 1993 conditions.

[278] § 16-15 deals with it; the § corresponds to § 12 of the 1972 and 1993 condi tions.

paired damage to the new owner, the insurance is cancelled on delivery to a new owner but the insurer remains liable for casualties which occurred before delivery even though the damage is repaired after delivery.

The claim against the insurer cannot be transferred in connection with a transfer of the ship to a new owner. This is a different solution from that which applies to hull insurance but follows previous practice. Consideration of the insurer's interests justifies the rule. In loss-of-hire insurance his position would be too exposed if he ran the risk of having to settle a claim from a party with whom he previously has not had any contact.[279]

4.9. Mortgagee's interest insurance and the measure of indemnity

The mortgagee's interest insurance is worth examining due to its scope and also because of the nature of the measure of indemnity offered under it. When the purchase of the insured object is financed by a bank or similar institution, the lender's security over the subject-matter is meaningful only if some form of insurance exists in the lender's favour.

Banks and other institutions providing ship finance require insurance protection just as much as other entrepreneurs, and it is often in such cases that the cover under a mortgagee's interest insurance is engaged. [280] It was as a result of *The Alexion Hope*[281] that the initial Institute Mortgagees Interest Clauses Hulls (30/5/86) were produced. The plaintiffs were mortgagees of the *Alexion Hope*. As such they were the assignees of the benefit of the hull and machinery policy on the vessel. The ship was lost by fire. The hull underwriters sought to defend the plaintiff's claim on the

[279] Ch. 16§15 Norwegian Marine Insurance Plan (1996) Commentary <http://exchange.dnv.com/nmip/index.htm>.

[280] The insurable interest of a mortgagee bank is defined in s.14(1) of the Marine Insurance Act 1906. The mortgagees' initial requirement is for cover against the perils customarily insured by the shipowners' hull policies and the risks normally covered by the shipowners' P&I entries. Theoretically, cover is obtained by the mortgagee: by effecting a separate insurance to cover his own interest; in hull insurances, policies are effected in such a way that both the shipowner's and the mortgagees' interests are covered as co-assured; by requiring the mortgagor shipowner to assign the hull policies and P&I entry in his favour (this is done by endorsement on the shipowners; policies and P&I Club entries noting the interest of the mortgagee).

[281] *Schiffshypothekenbank Zu Luebeck AG v Norman Philip Compton ("The Alexion Hope")* [1988]1 Lloyd's Rep 311.

ground that the fire had been deliberately caused by the shipowner. The prospect of a trial against the hull underwriters had arisen and the plaintiffs sought an order on preliminary issues against the defendants, their mortgagee's interest underwriters, taking the view that, if they could recover their mortgagees' interest insurance, then the plaintiffs need not continue with an action against the hull underwriters. This required an interpretation of the mortgagees' interest insurance. The crucial issue was to establish the effect upon the mortgagees' interest cover of a refusal by the hull underwriters to pay for a constructive total loss of the vessel on the ground that it was attributable to the willful misconduct of the owner. The underwriters argued that a loss by fire occasioned through willful misconduct was not an occurrence within the meaning of the clause and that an average adjustment had to be accepted as correct by the hull underwriters before it was *"passed"* within the meaning of the clause. The argument was rejected at first instance and in the Court of Appeal on the ground that the word fire covered not only a fortuitous but also a deliberately set fire. The second argument was also rejected as the word *"passed"* had to be given its practical commercial meaning and in that sense it had to mean *"issued"* and not *"accepted as correct"* by the hull underwriters. The provision had the purpose of triggering a claim against the defendants. This required that an average adjustment had been issued and that the hull underwriters had declined to pay.

Since the *Alexion Hope*, the Institute of London Underwriters has produced a standard English Form of Contract, the Institute Mortgagees Interest Clauses Hulls 30/5/86 which have been further revised and nowadays are referred to as the Institute Mortgagees' Interest Clauses-Hulls 1/3/97.

Similarly, it was held in *The Captain Panagos*,[282] that a mortgagee's interest insurance policy, insuring against non payment following loss or damage to a vessel, was a marine and not a financial guarantee policy. This view was reinforced by the consideration that the mortgagee's loss could be regarded as incidental to the navigation of the seas as provided by s.3 (2) of the Marine Insurance Act 1906, even though it was not a loss by a *"peril of the seas"*. The insurer was liable as a result of this, for a measure of indemnity based on the value of the vessel rather than the amount of the mortgagee's financial loss. As a result of this ruling, the majority of mortgagee's interest insurance policies written on the London market are now in the Institute Mortgagee's Interest Policy Hull form and

---

282 *Continental Illinois National Bank & Trust Co of Chicago v Bathurst (The "Captain Panagos DP ")* [1985]1 Lloyd's Rep. 625.

are marine in that they insure the mortgagee's interest in hull although the measure of indemnity is based on financial loss.[283]

The event insured against is non-payment by owners' hull underwriters or P&I Club as a result of any of these insured perils. The policy is not a valued one as per s.27 of the Marine Insurance Act 1906. Indemnity is not available to the mortgagee where there has been any loss caused by a termination of the hull or P&I insurance by virtue of the non-payment of the premium or any financial default on the part of the owners' underwriters. The mortgagee only recovers if the insured peril occurs or if it exists without the privity of the mortgagee. The intention is to allow the insured to recover whenever the hull insurer refuses to pay, subject to exceptions listed.

The mortgagees' interest insurance contract is dependent on compliance with the warranties that valid contracts of insurance are in place on behalf of the owners with their hull and P&I insurers, which shall be maintained except as a result of an insured peril throughout the currency of the mortgagees' interest insurance; that those policies are endorsed to the extent of the assured's interest; and that the assured has procured and registered a valid first mortgage. The normal period of insurance for the policy is 12 months. The amount payable is the lesser of the amount of the assured's net loss and any amount recoverable under the *"sue & labour"* clause collectively exceeding the sum insured on the mortgaged vessel, or

[283] The form is usually drafted on the basis that a separate insurance is issued for each named individual vessel. The main aspects of this type of insurance are encapsulated in the following clauses. Clause 1 summarises the purpose and effect of the insurance. A loss, damage or liability is *prima facie* covered by the owners policies and club entries if it were not for a defence based upon the assured's misconduct. There is also an important proviso in bold type that the insured peril relied on by the mortgagee must occur or exist without the privity of the mortgagee assured. Privity here includes actual privity and *"blind-eye"* knowledge. The indemnity payable is the lesser of either the mortgagees' actual net loss plus any claim under the duty of assured (*"sue & labour"*) clause, the total not exceeding the sum insured; or the claim (or part of the claim) which is not recoverable under any of the owners policies and club entries. Clause 2 sets out a full list of the insured perils. Clause 6 deals with *"sue & labour"*. The assured shall take measures as may be reasonable to avert or minimise a loss. The underwriters reimburse the assured for the cost of such measures and neither party is prejudiced thereby. The assured must report in writing to the underwriters any circumstances which may give rise to a claim under the insurance within thirty days of these circumstances coming to the assured's notice and thereafter to keep the underwriters informed of the developments.

the amount of any unrecoverable claim or part thereof under any of the owners policies and Club entries.

There is an express subrogation right upon the mortgagees' interest insurance. The assured has a right, as the assignee of the owner, to proceed against the hull insurer, and the mortgagee's interest insure may proceed against the owner of a vessel as the assured's debtor, because ultimately, the policy protects the assured against the debtor's default.

In Greece, in case of mortgage insurance related to the aspect of financing of the purchase of the vessel, satisfaction of mortgagee is secured by his mortgage right on the insured property.[284] The mortgagee has also his own legal interest (mortgage interest) which may become the object of marine insurance. The object of this interest, held by a mortgagee, is a right which is indirectly exposed to maritime perils since the occurrence of insured risks may result indirectly in the forfeiture of the mortgagee right or in complete elimination of its economic value. This kind of insurance transaction provides the mortgagee with a more complete security, but at his own expense, the mortgagee is the second contracting party, the insured and the beneficiary of the insurance indemnity.[285]

4.10. Double Insurance and the measure of indemnity

4.10.1. Double insurance and the measure of indemnity in England

When property is insured for the same adventure under more than one policy, double insurance exists. The Marine Insurance Act 1906 provides in s. 32 certain rules to be applied. In order to constitute double insurance, the first requirement of the Act is that the insurances must have been effected by or on behalf of the assured on the same adventure and interest or on any part thereof. The policies do not have to be the same in all respects. As

284 By law or agreement he has the right to insure the mortgaged ship on behalf and at the expense of the owner if the ship is uninsured or partly insured. This is the case of insurance of another person's interest and the mortgagee has the right to claim immediate payment of the debt if the debtor does not pay the insurance premium.

285 Argyriadis A(1979) Marine Insurance:A General Comparative View in the Light of Greek Law, Revue Hellenique de Droit International 32: 28-40.

long as they overlap in their scope sufficiently to cover the assured's interest on the same adventure then this first requirement of double insurance will be satisfied.[286] The second requirement set by the Marine Insurance Act is that through the effecting of double insurance, the facts insured exceed the indemnity allowed by the Act. It is with this subsection of the Marine Insurance Act 1906 s.32(1), that the indemnity principle is correlated.

Although double or multiple insurance of the same risk is lawful, however, the assured is entitled to satisfaction of his loss only once. He may proceed against any one insurer or combination of insurers for the whole sum due, leaving any insurer who pays more than his rateable proportion of the loss to recover contribution from the other insurers.[287] In practice, double insurance is mostly encountered in respect of cargo and rarely with ships.

Double insurance will arise where two policies provide that the insurer is not liable if the assured is entitled to indemnity under another policy. The presence of such a clause in one policy prevents that clause in the other from taking effect so that each insurer is liable. Thus, a clause of exclusion by reference to another policy is effective only if there is another policy on which the assured can obtain indemnification, the insurer bearing the burden of proving the existence of such a policy.

In contrast, double insurance is avoided by rateable proportion clauses, by virtue of which the insurer's liabilities to the assured are all reduced to the appropriate percentage of the loss.[288] These clauses are nowadays contained in insurances as standard clauses. In relation to their function, it is worth discussing the ruling in *Drake Insurance Plc v Provident Insurance Plc*.[289] In this case, the appellant *"Drake Insurance Plc"* sought to recover a contribution in equity from the respondent Provident Insurance plc on the basis that both companies were insurers of the same loss.[290]

---

[286] Lambeth RJ (1986) Templeman on Marine Insurance: Its Principles and Practice, 6th edn, Pitman, pp 438-439.

[287] Bennett H (1986) The Law of Marine Insurance, Clarendon Press, Oxford, p 425.

[288] Bennett H (1986) The Law of Marine Insurance, Clarendon Press, Oxford, p 427.

[289] [CA 17 Dec 2003].

[290] A third party, Mr Beach, was injured by a car driven by Mrs Kaur who was driving her husband's car and was insured under her policy with Drake in respect of any car driven by her with its owner's consent. Her husband, Dr Singh, was insured under his policy with Provident in respect of the car which Mrs Kaur was driving at the time of the accident and Mrs Kaur was a named driver on his policy.

However, Provident purported to avoid its policy. Provident disputed its liability towards Drake, to share in that loss, alleging that there is no double insurance and even if there is such, a special clause in Drake's policy limited Drake's liability in a case of double insurance to only half of the loss; so that by paying the loss in full, Drake was a volunteer and cannot recover. At First Instance the judge agreed with this defence; however, the Court of Appeal allowed Drake's appeal on the grounds that Provident was not entitled to avoid its policy and Drake was not a volunteer. In reaching his decision, Lord Justice Rix stated - in relation to the question whether the rateable proportion clause excludes the right to contribution and subject to the question of voluntary payment - that the mere existence of the rateable proportion clause is not excluding the operation of the equitable rule of contribution. His Honour, further on, went to state that the clause does not of itself exclude a right to contribution -seeing that the essence of the clause is to apply a rateable liability as a matter of contract- that it would be surprising if it had the effect of prejudicing one insurer who had paid too much, and that each insurer has not ceased to insure for the same loss just because he cannot be forced by contract to pay more than the rateable proportion or because the clause in effect requires the insured to involve both his insurers at once in order to obtain a full indemnity. Justice Clarke, agreed and added that Provident, by its argument that Drake paid as a volunteer, was only seeking to achieve a result by which Drake remains liable for the whole claim, when in equity the former should be shared between them. His Honour, being rather critical, stated that such a result would show the insurance industry in a very poor light, thus, Drake is entitled to a 50% contribution from Provident, following the correct construction of the *"rateable proportion"* clause. Where the assured claims under a valued policy, he must give credit as against the valuation for any sum of money received under any other policy regardless of the actual value of the subject-matter insured. The rule is uncontroversial where both policies contain the same valuation. In *Morgan v Price*[291] the two policies valued the insured ship at £2,500. Payment of £2,500 on one policy provided the assured with the full indemnity for which he had bargained and constituted satisfaction under both policies. Where the two policies contain different valuations, however, the case is different. In *Bruce v Jones,*[292] a ship was insured for four different sums under four policies containing three different valuations. The assured having recovered a total of £3,126 under three of the policies, the issue was the measure of indemnity recoverable under the fourth policy under which the vessel

[291] (1850)4 Exch 615.
[292] (1863)1 H & C 769.

was valued at £3,200. It was held that the assured was bound by the agreed valuation, had to give credit for the sums already received under the other policies, and was therefore entitled only to the balance of £3,200. With respect to unvalued policies, the same rule operates except that credit must be given against the full insurable value.[293] Should the assured receive more than the measure of indemnity allowed under the Marine Insurance Act 1906, the excess is held in trust for the insurers in proportion according to their contribution rights.[294] Increased value policies, common in cargo insurance, do not give rise to double insurance, because the subject-matter of the *"increased value policy"* is not the goods themselves but the increased value thereof. Thus, rights of contribution do not arise for the underwriters on the goods as against increased value underwriters.[295]

An assured may over-insure by taking up a *"p.p.i."* policy in addition to the standard hull, cargo or freight policy. This occurred in *The Gunford* where, in addition to the hull and freight policies, additional valued policies on disbursements and on hull and disbursements were also taken out by the assured and where the House of Lords held that even though the insurances on disbursements were *"p.p.i."* policies, nonetheless there was a double insurance, as much that was covered in the hull and freight policies being also covered by the policies on disbursements.[296]According to s. 84(3)(f) of the Marine Insurance Act 1906, if the assured has over-insured by double insurance, a proportionate part of the several premiums is returnable upon the fulfillment of certain conditions set out by the Act. This

[293] Section 32(2)c MIA 1906.

[294] Section 32(2)d MIA 1906.

[295] In the case of *Boag v Standard Marine Insurance Co Ltd* [(1936) 2 KB 121] a cargo was insured for its full value at the time of shipment. The value rose during the voyage and an increased value policy was taken out with other underwriters. The cargo was totally lost and the assured was paid in full by the primary underwriters and the Increased Value underwriters for their respective interests. Thus, a smaller sum than the one paid by the primary underwriters was received in general average which the primary underwriters claimed in full as subrogation. By the introduction of the Clause 14 of the Institute Cargo Clauses (A),(B),(C), the result of the decision in *Boag v Standard Marine Insurance Co Ltd [(1936)2 KB 121]* was altered and what were considered to be the inequitable consequences have been rectified. If the assured takes out increased value insurances on conditions more limited than the primary policy, not only might he find himself partially under-insured but certain indemnities which would otherwise be payable in full under the primary policy would be reduced (O' May D (1993) Marine Insurance Law and Policy, LLP p 463).

[296] Hodges, S (1996) Law of Marine Insurance, Cavendish Publications, pp 5-14.

provision is said to have largely codified *Fisk v Masterman* [297], a case concerning multiple insurance of cargo where five policies were taken out on the day preceding its safe arrival and a further six were concluded *bona fidae* after arrival. The main issue here was whether the underwriters on the first group of policies should contribute to the rebate of premium. No rebate was actually due from them, however, because the risk had attached. Thus, they were entitled to full premium as compensation for assumption of the risk.[298]

4.10.2. Double insurance and the measure of indemnity in Norway

Under Norwegian law, when the interest[299] is also insured with another insurer,[300] there is double insurance. The principle of primary joint and several liability is established, and it is applicable to three situations.

In the first place, it applies to double insurance in the form of ordinary co-insurance. In the second place, the provision becomes significant when there is *"double insurance"* in the traditional sense, i.e. where several parallel insurances are effected which in the aggregate will give the assured more compensation than the loss he has suffered. The third situation where there is double insurance is when a loss is covered partly under the primary cover of an insurance, partly as costs to avert or minimise the loss under another insurance.[301] In case one insurance has been made subsidiary, the primary rule is that the insurer who has sub-

[297] (1841) 8 M & W 165.

[298] Bennett H (1986) The Law of Marine Insurance, Clarendon Press, Oxford, p 431.

[299] As per § 2-6 of the Norwegian Marine Insurance Plan (1996).

[300] As per § 2-6 of the Norwegian Marine Insurance Plan (1996).

[301] In principle, this loss should be covered under the insurance which covers costs to avert or minimise the loss. Yet, here also the assured must initially be entitled to claim damages from both insurers according to § 2-6. The size of the compensation to which the assured *"is entitled"* will depend on the insurance conditions. If the conditions authorise cover of varying amounts, it is the highest amount which is decisive for the size of the claim. Until the assured has recovered this amount, he may bring a claim against any of the insurers he wishes within the terms of the conditions which the relevant insurer has accepted. The provision contained in subparagraph 1 is only applicable in the event of a conflict between two insurances covering the same peril.

sidiary liability is only liable for the amount for which the assured does not have cover with other insurers.[302]

4.10.3. Double insurance and the measure of indemnity in Canada

In Canada, when a loss occurs that is covered by two or more policies of insurance, it is known as double insurance. In such a case there is immediately a question as to which of the policies is primary and which is excess which will determine the rights of the insurers as between themselves with regards to contribution.

To resolve these problems *"other insurance"* clauses were developed, also, in Canada. These clauses generally fall into one of three categories: the first type of clause is a *"pro-rata clause"*, which provides that both policies shall share the loss pro-rata. The second type of clause is an *"excess clause"* which stipulates that the policy in which the clause is contained is excess and the other policy is primary. The third type of clause is called an *"escape clause"*. It provides that in the event of other insurance, the policy will be void or will not contribute. There has been a good deal of case law dealing with competing *"other insurance"* clauses. Most of this case law has involved situations where the two policies have contained similar "other insurance" clauses, i.e. where both policies contain a pro-rata clause or both contain an excess clause. In those situations, the courts have held that the two clauses cancel each other out with the result that both insurers must contribute rateably to the loss.[303] There have also been some cases that have considered situations involving two different types of *"other insurance"* clauses. One of the leading cases is the British Columbia case namely *Seagate Hotel Ltd v Simcoe & Erie General Insurance Co*

[302] If several insurances are made subsidiary, there is a risk that the assured may be left without settlement because both or all of the insurers may invoke their subsidiarity clauses. During the Plan revision, it was decided that in such cases a primary joint and several liability should be imposed on the insurers vis-à-vis the assured. § 14 of the Norwegian Marine Insurance Plan 1964 contained a provision relating to the duty of the person effecting the insurance to disclose any other insurances he might have. The provision has, therefore, been deleted. If the insurer in a recourse settlement should need to know about other insurances, he can ask the person effecting the insurance after the loss has occurred.

[303] *Weddell v Road Transport & General Insurance Co* [1932] 2 K.B. 563; *McGeough v Stay 'N Save Motor Inns Inc* (1994) 92 B.C.L.R. (2d) 288; *Simcoe & Erie General Insurance Co v Kansa General Insurance Co* (1994) 93 BCLR (2d) 1).

et al,[304] which was affirmed on appeal.[305] This case concerned a personal injury, the liability for which was covered by two policies of insurance. Both policies contained *"other insurance"* clauses. One policy contained a pro-rata clause and the other contained an excess clause. The court held that the resolution of the issue depended on the precise wording of the two clauses and when this wording was taken into account the policy with the pro-rata clause was held to be the primary policy and the policy with the excess clause was the excess one.

4.11. General conclusive remarks and comparative discussion

English law, having enjoyed long enough a dominant position in the area of marine insurance, has developed a law regime to regulate marine insurance with the aim to create a perfect and absolute indemnity.

Certain peculiarities, which exist by nature in this rather technical area of law, have imposed the requirement for prerequisites to be met and for assumptions to be made and, in effect, the perfection sought has been partially impaired. Thus, under English law, a distinction needs to be drawn between a sum insured and an agreed value, the former delimiting the financial cover by stating the maximum potential liability of the insurer under the policy and the latter being conclusive evidence of the insurable value of the insured property so valued and - as such - playing a crucial role in determining the precise amount of the insurer's liability. The mechanism of agreed valuation has proved beneficial to the interest of the assured and the insurer and, although it is departing from the indemnity principle, courts have agreed to implement it for the sake of commercial convenience. The law, however, prevents over-indemnification and to this extent valuation is contested and re-opened in case it is excessive and amounts to fraud and material non- disclosure.

Similarly, in double insurance the assured can recover against the various insurers but he is overall limited to indemnification once and only for the loss sustained.

Overall, the means have justified the goal with regards to valuation and the measure of indemnity offered in marine insurance. An over-valued subject-matter insured does not imply an automatic re-openness of the valuation but, at the same time, it does not necessarily imply that the latter is not fraudulent. We notice that agreed valuation, by nature and by defini-

[304] (1980) 22 BCLR 374.

[305] At (1981) 27 BCLR 89.

tion, entails the overvaluation danger which in its turn attributes to the indemnity flaws; nevertheless courts, today, support valued policies and sanction overvaluation in the existence of insurable interest and in the absence of underwriting on *"p.p.i."* terms. Similarly, judging the law on the measure of indemnity, we note that it has managed to serve well its goal and has enhanced the award of fair, though imperfect, indemnification.[306]

The same aim dominates the regulation of marine insurance law, in the rest of the jurisdictions examined in relation to the measure of indemnity. All jurisdictions impose severe sanctions to tackle fraud in the valuation process.

In Greece and in France, the Courts approve the use of valuation despite its flaws and the law protects the insurer in case of fraud in valuation, by enabling him void the contract. Under Greek law, he may also sue for damages on the basis of the fraud occurred. Similarly under American law, as well as in the case of Canada and Australia there is voidance of the contract in the presence of fraud. In Norway, fraud in valuation leads to an extra sanction if compared with the case of simple non fraudulent overvaluation, i.e. not only valuation is eliminated, but there is also voidance of the contract.

Not least - as an illustrative example of the effort to establish the fairest possible measure of indemnity - from the family of the common law jurisdictions, it is worth noting that Canada has established the use of *"other insurances"* clauses, to regulate the characterisation of policies as primary and excess in case of double insurance,[307] following the example of England where rateable contribution and excess clauses are used since long, and where rateable proportion clauses, in particular, are mostly common and standard in insurances nowadays.

[306] To this effect the various cases together with the Institute Clauses have contributed a lot, mainly as a means of keeping updated the text of law as the latter is set out in the Marine Insurance Act 1906.

[307] These clauses provide a solution to the problem of over-indemnification in the case of double insurance, either by setting a pro-rata clause as per which the loss is to be shared on a pro-rata basis between the two contracts; or by setting an excess clause, thus constituting the one contract as primary and the other with that clause as an excess one; or by setting an escape clause, so called because the contract with it is void or non-contributable, should there be any other contract.

5. Subrogation rights arising from marine insurance contracts

5.1. The rights of the insurer on payment in marine insurance contracts in England

5.1.1. The doctrine of subrogation: definition and perspectives

Subrogation literally denotes the substitution of one person in the place of another with reference to a lawful claim, demand or right, so that he who is substituted succeeds to the rights of the other in relation to the debt or claim, and its rights, remedies, or securities. In the context of marine insurance, subrogation is the right by which an underwriter, having settled a loss, is entitled to place himself in the position of the assured, to the extent of acquiring all the rights and remedies in respect of the loss which the assured may have possessed either in the nature of proceedings for compensation, or recovery in the name of the assured against third parties, or in obtaining general average contribution thereto.[1]

There is a disagreement as to the origins of the rights of subrogation in English law, with two conflicting views generally being advanced. One view is that subrogation is the child of equity, being imposed by the Courts so as to prevent unjust enrichment of the assured at the expense of the insurer.[2] The school of thought supporting this view, holds that subrogation is a principle of equity and that the insurer's rights of subrogation were acquired from the Chancery in the early case of *Randal v Cockran* [3] whereby it was stated that the insurer possessed *"the plainest equity"* on

---

1 This right extends, in cases where the underwriter has settled a total loss, to entitle him to take over what, if anything, remains of the property.

2 Green A (1995) Strengthening the Insurer's Subrogation Rights, IntILR 3(10): 348-352.

3 (1748)1 Ves Sen 97.

the recognition, by courts of equity in the 18th century, of the notion of subrogation.[4] The other view is that the rights of subrogation are terms implied into the insurance contract, with the role of equity being limited to force an intransigent insured to lend its name to an action against a third-party wrongdoer. This second school of thought supports that the insurer's rights of subrogation rest upon terms implied into the contract of insurance by operation of law, whereby the assured owes a duty to take proceedings against third parties to reduce his loss and to account to the insurer for any benefits, received by him, which do reduce it. This is an analysis which has been developed by Diplock J., in *Yorkshire Insurance Co Ltd v Nisbet Shipping Co Ltd*[5].

It is submitted, however, on the basis of the House of Lords authorities on *Hobbs v Marlowe*[6] and *Napier & Ettrick v Hunter*[7], and as a matter of legal history, that subrogation in insurance law is a legal doctrine by origin. Equity developed later to support the development of the doctrine and thus may have created the impression that the doctrine was an equitable one; however it should not upstage common law at all, for,[8] the courts' task nowadays is to see the two strands of authority -at law and in equity- moulded into a coherent whole.[9] From a practical point of view, the origins of subrogation make little difference. The important point is that the rights of subrogation can be extended or reduced by the express terms of the insurance contract, with the result that it is always open to the insurer to improve his position by the use of a widely drafted subrogation clause.[10]

5.1.2. The rights in respect of which subrogation arises and their extent; the persons upon which subrogation rights may be effected

Subrogation, being one of the first principles of insurance, applies equally to all contracts of indemnity. It is therefore well settled law that subrogation is a corollary of the principle of indemnity, since it precludes the assured from recovering from two sources in respect of the same loss and is

---

[4] Jones NL (1997) MacGillivray on Insurance Law , 9th edn, S&M, Ch 22.
[5] [1962]2 QB 330.
[6] [1978] AC 16.
[7] [1993] AC 713.
[8] As also stated in the above cited cases.
[9] Jones NL (1997) MacGillivray on Insurance Law , 9th edn, S&M, Ch 22,.
[10] Green A (1995) Strengthening the Insurer's Subrogation Rights, IntILR, 3(10): 348-352.

ancillary only to indemnity contracts.[11] The principle was well defined in the case of *Simpson v Thompson*[12] and in the cases of *Castellain v Preston*[13] and *Burnard v Rodocanachi*[14].

It is also well established that subrogation arises once the insured has been indemnified.[15] It is submitted that the right may exist as a contingent one, at the time of effect of the contract, and later on arise, i.e. after the insurer has indemnified the assured and can subsequently exercise his subrogation right. In *Boag v Standard*[16], cargo owners had insured their cargo with a company for £685 but - due to market fluctuations - the net value of the cargo increased to £900 and the owners insured the increase in value with a Lloyd's underwriter. The cargo became a total loss and the assured received under both policies, as well as an additional sum in place of general average contribution. The issue here was whether the increased value underwriters had an equity in it, for an amount proportional to their share of the total insurance coverage. It was held that the initial insurance company had a right of subrogation when it effected the policy, in the sense of it being a contingent right.[17]

---

11 *Burnard v Rodocanachi* (1887)3 App.Cas 279, at 339 per Blackburn L.J.

12 (1887)3 App Cas 279, at 284 , per Lord Cairns who stated :
"...where one person has agreed to indemnify another he will, on making good the indemnity, be entitled to succeed to all the ways and means by which the person indemnified might have protected himself against or reimbursed himself for the loss."

13 (1883)11 QB 380, at 401, Bowen LJ stated:.
".....a person who wishes to recover for a total loss......if he has a means of diminishing the loss, the result of the use of those means belongs to the underwriters. If he does diminish the loss, he must account for the diminution to the underwriters."

14 (1882)7 App Cas 333, at 339, Lord Blackburn stated:
"...where there is a contract of indemnity, and loss reduces or diminishes the amount which the indemnifier is bound to pay; and if the indemnifier has already paid it, then, if anything which diminishes the loss comes into the hands of the persons to whom he has paid it, it becomes an equity that the person who has already paid the full indemnity is entitled to be recouped by having that amount back".

15 In *Simpson v Thompson* (1887)3 App Cas 279, Lord Blackburn pointed out (at 293) that the right arose from the fact that the underwriters had paid an indemnity, and in *Darrell v Tibbitts* (1880)5 QBD 560, (at 563) , Brett J. observed that after the assured has been paid, is the insurer actually put into the place of the assured with regard to every right given to him by the law respecting the subject-matter insured; in *Page v Scottish* (1929) 140 LT 151, (at 578) Scrutton LJ stated that the underwriter has no right until and unless he indemnifies the assured under the policy.

16 [1937]2 KB 113.

17 Both insurers have the right of subrogation and the general average contribution has to be apportioned among them as per their insured value. It has been proposed that if an insurer has part of coverage of the subject-matter insured

Although the rule set in *Boag v Standard*[18] has been modified by the increased value clause[19], nevertheless, it is mostly in terms of academic terms that we distinguish whether the right arises upon conclusion of the contract or after payment, as it is only after payment that the insurer can exercise his right.

All the above are encapsulated in the Marine Insurance Act 1906 in s. 79. The Marine Insurance Act 1906 draws a clear distinction between cases where an underwriter has paid a total loss, where he is entitled to take over the interest of the assured *"...in whatever may remain of the subject-matter so paid for"*, and cases where he has paid only a partial loss, where no such proprietary interest as in the former case is acquired by the underwriter. The underwriter, in any case, is on payment subrogated to all the rights and remedies of the assured in respect of the subject-matter insured, with the qualification that in the case of a partial loss his rights may extend only so far as the assured may have been indemnified. Thus, the fundamental difference between the right of subrogation in cases of total loss as opposed to partial loss, is that in the former case - in addition to the right of subrogation - the insurer actually takes over the interest of the assured in the remains of the subject-matter, whereas in the latter he merely has the right to pursue claims against third parties without obtaining a co-existing interest in the goods.

However, an express clause of subrogation in a contract of insurance may modify the doctrine operated by law and give the insurer the subrogation right before the insured has been indemnified.[20]

The insurer is restricted to the rights incident to and arising out of the thing insured. Thus, in *Sea Insurance v Hadden*,[21] where the insured vessel was lost in collision with another vessel before the chartered freight was earned, the owners - although having given notice of abandonment - were paid for a total loss and the insurers were not held being entitled to the benefit of the compensation received by the owners of the vessel at fault in respect of the loss of freight. Similarly, if a vessel is damaged by collision and her owners recover, from those by whose negligence the collision was caused, damages in respect of matters which are not covered by a policy on ship, the underwriters cannot - by paying for a total loss - re-

and the other insurer has insured the other part, then both have a joint subrogation right (Chen S (1999) Subrogation in the Law of Marine Insurance, PhD Thesis, University of Southampton, p 14).

18 [1937]2 KB 113.

19 Institute Cargo clauses 1/1/82,clause 14.

20 Birds J (1979) Contractual Subrogation in Insurance Law, JBL, 124.

21 (1884)13 QBD 706.

cover from their assured sums paid to them by the wrongdoer but not paid as part of the value of the ship insured.

The underwriter is only entitled to the benefit of such remedies, rights or other advantages, as the assured would himself be able to enjoy.

The underwriter has no independent rights of his own, cannot sue in his own name and is not[22] liable to give discovery in an action brought in his interest in the name of the assured.[23] The advantages to which the insurer, by subrogation, succeeds are only advantages to which the assured is or was, by right, entitled.[24]

If an assured, who has sustained a loss in respect of which he has a claim against some third party, intends to make a claim upon his policy, he must take care not to come to any arrangements with such third party which may prejudice the insurer's rights of subrogation. If he effectually renounces any rights or remedies which he may have, he will be bound to give credit to his insurers for the value of such rights or remedies. There seems no reason however, why an assured should not give the third party a release, subject to the insurer's right of subrogation. In the same way, the insurer's rights of subrogation will not be diminished by any contract made by the assured with a subsequent insurer; for, just as the insurer is only entitled to the benefit of such remedies, rights or other advantages as the assured would himself enjoy, same, on subrogation he is entitled to that benefit unimpaired by dealings of the assured with other persons.[25]

In *BP Exploration Operating Co Ltd v Kvaerner Oilfield Products Ltd*[26], which is an application of the principles in *National Oilwell (UK)*

---

22 As he is distinct from the assured.

23 *James Nelson & Sons Ltd v Nelson Line Ltd* [1906]2 KB.

24 This was the ground of L.J.Brett's decision in the Case of *Castellain v Preston* (1888)11 QBD 380, and was considered also to have been the ground of the decision of the House of Lords, in the case of *Burnand v Rodocanachi* (1881)6 QBD 633; however, as it appears after more careful consideration of the ruling, it is to be said that the House of Lords justified these decisions not on the ground suggested by Brett LJ but because the payments, though voluntary, were –by the very terms of the declaration under which they were made – intended to compensate those who had actually been the losers by the Spanish depredations.

25 *Boag v Standard Marine Insurance Co* [1936]2 KB 121; Mustill, MJ, Gilman, JCB (1981) Arnould's Law of Marine Insurance and Average, 16th edn, vol I, Stevens, Ch 31.

26 *BP Exploration Operating Co Ltd v Kvaerner Oilfield Products Ltd* [2004] EWHC 999 (Comm)

Ltd. v Davy Offshore Ltd[27], *BP* was exploiting offshore oilfields, and ordered various items of equipment, including sub-sea control modules and directional control valves, which controlled the flow of production from oil wells on the seabed, from *Kvaerner*. These items were supplied by *Kvaerner* and *CC* under a series of contracts, most importantly a development contract.[28] *BP* claimed that the equipment provided was defective and was indemnified by its all risks insurers, who sought to recover the payment from *Kvaerner*. It was clear that if clause 10.5(b) was taken alone, there was an apparently unlimited obligation on *BP* to insure the property against all risks, with *Kvaerner* being named as a co-assured. However, if the opening words of clause 10.5 were taken into account, the position became different, because the that clause was restricted to specific circumstances post-delivery, and accordingly the obligation (authority) on the part of *BP* to insure would be limited to those circumstances. Colman J. held that clause 10.5(b) was free-standing and was not limited by the opening words of clause 10.5. He regarded each interpretation as plausible on the words used, but that there was no commercial sense in limiting the obligation to insure, and was persuaded by the surrounding documentation,

---

[27] *National Oilwell (UK) Ltd v Davy Offshore Ltd* [1993] 2 Lloyd's Rep 582 where it had been decided that if party A took out a policy which covered his own interests and those of party B, party B would only be regarded as a co-assured – and thus entitled to subrogation immunity – if he had authorised A to procure the insurance on B's behalf. The most important form of authorisation was the obligation in the agreement between A and B under which A was under an obligation to obtain insurance for B. In determining the scope of B's cover, it was necessary to consider the scope of the authorisation/obligation; if that were restricted to particular risks, then B's subrogation immunity was so limited.

[28] Clause 10.5 of the contract was stated to apply to:

"the performance of the Development Services under this Development Contract subsequent to the manufacture and delivery of equipment by the Contractor to BP with respect to any attendance by any member of the Contractor Group as may be required under the Development Contract in connection with the installation, assembly, testing, commissioning and start up of such delivered equipment or the carrying out of remedial work pursuant to clause 8 at BP's work locations onshore and/or offshore"

Clause 10.5(b) then stated that:

"Without prejudice to the Contractor's liabilities and obligations BP shall (at BP's cost) take out and maintain from the commencement of this Development Contract an insurance policy which will give subject to its terms and conditions, as outlined in Attachment 1 (Notes on Insurance), protection against risk of physical loss or damage and against general third party liability arising from the performance of the Development Services. The Contractor, Sub-Contractors and other contractors engaged in the installation of the Schiehallion Facilities will be covered under the policy as "Other Assureds" and therefore will have similar benefits under the policy to BP."

including the Notes on Insurance, which showed that *Kvaerner*'s price had not included the cost of construction insurance risks, that it was contemplated that *Kvaerner* would be covered and that the project was in the nature of a joint venture. There was also expert evidence demonstrating that it was a widespread – albeit not invariable – practice for all risks operators' contracts of this type to be extended to third party contractor. In reaching this conclusion, the court held that something had *"gone wrong"* with the layout of clause 10.5.[29]

In *HSBC Rail (UK) Ltd v Network Rail Infrastructure Ltd*,[30] *HSBC* leased rolling stock to a train operator, *GNER*, under a contract which provided that *GNER* was to assume all risk of loss, damage or destruction of the rolling stock from whatever clause, so that in the event of a total loss *GNER* was to pay the full agreed value of the rolling stock to *HSBC*. The contract also required *GNER* to take out all risks property insurance in the names of both itself and *HSBC* for their respective rights and interests: the proceeds were payable to *HSBC* and were to be applied in discharging *GNER*'s obligation to pay the full value to *HSBC*. The rolling stock was damaged due to the admitted negligence of the defendant, i.e. the successor to *Railtrack*. The insurers indemnified *HSBC*, and the insurers then sought to exercise subrogation rights against the defendant. The question was whether *HSBC* had a cause of action. The Court of Appeal held that it did not and ruled that a bailor who was not entitled to possession of goods could sue only for damage to his reversionary interest, and there had been no such damage because *HSBC* had been indemnified by *GNER*. The existence of the insurance made no difference to this conclusion. The person indemnified under the policy was *GNER* and not *HSBC*, given that the risk was borne by *GNER*: it was not necessary to decide whether *HSBC* would have had a claim under the policy.[31]

By virtue of the doctrine of subrogation, the insurer can also recover from the assured the value of any benefits received by him incidental to the loss. Where the assured receives some kind of compensation, from an outside source, which cannot be actually seen as a form of insurance, there needs to be clarified whether the compensation was intended to be a gift or a sort of indemnity for the assured, in respect of the loss he may have suffered. The insurers are entitled to the benefit of gifts made to the assured for the purpose of reducing the loss, provided they were not intended exclusively for the benefit of the assured. In *Burnard v Rodoca-*

---

29 Merkin R, Insurance Law Update 2003-2006.

30 *HSBC Rail (UK) Ltd v Network Rail Infrastructure Ltd*, [2005] EWCA Civ 1437

31 Merkin R, Insurance Law Update 2003-2006.

nachi Sons & Co,[32] underwriters paid the assured's claim in respect of a cargo destroyed by a Confederate cruiser. The claim was paid on a valued basis, which was less than the actual value of the cargo. Subsequently, an Act of Congress established a compensation fund out of which the assured was paid the difference between the actual loss and the sum received from underwriters. Under the provisions of that Act, no claim against the compensation fund was allowed for any loss which the injured party had received by way of indemnity from an insurer and no claim was allowed by or on behalf of any insurer, either in his own right or in that of the assured party. The House of Lords held that underwriters were not entitled to recover the compensation from the assured. In *Merret v Capitol Indemnity Corporation,*[33] the plaintiff was a representative Lloyd's underwriter who was reinsured under policies of reinsurance issued by the defendants. It was found that the plaintiff was entitled to recover $113,000 under various reinsurance contracts. However, about $45,000 had been paid to the plaintiff by their brokers, although these brokers were under no legal liability to make the payment. The payment was found to have been made to retain the plaintiff's goodwill and that the brokers expected to be reimbursed by the defendants. The payment was a gift even though it was made for commercial reasons. Although making it clear that it is a question of fact in each case whether or not a gift has been paid in diminution of the loss, Steyn J. said that if the assured can prove that the gift was intended solely for his benefit, it must be disregarded in assessing the assured's recoverable loss from the insurer. In *Colonia Versicherung AG v Amoco Oil Co,* [34] however, Amoco sold a cargo of Naptha on fob terms. The cargo was bought through a chain of contracts by ICI on cif terms. The cargo was found to be contaminated on delivery due to Amoco's negligence. The claim by ICI was settled in full by Amoco although there was no discernible claim against them by ICI and although Amoco may well have been entitled to limit their liability to other parties in the chain. The Court of Appeal said that the crucial question was whether, on the construction of the settlement documents between Amoco and ICI, it was the intention of Amoco to benefit ICI to the exclusion of underwriters. It was held that the payment by Amoco could not be regarded as a gift to ICI and it should be regarded as paid in diminution of ICI's loss. Underwriters were therefore not liable under the policy.[35]

---

[32] (1882)7 App Cas 333.
[33] [1991]1 Lloyd's Rep 169.
[34] [1997]1 Lloyd's Rep 261.
[35] Mance J, Goldrein L, Merkin R (1999) Insurance Disputes, London LLP.

It has been concluded, however, that it is incorrect to say that underwriters can under no circumstances be entitled to advantages received by their assured otherwise than as of right, and this view was supported in *Castellain v Preston*[36]. In addition, the decision in *Stearns v Village Main Reef Gold Mining Co*[37] is a clear authority for the rule that insurers are entitled to the benefit of gifts made to the assured for the purpose of reducing the loss, provided that they were not intended exclusively for the benefit of the assured.

Where the assured has rights both against his insurers and against a third party, in respect of a loss, he may recover from them an aggregate sum substantially in excess of his loss. If, after satisfaction from the insurers, the assured receives any further compensation in respect of his loss, he must hold it as a trustee for his insurer. The underwriter has the right to recover from the assured any sums, received by him, not only incidental to the loss but also those received in diminution of the loss. This further right reflects the principle that the assured is not entitled to receive more than a full indemnity for his loss. In *Castellain v Preston* [38] a vendor contracted with a third party to sell a house at a specific sum, the house having been insured by the vendor against fire. Under the terms of the contract, the purchaser completed the purchase paying the specified sum to the vendor. The underwriter, who had paid the vendor in respect of the loss, brought an action to recover the money paid by the purchaser and was held entitled to recover a sum equal to the insurance money from the vendor.[39]

It is an established principle of subrogation that an underwriter is entitled only to the assured's rights and remedies in respect of the subject-matter insured, in so far as he has indemnified the assured. Thus, if the sum recovered by the assured exceeds the amount paid under the policy by the underwriter, then the underwriter is entitled to have refunded to himself, under subrogation, only the sum he has paid.[40] In addition, he may be entitled to interest attaching to his payment. Yet, even where the underwriter has exercised rights of ownership, his rights are limited to the subject-matter insured.[41] The insurer cannot, by virtue of the doctrine of sub-

---

36 (1883)11 QBD 404.

37 [1905]10 Com Cas 89.

38 (1883)11 QBD 380.

39 The judgement of Brett LJ in this case, described later on by Diplock J as the *locus classicus* of the doctrine of subrogation in insurance law, has set out the full extent of the rights to which the insurer is subrogated.

40 *Yorkshire Insurance Co Ltd v Nisbet Shipping Co Ltd* [1961]1 Lloyd's Rep. 479.

41 In the case of *Attorney-General v Glen Line Ltd*, [1930]36 Com Cas 1., a dispute arose as to whether a claim by the Crown, as reinsuring underwriters, to

rogation, acquire rights which the assured never possessed. The rights and remedies brought about by way of subrogation may only be acted upon in the name of the assured who has been indemnified.[42]

Lord Jauncey stated in *Esso Petroleum Co Ltd v Hall Russell and Co & Others (The Esso Bernicia)*[43] :

"...Where an indemnifier is subrogated to the rights of someone whom he has indemnified he can only pursue those rights in the name of that person".

The insurer, on indemnifying against costs, may sue in the assured's name any person through whose default or wrongdoing the loss may have occurred. This applies whether the loss is a total or a partial one. Accordingly, where damage is done by a third party to the thing insured, he may be sued by the insurer in the name of the assured. The insurer, however, is entitled to sue in his own name where the assured has assigned to the insurer his right of action in respect of the subject-matter.[44]

As the foundation of the right of subrogation is payment under a contract of indemnity, in case the payment by an underwriter is not made

be entitled to a sum paid by the German Government as compensation to shipowners was well founded. It was held that the sum recovered by the former owners was not paid to them in respect of the loss of their ship but in respect of losses they might reasonably have expected to make by the use of their ship, and it was not therefore a sum to which the underwriters were entitled by reason of their payment of a total loss under policies insuring the ship itself (Lambeth RJ (1986) Templeman on Marine Insurance: Its Principles and Practice, 6th edn, Pitman, pp 451-462).

42 Hodges S (1999) Cases and Materials on Marine Insurance Law, Cavendish Publications, p 17.

43 [1988]3 WLR 730 HL; On this principle, it was held in *Simpson v Thomson* [(1877)3 App Cas 279] that, where a ship was sunk in collision with another ship of the same ownership, the underwriters - who had paid a total loss on the ship sunk had no right of recovery from the owner - although the other ship was at fault. Where a policy on cargo was effected by a ship-owner on behalf of the cargo-owner, it was held that the underwriters were entitled to pursue a claim under subrogation in the name of their assured, i.e. the cargo-owner, against the ship-owner in whose name as agent only the policy had been effected ("*The Yasim*" [1979]2 Lloyd's Rep 45 ; Lambeth RJ (1986) Templeman on Marine Insurance: Its Principles and Practice, 6th edn, Pitman, pp 451-462).

44 Ivamy ERH (1986) General Principles of Insurance Law, 5th edn, Butterworths, p 458.

under a legally enforceable contract of indemnity, he acquires no right of subrogation.[45]

Rights of subrogation are not acquired by underwriters under a *"p.p.i."* or *"honour"* policy. In *John Edwards Ltd v Motor Union Insurance Co. Ltd*[46] , the owners of a ship, which was sunk in a collision, obtained a declaration that the underwriters, who had paid them a total loss under a *"p.p.i."* policy, were not entitled to share in the recovery made in the collision proceedings. There was no legally enforceable right under the *"p.p.i."* policy to give rise to subrogation. Similarly, a liquidator of an insurer is bound to disallow altogether a claim by an assured based on a *"p.p.i."* policy, because it is unenforceable in law.[47]

The doctrine of subrogation is applied to all insurers, including the assured himself if he is his own insurer for part of the loss. Thus, in *The Welsh Girl* [48] a vessel was insured for £1,000 being valued at £1,350 in the policy. She was sunk in a collision and became a total loss. The insurers paid the assured the £1,000 and on suing the vessel at fault recovered £1,000. It was held that the assured could recover from the insurers 350/1,350 of the £1,000 since he was his own insurer for the amount of £350. On the other hand, in *Thames and Mersey Marine Insurance Co v British and Chilian SS Co*[49] the insurers paid a total loss on a vessel insured for £45,000 on an agreed value of that amount, after she had collided with another vessel. Proceedings were taken against the other vessel and the assured was awarded 3/5 of the actual value of his vessel, which was £65,000. It was held that the insurers were entitled to the whole of the amount recovered in the collision action.

The doctrine of subrogation also operates in favour of a reinsurer. Thus, in *Assicurazioni Generali de Trieste v Empress Assurance Corpn Ltd* [50], person A reinsured person B in respect of certain risks on which person B had insured person C. Person B paid person C, and person A paid person B in respect of losses in the policy. It was held that when person B recovered person C, the amount was paid on the basis that he had been induced to pay as a result of a fraudulent misrepresentation; the losses paid not being in fact risks under the policy. Thus, the principle of subrogation

---

45 This was made clear in the case of *Edwards & Co Ltd v Motor Union Insurance Co Ltd* [1922]2 KB 249; Lambeth RJ (1986) Templeman on Marine Insurance: Its Principles and Practice, 6th edn, Pitman, pp 451-462.

46 [1922]2 KB 249.

47 *Re London County Commercial Reinsurance Office Ltd* [1922]2 Ch 67; O'May D (1993) Marine Insurance Law and Policy, LLP, p 463.

48 [1906]22 TLR 475.

49 [1916]1 KB 30.

50 [1907]2 KB 804.

operated to entitle person A to recover from person B the amount so recovered. But it was also held that person B was entitled to deduct the costs properly incurred in recovering the money from C.[51]

Another distinction need be drawn between subrogation and abandonment. Abandonment is a corollary of the doctrine of subrogation and Arnould (1981)[52] has also pointed out that the two doctrines are closely related. Although the doctrine of abandonment is in its origins linked to that of subrogation, both share the objective of preventing the assured to receive more than an indemnity and the former is frequently regarded as the sub-rule of the latter.

The rights of subrogation and those resulting from abandonment are not identical but complimentary: whereas abandonment has effect only in cases of total loss, subrogation applies to all contracts of indemnity and to all cases in which any loss is reimbursed by the party indemnifying, whether it be partial or total.[53] Subrogation confers upon the insurer rights to pursue the assured's claims against the third parties for the loss of the subject-matter, whereas abandonment merely confers on the insurer rights over remains of the subject-matter and the proprietary right incidental thereto. Subrogation does not permit the insurer to sue in his own name, whereas - upon acceptance of the abandonment - the insurer becomes owner of the remains of the subject-matter insured and all rights and obligations arising from it are conferred upon him. Thus, another difference is

---

[51] Ivamy ERH (1986) General Principles of Insurance Law, 5th edn, Butterworths, pp 458-460.

[52] Mustill MJ, Gilman JCB (1981) Arnould's Law of Marine Insurance and Average, 16th edn, vol I, Stevens, § 1298.

[53] Mustill MJ, Gilman JCB (1981) Arnould's Law of Marine Insurance and Average, 16th edn, vol I, Stevens, Ch 31: In practice, insurers rarely accept abandonment, for it carries with it not only rights but also liabilities in respect of the abandoned property. Obvious liabilities are expenses incurred for the removal of the wreck and damage caused by oil pollution. (*River Wear Comrs v Adamson* (1877)2 App Cas 743, *The Mostyn* [1928]AC 57, *Arrow Shipping Co v Tyne Improvement Comrs* (1894)AC 508) Should, however, the insurer agree expressly or implicitly to assume ownership over the remains of the subject-matter insured, he would be able to retain any profit made on its sale. (*Attorney General v Glen Line Ltd* [1930]36 Com Cas 1, *Yorkshire Insurance Co v Nisbett Shipping Co Ltd* [1961]1 Lloyd's Rep. 479) It may be contended by some that, in this respect, the principle of indemnity has failed to realise its full potential and that the contract is not one of perfect indemnity. In accepting the abandonment, the insurer takes over not only rights but also liabilities in relation to the remains of the subject-matter insured. It could, therefore, be validly argued that as he had assumed all responsibility in respect of the subject-matter insured, he should be allowed to keep any reward arising there from.

that any profits earned by the insurer from abandoned property will accrue to him, whereas the subrogated insurer is only allowed to retain what he has paid for. Finally, subrogation operates automatically - by operation of law - as a result of the principle of indemnity to confer rights upon the insurer, whereas abandonment does not automatically divest the ownership of the assured to the insurer and it is the insurer who has the option to take over the remain of the subject-matter insured upon payment of the loss.[54]

5.1.3. Recovery in the case of under-insurance or partial insurance

The right of the insurer against third parties arises where the assured has been fully indemnified and only then.

A point for debate is whether the insurer - who has met in full his own obligations to the assured under the contract - can exercise his rights of subrogation where the sum insured under the policy is not adequate to meet the assured's total loss. In the absence of an express policy provision conferring subrogation rights on the insurer upon him meeting his full contractual obligations to the assured, irrespective of whether the assured has been indemnified overall, the question is open to doubt but the situation has been clarified with the ruling in *Napier v Hunter*[55], discussed further below[56].

In the case of underinsurance the assured is entitled to be *dominus litis*, even if the insurer has made a full payment under the policy terms, and any recoveries from third parties are then to be shared between underwriters and assured in proportion to the insurance burden each one bears[57]. In the case of *The Commonwealth*,[58] a policy was taken out for £1,000 on a vessel valued at £1,350. The vessel sunk and underwriters paid a total loss of £1,000 under the policy. Subsequently, the sum of £1,000 was recovered from a third party and the court held that underwriters and insured were entitled to share the recovery *pro rata*. However, following the deci-

[54] Chen S (1999) Subrogation in the Law of Marine Insurance, PhD Thesis, University of Southampton, pp 158-160.

[55] *Napier and Ettrick v RF Kershaw Ltd* [1993]1 Lloyd's Rep. 10.

[56] It would be inferred from *Napier v Hunter* [1993]1 Lloyd's Rep. 10 that the-Courts will hold in future that insurers are entitled to be simply subrogated to their assured's right of action from the moment the latter is fully indemnified under the policy terms, even though he may not have been fully compensated for his loss.

[57] *The Commonwealth* [1907] P 216.

[58] [1907] P 216.

sion in *Napier v Hunter*,[59] a different approach has been established. In this case a Lloyd's syndicate took out a *"stop loss"* policy with insurers containing both an *"excess clause"* and an agreed limit on liability. The syndicate suffered a loss and recovered on the policy. The members also sued their own managing agents for breach of contract and negligence. A settlement was reached and a sum of money was held representing the settlement money. The purpose of proceedings between insurer and the persons assured was to establish the respective claims on that sum, given that it was not sufficient to meet the totality of insured and uninsured losses. A further issue was whether the insurers could exercise any proprietary rights by way of trust or lien over the money. It was determined in the House of Lords that the assured should stand behind the insurer so far as recovery in respect of the excess was concerned. As inferred from *Napier v Hunter*,[60] courts will not regard the contract of insurance with an excess or deductible clause as underinsurance and it will be sufficient for the courts to award a subrogation right so long as the assured has been fully indemnified under the policy and the insurer, meanwhile, remains *dominus litis*. It is also inferred that courts will most probably hold, in future, that insurers are entitled to be simply subrogated to their assured's right of action, from the moment the assured is fully indemnified under the terms of the policy even though they may not have been fully compensated for their loss.

The assured's partial indemnity should not also affect his position as *dominus litis* in the claims for entire loss against the third party, even if the insurer has met his full liability under the policy. However, an express clause could provide for the insurer to be *dominus litis* and control the proceedings even before the insurer has received full indemnity and, indeed, it may enable the insurer to exercise a right of subrogation before payment has been made.[61] A provision to this effect would merely constitute an agreement between the parties, that an existing but unenforceable right of subrogation should be treated as an enforceable right. Nevertheless, it may be that it is not possible to confer a subrogation right in situations where one otherwise does not exist, because of the danger that a clause purporting to do this could be said to be champertous.[62]

Certain types of policy contain an aggregate limit of liability that is less than the total value of the insured property, for example fleet policies

---

[59] *Nappier and Ettrick v Hunter: Lord Napier and Ettrick v RF Kershaw Ltd* [1993]1 All ER 385; [1993] AC 713, HL.

[60] *Nappier and Ettrick v Hunter: Lord Napier and Ettrick v RF Kershaw Ltd* [1993]1 All ER 385; [1993] AC 713, HL.

[61] Birds J (1979) Contractual Subrogation in Insurance Law, JBL, 124.

[62] Derham SR (1985) Subrogation in Insurance Law, p 145.

(on ships or aircraft) and cargo open covers. The purpose of such aggregate limits is to protect underwriters from an aggregation of risk such as may occur if many ships, aircraft or cargoes accumulate at a particular place where a significant loss occurs at one time. Where a loss exceeds the aggregate limit, any recoveries in excess of the limit will accrue entirely to the assured on the *"top down"* principle until the limit is reached. In *Kuwait Airways Corporation (KAC) v Kuwait Insurance Co (No 2)*,[63] KAC insured 15 aircraft against war risk. In so far as the aircraft cover was concerned, the policy was subject to a limit of US$300m per occurrence. Each aircraft was separately valued in a schedule to the policy, the total value for all the aircraft being US$692m. All the aircrafts having been lost, as a result of the Iraqi invasion in 1990, insurers paid the limit of US$300m. Eventually, KAC recovered eight of the 15 aircraft insured under the policy, the agreed insured value of which was about US$375m net of certain recovery expenses. Underwriters contended that credit for the insured value of the recovered aircraft should be shared proportionately in the ratio 300/692 parts to insurers and 392/692 parts to KAC. The Court held that underwriters were not entitled to share in the recovery. KAC was entitled to apply the value of the recoveries to the uninsured loss of aircraft (£392m) and no credit was due to underwriters so long as the recoveries did not exceed that sum.

The distribution of recoveries may create controversies, in case of an excess clause in the policy. Few scholars have tackled this point, except Derham (1985),[64] who expressed the view that if - in case of underinsurance - a policy has an excess clause, the assured should be entitled to recoup the amount of his excess before the insurer is subrogated to any recovery from a third party. Further, the assured is entitled to a full indemnity for his actual loss including the excess. The rule similarly applies where there is a deductible clause in the policy.[65] In a fully insured policy with excess clause, the rule inferred from the *Nappier*[66] case in the House of Lords is that that the insurer has the first claim up to his payment. The fact that English law has not treated the assured as his own in-

63 [2000] Lloyd's Rep IR 439.

64 Derham SR (1985) Subrogation in Insurance Law.

65 Derham SR (1985) Subrogation in Insurance Law, p.134; What applies in practice in case of a deductible is that recoveries against any claim subject to a deductible are credited to the underwriters in full to the extent of the sum by which the aggregate of the claim unreduced by any recoveries exceeds the deductible.

66 *Nappier and Ettrick v Hunter: Lord Napier and Ettrick v RF Kershaw Ltd* [1993]1 All ER 385; [1993] AC 713, HL.

surer in the event of excess or deductible clause has been also criticised by the UNCTAD.[67]

5.2. The rights of the insurer on payment in marine insurance contracts in Greece

Under Greek law, subrogation is a legal cession or assignment of rights generally provided by law (Law 2496/1997 art. 14). It is based on the concept that the assured can only be once indemnified. Insurers who compensate their assureds, in respect of loss or damage, are automatically subrogated and can sue in their own name the person or entity responsible for the loss or damage, provided that the assured was entitled to indemnification by a third party.[68] The insurer cannot be subrogated against the assured's rights against his ascendants or descendants or spouse or persons living with the assured, or his legal representatives, unless they have acted in bad faith. The assured must preserve rights against third parties for the benefit of the insurer. If not, the latter can seek damages. In the case of sale, alienation or liquidation of the subject-matter insured, as per art. 277 of the CPML (ΚΙΝΔ), the new owner is automatically subrogated to the rights and obligations of the prior assured. For this to happen, the prerequisites are that an insurance contract must have been concluded and also that the subject-matter insured has been either sold or alienated or liquidated.[69] If it be a vessel, the new owner owes the full premium as well to the insurer and is only not liable to pay it only if he waives the contract within

67 UN: UN Conference on Trade and Development: Report on Marine Insurance, Legal and Documentary Aspects of the Marine Insurance Contract, UN, NY p 57, 20/11/1978,TD/B/C.4/ISL/27, where it is reported: *"....It is suggested that the English practice is inequitable to the assured. It is clear that both parties suffer loss whenever hull damage occurs and the insurer pays the claim and the assured bears the deductible. Just as the insurer desires to diminish his losses by offsetting recoveries from third parties, it seems inequitable to deny the assured the same opportunity. It would seem in this respect that the insurer, who is in the business of running the risk of loss, does not merit preferential treatment over the assured, who has attempted to eliminate the risk of such losses by buying the insurance in the first place."*

68 Spaidiotis K (1999) Marine Insurance Law in Greece, Maritime Advocate, Issue 7; Cases: *Piraeus Court of Appeal: 1741/1990ΕφΠειρ,ΕΝαυτΔ 1991,159 ; Piraeus Court of First Instance: 1848/1990 ΠΠρΠειρ, ΕΝαυτΔ91,219; Piraeus Court of Appeal : 722/1993 ΕφΠειρ, 1994,750. Athens Court of Appeal: 7230/199700 Εφ Αθ, Αρμ 1978,255; Piraeus Court of First Instance: ΠΠρΠειρ 122/1990, ΕΝαυτΔ 1990,243.*

69 Kiantos BD (1998) Insurance Law, 6th edn, Sakkoulas Publications, Thessaloniki, Greece.

thirty days. The insurer is not liable, if the occurrence of the events due to maritime perils would not have happened, had the subject-matter insured not been sold, as per art. 277§2 CPML (ΚΙΝΔ). In the case of cargo insurance, the insurer is not liable unless the new assured has not paid the premium, acting in bad faith.[70]

5.3. The rights of the insurer on payment in marine insurance contracts in Norway

In Norway, as per the Norwegian Marine Insurance Plan,[71] the insurer has a right of subrogation. More specifically, when the assured has a claim for damages against a third party on account of a loss, either wholly or in part,[72] the insurer is automatically subrogated to the assured's claim against the third party from the moment that he pays compensation under the insurance contract.

The insurer is subrogated to *"the rights of the assured against the third party concerned"*. This entails, that he takes over the claim for damages regardless of the basis on which it is founded. This does not, however, apply where the assured has a claim by virtue of another insurance contract. The insurer is subrogated to the claim as it is in the assured's hands. If there is a maritime lien or some other security connected with the claim, the insurer may exercise this right. The insurer only takes over claims for damages that are connected with the interest insured and refer to

---

[70] Velentzas I(1998) The New Law of Private Insurance, Ius Publ., Athens.; The insurer is also bound by a valid arbitration or choice of jurisdiction clause that had been agreed between the assured and the third party responsible for damages. If the insurer indemnifies the assured after the latter has initiated a trial against the third party, it continues the trial at its place of jurisdiction. Subrogation also entails the assured's procedural rights as well. The courts are not in accordance whether the assured has to initiate proceedings against a third party before the insurer pays him, so that these rights do not prescribe due to lapse of time barring set by law, given also the fact that the insurer cannot initiate proceedings before paying. Thus, in this matter courts decide on a case by case basis; however, the fact that the delay of the insurer may have been due to material reasons plays a decisive role. (Campbell D (2001) International Insurance Law and Regulation, Vol. I, Oceana Publications 2001, Section GRE,p.6.)

[71] Ch. 5 sections 3,4 Norwegian Marine insurance Plan 1996 Commentary <http://exchange.dnv.com/nmip/index.htm>.

[72] For example, as general average contribution or compensation for collision damage.

the very losses that the insurer has covered. If the assured has suffered any other loss, not covered under the insurance,[73] he retains the claim for damages or the claim for contribution in respect of these items. Where the insurer is only partly liable for the loss, the situation will often be that the insurance conditions provide that the assured shall bear part of the loss in the form of deductions or deductibles and in such a case, the assured shall retain a proportion of the claim for damages against the third party concerned equivalent to the loss he has sustained himself. The claim shall also be divided when the value of the interest affected by the loss is estimated to be a higher amount in the relationship between the assured and the third party than in that between the assured and the insurer and the third party is only liable for a proportion of the loss or is unable to cover the full value of the interest. Hence, the claim for damages shall be divided proportionately if the ship becomes a total loss as the result of a collision and its value is estimated to be higher than the hull valuation, whilst the third party – in accordance with the rules relating to limitation of liability - pays a smaller amount in damages than what the insurer has paid to the assured. Conversely, if the value of the ship in a collision case is estimated to be an amount equivalent to or lower than the hull valuation, the insurer shall keep the entire claim for damages, unless the assured has also suffered other losses.

It is the assured's claim against third parties which may be subjected to a proportionate division, and not the amount of damages which may be paid. The insurer shall invoke his proportion of the claim in his own name. If the assured does not wish to pursue his part of the claim, he is free to drop it. If both the insurer and the assured invoke their claims, it would be natural to try these claims in the same action; such action shall then be conducted in the names of both parties. Where it is the assured's claim that is divided, it is superfluous to issue rules relating to the apportionment of the costs of recovery. Each of the parties shall bear the costs that have been necessary, in order to recover his own claim. If the claims brought by the assured and the insurer against the third party concerned are not met in full, [74] the assured competes on a par with the insurer.

The Norwegian Marine Insurance Plan has not adopted the rule that is common in types of insurance of a more social nature to the effect that the assured's claim for damages prevails over that of the insurer in the event of the relevant third party's bankruptcy. If the value of the interest insured is set at a higher amount in the relationship between the assured and the third party than in the relationship between the assured and the in-

[73] For example, loss of time in connection with a collision.

[74] For example because the third party only has limited liability or is insolvent.

surer, and the third party is furthermore liable for the full loss and is able to pay the entire amount, the insurer's proportion of the claim will be larger than the compensation he has paid to the assured. It would not be reasonable for the insurer to make a profit from his right of subrogation in this way, and therefore it is established[75] that such profit shall be transferred back to the assured. There will obviously be no question of any profit until the insurer has been reimbursed with the expenses covered in connection with the recovery of the claim and the interest accrued on the compensation he has paid to the assured. The loss of interest for the period following the claims settlement with the assured must also be taken into account. If the third party's liability is stipulated in another currency than the one set out in the insurance contract, the insurer shall bear the risk of any exchange loss during the period between the event involving liability and the enforcement of the recourse claim. On the other hand, the insurer shall also have the advantage of any exchange gain.[76]

A special question arises where several insurers are entitled to a proportion of the claim for damages. The problem poses no difficulties if the various insured interests are assessed separately in the claims settlement. However, if the ship is a total loss as a result of a collision, the compensation will be fixed at one specific amount representing the value of the ship.[77] In practice, it has been disputed how the compensation received shall be apportioned among the hull insurer, the hull-interest insurer and the freight-interest insurer. One solution is to make also an apportionment among the total-loss insurers. In the alternative, the traditional layer distribution of the total-loss insurances may be adopted and the hull insurer must be given first priority to compensation to the extent of his claim. The hull-interest insurer will then be given second priority, whilst the freight-interest insurer will only get his share if there is still anything left of the compensation. The reason for such a solution is that it would not be reasonable if, in the event of a total loss, the hull insurer's claim for damages were to be affected by the extent of the freight-interest insurance that the shipowner has taken out.[78]

---

75 Ch. 5 paragraph 5-13 subparagraph 3, Norwegian Marine Insurance Plan (1996) Commentary [http://exchange.dnv.com/nmip/index.htm].

76 Hence, the rule in subparagraph 3 shall not apply here.

77 Including the value of a lost charterparty, if relevant.

78 During the revision, there was general consensus that in the normal situation where the hull value is equal to or higher than the market value, the hull insurer should be given priority. If, however, the hull valuation is lower than the market value, an apportionment must be made so that each insurer receives a proportion of the compensation equivalent to his share of the market value.

5.4. The rights of the insurer on payment in marine insurance contracts in France

Subrogation is dealt with in art. 33 of the Law of 3/7/1967 and now art. L. 172-29 of the Insurance Code. According to these articles, an insurer who has paid an indemnity, is subrogated to the rights of the insured against third parties which, on their part, caused the damage incurring the insurer's responsibility. This shows the facultative character of subrogation. Subrogation also has a contractual character in virtue of art. 17 of the law of 3/7/1967, of the policy type, and of art. L. 121-12 of the Insurance Code.

The insurer's right of subrogation is limited to the amount he has paid. Before subrogation, the only thing that the insurer can ask from the insured is to notify the carrier to sue in his own name, where an indemnity - due to the assured's negligence - cannot be calculated in time for the carrier to prescribe to it.

A case brought before the Court of Appeal of Versailles,[79] clearly illustrates the pattern followed in many cases where the right of action of the subrogated insurer has been contested. In this case, a manufacturer assigned the transportation of textile machines, from France to Argentina, to a broker. Upon the opening of the cases containing the machines, damage due to mould were discovered. The insurer indemnified the transporter and, following up, sued the broker. The court rejected the insurer's plea, noting that one damage occurred during packing which was a risk not covered by the marine policy. The insurer should not, therefore, have had indemnified the transporter and by having done so he was deprived of his legal subrogation rights as per art. L-172.29 of the Code of Insurances.[80]

5.5. The rights of the insurer on payment in marine insurance contracts in the USA

The US law's position, in relation to subrogation, resembles the one under English law. Hence, under US law, as well, subrogation has been defined as the right by which an underwriter, having settled a loss, is entitled to place himself in the position of the assured to the extent of acquiring all the rights and remedies in respect of the loss which the assured may have possessed. Subrogation is an equitable doctrine firmly established in ma-

---

[79] CA Versailles 12e Ch, Sect 2-8 Novembre 2001.

[80] Tantin JF(2002) Le Droit d'Action de l' Assureur Subrogé: Pièges at Parades , DMF 630:803.

rine insurance law.[81] As a general rule, the insurer has no right of subrogation until he has already made a payment to the assured.[82] Subrogation avoids the unjust enrichment of the assured by giving the insurer the right to recoup payment for expenses he has already paid that are subsequently collected by an insured from the exercise of his rights against a liable third party. There are two kinds of subrogation: *"legal subrogation"*,[83] which arises by operation of law, and *"contractual subrogation"*,[84] which results from an agreement between the parties, usually as a clause in the insurance policy. This distinction may be important. If the requirements for legal subrogation are not met under the facts of a particular case, subrogation can still occur if the right is given by contract.[85]

Although the right of subrogation arises when the insurer has paid the assured's loss, in *Welded Tube v Hartford*[86] it was held that a cargo underwriter could plead an ocean carrier in an action brought by its assured even if it had not technically acquired any subrogation rights by making payment to the assured. Further, in *Blasser v Northern Pan-Am*[87] it was held that although a cargo insurer generally has no right to sue the ocean carrier until it has become subrogated by payment of its assured's loss, such subrogation occurs where the assured has sued both the insurer and the carrier in the same action and both are found liable. The insurer was permitted to recover on its cross-claim against he carrier for cargo damage found to have been covered by its policies.[88]

By operation of the rule namely the *"real party in interest"* rule - pursuant to Art. 17(a) of the Federal Rules of Civil Procedure - an insurer sues in subrogation in his own name if he has fully indemnified the assured for his loss. Difficulties arise when the assured is only partially compensated by the insurer. Many state courts allow the assured to sue alone, for

---

81 See *Aetna Ins Co v SS Ortiguera* 583 FSupp 671 (SDNY 1984), where a marine liability insurer, having paid the insurance claim, sued as subrogee the defendant stevedore and it was held that he was a proper subrogee, not a volunteer.

82 The insurer becomes subrogated to the insured's rights only to the extent actually paid on the policy. See *Aetna Ins Co v United Fruit Co* 304 US 430 S.Ct.959,82L.Ed. 1443 (1938).

83 Sometimes called *"equitable subrogation"*.

84 Sometimes called *"conventional subrogation"*.

85 Johnson JF IVth, Brown DR (2001) International Insurance Law and Regula tion: United States, Oceana Publications Inc., Dobbs Ferry, NY, USA.

86 1973 AMC 555 (ED pa)

87 628 F2d 376, 1982 AMC 84 (5th Circ).

88 Chen S (1999) Subrogation in the Law of Marine Insurance, PhD Thesis, University of Southampton, p 178.

the whole loss, in cases of partial payment but in doing so the allocation of the recoveries is then uncertain as to who should have the first claim and it is also less clear whether the assured is liable to the insurer in damage if he does not *bona fide* consider the insurer's interests.[89] The *"real party in the interest"* rule was designed to avoid splitting the cause of action and making the tortfeasor defend two suits for the same wrong. Federal Courts purport that the insurer remains the *"real party in interest"* and should prosecute the action in his own name jointly with the assured.[90]

Subrogation may not be invoked against a person directly or indirectly covered by the contract of insurance.[91] Subrogation may also be waived with respect to additional named insured parties as a way of allowing two or more parties to a marine venture to be insured under one policy of insurance.[92]

It is also established that the doctrine of subrogation is different to the concept of abandonment in marine insurance.[93] This was also the finding in *The Livingstone.*[94] In this case, a vessel -whose insured value was less than the real one- was sunk by collision and the underwriters paid for a total loss. Afterwards, the assured recovered the amount of her real value

---

[89] In *North River Insurance Co v Mackenzie* [74 So 2d 599 (Ala. 1954)], the assured suffered property damage and received $2,357 which was the limit payable under the policy. Then the assured sued the tortfeasor alleging total property damage of $7,500 and without notifying the insurer settled the claim for $5,982.15. The insurer subsequently sued the assured foe repayment of the proceeds from insurance paid to the assured initially. The court held for the insurer that when an assured accepts from the insurer the amount of the policy damage to his property and thereafter settles his claim against the tortfeasor to the prejudice of the insurer, the insurer may recover from the assured the amount paid in the policy without necessarily demonstrating that he settlement exceeded the actual loss less the amount paid on the policy.

[90] Chen S (1999) Subrogation in the Law of Marine Insurance, PhD Thesis, University of Southampton, p 174.

[91] *Atlas Insurance Co Ltd v Harper, Robinson Shipping Co*, 508F2d.1381, 1975 AMC 2358 (9th Circ 1975).

[92] See Schoenbaum TJ (2001) Admiralty and Maritime Law, 3rd edn, Hornbook Series,West Group, St.Paul ,Minn. USA; See Cases: *Dillingham Tug & Barge Corp v Collier Carbon & Chem Corp* 707 F2d 1086, 1984 AMC 1990 (9th Circ 1983).; *Twenty Grand Offshore Inc v West India Carriers Inc* 492 F2d 679, 1974 AMC 2254 (5th Circ 1974).

[93] Following abandonment, if the thing abandoned proves to be of greater value than the amount paid to the assured, the underwriter is still entitled to retain possession of the whole proceeds; whereas subrogation can never entitle the insurer to recover more than he has paid the assured.

[94] 130 Fed Rep 746.

as damages from the vessel in fault and the court held that the insurers were only entitled to receive the amount they had actually paid with interest.

5.6. The rights of the insurer on payment in marine insurance contracts in Canada

The insurer is subrogated to the rights of the assured upon effect of the act of indemnification. The former is, therefore, a consequence of the indemnifying character of the contract of marine insurance.

Pursuant to section 81 of the Federal Marine Insurance Act, an insurer is subrogated to all of the rights and remedies of the insured upon payment of a loss. Once he has fully indemnified the assured, the insurer is subrogated to the rights of the assured on the subject-matter insured which in its turn has been the object of indemnity.[95] This right of subrogation entitles the insurer to commence action against the wrongdoer, in the name of the insured. Where the insured has not received a full indemnity, either because of the existence of uninsured losses or because of the application of a deductible, the insurer does not have the right to control the action. An insured who has not been fully indemnified retains the right to hire and instruct lawyers and to control the litigation. The insured who does so owes a duty to the insurer to pursue the claim with diligence and in good faith. The distribution of the proceeds from a subrogated action as between the insurer and insured is dictated by s. 88 of the Federal Marine Insurance Act, which provides that the insured is deemed to be self insured with respect to his uninsured losses. Thus, the insured and insurer share in ratio, in relation to the proceeds from the subrogated action.

5.7. The rights of the insurer on payment in marine insurance contracts in Australia

Under Australian law, subrogation is perceived as being merely one facet of the principle of indemnity and has no application to contracts of insurance which are not contracts of indemnity.[96]

---

95 Braen A (1992) Le Droit Maritime au Québec, W&L.

96 Sutton K (1991) Insurance Law in Australia, 2nd edn, Law Book Company Ltd.

In *British Traders' Insurance Co Ltd v Monson*[97] the High Court of Australia, in discussing the decision in *Castellain v Preston*,[98] pointed out that the decision was not a case of subrogation in respect of an outstanding right of action as in the ordinary sense of the word, but was one where the assured had been paid the amount of his loss by the insurer and had later received a payment from a third party which eliminated that loss.[99] The principle embodied in the dictum of this case was applied to defeat the claim of the assured in *Sydney Turf Club v Crowley*,[100] where the assured had been indemnified by one insurer so that he had suffered no loss and there was therefore no right of action available to him against the second insurer to which the first insurer could be subrogated. It was also in *Santos Ltd v American Home Assurance Co*,[101] where it was emphasised that the exercise of subrogation was dependent upon payment of the claim by the insurer. It was pointed out that until payment in full, the assured was entitled to remain *dominus litis*,[102] although partial payment -or payment of so much as was due under the policy- would give the insurer certain rights. White J. referred to and applied certain passages to that text to the situation with which he had to deal. His Honour listed the conditions precedent to the exercise of rights of subrogation as (a) that the insurance was indemnity insurance (b) that payment of the insurer had been made under it; and (c) that the insurer's rights of subrogation had not been ex-

---

97 (1964) 111CLR 86 at 94-95.

98 (1883) 11 QBD 380.

99 The judgements made it clear how heavily important it was that the right of the insurer be placed in the position of the assured in relation to both his rights against third parties and the fruit of those rights. The decision rendering the assured accountable to his insurer for the amount paid by the third party was arrived at on the basis that the insurer's obligation had been only to indemnify the assured against his loss, and the payment originally made by the insurer to the assured had been made, not because it was in fact required for indemnification, but because of mutual assumption, which had turned out to be erroneous, that it was required for indemnification. The money had to be brought to account by the assured because it diminished the loss against which the insurer merely undertook to indemnify him. Their Honours added: *"If the assured in that case had received the payment from the third party while still unpaid by the insurer, and had thereafter sued the insurer on the policy, we should be of opinion, notwithstanding the doubt suggested in MacGillivray on Insurance Law, (5th ed., 1961), para. 1798) that the fact of his having received the payment from the third party would have constituted a bar to his claim, as distinguished from affording the insurer a right by way of cross-action to have him account for the amount so received."*

100 (1972) 126 CLR 420.

101 (1987) 4 ANZ Ins Cas 60-795 (SCSA) at 74,874-875.

102 i.e. in control of any litigation

cluded by a term of the parties' contract. He regarded it as firmly established that payment under the policy was a prerequisite to the exercise of rights of subrogation and, as an illustration of the strictness of the principle, pointed to the fact that if an insurer was liable under the one policy for several different types of loss to the assured, he was required to pay for all the types of damage before he could be subrogated to any particular right of the assured. In the case before him the policy gave only partial indemnity against loss, but his Honour found it unnecessary to consider whether the right of subrogation arose prior to there being a full indemnity, since liability had been denied and in consequence no payment had been made at all. He, nevertheless, appeared to approve that *Commercial Union Assurance Co v Lister*,[103] was a case which decided that until full indemnity was received, the assured was entitled to remain *dominus litis*, but not as deciding that there were rights of subrogation at all. Further on, his Honour commented that this view would seem to be in line with SGIO *(Qld) v Brisbane Stevedoring Pty Ltd.*[104] On this view, it seems that in the case of partial indemnity the assured cannot refuse to take proceedings at the behest of the insurer on the ground that no rights of subrogation have arisen,[105] although the assured will remain in control of the litigation to enable him to protect his residual rights.The insurer's right of subrogation in case of payment by him for a partial or a total loss is dealt with in s. 85 of the Marine Insurance Act 1909. In particular, the insurer may bring an action in the assured's name against any third party who has caused the loss.[106]In terms of the attempted reform in marine insurance law, subrogation has been one of the issues the Australian Law Reform Commission has dealt with.

5.7.1. The main areas of the reform in relation to subrogation under the Australian law regime

The issues on subrogation are dealt with in Chapter 12 of the Australian Law Reform Commission's Report. The Commission's recommendations propose changes on two topics.

---

[103] (1874) LR 9 Ch App 483.

[104] (1969) 123 CLR 228.

[105] Sutton K (1991) Insurance Law in Australia, 2nd edn, Law Book Company p 884.

[106] "The Australian Law Reform Commission Reform: 91: Report" in http://www.austlii.edu.au/au/other/alrc/publications/reports/91/

The Marine Insurance Act 1909 is silent on the distribution between the insurer and insured of the sum recovered by third parties, whether by the insurer exercising its rights of subrogation or by the assured itself. The Common law provides limited guidance and the Insurance Contracts Act does not provide a comprehensive regime although having modified the Common law in relation to non-marine insurance.

The Commission's proposals set out a complete system for the distribution of money received from third parties, though this may be modified by agreement of the parties. Secondly, the Commission proposes the insertion into the Marine Insurance Act of a new section reflecting the provisions of s. 68 of the Insurance Contracts Act which relates to the effect on an insurer's rights of subrogation of contracts, entered into by the assured with third parties, that limit or exclude the assured's right to recover from the third party in the event of loss or damage to the insured property. Such contracts also limit or exclude the insurer's right to recover from the third party under the assured's rights of subrogation. Section 68 of the Insurance Contracts Act, prevents the insurer from relying on a term of the policy that limits its liability to indemnify the assured by reason of the existence of any such third party contract, unless the insurer has clearly informed the assured of that term before the contract of marine insurance was concluded. The section also stipulates that the existence of such contracts, need not be disclosed by the assured before the contract is concluded.[107]

In summary, the Australian Law Reform Commission's report has the following recommendations with regard to subrogation, the Marine Insurance Act should be amended to provide that, subject to any agreement between the insured and insurer, money recovered from third parties either by the insurer under its rights of subrogation or by the insured is distributed in the following order; firstly, the party or parties funding the recovery action are reimbursed for the administrative and legal costs of that action, pro rata if there is more than one such party and there are insufficient funds to reimburse them in full; secondly, (a) if the insurer has funded the recovery action, he is entitled to retain an amount equivalent to the amount it has paid to the insured under the contract of marine insurance. The assured is then entitled to be paid an amount so that the total amount that he receives under the contract of marine insurance and from the recovery action equals its total loss. (b) if the assured has funded the recovery action, he is entitled to retain an amount so that the total amount received under the contract of marine insurance and from the recovery action equals its to-

[107] "The Australian Law Reform Commission Reform: 91: Report" in http://www.austlii.edu.au/au/other/alrc/publications/reports/91/.

tal loss. The insurer is then entitled to be paid an amount equal to the amount he has paid under the contract of marine insurance. (c) if the insurer and the insured have both funded the recovery action, they are entitled to the amounts referred to in (a) and (b) above, *pro rata* if there are insufficient funds to reimburse them in full; thirdly, any excess or windfall recovery is paid to the parties in the same ratio that they contributed to the administrative and legal costs of the recovery action; fourthly, notwithstanding the statements of principle above, any separate or identifiable component in respect of interest should be paid to the parties in such proportions as fairly reflect the amounts that each has recovered and the periods of time for which each lost the use of its money.

The Insurance Contracts Act s. 68 should be re-enacted in the Marine Insurance Act 1909 as a *"new"* section 85A to provide that the insurer cannot rely on a term of a contract of marine insurance that has the effect of limiting or excluding the insurer's liability under the contract of marine insurance because the insured is party to an agreement with a third party that limits or excludes its rights to recover damages from the third party unless the insurer clearly informed the insured of that term before the contract of marine insurance was concluded and, also, that such agreements with third parties do not have to be disclosed by the insured before the contract of marine insurance is concluded.[108]

5.8. General conclusive remarks and comparative discussion

As a general conclusive remark, regarding subrogation in marine insurance under the English law regime, we note that subrogation is a corollary of the principle of indemnity and as such it is applicable to all insurance contracts which are by their nature contracts of indemnity.[109] The two existing old schools of thought, in relation to its origins, are surpassed nowadays by the fact that subrogation has come to be perceived and accepted as a legal doctrine by origin and also by the fact that there is little practical importance embodied in the origins since subrogation is reduced or expandable by express contract terms.

---

108 "The Australian Law Reform Commission Reform: 91: Report", in http://www.austlii.edu.au/au/other/alrc/publications/reports/91/.

109 The assured is to be fully indemnified but no more and the insurer may not re cover through the existence of subrogation rights more than the sum paid out under the contract: neither assured nor insurer should make a profit.

It is of interest to note that the right is exercisable only after payment, and that in case of a total loss the insurer also overtakes any remaining proprietary right, whilst in case of a partial loss his rights are limited to the extent of indemnification of the assured. However, it is possible to have an express policy clause stipulating the operation of subrogation prior to indemnification. The insurer, upon payment in full, acquires the benefit of certain rights of action of the assured as well as a right to money recoverable or recovered from third parties so long as it was aimed to reduce the insured loss. It is also worth noting the existence of a big debate and of a doubt surrounding the question whether subrogation rights can arise prior to the assured's full indemnity for the loss sustained. No clear answers really existed in any decided English case and it was only sparsely, in other Commonwealth jurisdictions,[110] that case law[111] had supported a general view that the insured had to be fully compensated before the insurers were subrogated.[112] However, since *Napier v. Hunter*[113], insurance contracts with an excess/deductible clause are no longer taken for underinsurance and subrogation rights are granted provided the assured has been fully indemnified[114] although the indemnification may not be a total one. Implications, following this decision, are summed up in that the law has relaxed its criteria in relation to the time point of the operation of the doctrine in case of policies which are either valued, subject to average or have severe deductibles.We also note that, despite the great influence of the English law regulation on subrogation on the other legal regimes, there are still legal issues in the application of subrogation and criticism of the doctrine for being rigid and inequitable to the assured has been generated by academic scholars[115] as well as by the UNCTAD Secretariat.[116] In particular, generated criticism involves the characterisation as inequitable of the assured's deprivation from participation in recovery in respect of the deductible. The UNCTAD Secretariat has suggested that the clause denying the ship-owner a co-insurer status so far as his deductible extends and denying from him proportional rights of participation in recoveries from third parties -in hull policies- giving instead to the insurer preference in such re-

[110] Such as Canada.

[111] *Ledingham v Ontario Hospital Services Commission* (1974) 46 D.L.R. (3d) 699.

[112] Birds J, Hind NJ (2001) Bird's Modern Insurance Law, S&M p 292.

[113] [1993]1 All ER 385; [1993] AC 713 HL.

[114] By the insurer and under the specific policy.

[115] Hasson R (1985) Subrogation in Insurance Law-A Critical Evaluation, Oxford Journal of Legal Studies Vol 5, No 3.

[116] United Nations(1982) UN Conference on Trade & Development: Legal and Documentary Aspects of the Marine Insurance Contract, UN,NY.

coveries, is inequitable and should be amended.[117] Many have judged the real need for the existence and exercise of the right of subrogation. However, it is believed that the doctrine serves too good a goal and need remain albeit some changes which could probably be done, in view of eliminating its defects. Notwithstanding the existing defects, there has been some progress in particular points via inter-regulations amidst insurers, although there is still room for improvement.

From the rest of the common law jurisdictions examined, in the USA the position is similar to that under English law[118] but innovation lies in the existence and operation of a device namely the *"real party in interest"* rule which was mainly established to avoid the split of cause of action in case of partial compensation of the assured by the insurer. In Australia, the recent reform attempted by the Australian Law Reform Commission has resulted in a new proposal regarding the system for the distribution of money received from third parties, aimed to serve fairly both parties. In addition, the Commission's proposal – subject to prior clear information of the assured – to stop the insurer from relying on a policy term which limits his liability to indemnify the assured because of any contract with a third party, shows a clear move towards a wider protection of the assured's rights. From the group of the continental law countries, it is worth noting that under Greek law, the indemnifier insurer is directly subrogated and can claim loss by suing directly the responsible person or legal entity provided the assured was entitled to indemnification by the third party that caused the damage to the subject-matter insured.

In all jurisdictions examined, it appears that the goal of subrogation is to preserve the rights of the insurer upon him having indemnified the assured and to ensure that the assured is not over-indemnified. In essence, subrogation is dedicated to serving the main idea under the indemnity principle and, to this extent it is a fairly sound principle. On the other hand, there has been extensive criticism on the doctrine's application, i.e. in relation to subrogation actions due to the fact that there is only point in exercising subrogation against a defendant also insured and thus the right id rarely exercised in the adverse case scenario as it may be wasteful and expensive to do so, or because it encourages multiple insurances to cover both first and third parties, or because in case of a non-insured defendant -

[117] United Nations(1982) UN Conference on Trade & Development: Legal and Documentary Aspects of the Marine Insurance Contract, UN,NY.

[118] i.e. subrogation is deemed to be a form of legal substitution which avoids the unjust enrichment of the assured and at the same time enables the insurer to recoup expenses already disbursed by the insurer and collected by the assured as a result of his rights against a liable third party.

on whom liability is thrown - the insurer who has been paid is relieved from assuming the risk and from distributing the cost among the premium-paying public and in that case risk distribution , one of the most important facets of insurance, is undermined.[119] Perhaps a solution could be the deletion of the defects the doctrine carries mainly in terms of its English practice, with the aim to avoid the possibility of their application by courts in other jurisdictions too.

[119] Birds J, Hind NJ (2001) Bird's Modern Insurance Law, S&M, pp 314-315.

6. Discussion on the principle of indemnity in marine insurance contracts

6.1. General critique

If we compare the British insurance legal regime and its approach towards marine insurance with that of other national legal regimes, we notice that the latter ones often take different approaches with regards to particular aspects of marine insurance. Despite the similarities noted, there are numerous substantive differences between the different legal regimes which affect the type and degree of insurance protection the assured receives.

In England, the Marine Insurance Act 1906 has codified the then existing cases - at the time of its enactment - and at the same time has achieved a successful coverage of the various legal issues arising within marine insurance law and practice, whilst being supplemented by the Institute Clauses and by current case law. Indeed, the judiciary has played a crucial role in this achievement, by clarifying the weak points of the Act and, likewise, the Institute Clauses and their various amendments have largely innovated the way law is being formulated by Courts based on their interpretation.

In the US marine insurance had been regulated by federal maritime law until the Supreme Court's ruling in *Wilburn Boat Co v Fireman's Fund Insurance Co*,[1] as a consequence of which in the absence of an established federal admiralty principle state law should apply. It has been suggested that the application of *Wilburn Boat Co v Fireman's Fund Insurance Co* [2] could be avoided contractually, i.e. via clauses in the policy which would stipulate that the law of another country or federal maritime law will govern the interpretation and effecting of the contract. It has also

1 *Wilburn Boat Co v Fireman's Fund Insurance Co*, 348 US 310,75 S Ct 368, 99 LEd 337 (1955).

2 *Wilburn Boat Co v Fireman's Fund Insurance Co*, 348 US 310,75 SCt 368, 99 LEd 337 (1955).

been suggested that such clauses, if not unreasonable, are enforceable or at least possibly influential. In relation to the first of these suggestions, it seems rather uncertain the extent to which US Courts, particularly state courts, would accept choice of law clauses if the intent were to avoid a rule of local law. In relation to the second of these suggestions, however, it is doubtful that a choice of law (federal or non-US) rule or clause in terms of a wholly local (intra-state) issue would be effective. This reservation is justified by the fact in the US there is the almost axiomatic acceptance that state law is pre-empted by federal law and that regulations duly promulgated by a federal agency - pursuant to congressional delegation - have the same pre-emptive effect so that it could be argued that the choice of law clause stipulating federal law to apply could have no constitutional resistance. All that applies well in cases where there is an *"actual conflict"* between federal and state law, i.e. when federal and state enactments are directly contradictory on their face,[3] whereas the situation is different in the case of marine insurance. The ruling in *Wilburn Boat Co v Fireman's Fund Insurance Co*[4] merely enhanced the application of state law in the absence of suitable federal law. To simply impose a choice of law clause, especially in the case where it is one stipulating the application of federal law - but perhaps also in the case where it is one stipulating the application of international law - could be a problem in terms of constitutionality. In addition, state courts may oppose to their obligation to follow it and impose a constitutionality issue, merely on the basis that the present case scenario is different, i.e. we are not dealing with a case where state and federal law conflict, hence the latter prevails, but, instead, there is no federal rule to impose and as a result state law applies. Constitutionality issues could perplex more the situation already muddled, therefore, perhaps the best solution would be achieved if US. courts liberalised the standards based upon which they determine whether marine insurance law is *"established"*, and simply concluded that the law is *"established"* where analysis indicates the existence of a level of authority, equal to that which lawyers and judges normally consider adequate in assessing what the law is, combined with a realistic attitude towards the advisability of fashioning admiralty law in cases where the existing law lacks clarity.

In Canada, marine insurance was regulated by provincial statutes, until 1993 when the Federal Marine Insurance Act was enacted, being largely based on the English Marine Insurance Act 1906. In Australia, the

---

3 Tribe LH (1998) American Constitutional Law, 2nd edn, Foundation Press Inc, p.481.

4 *Wilburn Boat Co v Fireman's Fund Insurance Co*, 348 US 310,75 S Ct 368, 99 LEd 337 (1955).

Australian Marine Insurance Act, which was enacted in 1909, is said to have been almost an identical replica of the Marine Insurance Act 1906.

In Greece, marine insurance law is mainly regulated in two separate statutes, and where permitted, i.e. subject to the principle of *lex specialis*, general insurance and commercial law principles may also apply. In Norway, marine insurance is regulated through the Norwegian Marine Insurance Plans, which are, essentially, forms of private codification. In France, marine insurance is regulated primarily by the Insurance Code and secondarily by national laws which communicate European Directives, together with recommendations or rules encompassing customs.

It is notable, as a conclusion, that in the common law countries marine insurance is often regulated in a separate statute; whereas the continental law regimes have created their own statutes, which are significantly different in nature from those of the common law jurisdictions and are often supplemented by other parts of law as well. Apart from the differences existing in the regulatory framework, the general idea behind the principle of indemnity is common, i.e. that the assured gets indemnified only for the loss sustained, with the general aim of him not being over-indemnified.

Regarding the cover offered, the Marine Insurance Act 1906 offers a scope of cover which is quite analytical and exhaustive.[5] In the rest of the jurisdictions, the scope of cover offered has been regulated on the same basis. However, in contrast to the *"enumerated risks principle"* as per the English law, Greek law adopts the *"all risks principle"* and as such it affords a wider context wherein all possible risks are covered, with the exception of war risks and third party liability for which special insurance cover has to be agreed. Nevertheless, this width is, in fact, only superficial since most of the times it is eliminated in practice by the specific mention in the contract of the cover included, as well as due to the fact that part of the effected Greek marine insurance bulk is concluded within the English market. Similarly, in the rest of the jurisdictions examined, although primarily the *"all risks principle"* applies, the latter is eventually limited by exclusions or limitations stipulated by special clauses in the policy. Despite the differences in the text of law, in terms of practice the position comes to be the same as under the English law; however, a major difference is that in the other jurisdictions it is actually the parties which rescind to such limitations and exclusions and not the law itself *ab initio*.

5 Indemnity is offered for a loss occurred, caused by a covered peril, as well as for voluntarily occurred losses, charges or expenditure which have been effected with the aim to avert or to minimise a loss.

Regarding insurable interest, the latter was devised in the UK after the statutory prohibition on gambling policies, in order to help distinguish legitimate from wagering contracts ; yet the requirement of legitimacy has actually encouraged cases where agreed value policies with an excessive overvaluation of the subject insured were not deemed gaming and wagering ones. Today, however, the danger for wagers is no longer imminent and courts have come to accept a more relaxed approach towards insurable interest. As a result there have been cases with a substantial departure from the rule adopted in *Macaura v Northern Assurance Co*,[6] the strictness of a legal relation behind insurable interest has been bent and an economic interest has, in certain cases and law regimes, come to be considered enough in light of the need to abide with modern circumstances and commercial convenience. Along the same line, the Australian Law Reform Committee proposals recommend that what is essential is that the insured have an insurable interest in the goods insured at the time of the loss, even though this is not also required when the contract is concluded. Due to the anticipated strong resistance of the Australian market to the abolition of the requirement for an insurable interest, the Australian Law Reform Commission has also prepared alternative recommendations as per which the buyers of insurable property should acquire an insurable interest no later than the time when the buyer pays for it or is obliged to pay for it. In the US insurable interest is connected with ownership of the policy should have ownership or similar interest in or relationship to the thing or person insured. Similarly, in Canada insurable interest is required, when effecting marine insurance contracts, however the requirements set for it by were significantly relaxed in *Constitution Insurance Co of Canada v Kosmopoulos*[7] where the Court followed the view that a pecuniary interest is enough.

Within the continental jurisdictions, in Norway - where the concept of insurable interest is fundamental and partially regulated in mandatory law - insurable interest primarily has to be legal or lawful, i.e. the insurance should not cover illegal activity as such activities are taken for alteration of risk, and secondly it has to be capable of valuation in money terms. Greek law specifically states that the insurable interest has to be lawful and not illegal, otherwise the contract is void. Similarly, in France insurable interest is necessary to exist and be lawful. In US and French law, a stipulation that the insurer agrees to dispense with proof of interest, other than production of the policy itself, is considered to reverse the burden of proof thereby requiring the insurer - if he contests the existence of a

6 *Macaura v Northern Assurance Co Ltd* [1925] AC 619.

7 *Constitution Insurance Co of Canada v Kosmopoulos* (1987) 34 DLR (4th) 208.

valid insurable interest - to prove that no such interest exists. In light of the above, and especially of this latter remark in US and French law, it has been suggested that the British rule is eliminated for the sake of the adoption of a more relaxed approach, i.e. either that the combined proposal of American and French law is adopted or that the *"p.p.i."* clause becomes able of enforcement and also that reliance for criminal law sanctions against gambling in insurance policies is sought for.

If we are, however, to abolish *in toto* the requirement for insurable interest, we need, firstly, investigate the needs which lead to the adoption of a binding prerequisite for an insurable interest to exist, i.e. the difficulty to otherwise define moral certainty and the fact that the test of moral certainty of benefit from the preservation of the subject-matter would result in multiple insurances on the same property. More specifically, one main obstacle in relation to the latter is the indemnity principle. Today, however, not only courts award damages for the loss of a chance, but we have also come to terms with the imperfection of the indemnity principle; yet the distance between these facts and the point where we might allow expectation of benefit to be a ground of insurable interest, remains long enough to be traversed by the insurers easily. However, given also certain existing contemporary circumstances, it would seem axiomatic to relax the requirements for insurable interest and expect the latter to be lawful in the nature and mode of exercise and to also entail an economic benefit. Good grounds for such a proposal seem to be the fact that wagers are rare, nowadays, and the fact that the assured must actually have a justified economic interest either directly in the subject-matter insured or as a consequence of its loss, in order to claim for a loss covered for in a policy. Moreover, the path set for by Courts in *Constitution Insurance Co of Canada v Kosmopoulos*[8] has recently been reinforced by further litigation mirroring the tendency towards a more relaxed and wider approach, with regards to the requirements for insurable interest. Thus, it is highly probable that *Macaura v Northern Assurance Co Ltd* [9] would not have been followed nowadays, in light of contemporary cases such as *Feasey v Sun Life Assurance Co of Canada,*[10] *O' Kane v Jones & Others*[11], or more recently

8 *Constitution Insurance Co of Canada v Kosmopoulos* (1987)34 DLR (4th) 208.

9 *Macaura v Northern Assurance Co Ltd* [1925] AC 619.

10 [2002]2 All E R (Comm) 292, the first recognition by courts that insurable interest can be justified in cases where it is founded on an economic basis.

11 [2003] All ER (D) 510 (Jul), where strong considerations of commercial convenience where enough for the court to justify the existence of an insurable interest.

Linelevel Ltd v Powszechny Zaklad Ubezpieczen SA ("The Nore Challenger")[12] and *Murphy v Murphy*[13].

In relation to losses, English law offers a wide scope of categorisation of losses, the most distinctive being the classification of a total loss as a constructive total loss, a device basically created in marine insurance law for the sake of indemnification of the assured.[14] Recent case law[15] has indicated that tender of a notice may not be an essential component of a claim for constructive total loss where the insurer could not have possibly benefited from such a notice. In the US the concept of actual total loss is more restricted, the requirements for giving notice of abandonment being more relaxed and a valid tender exists even where the latter is deduced by the assured's conduct. In Greek law, the scope of the notion of abandonment is wider, for it is linked to total losses in general. In Norway, categorisation of losses affords a narrower scope and any loss which is not a total loss is either a damage or partial damage. Constructive total loss is termed differently, the insurer is in a stronger position[16] and the assured has extra obligations.[17] All legal systems have been influenced by the English law regime but there are differences in the criteria for constructive total loss, whilst recent English case law[18], following the position adopted in the USA, has revealed a further relaxation on the criteria for tender of notice of abandonment.

Regarding the measure of indemnity, English law offers a distinction between a sum insured and an agreed value, in cases of unvalued or valued policies accordingly. Although agreed valuation often departs from the indemnity principle, it is sanctioned by the courts on grounds of commercial convenience, but in an effort to avoid over-indemnification valuation may be contested and re-opened if it is extremely excessive or

12 *Linelevel Ltd v Powszechny Zaklad Ubezpieczen SA (The Nore Challenger)* [2005] EWHC 421 (Comm).

13 *Murphy v Murphy* [2003] [2004] Lloyd's Rep IR 774.

14 In case of constructive total loss the assured may recover the amount corresponding to an actual total loss, even when he has not suffered such a total loss, provided his loss fulfils certain criteria and he has given the insurer notice of abandonment.

15 Such as *Kastor Navigation Co Ltd v AGF MAT (The Kastor Too),* [2003]1 Lloyd's Rep, 296.

16 As he may opt at any stage to pay for a total loss and disentangle himself from future liabilities or he may elect to proceed and salvage the insured vessel.

17 On top of giving notice of abandonment, he must consult the insurer as to any future action aiming to prevent or minimize the possibility of further loss.

18 Such as *Kastor Navigation Co Ltd v AGF MAT (The Kastor Too),* [2003]1 Lloyd's Rep, 296.

amounts to fraud and material non- disclosure. Similarly, and in view of protecting the principle of indemnity, in case of double insurance the assured may recover against various insurers, yet only once and for the losses actually sustained. Thus, although indemnity has come to be perceived and accepted as imperfect, the law - alongside with the various Institute Clauses - enhances the award of fair indemnification and to this effect the existing imperfection is sanctioned by the goal achieved.

The same consensus governs the regulation of marine insurance law in this area in all the other jurisdictions examined and the only additional points worth noting are, the fact that under Norwegian law[19] the assured gets an extra sum as a means of compensation for the time lost in repairs, and the fact that in France a separate policy is effected in case of excess value, whilst in Canada *"other insurances"* clauses are used to resolve over-indemnification issues in case of double insurance.

The regulation of subrogation in the UK has also affected the other legal regimes. Subrogation being a corollary of the principle of indemnity, it is applicable to all insurance contracts which are by nature contracts of indemnity. The doctrine entails legal problems in its application and has been subjected to heavy criticism from time to time.[20] This has lead to the consideration that it is highly inequitable to deprive the assured from participating in the deductible's recovery, hence it has been suggested[21] that the clause denying a ship-owner the status of a co-insurer status on the extension of his deductible and also proportional rights of participation in recoveries from third parties,[22] should be amended.[23] Notwithstanding those drawbacks, the doctrine serves too good a goal to be abolished. In the US the position is similar in many respects, with the only additional element being the existence of the *"real party in interest"* rule, which was fashioned to avoid the split of cause of action where there is partial compensation of the assured by the insurer. Similarly, in Australia, the proposals of the Australian Law Reform Commission set out a complete system for the distribution of money received from third parties. In Greece, the in-

19 In case of ship-owner's insurance.

20 United Nations (1982) UN Conference on Trade & Development: Legal and Documentary Aspects of the Marine Insurance Contract, UN,NY p.36; Hasson R(1985) Subrogation in Insurance Law - A Critical Evaluation, Oxford Journal of Legal Studies Vol 5, No 3.

21 By the UNCTAD Secretariat.

22 Giving instead to the insurer preference in such recoveries.

23 United Nations (1982) UN Conference on Trade & Development: Legal and Documentary Aspects of the Marine Insurance Contract, UN,NY p 36.

demnifier insurer[24] is directly subrogated and may sue directly the responsible person or entity. All in all, the goal of subrogation is to better serve the main idea under the indemnity principle through the preservation of the rights of the insurer and the meeting of the prerequisite of non over-indemnification. By and large the doctrine operates well and should only be subject to amendments in terms of deletion of the defects it appears to have in terms of the English practice, with the view to eliminate the potential of their future implementation by Courts in other *forums*.

6.2. Advantages and disadvantages of the proposition for a future law reform

6.2.1. General remarks on the idea of unification and/or harmonisation

The main conclusion, derived from the above comparative analysis, is that the extent, degree and scope of insurance conditions vary from country to country, despite the major influence that the English law regime affords in the area of marine insurance law.[25]

Given the international character of marine insurance, there have been considerations to harmonise the legal regimes which govern the rights and obligations of the parties to an insurance contract. The issue of harmonisation, however, is not yet mature enough and there is an ongoing debate on the actual need of a reform, in view of harmonisation, as well as on the nature and format of such a reform. Arguments supporting a reform in light of harmonisation are the fact that there is still a remarkable diversity in the content of the legal regimes governing marine insurance, despite the existence of a virtually *de facto* international marine insurance legal regime, the main consequence of that being the inability of the assured wishing to purchase foreign insurance to easily comprehend the coverage offered by foreign marine insurance markets. To this effect, the assured has a strong case to support international harmonisation of marine insurance regimes. Harmonisation would also be useful to the party of the insurer, as it helps spread risks where policy conditions originate from a

---

[24] Where he is actually entitled to indemnification by the third party that caused the damage to the subject-matter insured.

[25] United Nations(1978) UNCTAD Report: Legal and Documentary Aspects of the Marine Insurance Contract, UN,NY, pp 19-38.

country other than his. Finally, the need for harmonisation is also assumed from the fact that although the British marine insurance legal regime is widely perceived and used as a *de facto* international marine insurance legal regime, in fact the internationalisation of its character is virtual and often limited by the national character often unavoidably entailed; thus, it can be said that it is inappropriate and unfair to the local law of other countries to use it instead of adopting an internationally recognised harmonised instrument.

6.2.2. The arguments for and against a law reform by means of new codification

Many would argue that the law reform of marine insurance law is not a task worth undertaking. Past attempts to reform insurance law[26]have lead to the belief that the production of a code of insurance law seeking to lay down entirely new principles is likely to be a long-term process. Moreover, similar past experiences of the Law Commission have demonstrated that alongside with the time-consuming factor, one need also consider that it might be almost impossible to achieve a consensus on how the law ought to deal with certain issues.[27] Nevertheless, the time consumed remains the biggest disadvantage.[28]

---

26 Such as the wholesale reform of insurance law has been since 2001 under consideration by the Department of Trade and Industry.

27 Croly C, Merkin R (2001) Doubts About Insurance Codes, JBL, Nov, pp. 587-604.

28 Even in cases where the objective is to produce no more than a codification of principle, there can exist substantial disagreement on points of fine detail leading to even more delay in the final passing of the codifying statute. In the case, however, of the Marine Insurance Act 1906, its history has shown that if the parties involved were let those disagreements overtake and drug even more in time length the codification process that would have been highly unbeneficial to their interests Already, the Bill - first introduced in 1894 - only became the Marine Insurance Act in 1906, there was too much negotiation and amendment in the intervening period involved and in addition a range of further amendments were made in the final Parliamentary stages of the Bill in 1906. Doubtless, there would have been a temptation for those involved to sneak through the odd change or two in the law and to give effect to what was perceived to be the law on points which had not been tested before the courts. These temptations were, however, resisted by Chalmers and the 1906 Act came to snapshot of the law as it was back then, with the unresolved issues having remained unresolved and with no effected changes to the law, at least intentional ones

In the case of the Marine Insurance Act 1906, the debate involved was between businessmen and lawyers, the prime demand of the former group being the achievement of certainty[29] and the prime aim being the achievement of simple and easily understood statements of principle,[30] whilst lawyers preferred the ability of the common law to adapt flexibly to changes in market practice and issues arising in other unforeseen circumstances. In effect, the desires of the business community prevailed over the caution of lawyers, and the Bill was won.[31] Today, modern demand for codification is underlined by the need for clarity of principle, the range of the sources of law and the desire of the London insurance market to retain its' control over international policy wordings and its' pre-eminence as a centre for arbitration and dispute resolution. However, the amount of time needed to be consumed - even for the codification of relatively clear matters - remains a process which is lengthy and most probable to lead into incompleteness and imperfection. In accordance with the view of Croly & Merkin[32], it seems unrealistic to switch away from identifying and reforming serious defects in the law, towards a generalised attempt to write down what already exists. Moreover, the introduction of any new Act of Parliament would produce a period of dislocation. But even if we were to introduce a new code which would retain much of the old law whilst amending some of it, the introduction of new terminology would not necessarily mean that the law has been changed, as old law often remains relevant in deciding whether or not there has been a change introduced by the new law. In addition, mixed statutes of such a type are often followed by short-term dislocation. By contrast, a pure code would not change the law but merely would reflect its' state at the date of enactment of the legislation.[33]

(Croly C, Merkin R (2001) Doubts About Insurance Codes, JBL, Nov, pp 587-604).

29 Those in favour of the measure recognised that commercial law acted as a default mechanism and that, as long as the law on any particular point was clear, a commercial contract could be drafted to adopt -generally by silence- or reject the common law's default rules.

30 Hence, they pressed for that case in 1906 and they were also supported by the consideration that at the time the law of marine insurance rested upon over 2,000 reported cases of varying degrees of obscurity and poor reporting.

31 Croly C, Merkin R (2001) Doubts About Insurance Codes, JBL, Nov, pp 587-604.

32 Croly C, Merkin R (2001) Doubts About Insurance Codes, JBL, Nov, pp 587-604.

33 The proper approach to the interpretation of a codifying act was set out in Lord Herschell's often cited speech in *Bank of England v Vagliano Brothers* [1891] AC 107, at pp 144-145 (Bills of Exchange Act 1882) where he stated: *"I think*

However, given the fact that the drafting of a new code can neither anticipate nor provide clear answers to all subsequently arising issues, we assume that the answers given by a code can never be totally conclusive. Thus, a new code might be expected to have had a relatively small effect on reducing the number of marine insurance disputes which might arise.

On the other hand, because the Marine Insurance Act 1906 has retained little relevance in the present market and has left non-tackled factual and important matters, the courts have been required to fill the gaps and in doing that they have had to constantly revise the wording of the marine market and to look not only at the common law but also at the original wordings and at the changes themselves - before ascertaining the purpose of the new wordings - also because of the development of the existing marine market and practice.[34]

Nevertheless, the Marine Insurance Act 1906 has not removed the need to refer to pre-Act authorities, and even where the wording of the Act is clear the courts have accepted the need to construe its terms flexibly in order to give the Act a sensible modern application. In effect academics,[35]

---

the proper course in the first instance is to examine the language of the statute and to ask what is its natural meaning, uninfluenced by any considerations derived from the previous state of the law, and not to start with inquiring how the law previously stood, and then, assuming that it was probably intended to leave it unaltered, to see if the words of the enactment will bear an interpretation in conformity with this view. If a statute, intended to embody in a code a particular branch of law, is to be treated in this fashion, it appears to me that its utility will be almost entirely destroyed, and the very object with which it was enacted will be frustrated. The purpose of such a statute surely was that on any point specifically dealt with by it, the law should be ascertained by interpreting the language used instead of, as before, by roaming over a vast number of authorities in order to discover what the law was, extracting it by a minute critical examination of the prior decisions." Therefore, only in the cases of ambiguity, construction of language with a technical meaning or statutory lacuna is it legitimate to resort to the previous case law. If this is right, then the Marine Insurance Act 1906 has proved to be peculiarly ambiguous and gap-ridden. This point is taken up in detail below, but it may be said in general terms that there are very few sections of the Marine Insurance Act 1906 which have been taken at face value by the courts. One area in which the *Vagliano Brothers* approach may provide assistance is to prevent a code from being rendered out of date almost as soon as it is enacted, a situation which may be posed in the event of a post-code judicial decision arising from facts taking place prior to the enactment of the code (Croly C, Merkin R (2001) Doubts About Insurance Codes, JBL, Nov, pp 587-604).

34 Croly C, Merkin R (2001) Doubts About Insurance Codes, JBL, Nov., pp. 587-604.

35 Such as Professor Cheshire, who spoke of "*the paralysing hand of the Parliamentary draftsman*"; and judges such as the one time Master of the Rolls, Lord

alongside many others, have supported the view that codification has been cast aside by a resurgence of the common law of decided cases. Amidst those opposed to codification, Lord Goff has supported the view the latter should only be undertaken where the good is perceived to outweigh the harm done and in relation to that he has specifically referred to the Marine Insurance Act as an example of codification which did not pass the test.

However, one should always bear in mind that every statute, code or even restatement is by its very nature dated and to simply discard the impact of the Marine Insurance Act 1906 on that basis seems rather harsh. Another objection is that related to what Lord Goff termed as *"the temptation of elegance"*, i.e. the temptation to adopt a solution because we are attracted by its elegance which also entails simplicity. Yet law cannot afford to dispense of complexity sometimes. Another considerable element of objection is what has been called as the *"temptation to tinker"*. Like in the old saying *"the best is the enemy of the good"*, the greater the code the less the chance of anything like success.[36]

It is, therefore, concluded by those who deny the need for a law reform through a new code, that the desire to have insurance law contained in a single piece of legislation cannot be fulfilled in practice, firstly because insurance law is embodied in other parts of law which may also apply and no complete codification can exist[37], secondly, because a code will always face interpretation by courts with the result of a body of outside court jurisprudence being developed[38], and thirdly because of the tendency of general law to move on.[39] Moreover, it is supported that[40] English courts have managed well in ensuring that the demands of the insurance market

Evershed, who once described the interpretation of statutes as *"intellectually exacting but spiritually sterilising"* (Quoted by Beatson (1997) CLJ 291, 299). That was said well back in the twentieth century, but such attitudes persist. As recently as 1997, Dame Mary Arden, herself an advocate of some degree of codification, wrote of the *"deep-seated fears of common lawyers about codification"*(1997) CLJ 516, 531) [Clarke M (2001) Doubts from the Dark Side-The Case Against Codes JBL Nov pp 605-615].

36 Clarke M (2001) Doubts from the Dark Side- The Case Against Codes JBL Nov pp 605-615.

37 Given also the proliferation of directives and conventions.

38 And it is easy to anticipate that within a relatively short period the experience of the Marine Insurance Act 1906 would be repeated.

39 Croly C, Merkin R (2001) Doubts About Insurance Codes, JBL, Nov, pp 587-604.

40 In view of the need for a flexible code to meet up with the non-static form and the new wordings of the insurance market.

have not been frustrated,[41] as they have refused to permit strict wordings to operate contrary to commercial common sense, whilst businessmen are better served by having a law which does not hark back to another era but responds to their needs in changing circumstances and is incapable of adaptation without bringing that law into disrepute.[42]

At the opposite side lie those who support codification, although their reasoning often contains weaknesses. One of the perennial arguments for codification is that it makes the law more accessible. Codes are supposed to contain plain and simple language, yet all of the meaning of the law embodied in them. It is doubtful, though, how this can be achieved in a simple language and given the modern era circumstances it is highly possible that the code will be lost in the sheer volume of information available. Another argument for codification is that it makes it quicker and easier to find the answer to a legal problem. In order for this to be feasible, however, the first assumption is that the problem does not raise new points of law but can be solved by the application of established rules and the second one is that the code is clear and unambiguous. Examples like the Marine Insurance Act 1906 - whose sections have triggered numerous litigation - have shown that the larger the body of case law the less successful the statutory provision.

Thus, the experience of the past offers scant encouragement to the codifier of the future. And in recent attempts, such as that of the Australians to reform *in toto* non-marine insurance law in Australia, the Insurance Contracts Act, which was produced, has already inspired huge amounts of litigation though its main aim was to benefit consumers. Further, the market men say that they do not need a code to make the law more accessible and more intelligible, and academics have described the endeavour of codification as a quest for utopia.[43] In addition it is doubtful that British insurers will treat a reform or codification of insurance law as a divine convergence of change and self-interest. Not least, another drawback is the lack of Parliamentary time and inclination for prioritising the passing of such laws. The reality is that, in a world with members of parliaments subject to re-election every few years, parliaments prefer to spend time and energy on legislation that is attractive to a significant section of the electorate and it is highly probable that marine insurance codes do not

---

41 Insofar as those demands have not distorted the policy of the general law and, more specifically.

42 Croly C, Merkin R (2001) Doubts About Insurance Codes, JBL, Nov, pp 587-604.

43 Clarke M (2001) Doubts from the Dark Side- The Case Against Codes JBL Nov pp 605-615.

fall in this category. Thus, statutory reform, nowadays, is likely to be limited to what has been called legislative microsurgery, i.e. the correction of particular defects of existing legislation.[44]

Perhaps the best solution would be the development of an international instrument to serve as a base for the conclusion of international marine insurance contracts, whilst affording a degree of national market flexibility without loosing the benefits gained from international uniformity. In addition, the contractual terms governing the marine insurance policy should be the central point towards harmonisation. Bearing in mind the difficulties addressed previously in the arguments against codification, it seems that uniform and international conditions are the most appropriate format for such an instrument. There is no need to give legal character to such an instrument, mainly to avoid perplex situations that accompany legislative codifications. If the conditions were to be given the form of a legislative instrument, all sorts of problems would arise and past experience - such as the attempt of UNCTAD to create a successful Convention which faced huge problems and resulted in failure - has shown that the disadvantages are far more than the advantages with the result being still one of a doubtful character. Such types of effort, which would most probably revive the Geneva debates, are therefore perceived as no n proper to be attempted, simply because whenever previously tried out they have failed. On the other hand, examples such as the one of general average, which, since the 1800's, is regulated and operates successfully via the General Average Agreement Forms, lead us to believe that the reform in marine insurance should follow a similar approach and shape up into the format of conditions non-legislative in nature and at the same time flexible, allowing a degree of national element embodied in them as per the parties' intentions.

The Norwegian Plans seem ideal in forming the basis for such uniform and international conditions from which all national variations could stem, their format being simple and easier to follow compared to a policy with attached separate clauses and their use being optional and subject to alterations by contract. Due to their nature as non-binding, such conditions could be altered to fit each national legal *forum* with the alterations taking the format of a separate stipulation in the national policy form without altering the core conditions with the aim to better serve uniformity and enhance comparison in all levels. International uniformity would also be preserved by means of basing the content of the policy conditions upon the English marine insurance regime, whilst at the same time ensuring that the

---

44 Clarke M (2001) Doubts from the Dark Side- The Case Against Codes JBL Nov pp 605-615.

relevant alterations, necessary in national level, appear on the content of the national insurance contract drawn upon the rules and specifications of the legal regime of the country involved each time.[45] In addition, similar to the Norwegian Commentary to the Norwegian Marine Insurance Plan, a set of explanatory comments - in the format of guidelines - would be needed for the best interpretation of the conditions and in order to facilitate the interpretation of difficult clauses and assist the successful achievement of accurately translating the conditions. Moreover, as a result of the latter, local judiciaries would be aided in their task of interpreting these conditions and objectivity would be served in the best possible way. Not least, following again the trend established in Norway, an internationally representative group of experts would be set up, to ensure constant and up to date uniformity.

6.3. Alternatives to legislative reform

Alternatives to the establishment of a new code exist, such as the adoption of a code of practice -as this has been established by long term experience in the field of marine insurance- which would be binding for the party of the insurer. Already such an alternative has been implicitly implied by the Australians and the Australian Law Reform Commission. However, there are difficulties within the spectrum of such an approach. Such a code of practice, if hypothetically adopted, would have the status of a self regulatory code, encompassing no actual legal force within it, but merely implying a communal observation for insurers.

Advantages with such a reform are the fact that such a statement could be more easily renewed as non subject to parliamentary approval, and the fact that the industry itself may be more flexible in identifying and sanctioning hypothetical breaches. On the other hand, a clear disadvantage is the fact that there is basically no way to monitor the frequency in the adoption and the use in actual practice of such a code like document.

---

45 Due to the fact that in some legislations exist binding rules on contractual relationships, and in order to ensure the ability to use the conditions as well as uniformity in their application, there might also be need for additional legislative provisions. The form of such legislative provisions could either be that of a legally binding international convention, or that of the creation of model legislative provisions to be enacted by each country as part of its domestic legislation[United Nations(1978) UNCTAD Report: Legal and Documentary Aspects of the Marine Insurance Contract, UN, NY pp 19-38].

Model laws and restatements form another category of alternatives; model laws comprising of a set of unofficial rules which may be incorporated into transactions, have many of the advantages of a code or codes without some of their disadvantages. For once, they do not have to conform to national drafting technique and thus are likely to arouse less local opposition. In addition, if they prove unworkable or need reform that could be done easily in the same unofficial way in which they were born in the first place. As in the case of codes of practice, skepticism has also been expressed in relation to the extent of their compliance in practice and the effectiveness of their monitoring.[46]

Institute Clauses could be amended by substituting the relevant sections of the Marine Insurance Act 1906 with the provisions provided in the Clauses, with the aim to cover all agreed areas of reform in marine insurance. However, the Committee, to undertake such a task, would have to consume a lot of time in order to successfully achieve such a challenge, if given certain parliamentary authorisation and it is not certain whether the industry would be prepared to devote a long time in respect of such a process.

Assuming that a hypothetical reform would be a legislative one in the format of uniform, international policy conditions, we will proceed to draft the content that such uniform policy conditions would have in areas related to the indemnity principle, such as the insurable interest, the measure of indemnity, and subrogation. For the purposes of this hypothetical reform, we assume that the conditions would for the most part restate and develop existing principles rather than seek to create entirely new principles. Thus, the pattern followed assumes - in terms of content - the articles of the Marine Insurance Act 1906 as the basis upon which reform is to take place,[47] and, as a result of this assumption, all suggested changes will be incorporated into the text of the Marine Insurance Act 1906.[48]

---

[46] Clarke M (2001) Doubts from the Dark Side- The Case Against Codes JBL Nov pp 605-615.

[47] Croly C, Merkin R (2001) Doubts About Insurance Codes, JBL, Nov, pp 587-604.

[48] The justification for the choice of such a pattern, in terms of the context, is the dominant position that the English law regime possesses in regulating this area of law, and in terms of the format chosen the fact that legislative reform seems the best route to achieve international uniformity and harmonization, and also the fact that policy conditions offer flexibility.

6.4. Provisions related to indemnity in need of reform

6.4.1. The discussion on possible reform of the sections on insurable interest

S.5 of the Marine Insurance Act 1906 states in subsection (1) that every person interested in a marine adventure has as an insurable interest and further in subsection (2) that a person is deemed as interested in a marine adventure where he stands in any legal/equitable interest to the adventure/any insurable property at risk therein, in consequence of which he may benefit from the safe/due arrival or may be prejudiced from the loss/damage/detention of the insurable property, or incur liability in respect thereof.

In Australia, the Australian Law Reform Commission has expressed the view in its report that the assured should not necessarily have an insurable interest in the subject-matter insured at the time of loss, and proposes that the only requirement is that there exists an expectation of acquiring one.

In Norway, as per the Norwegian Marine Insurance Plan, it is sufficient to have some clear possibility of economic loss. The position adopted in Norway is rather relaxed and the fact that insurance should not cover illegal activity is paramount only because the former is perceived as an alteration of risk.

In the rest of the legal systems examined, the prerequisite is that a lawful insurable interest exists at the time of effecting the contract or at the time of loss, and most often one is perceived as such when it exists at the time of conclusion of the contract or at the time of loss, i.e. when it is one that can be valued in money terms. It appears that this prerequisite of legitimacy and lawfulness was adopted mainly because of the vast influence from English law and also in order to tackle cases of fraud. Legitimacy, however, does not necessarily guarantee lack of fraud. The rather relaxed solution proposed by the Australian Law Reform Commission and adopted since long in the Norwegian Marine Insurance Plan seems rather attractive, in order to serve as a pattern for a reform in this section, and most of the criticism made upon the current law regime could be avoided if a solution combining the features of the various regimes' regulation were to be adopted.

Bearing all that in mind, insurable interest could be regulated in the proposed policy conditions as follows: [49]

Article 5.- Insurable Interest Defined.

(1) Subject to the provisions of this Act, every person has an insurable interest who is interested in a marine adventure.

(2) In particular a person is interested in a marine adventure ***where he has any sort of interest or any sort of expectation of such an interest, in the adventure or the property at risk therein ,either at the time of conclusion of the contract or at the time of the loss,*** *in consequence of which he may benefit by the safety or due arrival of the insurable property, or may be prejudiced by its loss, or damage thereto, or by the detention thereof, or may incur liability thereof.*

As proposed above, the set of explanatory comments accompanying the reformed text of the law - in relation to insurable interest - would be as follows:

Commentary:

The provision establishes the traditional precondition for a valid insurance contract, i.e. that the assured must have an interest or an expectation of an interest in the subject-matter insured either at the time of conclusion of the contract or at the time of the loss.

By "interest" any lawful or economic interest, i.e one that can be valued in money terms, is termed. There is no need for such an economic interest to exist as even an expectation of acquiring it is enough to entitle the assured to a claim for indemnification. Such an interest is therefore one that can be insurable. A "gambling insurance", where it has been clear from the outset that no insurable interest existed, is therefore invalid. Similarly, the assured must be precluded from invoking the insurance after the interest is no longer in his hands.

Due to the realisation that there is still a clear need for *"p.p.i."* policies, even in the case that a policy is a gaming or wagering policy, thus issued *"p.p.i."*, one solution would be to reform the law so that it be not considered as void, but be rendered enforceable. There would also be the option of adopting the measure of criminal sanctions against gambling cases, in case of proven intentional fraud in effecting such a contract in order also to serve and preserve the indemnity principle. The burden of proof of non existence of fraud should lie with the assured so as to preserve the insurer's party and prevent the latter from having to indemnify the assured even in cases of fraud. By shifting to the assured's party the burden of proving that the policy does not rely on fraud, the indemnity principle is

---

[49] The bold parts indicate the modified/newly-inserted parts.

also best served. The relevant section of the Marine Insurance Act 1906 would become, upon reform, as follows:

Article 4.- Gaming or Wagering Contracts.

(1) Every contract of marine insurance is deemed to be a gaming or wagering contract where the assured has no insurable interest, *as defined by this Act, and the contract is entered into with no expectation of acquiring such an interest, or where the policy is made "interest or no interest" or "without further proof of interest than the policy itself".* ***However, such contracts are not considered as void and are enforceable.***

(2) If such a contract is entered into with the intention of fraud, and without other legitimate reasons, the party affected by such a fraud can sue the fraudulent party for damages.

In relation to the above article, the following explanatory comments could be made:

Commentary:

Although contracts entered into without the existence of an insurable interest or expectation of such an interest are deemed as gaming or wagering, they are nevertheless valid and enforceable before Courts. The effecting of such contracts may be appropriate and/or unavoidable in extreme cases where legitimate reasons impose its use, such as when ascertainment of the insurable interest in respect or even of its expectation, is difficult to be achieved. In such or other similar cases, the parties agree to contractually be bound at their own risk. If such a contract is provoked to be concluded based on fraudulent intention(s) of a contractual party involved, the law provides the measure of the award of damages to the party affected by the fraud. Such a suit for the award of damages can be claimed before any appropriate Court.

6.4.2. The discussion on possible reform of the sections relating to the measure of indemnity

Another area which may be appropriate for a hypothetical reform relates to the measure of indemnity.

In all of the law systems examined under the scope of the present thesis, the rule followed is more or less the same as under the English law, and the measure of indemnity can extend up to the sum insured, i.e. the agreed value, in case of a valued policy, and up to the insurable value in case of an unvalued policy. There is a point of departure – in the regulation as per the French law regime – which might justify a hypothetical reform, i.e. the fact that under the French law if the insurable value is more than the actual value of the subject-matter insured, a second complimentary policy is then effected to cover the excess value.

The relevant section of the Marine Insurance Act 1906 would in this case become, upon reform having taken place, as follows:

Measure of Indemnity.

67. - Extent of liability of insurer for loss.

*(1)**The measure of indemnity is** the sum which the assured can recover in respect of a loss on a policy by which he is insured, **and it corresponds** in the case of an unvalued policy to the full extent of the insurable value, or, in the case of a valued policy to the full extent of the value fixed by the policy.. **In case the insurable value is more than the actual or market value of the subject-matter insured, a second policy should be effected covering the excess value.***

(2) *Where there is a loss recoverable under the policy, the insurer, or each insurer if there be more than one, is liable for such proportion of the measure of indemnity as the amount of his subscription bears to the value fixed by the policy in the case of a valued policy, or to the insurable value in the case of an unvalued policy.*

In relation to the above article, the following explanatory comments could be made:

Commentary:

Insurable value is determined by the actual or market value of the subject-matter insured. The second policy which is effected in order to provide cover for the excess value acts as a complimentary policy to the initial one.

Finally, with regards to subrogation, the only interesting point worth noting is that under the Greek law regime, an insurer can sue in his own name, when subrogated to the rights of the insured, upon indemnifying him. Such a point of departure is not considered as so important to trigger reform of the law.

6.5. General conclusions and future prospects

Following the CMI's Centenary conference in Antwerp, in 1997 - during which Lord Mustill suggested that the CMI puts marine insurance in its work programme for the new millennium - the CMI was given a flying start after an International Colloquium, organised by the Scandinavia Institute of Maritime Law, and held in Oslo, in May 1998. The Colloquium was the first opportunity for a number of lawyers from different countries, to identify the recurrent marine insurance problems with which their courts were confronted.

Following the Oslo symposium the CMI Executive Council decided to create an International Working Group, comprising of a good mix of academics, practitioners drawn from both common law and civil law systems, and an active underwriter. As it was not possible to tackle the whole of the area of marine insurance law, it was decided that the International Working Group would initially concentrate on some topics[50] and in accordance with the CMI traditions, a questionnaire was prepared and distributed to all 53 National Maritime Law Associations affiliated to the CMI and further on a report was produced on the basis of the responses received.

In the following CMI Conference, held in Singapore in November 2001, delegates were invited to discuss whether there is any support for harmonisation of the law of marine insurance by means of an appropriate international instrument. It was pointed out that for any attempt at harmonisation to have even the slightest chance of success it would need to be limited in scope and to have the broad acceptance of insurers and the shipping industry generally. Delegates were also invited to consider whether the CMI should seek to produce contractual model clauses on certain issues of marine insurance or simply produce a work of reference which would identify national solutions to particular problems, possibly identify the most frequently encountered solutions and even suggest some draft wording for use in contracts of insurance or in legislation. At the conclusion of the 37th Conference of the CMI in Singapore, it was resolved that work would continue so as to identify where a measure of harmonisation might be feasible and desirable so as to better serve the marine insurance industry.[51] That there is a need for change, there cannot be any doubt. The CMI, however, resolved at its Assembly in Singapore to continue with its work, and felt the need at that stage to state what the work product will not be, rather than what it will be.

In effect, the CMI, following also the publication of a "Perspective" by UNIDROIT[52] has agreed on a number of drawbacks associated with conventions. To begin with, it has been agreed that intergovernmental negotiations aimed at producing an international convention are always protracted and confrontational and disproportionate time and

50 Namely: (1) the duty of disclosure; (2) the duty of good faith; (3) alteration of risk; (4) warranties; and (5) special clauses having special consequences.

51 Griggs P (2001) Insurance Codes – A Middle Way, JBL, Nov, pp 616-622.

52 UNIDROIT (1997) Harmonisation of Commercial Law: Co-ordination and Collaboration, Rome.

effort are expended in order to produce an agreed text. In addition, the constant and rapid evolution of commercial law in the later part of the twentieth century has meant that any harmonising instrument borne in adversity is likely to be out of date before it comes into force. Furthermore, in many instances, in order to achieve an agreed text, it is necessary to insert reservation clauses allowing states to opt out of certain convention provisions which are inconvenient or not compatible with national law. This gives further opportunities for diversity within a document aimed at achieving uniformity. There is no government which will ratify or accede to a convention if, following consultation with businessmen in their own country, it is established that the proposed new law will not be appropriate. Ideally the process of such a consultation should take place during the negotiations leading up to the convention but in practice it often takes place after the text of the convention has been agreed with the result of the measure not getting beyond the post-convention consultation process with disastrous effects on the number of ratifications and accessions. Moreover, conventions carry with them treaty obligations which may, in time, prove to be an embarrassment and thus, rather than tie their hands for the future, states may well decide not to accede to or ratify a convention which may cause this sort of problem. Amendments to existing conventions, which are generally achieved by a protocol or new convention, often leads to diversification rather than unification of maritime law. A further problem with conventions arises from the tendency of some states to adopt a more recent convention without denouncing its predecessor and awkward treaty problems can thereby be created. Secondly, codes, rules and model laws also carry drawbacks: for example, a model law will only fulfil a unifying purpose if it really is a *"model"* law, i.e. one produced after extensive research into national laws and drafted with an eye to ensuring that it will create few fundamental conflicts with those existing national laws. Nevertheless, a further weakness of is that model laws carry with them no international treaty obligations leaving states free to change their domestic legislation if national circumstances dictate, thereby undermining the level of uniformity achieved by the model law.

The drawbacks related to the enactment of codes are numerous. Codes and rules are instruments which, by their very nature, can only apply when the parties are in a contractual relationship and have the opportunity of incorporating the code or rules into their contracts and are unlikely to be applied after a problem has arisen between parties who have no such contractual relationship.[53] Within the CMI, the possibility of a convention, a code or a model law has been dismissed and it is hoped that some draft

---

[53] Griggs P (2001) Insurance Codes – A Middle Way, JBL, Nov, pp 616-622.

provisions could possibly be produced, incorporating the best solutions from national laws which may aid those who are seeking to update their marine insurance legislation as well as those in the insurance market who are seeking to amend the terms upon which they write business. Similar to the CMI's proposal, the policy conditions, proposed by the author of the thesis, set the international base whilst, at the same time, leaving some space for flexibility at national level. In effect the result sought is the same, i.e. to aid – through the incorporation of the best solutions from national laws – those who are seeking to update their marine insurance legislation as well as those in the insurance market who are seeking to amend the terms upon which they write business.[54]

Enough has been said, to demonstrate that the foundation stone to be set by parties involved in any harmonising project, should be the decision, at an early stage, on the nature and format to be followed so as to produce the most effective harmonising instrument, whether it be a convention, model law, code, model clauses or policy provisions. For, each instrument has its advantages and disadvantages which must be weighed in the balance of decision.[55]

Turning into the present situation, amidst the options proposed in terms of reform, seems to be that of legislative reform in the form of conclusion of uniform international policy provisions which leave some space for national law intervention. Should for one reason or another, legislative reform be not feasible, then one should examine the option of amending the Institute Clauses, and last should come the option of adopting a Code of Practice as a reform without legal force is fated to be problematic as well as ineffective in the long run.[56]

---

54 Griggs P (2001) Insurance Codes – A Middle Way, JBL, Nov, pp 616-622.

55 Griggs P (2001) Insurance Codes – A Middle Way, JBL, Nov, pp 616-622.

56 Soyer B (2000) Warranties in Marine Insurance: A Comprehensive Study, PhD Thesis, University of Southampton.

Bibliography

ABI Marine Statistics (1995) Marine Insurance Report, Iss.133:46

Andal RV (1999) Insurance Law in Canada, Vol. II, Carswell Publications

Andrewartha J & Swangard M English Maritime Law Update: 2000, 32 JMLC 439

Argyriadis A (1986) Elements of Insurance Law, 4th edn, Sakkoulas Publications, Thessaloniki

Argyriadis A (1979) Marine Insurance:A General Comparative View in the Light of Greek Law,Revue Hellenique de Droit International :28-40

Australian Law Reform Commission (ALRC) (2001) The Australian Law Reform Commission Reform: 91: Report, Sydney

Balis G (1961) General Principles (of Civil Law) ,8th edn, Athens

Barrett J (1980) Policy Disputes in America: Damages Against Insurers, LMCLQ 131

Barstow CJ (1996) The Institute Time Clauses 1.11.95 IntML 129

Benjamin P (1997) Benjamin's Sale of Goods, 5th edn, London Sweet & Maxwell

Bennett H (1996) The Law of Marine Insurance, Clarendon Press, Oxford

Bennett H (1994) The Role of the Slip in Marine Insurance Law, LMCLQ 94

Bennett H (1996) The New Institute Time Clauses Hulls LMCLQ 379

Berg A (2000) Excluding Liability for Loss of Profit LMCLQ 20

Birds J & Hird NJ Bird's Modern Insurance Law, London S&M

Bockrath J Insurable Interest in Maritime Law, 8 JMarL&C 247

Born GB (1996) International Civil Litigation in the USA Courts: Commentary and Materials, 3rd edn

Brice G (2000) Salvage and the Role of the Insurer, LMCLQ 26

Briggs A (1990) The Formation of International Contracts LMCLQ 192

Brooke H (1985) The Regulation of Wet Marine and Aviation Insurance in the United States, LMCLQ 453

Brown A (1987) Hazard Unlimited: The Story of Lloyds of London, LLP

Brown C (1999) Insurance Law in Canada, Vol. I, Carswell Publications

Brown C & Menejes J (2000) Insurance Law in Canada, 2nd edn, Carswell Publications

Buglass LJ (1973) Marine Insurance and General Average in the US: An AverageAdjuster's View Point, Cambridge Maryland, Cornell Maritime Press Inc

Bull HJ (1999) The Norwegian Marine Insurance Plan of 1996 In Huychbrechts M (ed) (1999) Marine Insurance at the Turn of the Milenium, Vol. I, Intersentia, Antwerp

Campbell D (2001) International Insurance Law and Regulation, Vol. I, Oceana Publications

Chen S (1999) Subrogation in the Law of Marine Insurance, PhD Thesis, University of Southampton

Chiang EC (1986) Das Interesse im Seeversicherungsrecht, Frankfurt, V.P.Lang , 1986

Clarke MA (1997) The Law of Insurance Contracts, 3rd edn, LLP

Clarke MA (2001) Doubts from the Dark Side- The Case Against Codes JBL Nov: 605-615

Collier JC (2001) Conflict of Laws, CUP

Croly C., Merkin R. (2001) Doubts About Insurance Codes, JBL 587

Derham SR (1985) Subrogation in Insurance Law

Derrington SC (2002) Non-Disclosure and Misrepresentation in Contracts of Marine Insurance: A Comparative Overview and Some Proposals for Unification, LMCLQ 66

-, (2002) Marine Insurance Law in Australia: The Australian Law Reform Commission Proposals, LMCLQ 214

De Smet R (1960) Traite Theorique et Pratique des Assurances Maritimes, Tomes I,II,III, Paris

Doukas SI (1988) The Private Insurance, 2nd edn, Athens

Du Pontavice E (1989) Les Assurances Transport: L'Attraction Progressive de l' Assurance Maritime sur l' Assurance de Transport Terrestre , Annuaire de Droit Maritime et Aero-Spatial, Tome X : 11

Falkanger T et al (1998) Introduction to Maritime Law: The Skandinavian Perspective, Tano Ashehoug, Oslo

Fernandes RM (1987) Marine Insurance Law of Canada, Butterworths, Toronto

Fontaine M (1996) Droit des Assurances, Larcier

Furman AM (1998) Punitive Damages and Their Insurability under US Maritime Law IJOSL 4

Gauci G (2000) The Obligation to Sue & Labour in the Law of Marine Insurance- Time to Amend the Statutory Provisions? IJOSL 2

Goldman SE (2000) Recent Development in American Marine Insurance Law-1999 Reviewed IJOSL 11

Green A (1995) Strengthening the Insurer's Subrogation Rights IntILR 348

Griggs P (2001) Insurance Codes – A Middle Way, JBL, Nov: 616-622

Grime R (1991) Shipping Law, 2nd edn , S&M, London

Harrel-Courtes H (1968) Le Nouveau Droit Francais de l'Assurance Maritime et des Evenements de Mer , Argus, Paris

Hodges S (1996) Law of Marine Insurance, Cavendish Publications

-, (1999) Cases and Materials on Marine Insurance Law, Cavendish Publications

Huybrechts M (1999) Marine Insurance at The Turn of The Millenium, Vol. I,II, Intersentia, Antwerp-Groningen-Oxford

Ivamy ERH (1986) General Principles of Insurance Law,5th edn, Butterworths

Johnson JFIV, Brown DR (2001) International Insurance Law and Regulation: United States, Oceana Publications Inc., Dobbs Ferry, NY, USA

Karavas V(1962) Manual of Commercial Law, Athens

Kalantzis AK (1994) Law of Transportations, Nomiki Vivliothiki Editions, Athens, Greece

Kalantzis AK (1998) Private Insurance Law- Cases and Materials, Nomiki Vivliothiki Edn, Athens, Greece

Kiantos BD (1998) Insurance Law, 6th edn, Sakkoulas Publications, Thessaloniki, Greece

Lambeth RJ (1986) Templeman on Marine Insurance: Its Principles and Practice, 6th edn, Pitman

Legh-Jones N et al (1997) MacGillivray on Insurance Law , 9th edn London S&M

-, (2002) MacGillivray on Insurance Law , 10th edn London S&M

Lewins K (2002) Australia Proposes Marine Insurance Reform, JBL 292

Maclou C (1954) Le Delaissement dans L' Assurance Maritime , Rousseau, Paris

Mance J, Goldrein L, Merkin R (1999) Insurance Disputes, London LLP

Maslanka MP (1980) Punitive Damages in the Admiralty, The Maritime Lawyer , Vol. V, 21

Merkin R (1997) Colinvaux's Law of Insurance, 7th edn, S&M, London

-, (2002) Colinvaux & Merkin's Insurance Contract Law, S&M, London

-, (2000) Marine Insurance Legislation, LLP

Mustill MJ & Gilman JCB Arnould's Law of Marine Insurance and Average, 16th edn, Stevens

O'May D (1993) Marine Insurance Law and Policy, LLP

Papapolitis NI (1957) *Insurance of the Liability of the Shipowner*, Athens

Rodiere R (1971) Droit Maritime, Dalloz, Paris

Rokas I (1995) Introduction to the Law of Private Insurance, 4th edn, Oikonomikon Publications, Athens

Schoenbaum TJ (2001) Admiralty and Maritime Law, 3rd edn, Hornbook Series,West Group, St. Paul, Minn, USA

-, (1999) Key Divergences Between English and American Law of Marine Insurance: A Comparative Study, Cornell Maritime Press

Skantzakis AP (1970) Insurance Lessons, Athens, Greece

Skouloudis Z (1995) The Law of Private Insurance, 2nd edn, P. Sakkoulas Publications, Athens,Greece

Soyer B (1999) Warranties in Marine Insurance: A Comprehensive Study, PhD Thesis, University of Southampton,

Spaidiotis K (1999) Marine Insurance Law in Greece, Maritime Advocate, Issue 7

Tassel Y (1999) 25e Anniversaire de l' Annuaire du CDMO: Recension du Droit Maritime Prive , Annuaire de Droit Maritime et Oceanique, Tome XVII, 379

Thomas R (1996) The Modern Law of Marine Insurance, LLP

Tsatsos D, Dountas M, Zepos K (1954) Insurance Law Lectures, Sakkoulas Publications, Athens

United Nations (1982) U.N. Conference on Trade & Development: Legal and Documentary Aspects of the Marine Insurance Contract, UN, NY

-, (1997) UNIDROIT: Harmonisation of Commercial Law: Co-ordination and Collaboration, Rome

Velentzas I (1998) The New Law of Private Insurance, Ius Publications, Athens

Volk KK (1998) A Muddle in Marine Insurance, Maritime Advocate, 4

Wall DJ (2003) International Hull Clauses 1/11/02: A Commentary, Shipping & Trade Law, Vol.3, No 1

Wilhelmsen TL (1998) The Marine Insurance System in Civil Law Countries- Status and Problems, MarIus No 242, 15 Utgitt Av Sjorettsfondet, Oslo

Wilmot N (1975) The Contract of Marine Insurance in English and Norwegian Law:*Part I-IV,* Oslo

Witherby S (2001) Witherby's Refernce Book of Marine Insurance Clauses, 73rd edn, Witherby's, London

Wood J (1994) Maximising Recovery/Minimising Exposure: Recent Developments in Marine Insurance, IntILR 89

Wong J (1996) Marine Insurance from the Australian Perspective, IJIL 213

Wright J (1993) An Analysis of the Principle of Subrogation, IntILR 79

Table of Cases

A. Australia

B.England

C. Canada

D. France

E.Greece

F. Norway

G.USA

Table of Statutes

A. Australia

B.England

C. Canada

D. France

E. Greece

F. Norway

G. USA

Index

About the Author

Dr Kyriaki Noussia, Ph.D., LL.M., is C.S.E.T. Lecturer in Common Law at the School of Law of the University of Birmingham, UK. She is also a Barrister and Solicitor in Greece (Athens Bar Association) and a member of various associations and committees in the field of transport, maritime, and international commercial law. Her key research areas are international commercial law, arbitration, insurance/reinsurance law, maritime law and comparative law.